THE DREYFUS AFFAIR

THE DREYFUS AFFAIR

The Scandal That Tore France in Two

Piers Paul Read

BLOOMSBURY PRESS

NEW YORK • BERLIN • LONDON • SYDNEY

Published by Bloomsbury Press, New York

All papers used by Bloomsbury Press are natural, recyclable products made from
wood grown in well-managed forests. The manufacturing processes conform to
the environmental regulations of the country of origin.

LIBRARY OF CONGRESS CATALOGING-IN-PUBLICATION DATA

Read, Piers Paul, 1940–
The Dreyfus affair : the scandal that tore France in two / Piers Paul Read. — 1st U.S. ed.
p. cm.
Includes bibliographical references and index.
ISBN-13: 978-1-60819-432-2 (alk. paper)
ISBN-10: 1-60819-432-9 (alk. paper)
1. Dreyfus, Alfred, 1859–1935. 2. Dreyfus, Alfred, 1859–1935—Influence. 3. Scandals—
France—History—19th century. 4. Trials (Treason)—Political aspects—France.
5. Antisemitism—France—History—19th century. 6. Religion and politics—France—History—
19th century. 7. France—Politics and government—1870–1940. 8. France—History—Third
Republic, 1870–1940. 9. France—Intellectual life—19th century.
I. Title.
DC354.R33 2012
944.081'2—dc23
2011034456

First U.S. Edition 2012

1 3 5 7 9 10 8 6 4 2

Typeset by Hewer Text UK Ltd, Edinburgh
Printed in the U.S.A. by Quad/Graphics, Fairfield, Pennsylvania

France at the time of the Dreyfus Affair

ENGLAND

English Channel

BELGIUM

Calais

Le Havre
Rouen
Seine
Versailles ■ PARIS

St Malo

BRITTANY
Rennes ●

Vannes
Port Haliguen ●
Nantes
Angers
Tours
Loire

THE
VENDÉE
Poitiers ●
Île de Ré ●
La Rochelle ●

FRANCE

Pons ●

*Bay of
Biscay*

Bordeaux ●
Garonne
Dordogne
Lot
Garonne

Toulouse ●

Moulins ●

Dijon ●

Lyon ●
Saône
Rhône

Avignon ●
Montpelier ●
Narbonne ●

Carpentras ●
Aix-en-Provence ●
Marseilles ●
Draguignon ●

Sedan ●
Châlons-
sur-Marne ●

LUX.
Trier ●

GERMANY

LORRAINE
Metz ●
Nancy ●
Strasbourg ●
ALSACE
Mulhouse ●
Rhine
Basel ●

SWITZERLAND

ITALY

Mediterranean Sea

The Salvation
Islands
Île Royale
Devil's Island
(Île du Diable)

GUIANA

Île Saint-Joseph

SPAIN

ANDORRA

0   25   50   75   100 miles
0   50   100   150 kilometres

Contents

Preface

Many books have been written about the miscarriage of justice in France in 1894 which led to the Dreyfus Affair. A complete bibliography of the Affair published in 1970 listed 551 titles[1] and many more have been published since then. Few have contained startling revelations. Already by 1960 the French historian Marcel Thomas recognised that 'it would be vain to hope to solve in an entirely new way a "mystery" which, in fact, has no longer been a mystery for quite a time'.[2]

One reason for the continuing interest in the Affair is the intriguing nature of the story itself. A year before he himself became a protagonist by writing 'J'accuse', the French novelist Émile Zola saw its potential. 'What a poignant drama,' he wrote in *Le Figaro*, 'and what superb characters.'[3] Moreover the events took place at a period in French history – the *belle époque* – which saw an extraordinary flourishing of arts and sciences, flamboyant *fin de siècle* architecture and a sexual permissiveness that brought Edward, Prince of Wales and Oscar Wilde to Paris to escape the chilly moral climate of Victorian England.

However, as the Dreyfusard poet Charles Péguy realised at the time, the Affair was more than a dramatic story in a colourful setting. The tumult that divided France was of major and long-lasting significance in three interconnected histories – that of France, that of Israel and 'above all' that of Christianity.[4] When Péguy talked of Christianity he had in mind the Roman Catholic Church, and by Israel he meant not the state of that name, yet to be established, but the Jews. Captain

Alfred Dreyfus was a Jew and it was the anti-Semitic passions that erupted during the Dreyfus Affair that provoked outrage at the time and, after the Second World War, led some to regard it as 'a kind of dress-rehearsal'[5] for the anti-Semitism of Hitler's Third Reich.

Modern historians of the Affair dispute this linkage. 'The history of the Right during the affair', wrote Ruth Harris in her *The Man on Devil's Island: Alfred Dreyfus and the Affair that Divided France* (2010), 'has too often been distorted by attempts to press the *fin de siècle* into an inter-war mould, to find a dark teleology that does not really exist.'[6] However, the enormity of the Holocaust has affected some historians' perceptions. 'After the Nazi genocide,' wrote Stephen Wilson, 'the endemic prejudice of non-Jews against Jews has assumed a monstrously inhuman dimension that has unbalanced the study of the Affair.'[7] Vincent Duclert, in his *Alfred Dreyfus: L'honneur d'un patriote* (2006) wrote of 'a hyper-sensitivity' found in reputable Jewish historians which 'distorts their analysis'.[8]

As the title of Duclert's book suggests, he sees Alfred Dreyfus as a hero of the secular French Republic and of the values of the Enlightenment, rather than of the Jewish people or the Jewish religion. That is undoubtedly how Dreyfus saw himself. However, if Dreyfus had not been Jewish it seems unlikely that his case would have become a *cause célèbre* of such magnitude. The French historian Alain Pagès asked how the sufferings of Dreyfus could cause worldwide indignation at a time when France was committing crimes in Africa or in Indo-China that were 'without a doubt a thousand times more odious . . . without arousing much reaction from French political opinion'.[9] Nor was Alfred Dreyfus the only innocent man to be deported to the prison colonies of French Guiana: the case of Guillaume Seznec, pardoned by General de Gaulle in 1946 after twenty-four years imprisoned in French Guiana and posthumously rehabilitated by the Cour de Cassation only in 2005,[10] is as obscure as that of Dreyfus is well known.

In France the Dreyfus Affair remained contentious well into the twentieth century. Alfred Dreyfus's son Pierre wrote that his father would 'be recognised by future generations as one of the truest heroes in the history of our beloved France';[11] yet even today, writes Vincent

Duclert, 'Dreyfus is not to be found in the Panthéon of the national memory . . . and the French authorities remain hesitant when faced with the commemoration of the event.'[12] The historian Marie-Christine Leps describes how, in 1985, an offer made by the Socialist President Mitterrand of a statue of Alfred Dreyfus to be erected in the École Militaire was refused by the French military 'because it was perceived as a reminder of division and humiliation'. In 1994 the Director of the Historical Section of the Army was dismissed by the Minister of Defence for stating that Dreyfus's innocence was merely 'a thesis generally admitted by historians'. It was not until 1995 that the French Army officially declared through the then Director of its Historical Section that Dreyfus was innocent.[13]

On the centenary of the publication of 'J'accuse' in 1998, the then President of the French Republic, Jacques Chirac, wrote to the descendants of both Alfred Dreyfus and Émile Zola to mark the occasion. In 2006, a stamp was issued depicting Alfred Dreyfus, and the Socialist Minister of Culture Jack Lang proposed that the body of Dreyfus, like that of Zola, should be reinterred in the Panthéon. Dreyfus's grandson, Jean-Louis Lévy, said he thought his grandfather would rather remain in the Montparnasse cemetery. 'His grave is extremely modest and I think he was a man who would not like to have been Panthéonised.'[14]

The 'Panthéonisation' of Alfred Dreyfus has been left to historians. 'If Dreyfus and his friends become historians and write text-books,' wrote Maurice Barrès, the anti-Dreyfusard author and journalist, 'we shall be villains in the eyes of posterity.'[15] Albert S. Lindemann, in *The Jew Accused*, talks of 'the confident tone of moral superiority assumed by most Dreyfusards and accepted by later generations as wholly justified'.[16] The subtitle of Vincent Duclert's recent work, *L'honneur d'un patriote* – the honour of a patriot – conveys the author's view of Dreyfus in this volume of more than a thousand pages. Ruth Harris, in her recent book on the Dreyfus Affair, acknowledged that the subject has been overwhelmingly dominated by the Dreyfusard historians. She expresses an anxiety that her attempt to be fair to both sides 'might be seen as undermining a vision of French history that has galvanized French men and women to oppose oppression';[17] yet one reviewer judged that she herself never entirely abjures 'her own preference for the Dreyfusard cause'.[18]

Can anything be said for the anti-Dreyfusards? Because so many of them were Catholics, both tribal and devout, Catholic historians have been wary of writing about the Affair, and before starting this book I asked myself whether it was prudent for me, as a Catholic, to remind the world of their role. However, Péguy was right to see the Affair as a defining moment in the history of the Catholic Church. The Affair is intelligible only if it is seen in the context of the ideological struggle between the France of St Louis and the France of Voltaire. Moreover, as Albert S. Lindemann wrote in *The Jew Accused*, if 'anti-Semitism is to be comprehended, it must be through an analysis of the Gentile mind, a dissection of the pathologies of western Christian thought that have over the ages powerfully conditioned non-Jews to hate Jews'. Like Lindemann, I believe that 'a calm, balanced and unflinching effort to understand anti-Semitism and anti-Semites is in the long run the best defence against the views they propagate'.[19]

The Dreyfus Affair tells a story that needs no fictional embellishment and the account which follows is based either on the memoirs of those involved or on facts established by reputable historians. Unless otherwise indicated in the Notes and Bibliography, translations from the French are my own. I have been free in rendering dialogue to make it easy on the modern ear. I have used the term 'Prime Minister' rather than 'President of the Council of Ministers' for the same reason. 'Commandant' and 'Major' are used interchangeably. To make the story manageable, and yet render its complexities comprehensible for a general reader, I have started this account with the event that saw the birth of modern Europe – the French Revolution of 1789.

PART ONE

Before the Affair

The French Revolution

1: The Estates General

In 1788, King Louis XVI of France, faced with bankruptcy, was obliged to summon the Estates General to authorise new taxes. Last convened under King Louis XIII in 1614, this vehicle for democratic representation had fallen into desuetude. The Bourbons believed in their God-given right to rule as absolute monarchs, and even now Louis XVI was reluctant to concede to his people a say in how they were governed. The nobility and clergy, too, saw a potential threat to their privileges, in particular their exemption from existing taxes such as the *taille*. However, the government's financial predicament, and growing disorder throughout the country, left the King with no alternative and the Estates General was commanded to convene at Versailles in May 1789.

The First of the three Estates was chosen by the nobility, the Second by the clergy and the Third by the commons. Voting for the delegates took place in January. The novelty of an election meant a high turn-out and a surge of political debate in cafés, clubs and Masonic Lodges. Pamphleteers discussed and disseminated the ideas of Voltaire, Rousseau, the French Encyclopaedists and the English philosopher John Locke. All condemned the concept of royal absolutism, but none at this stage envisaged a nation without a king.[1] After much wrangling, it was agreed that the Third Estate, since it represented 96 per cent of the population, should have double the representation of the first two:

there were 610 members as against 291 for the First Estate, the nobility, and 300 for the Second, the clergy.

The first session of the Estates General was opened by the King at Versailles on 2 May 1789. On 17 June, after a number of disputes over its authority, the Third Estate declared itself a 'National Assembly' and was joined by some radical aristocrats and a majority of the clergy. Locked out of their usual meeting place by orders of the King, the members of the new Assembly retreated to an indoor tennis-court and took an oath never to disperse until they had established a democratic constitution. They then went to work to draw up such a constitution under the presidency of the Archbishop of Vienne.

The rejection of royal authority by the new National Assembly was supported by a mob of angry Parisians. On 14 July, a crowd of 60,000 seized 28,000 muskets from the military hospital, the Invalides, and then marched on the Bastille, a large, fourteenth-century fortress where prisoners were held on the whim of the King. At the time there were only seven inmates – four forgers, an Irish lunatic and an incestuous aristocrat imprisoned at the request of his family. However, the Bastille symbolised the despotic powers of the King. It fell to the mob with casualties on both sides. 'Is this a rebellion?' asked King Louis when told of the fall of the Bastille. 'No, sire,' replied the Duc de la Rochefoucault-Liancourt, who had given him the news, 'it is a revolution.'

There had been revolutions before. In 1649 the English had executed their king, Charles I, and in 1688 replaced his son, James II, with monarchs more to their liking – James's daughter Mary and her Dutch husband, William of Orange. More recently the British colonists in North America had broken their ties with their king, George III, and had established a republic. However, these revolutions were essentially conservative – a change of personnel at the top of a ruling class. None had the profound, far-reaching and long-lasting consequences of the French Revolution.

Rather, as the historian Michael Burleigh has pointed out, the French Revolution – that 'singular accomplishment of moralising lawyers, renegade priests and hack journalists'[2] – was the 'distant progeny' of an earlier upheaval in European history, the Protestant Reformation.

'Liberté, Égalité, Fraternité' – Liberty, Equality, Fraternity – took the place of 'sola scriptura, sola fide, sola gratia' – salvation by scripture, faith and grace alone – as a slogan for undoing the existing order. What transpired in France in the last decade of the eighteenth century would influence the course of European history well into the twentieth century and affect in particular those who became embroiled in the Dreyfus Affair – the Jews, the Germans and the Catholic Church.

2: The Liberation of the Jews

On 21 September 1791, the French National Assembly voted to remove all the existing discriminatory laws affecting Jews and admit 'those who took the civic oath and committed themselves to fulfil those duties imposed by the constitution' to full citizenship with the same rights as anyone else. It was a momentous change because for 1,200 years France had been a Catholic nation in which men and women from the different regions of France 'felt united and distinguished by their overwhelming Catholicism, even though the majority of them had still to learn how to speak or write the French language'.³ Protestants, at first tolerated under King Henry IV's Edict of Nantes, had been either driven into exile or obliged to convert to Catholicism when that Edict was revoked by King Louis XIV in 1685. Jews had been expelled from France in the Middle Ages; the only substantial communities at the time of the Revolution were in Alsace, annexed by France as recently as the seventeenth century. These communities had existed in and around the River Rhine since the time of the Roman Empire. 'After the conquest of Judah by Pompey,' we are told by Max Dimont, 'Jews and Romans became inseparable. Behind the Roman armies carrying the Imperial Eagles marched the Jews carrying the banners of free enterprise.'⁴ Trier, from which the name Dreyfus is derived, was the largest Roman city north of the Alps.

It would be more than fifty years before any other European nation would follow suit in extending full civil rights to Jews, and the new law was not passed without dissenting voices. Jean-François Rebel, a deputy from Alsace, begged the Assembly to consider the views of his gentile constituents, that 'numerous, industrious and honest class . . . ground down by cruel hordes of Africans who have infested my region'.[5] He warned that the Alsatian Jews had no desire to assimilate and, with their distinctive dress, dietary laws and Germanic dialect, would constitute 'a nation of aliens within France'. There were also rabbinical misgivings because 'implicit in return for this emancipation was a commitment to assimilation, the abandonment of the idea of a "Jewish Nation"'.[6] However, the overwhelming reaction of Jews living in France was one of joy. After centuries of oppression and discrimination, Jews were to enjoy the same liberty, equality and fraternity as the rest of mankind. When the French revolutionary armies threw back those of Prussians, Austrians and émigré French aristocrats and crossed the Rhine, they were welcomed by Jews. 'Jews even composed messianic hymns in honour of their liberators.'[7]

Full civic equality meant that Jews in France could attend schools and universities, and enter the professions, on an equal footing with any other citizen. They could also take advantage of the transformation of France in the course of the nineteenth century from a largely agricultural to a money economy. 'Economic changes', wrote Abram Sacher, 'were more crucial in winning political equality for Jews than all the glittering generality about the rights of man and the sanctity of the human personality.'[8] Jews emerged from the ghettos into a world in the midst of an industrial revolution that opened unimagined opportunities for social and material progress. Well equipped by their experience and connections, many Jews entered into commercial and financial enterprises and distinguished themselves.[9] In France, in the second half of the nineteenth century, there was a doubling of industrial production, a tripling of foreign trade, a fivefold increase in the use of steam power, a sixfold increase in the railways; and among the bankers and entrepreneurs who made huge fortunes 'there was a disproportionate number of "outsiders" – notably men of Protestant or Jewish origin',[10] a number from families with affiliates in other nations such the Rothschilds (Germany and Britain) and the Ephrussis (Austria and Russia).

The continuing restrictions imposed upon Jews in the Austrian Empire or the United Kingdom of Great Britain did not mean that

Jews in those nations were without influence. At the Congress of Vienna, held after the defeat of Napoleon, the question of Jewish emancipation was supported by the ministers of Protestant Prussia, Wilhelm von Humbolt and Karl-August von Hardenberg, and also by the British Foreign Secretary, Lord Castlereagh. During the negotiations Castlereagh received a letter on the matter from the head of the London branch of the Rothschild family, with a covering note from the Prime Minister, Lord Liverpool 'assuring him that "Mr. Rothschild has been a very useful friend" and adding, by way of postcript: "I don't know what we should have done without him last year"'.[11]

Prince Metternich, and many other members of the Austrian aristocracy, were also intimately involved with the Rothschilds. Salomon von Rothschild had been ennobled as Baron Rothschild and many of the grand aristocratic families banked with the Rothschilds, among them Metternich's relatives, the Zichys and the Esterhazys. Metternich's third wife, Melanie Zichy-Farrari, was a close friend of Salomon's sisters-in-law, Betty Rothschild in Paris and Adelheid Rothschild in Naples. Salomon's brothers served as honorary Austrian consuls in Frankfurt, London and Paris.

It was this power exerted over governments by bankers such as the Rothschilds that gave rise to the idea of a secretive supranational Jewish lobby known at the time of the Dreyfus Affair as the 'syndicate'. In France its influence was thought to have been responsible for the release of Jews in Damascus who had been charged with the ritual murder of a Capucin friar in 1840. The investigation had been conducted by the French Consul in Damascus, the Comte de Ratti-Menton. 'It is with real distress', he wrote in a dispatch to Paris, 'that, bit by bit, I have had to discard my scepticism in the face of the evidence.'[12] After torture by the Ottoman authorities, the suspects confessed. However, when the news reached western Europe, a radical Jewish deputy in Paris, Adolphe Crémieux, and a leading member of the Jewish community in London, Sir Moses Montefiore, lobbied for their release. A subscription was raised to send these two eminent representatives of their respective communities to Cairo: Nathaniel Rothschild in London contributed £1,000.

The French government led by Adolphe Thiers backed the French Consul but the British Prime Minister, Lord Palmerston, took up the cause of the Damascus Jews. Based on his premise that 'Britain has no permanent friends, only permanent interests', Palmerston sought to counter the influence that was exercised by Russia as protector of the Orthodox and by France as protector of the Catholic communities in the Ottoman Empire by championing the Jews living in the Middle East. Diplomatic pressure was put on the Ottoman Vizier in Cairo, Muhammed Ali, who, when he saw British gunboats off the coast at Alexandria, ordered that the Damascus Jews be set free.

In the course of the controversy over the Damascus Jews, the Talmud had been scrutinised by European scholars and, while nothing was found that called for ritual murder, certain passages 'damaging to the good name of the Jewish people' came to light such as that in which the enlightened codifier of the Talmud, Maimonides, ruled that 'it is forbidden to save a Kuti* when he is near death; for example, if you were to see that one of them has fallen into the sea, you should not pull him out'.[13]

In Britain, most newspapers followed the government line that the charges of ritual murder against the Damascus Jews were vile calumnies; however, *The Times* declared itself to be open-minded on the Damascus Affair, and some of the readers' letters showed that the government's judgement was not necessarily accepted by the public at large. 'I, and I firmly believe, nine-tenths of my fellow-countrymen', wrote one reader, 'share the perception of the enormous guilt of the Jews of Damascus, brought home to them by proofs which, had they been before an English tribunal, would long ere have sealed their fate.'[14]

'Anti-Semites,' wrote Albert S. Lindemann, 'and even some Europeans who were not particularly hostile to Jews, saw in the Damascus Affair evidence of a central contradiction in the ideal of Jewish emancipation. A Jewish nation remained Jews; no matter in which country they lived and in spite of their protestations of modern-style patriotism, they still

---

* Idolater, 'interpreted by later commentators, such as Rashi and Maimonides, as applicable to Christians' (Jonathan Frankel, *The Damascus Affair*, p. 273).

held the interest of their Jewish brethren to be higher than those of their adopted country.'[15] This was felt most acutely in France, humiliated and discredited throughout the Middle East. It also revealed the limitations to the power of their elected representatives. When objections were raised to the appointment of the Comte de Ratti-Menton as French consul in Canton, his cousin, Vicomtesse Vadresse de Sur, wrote pleading that this new posting should be allowed to proceed. With a proper appreciation of where power now lay, she wrote not to France's Prime Minister or Foreign Minister but to Baron James de Rothschild who replied magnanimously that he would not veto the appointment. 'My sentiments never permit me to hit a man when he is down.'[16]

3: The Catholic Church

At the time of the French Revolution, it was not Jewish bankers who were perceived to own a disproportionate share of the nation's wealth but the Catholic Church. Endowments by the devout over the centuries had made Catholic dioceses and monastic foundations substantial landowners: the abbey of Saint-Germain-des-Prés in Paris owned land equivalent to two arrondissements of Paris.[17] Moreover, bishoprics, abbacies and other ecclesiastical posts had become sinecures for the aristocracy. The future statesman Charles Maurice de Talleyrand-Périgord, forced to become a priest by his family because he had a club foot, secured an income of 18,000 livres a year as the absentee abbot of Saint-Denis in Rheims even before he was ordained a priest and, at the age of thirty-five, was consecrated bishop of the wealthy diocese of Autun. The young François-René de Chateaubriand obtained an income of 200,000 livres a year as a notional Knight of Malta. Many of the ordinary parish priests were poor, and 'the incomes of the 135 bishops varied from ten thousand livres per annum to two hundred thousand', but only 'One bishop in 1789 was from a bourgeois background; the rest were aristocrats, 65 per cent of them from families whose nobility emerged in illustrious mists before the year 1400.'[18]

The lower clergy during the eighteenth century were 'on the whole chaste, resident and conscientious',[19] and many priests initially supported the Revolution. However, on 12 July 1790, the National Assembly enacted a Civil Constitution of the Clergy which stipulated the popular election of priests and bishops and severed all links between the French Church and the Pope in Rome. An oath of loyalty to this new Civil Constitution was demanded of the Catholic clergy: all but seven of the bishops refused to take it; so too half of the lower clergy. This led to a violent persecution. Non-juring priests, members of religious orders and lay Catholics were imprisoned and in the autumn of 1792, when an army of royalist émigrés threatened Paris, mobs broke into abbeys and convents where Catholics had been interned: between two and three thousand were murdered, among them three bishops and 220 priests.[20]

In Paris, 150 priests held in the Carmelite convent off the rue de Vaugirard were 'summoned before a makeshift tribunal' and when they refused to take the oath 'were taken away to be killed'.[21] Mme du Barry, the ageing mistress of King Louis XV, went to the scaffold in the company of eight Carmelite nuns. Priests who refused to take an oath of allegiance to the Civil Constitution of the Clergy were sentenced to deportation to New Guinea in West Africa. Others were 'interned for years in deplorable circumstances on ships anchored off Bordeaux or Rochefort'.[22] Few of the deportees survived the voyage to West Africa, and of the 762 priests incarcerated in one of the 'floating bastilles', 527 died of disease.

The alienation of devout Catholics by the French revolutionaries led to an uprising in the Vendée in the west of France, which later spread to other parts of the country and led to the most sanguineous reprisals by the revolutionaries. In Nantes, to economise on musket balls and powder, prisoners were drowned in the Loire – either trapped in scuttled barges or thrown off boats. Those who tried to save themselves by clinging on to the boats had their hands cut off by the soldiers' sabres. Many Catholic priests were among those receiving these 'patriotic baptisms'. Also in Nantes, men and women were stripped naked, tied together and then flung off boats in what the revolutionaries called 'republican marriages'. There were 1,800 victims of these so-called *noyades*. Those on dry land witnessed such scenes as 'young women stretched upside down on trees and almost cut in half'. As a result of the suppression of the royalist insurrection in the west of France, and the persecution of Catholics, 'up to a third of the population perished, a statistic roughly equivalent to the horrors of twentieth-century Cambodia'.[23] It was, in the view of the historian Michael Burleigh, tantamount to genocide.[24]

Not all the revolutionaries wanted to abolish religion as such. The Jacobin leader Maximilien Robespierre organised festivals of the 'Supreme Being': churches and cathedrals, including Notre Dame in Paris, were turned into 'Temples of Reason'. The Catholic Mass was replaced by ceremonies in which a lightly clad young woman was displayed as the Goddess of Reason. A number of Catholic priests took the oath of allegiance to the Civil Constitution and continued to say Mass, but 'even those clergy who sought to collaborate with the Revolution were eventually persecuted too . . .'[25] and the loathing of Catholicism provoked the same iconoclasm shown by French Protestants during the wars of religion: carvings were hacked off the portals of churches and cathedrals, and statues and stained glass destroyed. By the spring of 1794, Mass was being celebrated in only around 150 parishes in the whole of France.[26]

The atrocities perpetrated in the name of the Republic remained embedded in the collective memory of future generations in the west of France. They also forged a bond between the Catholic Church and the émigré aristocracy. 'A counter-revolution hitherto perhaps too facilely identified with the defence of mere privilege could thenceforth claim with reason to be about fundamental issues of conscience.'[27] 'For Catholics in the nineteenth century', wrote Ralph Gibson, the Rights of Man meant not 'liberty, equality and fraternity . . . but the September massacres, the *noyades* of Nantes, the *pontons de Rochefort*, the dry and wet guillotines. Only by keeping these things in the front of our minds can we understand what sometimes seems the mindlessly reactionary politics of Catholics in nineteenth century France.'[28]

The persecution of the Catholic Church diminished under the Directory* and ceased under Napoleon when irreligion came to be seen

---

* The executive form of revolutionary government in France between 1795 and 1799.

as a source of disorder. 'Children', reported the Prefect of the Aisne in 1800, 'have no idea of the Divinity, no notion of what is just and unjust; hence their wild and barbarous behaviour and their resemblance to a people of savages.'[29] François-René de Chateaubriand made the same point in his *Génie du christianisme*. 'Think of all those children who, born during the revolution, have neither heard anything of God, nor of the immortality of their souls, nor of the punishments or rewards that await them in a future.'[30] In 1801, Napoleon negotiated a Concordat with Pope Pius VII which restored Catholicism, 'the religion of the majority of Frenchmen', as the established Church of the French state. It was to remain in force until 1906.

4: Germany

At the time of the French Revolution, the German-speaking peoples of Europe lived under a number of different jurisdictions. The largest was the Austrian Empire which incorporated multiple races and nationalities, notably Magyars and Slavs. Next came Prussia, essentially German but, prior to the French Revolution, a minor state. It was clear to patriotic Germans that their weakness in the face of the French since the time of King Louis XIV lay in their disunity; but, when Europe was reordered at the Congress of Vienna after the defeat of Napoleon, the German-speaking people remained divided into thirty-nine states. The country that gained most was the Kingdom of Prussia: as a reward for its contribution to the defeat of Napoleon, and in return for ceding its Polish provinces to Russia, it was given territory in Westphalia and the Rhineland which brought it a greatly increased industrial potential and a common border with France.

The French were aware of the dangers they faced should the aspirations of German nationalists be realised. In 1851 Napoleon's nephew, Louis-Napoléon Bonaparte, elected President of France in 1848, had proclaimed himself sovereign of a Second Empire as Napoleon III. He had quickly made France the predominant military power in Europe, defeating Austrian armies in northern Italy in 1859. However, even without the German-speaking population of the Austrian Empire, the combined population of the small and medium states of the German Confederation – such as Bavaria, Saxony, Hanover and Hamburg – was twenty million. Were they to unite with Prussia, the new state would be the most powerful in Europe.[31] But the smaller German states showed no inclination to abandon their independence, and anyway their inhabitants were seen as no match for the belligerent French. The Russian diarist Alexander Herzen dismissed the Germans as *pantouflards*.* The French saw Germany, wrote Paul de Saint-Victor, as 'the land of innocence and good nature, the sentimental nest of platonic love'.[32]

This view of Germans as cosy, romantic and unwarlike was shown to be illusory. In 1862, the Chancellor of Prussia, Graf Otto von Bismarck, told his compatriots that 'not through speeches and majority decisions will the great questions of the day be decided . . . but by iron and blood [*Eisen und Blut*]'. In 1864 Prussia won a short war against Denmark and in 1866 defeated Austria at the Battle of Königgrätz. The possibility of a united Germany was now real, and Napoleon III saw the threat posed to France only too clearly. 'I can only guarantee the peace of Europe', he told the British Foreign Secretary, 'so long as Bismarck respects the present state of affairs. If he draws the South German states into the North German Confederation, our guns will go off of themselves.'

This was precisely what Bismarck hoped would happen. Nothing would be more likely to bring the smaller German states on side than a war with France. Diplomatically, he subjected the French Emperor to minor provocations. Napoleon III might not have fallen into his trap had he not had his own reasons for wanting a war. In elections for the legislature in the spring of 1869, three-quarters of the votes were cast for opponents of the regime. It was thought that a war against Prussia would rally public support for the Second Empire and militarily 'the odds were in France's favour'.[33]

Great confidence was placed in France's new Chassepot rifle, as superior to the Prussian Dreyse needle gun as the Dreyse had been to the

* Stay-at-home types, what we might now call couch potatoes: from *pantoufle*, slipper.

Austrians' muzzle-loading Lorenz rifles at the Battle of Königgrätz. The French had also developed the world's first machine-gun, the Montigny *mitrailleuse*. These advantages, however, were outweighed by the superiority of the Prussian artillery – the breech-loading, steel-tubed Krupp guns which were faster, more accurate and had a greater range than France's bronze muzzle-loaded cannon.[34]

Also the Prussians, with universal conscription, had a larger army than the French. The south German states contributed contingents which showed themselves to be more than mere *pantouflards*. The Prussian commander, Helmuth von Moltke, used mobile batteries to blast holes in the French lines. The French were defeated – the armies in the south under Marshal François Bazaine driven into the fortress of Metz, and those in the north routed at Sedan and their commander, Napoleon III himself, taken prisoner.

When the news of this defeat reached Paris, the imperial government fell in a bloodless coup and a republic was proclaimed. A Government of National Resistance was formed to continue the war; an Army of the Loire was raised and fought a semi-irregular war against the German invaders. This resistance provoked brutal retaliation which does much to explain the fear and loathing of the Germans felt at the time of the Dreyfus Affair. Though Bismarck never went so far as his wife – 'shoot and stab all the French, down to the little babies' – he insisted that there be no 'laziness in killing' so long as France continued its futile resistance. If a French village refused German exactions, Bismarck wanted every male inhabitant hanged. If French boys spat at German troops from bridges or windows, Bismarck wanted the troops to shoot them dead. So too when French women and children picked through the trash or scavenged for potatoes on the fringes of Paris. Troops who quailed would be executed. Bismarck only voiced the threat; his troops implemented it. 'Ironically,' wrote Geoffrey Wawro, 'a Prussian army that had deplored the atrocities and mass casualties of the American Civil War was now grimly embarked on a wholesale Americanization of the Franco-Prussian War . . .'[35]

Paris was besieged. The Radical leader, Léon Gambetta, escaped in a hot-air balloon to raise armies in the interior but all attempts to drive out the Germans failed. With the Parisians starving, the remaining members of the republican government went to the German headquarters now installed in Louis XIV's palace in Versailles and asked for an armistice. It was at Versailles, on 18 January 1871, in Louis XIV's celebrated hall of mirrors, that Bismarck's ambition was at last accomplished: a united German empire was proclaimed under the Prussian monarch, now Kaiser Wilhelm I.

Elections in France held a few weeks later, on 8 February, returned a conservative majority which chose Adolphe Thiers as President, the politician who had lost office thirty years earlier because of the Damascus Affair. Adolphe Crémieux, who had been instrumental in Thiers's fall, described the new parliament as 'an Assembly of country bumpkins'.[36] Businessmen were well represented, and one of its first measures was a law ending the wartime moratorium on the repayment of debts.

This was greatly resented by Parisians, many of whom had borrowed money and pawned their possessions to buy food at astronomical prices during the siege. The Parisian militia mutinied and the government of Thiers, which had prudently retreated to Versailles, was repudiated. In March, a Commune was proclaimed in Paris. An attempt by a detachment of the regular army to reclaim cannon seized by the Communards was repulsed and the general commanding the detachment put up against a wall and shot.

The general was only the first of a number of victims of the Communards' fury. When Thiers, backed by the conservative and largely Catholic Assembly, determined that the Commune had to be suppressed, reprisals and counter-reprisals took place on both sides. On 24 May, as the troops of the Versailles government advanced down the barricaded boulevards into the city, the Archbishop of Paris was taken from the prison of La Roquette, where he had been held hostage, and shot. During the next two days, fifty priests were either shot or bayoneted. The clergy in their soutanes were more easily identified as the enemy than the bourgeoisie, who had mostly left the city. 'The dying commune, ever old-fashioned, had been too busy with priests to bother with bankers.'[37]

The troops of the Versailles government took a disproportionate revenge. The brash Colonel Gaston de Gallifet, who had led his 3rd Chasseurs in a famous charge at the German lines at Sedan, now directed his men against their fellow countrymen. Between 21 and 28 May, in what came to be called *la semaine sanglante*, the bloody week, between 20,000 and 30,000 Communards were slaughtered – either shot on sight or after a trial by kangaroo court. Many thousands of those whose lives were spared were transported to penal colonies overseas. The army lost less than a thousand men.

Édouard Drumont, in *La France juive*, called the suppression of the Commune an act 'of savage iniquity' and blamed it on the Catholic majority in the National Assembly. Unquestionably there were Catholics who saw in the mix of anarchists, socialists and feminists – women were prominent among the Communards – the heirs to the Jacobins who had slaughtered Catholics during the Terror less than a hundred years before; and the execution of the Archbishop and fifty priests confirmed that perception; but Thiers's ruthless suppression of the Commune also reassured the men of property and the 'wary French peasants' that republican government could maintain order as well as an emperor or a king.[38]

It also ensured that Thiers could deliver a national consensus when it came to agreeing terms with the Germans. On 10 May, eleven days before the start of the *semaine sanglante*, a treaty was finally signed in Frankfurt. The terms proposed by the Germans included an indemnity of five million francs and the annexation by Germany of Alsace and a large part of Lorraine. Thiers's government had no option but to accept. It was a profound humiliation for the French and was seen as something that would be reversed as soon as France had regained its strength. France, said Victor Hugo, would one day 'exact a terrible revenge'.[39]

The Third Republic

1: Church and State

The National Assembly, elected in haste after the defeat at Sedan, was largely Catholic and royalist in its composition. The 'notables' who made up the majority wanted a monarchy but could not agree upon who should be king. The legitimist pretender was the Comte de Chambord, a childless old man living in Austria; the Orléanist pretender was the Comte de Paris. While the royalists bickered over the rival candidates, support for a royalist restoration dwindled. A number of by-elections in 1871 suggested that the peasants and bourgeoisie of *la France profonde*, reassured by Thiers's ruthless reimposition of order and fiscal competence, were warming to the idea of a republic.

A delegation was sent to Austria to negotiate a return of the legitimist pretender, the Comte de Chambord, as King Henry V of France. The old Count was willing to accept the crown but only on his terms. A compromise, thought possible on constitutional matters, foundered on the question of a national flag. Chambord insisted that it should be the white banner with the fleur-de-lis of the Bourbon kings. This was unacceptable to the French Army whose famous victories had been won under the tricolour. The negotiations collapsed.

In 1875, with no prospect of a king, the Assembly passed a number of laws establishing a directly elected Chamber of Deputies, an indirectly elected Senate, a cabinet or Council of Ministers and a President elected by the National Assembly. By a single vote the state created by these constitutional provisions was given the name 'republic' – the third since the Revolution of 1789. By the time the first elections to the newly constituted Chamber of Deputies were held in 1876, the mood of the country had changed. The voters returned a republican majority led by Léon Gambetta, the patriotic Radical who had escaped from besieged Paris in a balloon. However, for Gambetta the enemy was no longer the Prussians: 'Le cléricalisme, voilà l'ennemi.' The enemy of the Republic was now the Catholic Church.

The battle between left and right, anti-clericals and conservatives, was fought over education. For the secularist republicans, the establishment of a system of universal state education known collectively as 'The University' – the secondary schools, the lycées, the universities and the elite colleges of higher education (the Grandes Écoles) – was considered one of the greatest and most enduring achievements of the First Empire. However in 1850, under the then President, Louis-Napoleon, the Minister of Education Alfred Falloux had ended the state's monopoly on educational provision, leading to a rapid expansion of Catholic schools 'with relative freedom from official interference and hostile criticism'.[1]

These Catholic schools were run by religious orders – above all the Jesuits and the Assumptionists, two orders that were to play important roles in the Dreyfus Affair. The Society of Jesus, founded by Ignatius Loyola in the sixteenth century, had provided the shock-troops for the Catholic Counter-Reformation. With strict discipline and a long and rigorous training, and drawing recruits from the European nobility, it had sent missionaries to every corner of the world, and boasted of those who had been martyred by the enemies of the Church such as the Iroquois of North America and Queen Elizabeth I of England.

Taking vows of obedience to their General in Rome, who in turn swore to obey the Pope, the Jesuits were considered by their enemies to be unscrupulous in pursuit of what they termed 'the greater glory of God'. They were the implacable adversaries of Protestants, atheists, secularists and free-thinkers. Those who were 'of Hebrew or Saracen descent'² were ineligible to join the Society.* In 1773, under pressure from liberal European monarchs, Pope Clement XIV dissolved the order: it was reconstituted in 1814 by Pope Pius VII. The Jesuits' celebrated dictum, 'Give us a child until he is seven and he will be ours for life,' led them to establish schools for those who would be influential as adults – the sons of the aristocracy and *haute bourgeoisie*.

At the other end of the social scale, schools for the sons of peasants and artisans were started by the Augustinians of the Assumption – the Assumptionists – an order founded by Emmanuel d'Alzon only in 1850 'to combat the spirit of irreligion in Europe and the spread of schism in the east'. The Assumptionists built the first Catholic church in Istanbul since the fall of the city to the Turks in 1452 and equipped a hospital ship to be sent to the coast of Newfoundland so that French Catholic fishermen should not have to depend 'upon the hospital ships of Protestant nations which go to the aid of these unfortunate men and, while ministering to their material needs, draw their souls to heresy'.³

In France the Assumptionists published books, pamphlets and periodicals to disseminate the Catholic faith. Their newspaper, *La Croix*, overtly and crudely anti-Semitic, was sold outside every parish church on a Sunday morning and, at the peak of its success, achieved a circulation of four million copies. The Assumptionists also took advantage of the development of the railways under Napoleon III to organise mass pilgrimages to Lourdes, the village in the Pyrenees where, in 1858, Bernadette Soubirous had visions of the Virgin Mary. Miracles of healing ascribed to water from the spring in the grotto where the Virgin had appeared drew large numbers of pilgrims from all over France. With these manifestations of mass piety, the Assumptionists meant to confront secular republicanism. 'Pilgrimage was a way of proclaiming Christian values in public, and this often self-conscious attempt to return to the religious pageantry of the Middle Ages was one of the defining features of the movement.'⁴

The idea of miraculous cures at Lourdes was an affront to the scientific spirit of the age, and was dismissed most vigorously by the medical

* This was from fear of infiltration by Spanish Moriscos or Marranos, insincere converts from Islam and Judaism. The ban was not lifted until 1946. An exception seems to have been made for Leo Naphta in Thomas Mann's *The Magic Mountain*.

profession; but while French doctors trained in science were likely to be atheists, most of the nurses in French hospitals were Catholic nuns. With the idea of a welfare state still a pipe dream, the care of the old, the poor, the sick, the orphaned, the insane, the imprisoned, was largely undertaken by Catholic agencies funded by charitable donations. 'In the 1870s, the wards of almost all of France's 1,500 hospitals were run by about 11,000 members of active religious congregations.'[5] This provision of cheap labour by the Catholic nuns for social care raised no objections among the bourgeois republicans who, time and again, turned down the idea of an income tax to increase the government's resources. It was tacitly understood by successive republican governments that, as the political commentator André Siegfried put it, 'a Frenchman's heart is on the Left but his purse is on the Right'.[6]

It was a different matter when it came to education. 'Against the Catholic myth of a Christian France had arisen the counter-myth of a revolutionary France, the standard bearer of Liberty.'[7] Pope Pius IX's *Syllabus of Errors*, issued in 1864, had condemned 'progress, liberalism and modern civilisation', confirming in the minds of the secular republicans that the Catholic Church was the source of bigotry and reaction. Catholics became subject to a political discrimination that was inconsistent with those Rights of Man supposedly established by the French Revolution. After the elections of 1877, the republican victors unseated seventy-two deputies for supposed electoral irregularities, and 'for many years to come', observed the wry historian Denis Brogan, 'France was faced with the odd political phenomenon that corruption always came from the Right'.[8] However, the pre-eminent struggle between conservatives and republicans was not over electoral irregularities but over the formation of the minds of the young. Zealous republicans found it intolerable to have two rival systems of education teaching two different views of the French nation 'with different political beliefs and different attitudes towards progress'. They believed that the French peasantry was being indoctrinated by the fanatical Assumptionists and the bourgeoisie by the urbane and sophisticated Jesuits, whose schools were favoured by many non-Catholic parents because it was here that their children 'would learn good manners and form useful friendships'.[9]

In 1879 a government led by Jules Ferry, with a cabinet in which six out of the ten members were Protestants,[10] passed laws banning Catholic clergy from teaching in either state or private schools and dissolving unauthorised religious orders. As a result 261 religious houses were closed and 5,643 monks were expelled; they were only permitted to return ten years later, in 1889. Two hundred magistrates resigned their posts rather than take part in the expulsions, and their names were inscribed by the Catholics in a 'Golden Book'.[11] These anti-clerical laws were not directed against religious education as such: Jewish and Protestant children in Parisian primary schools continued to receive instruction in their faiths. The faculties of Catholic theology in French universities were finally abolished in 1884, but the Protestant faculties were encouraged.[12]

Catholics from families who had traditionally served in the French administration were now debarred. The higher strata of the old bourgeoisie were excluded from power in this generation, as far as it was Catholic or royalist, and on the whole it was both. The gap they left was filled by Protestants, to a lesser degree by Jews.[13] 'French Jews,' wrote Albert S. Lindemann,

> like German Jews, were among the most ardent and articulate supporters of the notion of removing public education from the control of the Catholic Church. It is also beyond question that Catholics had good reason to feel pushed aside by a new political class, within which there were many Jews . . . The Republican purging of the administration of justice . . . resulted in the prominence in the courts of Jews and Protestants, and the anti-clerical policy of the Ferry government meant that the decrees had often had to be enforced on Catholics by Jewish and Protestant officials.[14]

A Jewish prefect could, with impunity, observe Passover, but a prefect who was openly zealous in observance of Easter might find himself under violent attack. 'Taking Easter communion under the Third Republic was a much more affirmative, even courageous, act than it had been in (say) the 1850s: government employees who did so were unlikely to be promoted . . .'[15]

2: The Freemasons

For France's Catholics, those who were conspiring to destroy the Church in France – the atheists, Protestants and Jews – came to be subsumed in a single group: the Freemasons. Although Freemasonry claims an exotic pedigree, dating back to antiquity, it first appears in a way susceptible to historical examination in eighteenth-century England as a fraternity of high-minded men from the aristocracy and upper classes intent on the betterment of mankind. Freemasons are found among the American revolutionaries and played a significant role in the French Enlightenment and its political child, the French Revolution. It was not atheist in its inception but nor was it Christian: the Supreme Being recognised by the Freemasons was not the God of Israel, let alone the Trinitarian God of the Christian religion, but a philosophical notion, and in France it was the *philosophes* – those writers whose sceptical attitude towards feudal institutions and revealed religion paved the way for the Revolution – who became its apostles. On 7 February 1778, Voltaire was solemnly initiated in Masonic garb by 'Brother' Helvetius, who was in fact an atheist; uniquely in France, atheists were admitted as Freemasons. They did not have to subscribe to a belief in a Supreme Being.

One of the main attractions of Freemasonry to its members was a commitment to mutual assistance. Masons took a vow to come to one another's aid. They made useful contacts in the Lodges and supposedly identified one another outside by secret handshakes. Because of the oath of secrecy, non-Masons had no way of knowing whether they were denied a promotion or lost a contract because their competitors were Freemasons and they were not.

A contemporary historian of nineteenth-century France, Robert Tombs, judges the influence of Freemasonry to have been relatively benign, 'a federation of clubs for aspiring left-wing politicians, a place for networking rather than conspiracy, and a discreet refuge for political discussion when the atmosphere outside was unfavourable'.[16] However, even the pragmatic Bismarck regarded the secretive nature of Masonic networks as 'detrimental to civic equality and to public interests'.

Masons were suspected of putting loyalty to their fellow Masons over loyalty to the nation or society in which they lived.

Freemasonry was also perceived as a conspiracy against the Catholic Church. As early as 1738 Pope Clement XII had published a papal constitution, *In Eminenti*, condemning Freemasonry for its secrecy, its religious indifferentism and its promotion of humanistic values detached from Christian revelation. Catholics were forbidden to become Masons. The spread of the ideas of the French Enlightenment confirmed, in the eyes of subsequent popes, the prescience of Clement's warnings. Freemasonry 'was officially blamed for the calamities that had befallen the Church since the French Revolution, for example in the Encyclical *Quo Graviora* of 1826'.[17]

In 1884 Pope Leo XIII, who had succeeded Pius IX in 1878, repeated his predecessor's warnings about Freemasonry in an encyclical, *Humanus Genus*. Leo was already aged sixty-eight and in poor health when he was chosen as pope but was to reign for seventeen years. He would go down in history as the pope who came to terms with many of those aspects of modernity that his predecessor, Pius IX, had rejected – in particular the idea of democracy. To the consternation of the royalists in France, he initiated what came to be called the *ralliement* – the rallying of Catholics to the Republic – and in May 1881 had issued a historic encyclical, *Rerum Novarum* ('New Things'), which condemned socialism, upheld the right to private property but insisted upon the Church's commitment to social justice, including the right of workers to form trades unions and receive a just wage.

However, Pope Leo remained a man of profound personal piety and he looked with horror upon the assault on Catholic schools in Germany and above all in France, for which he held the Freemasons largely to blame. *Humanus Genus* was unambiguous and uncompromising in its condemnation of 'that strongly organized and widespread association called the Freemasons that was planning the destruction of holy Church publicly and openly, and this with the set purpose of utterly despoiling the nations of Christendom'. Freemasonry was a 'vast evil' and a 'fatal plague'. 'The teaching of morality which alone finds favour with the sect of Freemasons, and in which they contend that youth should be instructed, is that which they call "civil" and "independent", and "free", namely, that which does not contain any religious belief.' Leo warned that if Christian principles be 'taken away, as the natural-ists* and Freemasons desire, there will immediately be no knowledge as to what constitutes justice and injustice, or upon what principle morality is founded'.

Although no mention is made in *Humanus Genus* of a link between Freemasonry and the Jews, there is no doubt that throughout Europe, and particularly in France, it 'was generally regarded as a Jewish organization' by its critics. In an attack published in 1893, the French Bishop Meurin referred to Freemasonry as 'the *Synagogue de Satan*',† and had portrayed it as 'a Satanic cult, with which the Jews and Judaism were closely associated'.[18]

Four years before, in 1889, on the 100th anniversary of the French Revolution, the authoritative Jesuit journal published in Rome, *Civiltà Cattolica*, published a series of articles describing the ascendancy of the Jews in France as God's punishment for the nation's apostasy at that time. 'Heaven's chosen instrument of anger for punishing the degenerate Christianity of our time is the Hebrews. Their power over Christianity is continually increasing, along with the predominance of that evil spirit' that replaced the Rights of God with the Rights of Man. Once granted equal rights with Christians, 'the dam which previously had held back the Hebrews was opened for them, and in a short time, like a devastating torrent, they penetrated and cunningly took over everything; gold, trade, the stock market, the highest appointments in political administrations, in the army and in diplomacy; public educa-tion, the press, everything fell into their hands or into the hands of those who were inevitably depending on them'.

The tone of the articles was intemperate and singled out France, not just as the source of the ungodly notion of 'liberty', but also as the nation in which it had been most effectively exploited by the Jews. In France,

* Those who look upon nature as the sole source of all that exists and seek to explain everything in terms of nature.
† A term from the Book of Revelations (2: 9) used to refer to those Jews who maligned the early Christians.

the entire so-called High Finance is in the grip of non-French Jews who possess inestimable wealth. The litany of these princes of Israel is long and all have last names which sound as French as those of Arabs or Zulus. The Dreyfuses, Bischoffheims, Oppenheims, Erlangers, Hottinguers and so on, altogether form a banking Sanhedrin that represents a value of at least 10 billion francs, entirely extracted from the veins of France thanks to the *rights of man*, invented by this cosmopolitan and insatiable race.

Jews planned to 'take over the means of controlling public opinion . . . Journalism and public education are like the two wings that carry the Israelite dragon, so that it might corrupt and plunder all over Europe . . . The Jews buy the press, over half the newspapers are in their power, and they use it' to promote pornography and irreligion. The Jews 'tear down the crucifixes from the walls of the Paris schools, breaking them and giving orders to throw them into the sewers, and they defend sword in hand, children's obligatory attendance of secular schools, that is of those without and against the Christian God'.

3: The Army

In the view of the authors of this series of articles in *Civiltà Cattolica*, Jews might be taking over French journalism, the civil service, the judiciary, the schools and the universities, but there was one French institution where the conservative, Catholic Frenchman had reason to believe that he was still in control – the army. A Jew might be well equipped by inherited aptitudes to be a banker, a lawyer, a businessman, a doctor, a journalist, a teacher or a civil servant – but in a nation where the defence of the realm had historically been the prerogative of the aristocracy, and where Jews had been confined to civilian pursuits since the defeat of Simeon Ben Koseba in the second century AD, the French Jew was hardly credible as a soldier.

However, even here the pre-eminence of conservative Catholics was under threat. There was a new spirit of professionalism in the army and the introduction of universal conscription changed the nature of the rank and file from 'middle-aged, illiterate sots' to 'fresh-faced, educated' youths.[19] The army was infected with the spirit of modernity that had brought new roads, railways, banks, business and literacy into every corner of France and there was a difference of opinion between the modernisers and the traditionalists – not on questions of weaponry, strategy and tactics but on the composition of the officer corps.

There were two routes to a commission. One was via the military academy at Saint-Cyr, the other via the École Polytechnique. The feeder schools for Saint-Cyr were often Catholic establishments run by Catholic religious orders, in particular the Jesuit school of Sainte-Geneviève in Paris. The feeder schools for the École Polytechnique were the lycées or secular private schools such as the Collège Sainte-Barbe in Paris. There was intense competition for all the Grandes Écoles of the University with 'the examination for entrance to the École Polytechnique being the most revered of these tests'. As a result, the officers who joined the army from the École Polytechnique were from a wide range of backgrounds, and were very clever.

Graduates from Saint-Cyr had, since 1871, come increasingly 'from the aristocracy and the conservative and Catholic bourgeoisie. In 1868, the yearbook of Saint-Cyr counted among its graduates 89 names "with the noble particle"* out of 284. Ten years later, there were 102 aristocrats out of a class of 365.'[20] This was partly because income from land had declined, but also because 'the practical exclusion of the Conservative and Catholic classes from most branches of public life made the Army more than ever the natural career of the sons of these classes'.[21] Republicans had gradually displaced the older monarchist and Bonapartist cadres in the civil service and government bureaucracy. This displacement entailed a change in social class as well, from aristocrats to bourgeoisie, and in religion from Catholic to Protestant or non-believer – or Jew. In short, a new governing class began to come to power in France.

Catholics ascribed this to prejudice, but the politician and journalist Yves Guyot thought that all too often 'people of Catholic origin, but

* That is, 'de'.

now more or less agnostic', blamed discrimination rather than their own shortcomings for their failure in life.

> They don't want to take the trouble to learn a foreign language; they don't want to submit themselves to the tedium of hard work; they don't want to strain themselves by mastering the complexities of high finance; they want jobs and positions to come to them without effort in the traditional way. They are thus very jealous of the Jews who demonstrate in these jobs and positions the qualities of perseverance and know-how that they lack; and, like good protectionists . . . they demand that their rivals be removed; they pretend that they are persecuted, while in fact, it is they who want to persecute those whom they blame for their own lack of success.[22]

Whether they were excluded from the civil service as a result of incompetence or discrimination, many of those from a conservative Catholic background turned to the one major area of employment by the state that remained open to them, the army.[23] This increased representation in the officer corps of men of questionable loyalty to the Republic and revived 'myths about power-mad Jesuits' who were said to have 'packed the General Staff with their pupils'. In fact, 'in 1898, only a dozen General Staff officers out of 180 had attended their schools'.[24] However, the myths were potent and in 1888 the first civilian Minister of War, Charles Louis de Freycinet – himself a Polytechnicien – instituted a number of reforms. The École Militaire Supérieure was renamed the École Supérieure de Guerre and, in October 1890, Freycinet created the post of Chief of the General Staff, appointing to fill it General François de Miribel, also a Polytechnicien – indeed, 'the son, brother, and father of Polytechniciens' and 'a reformer by temperament and conviction'.

To open up access to officers with talent but no connections, General de Miribel ruled that each year the top twelve graduates of the École Supérieure de Guerre should serve as interns on the General Staff. This would not necessarily lead to a permanent appointment but it would make it more difficult for graduates of Saint-Cyr to advance through the old-boy network. However, Miribel himself was considered to be a poor judge of men. He appointed as his deputy General Raoul François Charles le Mouton de Boisdeffre, later described by General Edmond Legrand-Girard in his memoirs as 'refined, cunning but a lazy slug who directed things in a dilettante way'. Miribel promoted to the General Staff General Charles-Arthur Gonse, characterised in the same memoirs as 'a nullity made man'.[25] These republican officers were denigrated by their enemies as 'drawing-room intriguers', and appointments were made, according to Legrand-Girard, for 'their name or their connections'. General Félix Saussier, who was esteemed by republicans because he had seen off the potential putschist General Georges Boulanger, remained the Military Governor of Paris despite his louche private life.

Miribel's appointment of General de Boisdeffre as his deputy was, according to the first historian of the Dreyfus Affair, Joseph Reinach, made precisely *because* of his indolence. 'Miribel appointed him to the General Staff not because of his positive qualities but because of his nonchalance. This great worker, jealous of his work, wanted to do everything himself. De Boisdeffre's laziness didn't annoy him.' However, Miribel died suddenly of an apoplectic fit on 8 September 1893, and, wrote Reinach, 'the ignorance of Republicans about the armed forces allowed Boisdeffre to succeed him. He was installed like a prebendary, spending at most a few hours in his office, leaving his work to his subordinates, immersing himself rather in worldly affairs, indulging in expensive pleasures, and representing the army at various functions – something at which he excelled with his height, his having the manner of a military and diplomatic gentleman, his decorative quality, with something deep and serious in his expression which made him seem profound.'[26] The death of Miribel 'unquestionably weakened the position of the interns at the General Staff, particularly the Polytechniciens',[27] because Boisdeffre reverted to the old system of co-option.

3

Édouard Drumont

1: La France juive

The champion of those who were, or imagined themselves to be, disadvantaged by the rise of the Jews was Édouard Drumont, who in 1888 published an anti-Semitic polemic, *La France juive* (Jewish France). Drumont, though born in Paris, came from a family of porcelain painters in Lille. His father died when he was seventeen. After graduating from a lycée, he worked for a while as a civil servant in the Prefecture of the Seine, but soon left to try his hand at journalism. The growth of literacy under the Third Republic, the absence of censorship, the volatility of politics and the relatively lax laws of libel had created a flourishing newspaper industry. Drumont wrote for a number of papers, including *Le Gaulois*, *Le Petit Journal* and *Liberté*, the last owned by the Péreires, Sephardic Jewish rivals of the Rothschilds. In 1886, irked by the predominance and power of Jewish press proprietors, Drumont resigned from the staff of *Liberté* and started work on his book, *La France juive*. He was by now a widower, shy and self-effacing, a closed personality, set in his ways, very old-fashioned, rather eccentric, excessively introspective, contemplative, scholarly – 'a kind of secular monk'.

La France juive was a call to arms. France was a conquered nation, wrote Drumont, and was ruled by an alien minority, the Jews. Just as the Saxons in England had been enslaved 'by sixty thousand Normans under William the Conqueror', so the French had been enslaved by half a million Jews.* However, rather than conquer courageously with the sword, the Jews had worked deviously to establish themselves as a ruling caste – 'Nothing brutal . . . but a sort of gentle occupation, an insinuating way of evicting the indigenous population from their houses, from their jobs, a smooth way of depriving them first of their goods, then of their traditions, their morals and finally their religion.'[1]

The subtitle of *La France juive* was *Essai d'histoire contemporaine* – an essay on contemporary history – and Drumont presented his work as scholarly, reaching back far into the past to clarify the present, illustrating his theme with innumerable anecdotes and case histories which were described by Jean-Paul Sartre sixty years later as 'a collection of ignoble and obscene stories'.[2] The Jew's compulsion to dominate and exploit non-Jewish peoples, wrote Drumont, had been drummed into him over generations of studying the Torah and Talmud. Contempt for the gentile and a hatred of Christianity were unalterable features of his genetic make-up. 'This hereditary transmission of religious hatred and anti-social instincts is one of the things which has most struck us in the course of writing this book. Without giving to heredity the fatal character which is attributed to it by modern science, one must admit that it plays a considerable role in the make up of a people.'[3]

The Jews, wrote Drumont, took full advantage of the Enlightenment. 'To succeed in their attack against Christian civilisation, the Jews in France have had to be clever, to lie and disguise themselves as free-thinkers . . . For a long time they remained in a vague condition, working through Freemasonry, and hiding behind fine phrases: emancipation, enfranchisement, the struggle against superstition and prejudices of another age.'[4] Given full rights as citizens at the time of the French Revolution of 1789, they established an ascendancy through banking, trade and commerce, creating monopolies 'over all basic necessities, not only of industry, but of life itself' – wheat, sugar, coffee, copper, the press, the publishing industry and the new department stores – and, with the collusion of French Protestants, crushing any competition from French Catholics.

* Drumont greatly exaggerated the number of Jews living in France.

The collapse of the Union Générale bank in 1882 had been a case in point. The initial success of this financial conglomerate had been precisely because its founder Paul Eugène Bontoux had presented it as a vehicle for the savings and investments of Catholics that was not run by Protestants or Jews. 'Its operations were followed with blind faith by all classes of Catholics; its stock soared to fantastic heights and its activities had a great deal to do with the boom of 1880 and 1881 . . . Within a year the decline had set in and it turned into a collapse, whose consequences spread to every part of the French financial system.'[5] Drumont maintained that this collapse had been deliberately engineered by Jewish bankers such as the Rothschilds.

The name Dreyfus frequently crops up in Drumont's polemics. Among his *bêtes noires* were not just Auguste Dreyfus, who had made a great fortune importing guano from Peru and embroiled the French state in his enterprises, but also the Radical journalist and Deputy Camille Dreyfus – at one time editor of the anti-clerical *La Lanterne* and founder of *Le Matin* – and the proprietors of Dreyfus Frères, a Jewish meat supplier, whom he accused of supplying rotten meat to the army, a charge for which he was sued for libel and condemned to three months in gaol.

Drumont believed that he was championing Catholicism in France, and described in *La France juive* his own reconversion – how, after having 'denied the divine aspect' of Catholic dogmas and lived outside the Church, 'it had pleased God, in his infinite mercy, to call the poor writer by his name, to exercise on him a sweet and irresistible pressure which one does not resist, to tap him fraternally on the shoulder . . .' and call him back to the practice of his faith. He talks of Jesus of Nazareth as 'the most faithful of friends',[6] but, as John McManners points out, 'no one could mistake his tirades for over-flowings of Christian charity'.[7] Drumont himself seems to have found no incongruity between his abusive stereotyping of Jews and his Catholic beliefs. In old age, he rebuked God for the loss of his sight – 'after all that I have done for him!'; and he frequently complained that in his struggle he was given no support by the Church. 'I am not the intimate of any cardinal, bishop or Jesuit . . . On the contrary, the members of the upper clergy are hostile rather than friendly towards our ideas. They are servants of the Jews like many of our magistrates and our politicians.' He could not understand why, 'when he presented himself as an antisemitic candidate in the municipal elections in Paris in 1890, Catholic leaders had organized to oppose him: "all the Catholics [voted] against a man who defended the Church . . .".'.[8]

There were certainly Catholics who accepted that element of Drumont's conspiracy theory which matched the attack on Jewish influence in the Jesuit *Civiltà Cattolica* in 1889, and the anti-semitic polemic of the Assumptionist paper *La Croix*. And Drumont had his admirers among the lower clergy: almost a third of the anti-semitic books published in France between 1870 and 1894 were written by Catholic priests.[9] But there is a distinction to be made between theological anti-Semitism on the one hand and the pseudo-scientific theories found in Drumont; and there was friction at the interface as when, for example, the influential Jesuit priest Père du Lac rebuked one of Drumont's friends, Jules Guérin, for attacking a Catholic convert called Dreyfus, while another, Jacques de Biez, 'went about asking priests if it were really true that "Jesus Christ was a Jew? Drumont doesn't seem to mind, but I can't swallow it."'[10]

La France juive was a phenomenal success, selling over a million copies and going through 200 printings in twenty-five years. Some, like Léon Bloy, thought that Drumont deliberately exploited popular prejudice to make money and further a political career. He had 'found the goose that lays the golden egg' and realised that 'by far the easiest way to influence and to please people is to fill their bellies with their favourite swill'.[11] But 'what Drumont did have was great skill as a propagandist and an uncanny rapport with his public'. As he himself put it, his only merit was to have 'committed to print what everyone was thinking'.

2: La Libre Parole

In 1891, encouraged by the success of *La France juive*, Édouard Drumont founded a daily newspaper, *La Libre Parole* (Free Speech) to promote the ideology of anti-Semitism and expose the corruption and disloyalty of Jews. Soon after the publication of the first issue it had a scoop of spectacular proportions: the paper received a list of members of the Chamber of Deputies who had been bribed to vote in favour of a national lottery to bail out the bankrupt Panama Canal Company.

The Compagnie Universelle du Canal Interocéanique – the Panama Canal Company – had been founded by the French engineer Ferdinand de Lesseps, who thirty years or so earlier had built the Suez Canal. Now aged seventy-four, de Lesseps remained a man of prodigious energy and drive.* He was also an 'incurable optimist': as Ernest Renan, the author of *La Vie de Jésus*, said when receiving de Lesseps into the French Academy – quoting scripture as befitted the former seminarian – he had the faith to move mountains. But it took more than faith to move the mountains of the isthmus of Panama. De Lesseps's determination to do without locks and build a sea-level canal, 'a new Bosphorous', was thwarted by the mountainous terrain. Moreover, the tropical conditions made it a death-trap for the labourers and engineers. 'Yellow fever killed Europeans as fast as they could be sent out. The boast of the chief engineer, Dingler, that Panama was really healthy, was refuted by the loss of his own family,' despite their being housed in a large villa built at the shareholders' expense known as 'Dingler's Folly'.

But what threatened the Panama Canal project was not so much loss of life as a lack of money. De Lesseps had grossly underestimated the cost of the canal, and the company was obliged to raise new capital, thereby diluting the holdings of the original investors. Increasingly, a portion of the funds raised was used not to pay for the canal but to buy the silence of French journalists. A report written for the French government by an engineer called Rousseau was delivered to the Minister of Public Works, Charles Baïhaut, also an engineer and, as an officer of the Society for the Promotion of Good, a high priest of the new secular morality. Predictably, in the eyes of anti-republicans, the minister did not practise what he preached, first 'seducing the wife of an old friend who was not of a forgiving temper and then by allowing himself to be

* Ten years before, aged sixty-four, he had married his second wife who was aged twenty-one at the time. They had twelve children, the last born when de Lesseps was eighty-four.

tempted by the opportunities open to a Minister of Public Works to get his share of the spoils of Panama'.[12] Since no more money could be obtained from investors, a lottery was proposed of the kind that had raised funds for the completion of the Suez Canal under the Second Empire.

The price for Baïhaut's complicity in raising money from the public on a false prospectus, and throwing good money after bad, was to be one million francs. The raising of such large sums to pay off the politicians required expert attention. The company's first financier, a banker called Lévy-Crémieux, was replaced by Baron Jacques de Reinach – a German Jew with an Italian title, now a naturalised Frenchman, who had made his fortune with investments in French and Canadian railways. He had a chateau in Picardy and, like the guano-king, Dreyfus and the grain millionaires, the Ephrussis, a mansion overlooking the Parc Monceau in Paris. He was thought to be the model for Baron Duvillard, a character in Émile Zola's novel *Paris*.

Reinach had a nephew, Joseph Reinach, who sat in the Chamber of Deputies for the Seine et Oise, had been a close associate of Gambetta's and retained good contacts with the majoritarian Opportunists.* Jacques de Reinach himself had his own friends among politicians such as Camille Dreyfus and Léon Say. He 'spent lavishly in splendid hospitality, in fostering the arts, especially those arts which, like the opera and the ballet, brought him into contact with young women'.[13]

In oiling the wheels for the Panama Canal Company, Jacques de Reinach enlisted the help first of a fellow German Jew, Émile Arton, 'who looked after those aspects of the financing of Panama that would look oddest on the balance sheet', and next, to win over Radical deputies, of a French Jew from the Franche-Comté, Cornelius Herz, who had spent some of his life in the United States, as had his close friend the French Socialist politician Georges Clemenceau. Clemenceau had worked as a teacher in Greenwich, Connecticut, and had married a pupil, Mary Plummer, but by the time of the Panama Canal crisis

---

* Centrist republicans, known as 'Opportunists' because they postponed the radical reforms they supposedly supported until the time was opportune.

he had run through her money* and was in need of cash to pay for his newspaper and a mistress whose previous lover had been a multi-millionaire and prince of the blood, the Duc d'Aumale.

Herz, though not in the same league as Reinach, cut a considerable figure in Parisian society, and splashed money around to make friends and influence people, giving two expensive bracelets to the grand-daughters of the President of the Republic, Jules Grévy. He now began to augment the funds he received as a lobbyist for the Panama Canal Company with money paid to him by Reinach to keep quiet about some past treachery, sin or scandal, the exact nature of which never became known. The web of corruption grew ever larger with 510 members of the National Assembly, among them six government ministers, eventually accused of accepting inducements via Reinach and Herz to hide from the public the disastrous financial position of the Panama Canal Company and pass a law to permit a lottery to bail it out. The bill was passed by both the Senate and the Chamber of Deputies to raise 720 million francs, but it was under-subscribed by more than 50 per cent. The money raised was not enough. The company was bust.

The bankruptcy of the Panama Canal Company, with the loss of almost a billion francs by its French investors, 'was the greatest disaster since the collapse of the Empire, the greatest purely financial disaster since the Mississippi scheme of nearly 200 years before'.[14] There was a fear among government ministers, who had so recently seen off the threat of an authoritarian coup by General Boulanger, that if the truth became known about the means employed to cover up the true state of the company's finances before its collapse, the opprobrium would mean the end of the Republic. They therefore procrastinated over demands for an inquiry, and hoped that the truth might never come to light; but those hopes were dashed when a series of articles began to appear in *La Libre Parole* under the headline 'The Dirty Linen of Panama' – 'Les Dessous de Panama'.

The articles were written by a journalist, Ferdinand Martin, under the name 'Micros', but the material was supplied by Jacques de Reinach

---

* He later got rid of her by ordering the Prefect of Police to have her followed and, after she was caught with a young lover, threaten her with imprisonment for adultery unless she returned to the United States.

himself in return for an assurance that his name would be kept out of the ensuing scandal. It was too late. The conspiracy was unravelling. Reinach realised he would be exposed and, after an unpleasant interview with his nephew and son-in-law, Joseph Reinach, he returned home where, the next morning, he was found dead in his bed.

Was it suicide? Or was he silenced by powerful interests because he knew too much? It was said that Reinach had been poisoned, and Herz claimed that Reinach had earlier tried to poison him. Charges of fraud were brought against directors of the Panama Canal Company, among them de Lesseps, his son Charles and the contractor Eiffel whose tower dominating the Paris skyline symbolised the triumph of secularism, modernity and progress. The Chamber of Deputies was forced to vote for a public inquiry. Governments rose and fell, though all were formed from the same coalition of cronies – 'la République des Camarades'. The arraigned directors refused the role of scapegoats and produced the stubs of the cheques paid to the politicians. The parliamentary immunity of five deputies was lifted so that they could be charged with corruption; so too that of five members of the Senate. Some of the chief culprits had fled abroad – Arton, Reinach's first gofer, over the Rhine to wander around Europe, and Herz over the Channel to settle in Bournemouth on the south coast of England.

In the event, there were few convictions and, in the elections of 1893, remarkably few of the tainted deputies lost their seats. There was no credible alternative to the Opportunists. If they had 'been shown to be knaves, their enemies had been shown up as fools; and a peasant elector prefers a knave to a fool'.[15] There were Socialist gains and conservative losses. The only exception among the victorious Socialists was Georges Clemenceau, who had made his friend Cornelius Herz a Grand Officer of the Légion d'Honneur. Because Clemenceau spoke English and was known to support a policy favourable to England, he was accused of being an English agent and personal protégé of Queen Victoria. His speeches were interrupted by shouts in English of 'aoh yes' and, though the Socialist representation in the Chamber of Deputies rose from twelve to fifty, Clemenceau lost his seat.

3: Matters of Honour

The charge that Clemenceau was an English agent was made in the Chamber of Deputies by the leader of the French League of Patriots, and supporter of General Boulanger, Paul Déroulède. For this affront to his honour, Clemenceau challenged Déroulède to a duel. Clemenceau was a skilled and experienced duellist but in this instance his three shots missed their mark. So did those of Déroulède.

It was an incongruous feature of the French Third Republic, which considered itself in the vanguard of progress and civilisation, that this medieval way of settling differences should still be in force. In the course of the twentieth century the concept of honour – that is, a man's reputation for honesty and integrity – was to pass into abeyance, but in the late nineteenth century it was very much alive, and impugning it was still a reason for one man to challenge another to a duel.

Duelling had been accepted as a judicial process among the Germanic tribes outside the Roman Empire, and even by Christian kingdoms in the early Middle Ages: it was assumed that God would always ensure that the innocent would triumph over the guilty. Cardinal Richelieu, whose brother had been killed in a duel, persuaded King Louis XIII to ban it in 1626, and the Comte de Montmorency-Bouteville and his second, the Comte de Chapelles, were executed for fighting a duel in the Place Royale in Paris.[16] However, this means of settling 'affairs of honour' had survived the demise of the *ancien régime*. The contrast between the social status of swashbuckling French aristocrats and the middle-aged and often portly bourgeois journalists and politicians clearly did not deter the latter from throwing down the gauntlet to those who had insulted them – even if that gauntlet was no longer a chain-mail glove but rather a rolled-up newspaper. Clemenceau would later fight a duel with Édouard Drumont, and Déroulède with Jean Jaurès. Joseph Reinach, the nephew of Baron Jacques de Reinach, would fight thirteen duels in the course of his career.[17]

In some countries in central and eastern Europe, Jews, because of their lowly status, were not considered *satisfaktionsfähig* – capable of giving satisfaction to a man of honour[18] – but this was not the case in

France. Drumont, because of the numerous libels and insults published in *La Libre Parole*, was frequently challenged.* In 1886 he was challenged by Arthur Meyer, the editor of *Le Gaulois*, for reprinting an old article in *La France juive* which accused Meyer of cheating at cards. Edmond de Goncourt describes Drumont on the day of the duel as being in

a nervous, excited, gay mood. 'Today,' he exclaimed, 'I had fifty-five callers . . . The bell never stopped ringing. Crowds have started gathering in the street at the sight of all the people coming in . . . people who come to say to me: "How grateful we are to you for saying what we think!" There are some Carmelites who sent word to me that they would pray for me on Saturday . . . and somebody told my housekeeper, who's a pious old thing, that I was a sort of lay priest . . .'[19]

The obsession with duelling of this 'lay priest' and 'secular monk' reached absurd proportions. 'The mania for fighting which has taken hold of Drumont', wrote Goncourt,

is turning him into a figure of fun. Nature is nothing for him now but a setting for affairs of honour. When he took the lease of his house at Soisy, he exclaimed: 'Ah, now there's a real garden for a pistol-duel!' A certain walk in Daudet's park called forth the comment: 'Oh, what a splendid spot for a sword-fight!' And when, recently, his friends were discussing a marriage they wanted to arrange for him, he suddenly said: 'Yes, everything you say about the girl is perfect . . . But do you think she is likely to get upset when two gentlemen call for me in the morning?'[20]

* Prior to his duel with Clemenceau in 1898, Drumont had fought duels with Arthur Meyer in 1886, André Crémieu-Foa in 1892, Camille Dreyfus in 1893 and Bernard Lazare in 1896. Other duels fought by Jews include those between Catulle Mendès and Paul Foucher; Camille Dreyfus and Henri Rochefort; Joseph Reinach and Paul Déroulède; Henri Bernstein and Léon Daudet; Baron Robert de Rothschild and the Comte de Lubersac; and Armand Mayer and the Marquis de Morès.

A charge more serious than card-sharping, made over and over again in both *La France juive* and *La Libre Parole*, was that Jews could not be trusted as officers in the French Army. Up to that point, wrote Drumont, the Jews had infiltrated and now dominated every branch of the French state. 'France, thanks to the principles of '89 easily exploited by the Jews, fell to pieces. The Jews monopolised the public finances, took over everything, except the army.'[21] Now they were moving in on that most sacred of French institutions. In May 1892, *La Libre Parole* began publishing a series of articles, with the byline of the Comte de Pradel de Lamaze, under the headline 'The Jews in the Army'.

> No sooner have the Jews gained a foothold in the army than they have sought in every different way to gain influence. Already masters in finance, in the administration, promoting their interests in the law courts, they will be definitively masters of France on the day when they command the Army. Rothschild will be given the plans of mobilisation and one knows well to what end.[22]

One of the articles, 'The Jews at the École Polytechnique', stated that 'among the members of the society of former pupils, one finds 18 Martins, the most common name in France, but there are 19 Lévys. The Mayers and Meyers are 13.'

La Libre Parole had particular targets among the military, either officers who were Jewish or gentile officers who protected them. One of the latter was General Saussier, the Military Governor of Paris, Vice-President of the High Council of War and, in fact if not in law, because the title did not officially exist, 'generalissimo' elect of the French armies in time of war. Saussier was not Jewish but had a Jewish mistress, the wife of a Jewish officer, Maurice Weil. For *La Libre Parole*, Weil epitomised all that was wrong and risky in a Jewish officer. Born in 1844, and with a reasonable record in the Franco-Prussian war (he received the Légion d'Honneur), Weil had worked for a while in army intelligence, then commanded by a fellow Jew, Colonel Samuel. He was an amateur historian, played the stock market, loved horse-racing and was a popular guest in 'the salons of Jewish high finance . . . an assiduous visitor at the Rothschilds, the Ephrussis, the Cahen d'Anvers, the Camondos; he was even said to be the lover of a beautiful Jewish countess, the wife of a Jewish banker'.[23]

In 1876 he married 'an elegant Viennese, a co-religionist'. He developed a passion for horse-racing and was 'regularly to be seen at the paddock at Longchamp, Auteil and Deauville'. He frequently laid bets on the horses, either for himself or for his rich friends. In 1881, one of these rich friends, Baron de Schickler, accused Weil of cheating him and the ensuing scandal, exposed in the periodical *La Vie Moderne*, meant that Weil had to resign his commission in the army reserve. He fled to Spain to avoid judicial proceedings. 'The brilliant situation which he had built up for himself in Paris', wrote Maurice Paléologue,

> was in ruins. But, with that mixture of flexibility and tenacity which is one of the marks of his race, he set about gradually re-establishing it. By a stroke of brilliant cynicism, he secured the friendship of the Commander-in-Chief, the Governor of Paris, General Saussier, who, having a lively sensual appetite in spite of his sixty years, became the lover of the attractive Mme Weil. Thus, on 8 January 1890, the complaisant husband was restored to the army with the rank of major in the territorial cavalry and posted as adjutant to the Commander-in-Chief's staff. Henceforward he was his chief's inseparable companion; General Saussier dined with his good friends two or three times a week.[24]

This mix of sex, money and favouritism in high-ranking officers was a godsend for Drumont and his anti-Semitic friends. Senior officers' weakness for women, and consequent favouring of their *maris complaisants*, was not limited to Weil: according to *La Libre Parole*, Saussier also kept in post a senile and incompetent general named Édon whose wife's favours he also enjoyed. For Saussier, all this was water off a duck's back, but the constant repetition of the charge that the 300 or so Jewish officers in the French Army were incapable of true patriotism, and were therefore untrustworthy, outraged the Jewish officers in question, and in May 1892 one of them, Captain André Crémieu-Foa, wrote to Drumont laying down the gauntlet: 'in insulting the three hundred officers on active service who belong to the Jewish faith, you are insulting me personally'. Drumont replied: 'if Jewish officers are wounded by our articles, let them choose by lot as many representatives as they will and we will oppose them with an equal number of French swords'.[25]

A duel between Crémieu-Foa, who 'was rated as one of the best duellists in the army',[26] and Drumont was fought on 1 June 1892. The weapons chosen were swords. The fighting was intense; both men were wounded and Drumont's doctor, Poquelin, intervened to stop the fight. This 'semi-defeat' of Drumont led his seconds, the Marquis de Morès and the Comte de Pradel de Lamaze, to challenge Crémieu-Foa to a second duel. It was agreed by the duellists and their seconds that, to protect Lamaze's wife and children from anxiety, the duel should remain secret. However, Ernest Crémieu-Foa, the brother of André, sent a report of the duel to the Dalziel news agency.

To Drumont and his friends, this leak to the press confirmed the view that 'in Semitic eyes, probity and honour are meaningless'.[27] However, the culprit was thought to be, not Ernest Crémieu-Foa, but André Crémieu-Foa's second, Captain Armand Mayer, and it was therefore Mayer who was called out by Drumont's second, the Marquis de Morès.

Antoine Amédée-Marie-Vincent Manca de Vallombrosa, Marquis de Morès and de Montemaggiore, was the eldest son of the Duc de Vallombrosa. He was an elegant, swashbuckling figure with an arrogant tilt to his head and a fine, twirled moustache. At the military academy of Saint-Cyr, his fellow students had included the future Marshal Pétain and Blessed Charles de Foucauld, who later became a Trappist monk and was murdered by Bedouin in the Sahara. Morès was married to an American heiress, Medora von Hoffman, and with her dowry had bought large tracts of land in North Dakota. He had founded a town called Medora after his wife, and built an abattoir and meat-packing plant connected by a spur to the Northern Pacific Railway. His plan was to deliver dressed carcasses packed in ice to the major cities on the east coast, thereby cutting out the Chicago stockyards and the middlemen of the Chicago beef trust. The plan failed. The hold of the Chicago meat trust could not be broken: Morès believed it was dominated by Jews.

Morès returned to France and entered politics on an anti-republican, anti-Semitic ticket. As with Drumont, there was a measure of populism, even socialism, in his stance: he called for an alliance between France's ancient aristocracy and the French people against a republic dominated by the Jews. Teaming up with Drumont and writing for *La Libre Parole*, he accused Jewish butchers of selling rotten meat to the French Army's garrison at Verdun, a claim which made him popular among the workers in Paris's meat markets: they formed a small private army, 'the friends of de Morès', with a uniform of cowboy shirts and Stetson hats.

The duel between the Marquis de Morès and Captain Armand Mayer was fought with swords on 23 June 1892 on the Île de la Grande Jatte on the Seine west of Paris. Mayer, a professor at the École Polytechnique, gave lessons in fencing: the assailants were considered evenly matched. Mayer attacked Morès, who parried his thrust but, as Mayer continued his lunge, Morès's épée penetrated Mayer's body, went through his lung and was stopped only by his spinal column. The duel was stopped. The two men shook hands. Mayer was taken to a hospital but died at five in the evening.

Captain Armand Mayer's death provoked feelings of horror and revulsion throughout France. More than 20,000 people attended his funeral: the Chief Rabbi of France, Zadoc Kahn, gave the address. The Minister of War, Charles de Freycinet, stated in the Chamber of Deputies that 'the army must not make any distinction between Jews, Protestants and Catholics. Such a division in the army is a crime against the nation.'[28] Morès was charged with homicide. He retained a prominent lawyer, Maître Edgar Demange, to defend him: Demange had acted for him before when, in 1890, Morès had been charged with riot and inciting mutiny among French troops. In that case, Morès had been found guilty and sentenced to three months' imprisonment; but when it came to the killing of Captain Mayer, the jury decided that the fight had been fair and Morès was acquitted.

'We are only at the beginning of a civil war,' Morès wrote in *L'Écho de Paris* after his acquittal. He now joined forces with those trying to unseat Georges Clemenceau in the 1893 election during which much muck was raked up by either side. Some of the mud thrown at Morès by Clemenceau was not easily brushed off. It turned out that Morès, to pay off a gambling debt which he could not at the time settle from his own resources, had borrowed money from the Jewish fixer of the Panama Canal Company, Cornelius Herz.

After this humiliation, Morès thought it best to leave France. His plan was to travel across the Sahara from Tunisia to Sudan to open up a trade route that would bypass the British-controlled Suez Canal, enlist nomadic tribes under the tricolour and form an alliance against the British with the Mahdi. Morès's expedition had no official backing, but he proceeded all the same. He sailed to Gabes on the coast of Tunisia from where his caravan set off south towards Sudan. Four days into his journey, he was murdered by his Tuareg guides – 'robbed, stripped, his body mutilated, and all but one of his servants slaughtered'.[29] Many believed, among them his wife Medora, that this was not a case of mere banditry but was a judicial assassination instigated by ministers in the republican government in Paris.

André Crémieu-Foa also died in Africa. Feeling himself dishonoured by the whole imbroglio that had led to the death of his friend Armand Mayer, he requested a transfer to Dahomey. There he was injured during an engagement with hostile natives and later died of his wounds.

Among the letters of condolence received by his grieving mother in Paris was one from the man who had served as a second in her son's duel with Drumont, the Comte Marie-Charles-Ferdinand Walsin-Esterhazy. Esterhazy had encouraged the younger Crémieu-Foa, Ernest, to send an account of the duel to the Dalziel news agency – the 'dishonourable' act that had precipitated the duel between Morès and Armand Mayer – but that was not held against him by Mme Crémieu-Foa. 'I have the supreme consolation', she wrote back to Esterhazy,

> that my beloved son André has died as a soldier. The war in Dahomey is finished: seventeen officers died, two of them Jews! That is our response to the attacks of *La Libre Parole* . . . There will be a memorial service on Thursday in the Jewish synagogue for these brave young men who died

in the service of their country. It would make me happy to see you there among our friends – you who remained true amidst all these sorrows, you who are among those courageous men who, like me, put honour before life itself.[30]

The death of André Crémieu-Foa and another Jewish officer in the service of their country did not make a headline in *La Libre Parole*. The death of Armand Mayer had discredited the anti-Semites and put Drumont and his friends on the defensive. The circulation of *La Libre Parole* started to decline: the paper was in need of a dramatic new outrage like the Panama scandal.

In December 1893, a new government was formed by Jean Casimir-Perier with General Auguste Mercier as Minister of War. Despite a reputation for competence and a distinguished military career, Mercier did not meet with the approval of Drumont and his colleagues on *La Libre Parole*. He was a republican and graduate of the École Polytechnique, not of Saint-Cyr. Though nominally a Catholic, his wife was English and Protestant: Mercier did not go to Mass. He was known to have liberal opinions and thought to be covering up the corruption of a Jewish army doctor, Schulmann, by ordering a second inquiry when the first had condemned him. If Schulmann's conviction is confirmed, thundered *La Libre Parole*, then Mercier would have to resign. 'That would be the only act in his ministerial career that a good Frenchman could applaud.'[31]

However, the case of Schulmann was not enough to rouse the nation or increase the circulation of *La Libre Parole*. Something more dramatic was required, and something more dramatic turned up. At the end of October 1894, an anonymous letter was received by the paper which vindicated all the warnings and forebodings of Drumont and *La Libre Parole*. On 1 November, under a banner headline, the paper announced the arrest of a Jewish officer on a charge of espionage. 'Arrested fifteen days ago, he has confessed all and there is ABSOLUTE PROOF that he has sold our secrets to Germany.' It named the Jewish officer: Alfred Dreyfus.

PART TWO

Alfred Dreyfus

4

Evidence of Treason

1: The Statistical Section

After its humiliating defeat in the Franco-Prussian war, the French Army had been reorganised along the lines of its German counterpart which had so emphatically demonstrated its superiority in the field. Conscription was introduced and the High Command was divided into four departments, or *bureaux*. Attached to the Second Bureau was a secret unit for intelligence and counter-intelligence with the obfuscating name of the Section for Statistics and Military Reconnaissance. Its first commander was a Jewish officer, Major Samuel, who set up espionage networks in Berlin and the lost province of Alsace.

It was generally accepted in France that the Treaty of Frankfurt was not the end of the matter so far as Franco-German relations were concerned: sooner or later there would be another war. The Statistical Section's energies were therefore directed mainly towards Germany rather than other great-power rivals such as Britain, Italy or Russia, and its office in Paris was close to the German Embassy on the rue de Lille. It worked in concert with the Prefect of the Parisian police, and used methods employed by French intelligence since the time of Henri IV – in particular, the interception of correspondence. The intelligence gathered in this way was not limited to military matters but included compromising information on courtiers and statesmen.* The post-war Prefect of the Paris Police, Léon Renault, set up a parallel network of informers in France and also agents abroad: a memorandum from the Prefecture dated around 1872 recommended 'as suitable for future recruitment . . . *les Israélites allemands, presque tous achatables mais tous à surveiller*'¹ – 'German Jews, almost all venal but all to be watched'. The Paris correspondents of foreign newspapers were particularly suspect, with the Danish journalist Hansen and Blowitz, the Paris correspondent of the London *Times*, 'international celebrities known as double agents throughout Europe'.²

French anxiety about espionage increased in the 1880s when it became apparent that, even after the reforms, the French Army remained inferior to that of Germany. A demographic disparity meant a smaller pool for recruits; and despite new plans for rapid mobilisation, a reconfiguration of defensive fortifications in the east and development of new weaponry, doubts remained that France could win a new war with its enemy across the Rhine.

The proposed solution was diplomatic – an alliance with Tsarist Russia – and in 1893 the Chief of the General Staff, General de Boisdeffre, went to St Petersburg to negotiate a treaty of mutual assistance. In the short term, however, this increased rather than diminished French anxieties. Was it not possible that the Germans, realising that the Russian alliance would put them at a disadvantage, would find some excuse for a pre-emptive war before it could become effective?

A sense of responsibility for the security of the nation weighed heavily on the French Army's High Command. In almost all the other nations of Europe, the army and people were united behind a monarch; Germany in particular was a semi-militarised nation under the Kaiser. France, however, had known many different regimes in the course of the nineteenth century – the First Republic, the Directory, the Consulate, the First Empire, the Bourbon Restoration, the July Monarchy, the Second Republic, the Second Empire and now a Third Republic whose

---

* Under Napoleon III Victor Hugo, an opponent of the regime, would send several letters in a single packet with a request that, after it had been opened, they be forwarded by the police.

governments came and went, and whose stability, on many occasions, seemed precarious. With no king or emperor at the head of the nation, and presidents who, for fear of a coup, were deliberately chosen for their lack of military stature, officers in the French Army developed the view that 'they served the French state, not a particular regime'.[3]

This was especially true of the Statistical Section. Like other intelligence services the world over, the need for secrecy led to an isolation of its personnel from the rest of the army, and created among them an elitist *esprit de corps*. The Statistical Section came to consider itself to some extent superior to other state institutions, including the government, and felt authorised to subject ministers to surveillance and an assessment of their loyalty to France. There was a file on the civilian Minister of War, Charles de Freycinet; and, when a senior general, Gaudérique Roget, asked the Section to help him get rid of a troublesome mistress, he discovered it already knew all about the affair.[4]

The man who came closest to imposing an authoritarian form of government on the Third Republic, General Georges Boulanger, had served as Minister of War in 1886–7. Known as 'Général Revanche' for his bombastic speeches about the recovery of Alsace and Lorraine, he ordered a shake-up of counter-intelligence and the establishment of contingency plans for dealing with unreliable elements in the event of war. There was a national census in 1886 which Boulanger wanted to use to establish how many foreigners were living in the border zones of France.

The chief of the Statistical Section at the time was Colonel Jean Sandherr, an Alsatian from Mulhouse. His father had been a convert from Protestantism to Catholicism who, during the industrial unrest in 1870, had demonstrated against 'the Prussians of the interior' – that is, the Protestants and Jews. The son, Jean, was said to be the most handsome man in the French Army. He was a graduate of Saint-Cyr, served as a regimental officer until 1885 and subsequently taught at the École de Guerre. As an Alsatian, Sandherr was aware of the particular problems of security in the border areas of eastern France, and he diligently followed Boulanger's instructions to form a register of aliens and potential spies.

When Boulanger fell from power, Sandherr pursued the project on his own initiative. He drew up lists of those whose loyalty to France was suspect. Carnet A contained the names of resident aliens, most of them Germans, and Carnet B of non-resident aliens and suspect French citizens. Corps commanders were instructed to prepare premises where, in the event of war, those on the lists could be interned. At a meeting of the High Council of War held on 1 April 1889, it was agreed that in the event of war Sandherr's plan would be put into effect, with all enemy aliens of military age interned as prisoners of war and the women and children deported.

General Auguste Mercier, appointed Minister of War in December 1893, enthusiastically endorsed Sandherr's plans for the mass internment of up to 100,000 people in the event of war. The civilian prefects and army regional commanders were warned that the enemy aliens listed on Carnet A as Germans would often claim to be 'Alsatians, Lorrainers, Luxembourgeois, Swiss, Belgians, etc.'; and they were told that potential spies on Carnet B 'should be considered as criminals'. Inevitably Alsatians 'figured prominently' in Sandherr's list of suspects, his Carnet B.[5] And 'for Sandherr and Mercier . . . the distinction between indictment and conviction for spying was a mere legal formality. The assumption of guilt would hang heavily indeed on the accused.'[6]

Sandherr's plans for mass internment without due process of law have been considered a sign of paranoia in the French High Command, as have the elaborate measures taken to weed out spies. Douglas Porch, in writing about the French secret services, states that 'paranoia becomes an occupational hazard in counter-intelligence' and that the Statistical Section at this time was 'suffused with an atmosphere of exaggerated spy mania'; but Sandherr and his subordinates had to deal with the unique and complex questions of loyalties that followed the annexation by Germany of Alsace and Lorraine. With an ever increasing pitch in nationalistic rhetoric among the European powers, the ambivalent status of Frenchmen from these 'amputated provinces' made them either super-patriots or potential traitors. There was a disproportionate number of Alsatians in the Statistical Section not just because they spoke German but because they were thought best able to smoke out the traitors among those fellow Alsatians who had opted for French nationality.

Much was at stake. One of the lessons learned from the Franco-Prussian war was that superior weapons such as the breech-loading, steel-tubed Krupp guns could tip the balance in armed engagements. France had made significant advances in the design of weaponry: in 1892, the artillery had been revolutionised by the advent of the new 120mm howitzers and 155mm cannon; in 1893, the Lebel rifle was modified; and finally, from 1894 onwards, a rapid-firing breech-loading cannon, the 75, with revolutionary recoil mechanism, was brought into service: it could fire twenty rounds a minute instead of the seven of the cannon it replaced.[7]

Keeping such advances in weaponry from the Germans was of paramount importance and there were Frenchmen who were venal. In 1888 the Paris correspondent of the London *Daily Telegraph* reported that 'traitors seem to abound in the French army. The War Office authorities are at their wits' end.'[8] In 1890, a senior civil servant working in the technical section dealing with artillery in the Ministry of War was caught passing secret information to the then German military attaché, Hühne, on a park bench on the avenue Friedland in Paris. Boutonnet, the civil servant, was sentenced to five years in prison and a fine of 5,000 francs, and Hühne, at the request of the French government, was recalled to Berlin. Two years later, in 1892, a civil servant in the Naval Ministry, Greiner, was charged with selling documents to the American military attaché, Borup, who had passed them on to the Germans.[9]

The network of German agents was directed by the military attaché in the German Embassy in Paris. In 1894, this post was occupied by a charming and cultivated officer, Maximilian von Schwartzkoppen. Schwartzkoppen was already known to the French: he had done a previous tour of duty in the Paris Embassy, and Colonel de Sancy, director of the General Staff's Second Bureau, had got to know him when serving in the French Embassy in Berlin. It was accepted that, as the German military attaché, Schwartzkoppen would seek to inform himself on the French Army's potential; he was invited to attend manoeuvres, but suborning traitors was considered dishonourable, not just by the French Foreign Office, but also by the German Ambassador, a veteran diplomat, Georges-Herbert, Graf Münster von Derneburg. After the embarrassment of the Hühne affair, Münster gave strict instructions to Schwartzkoppen that he was not to indulge in espionage, and felt able to reassure the French government apropos of the new attaché: 'You won't have any trouble with him.'[10]

Schwartzkoppen had indeed promised Münster that he would conform to the code of conduct that the ancient and distinguished Ambassador felt proper, but there were higher powers than the Ambassador, notably the Director of Military Intelligence in Berlin who, with the Kaiser's approval, instructed Schwartzkoppen to ignore Münster's scruples. The interests of the German Empire were paramount, and Schwartzkoppen was to proceed on that assumption.

Schwartzkoppen was flexible when it came to matters of honour. The Statistical Section intercepted eighty of the letters in his correspondence with his mistress, Hermance de Weede, the wife of the Counsellor at the Dutch Embassy, described by Maurice Paléologue as a 'charming Dutchwoman, with feline movements and big, passionate eyes'.[11] They also intercepted the correspondence of Schwartzkoppen and his Italian opposite number in the Italian Embassy, Major Alessandro Panizzardi, which seemed to confirm the rumour picked up by a French agent working in the Spanish Embassy, the Marquis de Val Carlos, that the two men were lovers.

Dear Maximilienne, am I still your Alexandrine? When will you come to bugger me? A thousand salutations from the girl who loves you so. Alexandrine

My darling . . . all yours and on the mouth . . . Maximilienne

Yes little red dog, I shall come to your pleasure. I would be capable of stuffing a metre of swaddling in you and all the fourteen-year-old commandants if needed. Oh, the filthy beast. All yours, still coming. Maximilienne[12]

Other exchanges between the two military attachés intercepted by the Statistical Section were of a less personal nature. In April 1894, Panizzardi sent Schwartzkoppen the blueprints of the fortifications of Nice close to the border with Italy, apparently supplied by a spy he had recently spurned. 'Attached are 12 master plans of Nice which that scoundrel D. gave me in the hope of restoring relations.' Who was D? Two suspects, one named Dacher, the other Dubois, were investigated but both were cleared of suspicion.

Given the importance attached to counter-espionage by the French General Staff, it is remarkable that the number of officers serving in the Statistical Section was so small. Colonel Sandherr's second-in-command was Commandant Albert Cordier, who, had he not been an old friend and protégé of Sandherr's, would almost certainly not have remained in such a demanding post. Father Josué, as he was known in the office, was lazy, sloppy and fond of a tipple. Beneath Commandant Cordier came Lieutenant-Colonel Hubert Joseph Henry,* who, as an officer who had risen from the ranks, was an anomaly in such an elite group.

Henry was the son of a farmer in the Tourenne and his appearance, according to Maurice Paléologue, betrayed his origins: he was stolid, sturdy, thickset, with a fine moustache, florid cheeks and a look of gruff candour that concealed his peasant cunning. He had an impressive record. As a sergeant-major in the Franco-Prussian war, he had twice been taken prisoner, had twice escaped, and his brave conduct under fire had led him to be commissioned in the field. In 1876 he had served as aide to the reforming Minister of War, General de Miribel, and it was Miribel who first appointed him to the Statistical Section at the time when Charles Ferdinand Esterhazy, who had acted as second to André Crémieu-Foa, was serving there as a translator.

In 1882 Henry left the Statistical Section for a period of active service in Tunisia and Tonkin. He was promoted to the rank of major in 1891 and returned to the Statistical Section in 1897 as third-in-command. Henry knew no foreign languages and at first sight would seem unsuited

* Pronounced 'onrri'.

to work in army intelligence, but his peasant cunning and familiarity with the kind of low-life that he had encountered in the ranks enabled him to pick up information and recruit agents in circles of society inaccessible to those born into the officer class. 'In daily contact with venal servants, procuresses, former policemen and commercial travellers, he knew how to find the tone which would bring the reluctant into his confidence, bring the intractable to heel, persuade the reluctant to talk and terrorise as necessary those tempted to play a double game against the interests of the Section.'[13]

Despite the ease with which he moved among Parisian low-life, Major Henry was first and foremost a soldier, a strict disciplinarian with a profound respect for his superiors in the military hierarchy. He revered the senior officers of the High Command, and saw it as his duty not just to obey their direct orders 'but to execute the orders he had been given obliquely' with a nod and a wink, or even to anticipate orders that had yet to be given.[14]

Henry had a wife named Berthe who was to play a significant role in the Affair. According to Maurice Paléologue, he had fallen in love with this daughter of an innkeeper in his home village of Péronne. 'Pretty and attractive with a beautiful complexion, she kept him dangling so skilfully that he ended up marrying her.'[15] Once she had hooked her older husband and was installed in Paris, she had – so Commandant Cordier told Paléologue – taken up with another officer serving in the Statistical Section, Captain Jules Lauth.

Like his chief Sandherr, Lauth was handsome – a tall, trim, distinguished-looking ex-cavalry officer, always correctly dressed, highly intelligent, fluent in German, but cold, frigid, reticent. Again like Sandherr he was an Alsatian, born in Saverne north of Strasbourg, a Protestant though 'he wished he was not'.[16] His reticence helped to contain a short temper. He did not brook contradiction, which made his bond with the pig-headed Henry difficult to understand. Did Lauth's liaison with his wife Berthe give Henry a hold over Lauth, or was it Lauth, as Cordier believed, who had a hold over Henry? 'Be on your guard against Henry,' he told Paléologue, 'or rather be on your guard against Lauth, for he's the one who holds all the strings.'[17]

Among the officers serving in the Statistical Section there was also a Captain Pierre Matton who dealt with the Italians, and an archivist, Félix Gribelin – described by Paléologue as 'gentle, modest, self-effacing, the perfect servant, monastic in his docility'. Gribelin had an excellent memory and knowledge of the different dossiers, which was just as well because there was 'chronic disorder in the Statistical Section with a failure to date items of intelligence as and when they came into the office'.[18]

2: The Bordereau

Among the agents recruited by Major Henry from the Parisian low-life was an Alsatian, Martin-Joseph Brücker. His task was to keep foreign diplomatic personnel under surveillance, and to suborn clerks, valets and chambermaids working in the embassies so that they would assist him. One of Brücker's most useful recruits was a neighbour, Mme Marie-Caudron Bastian, who was employed on a daily basis by the German Embassy. Her job was to clean the offices, light the stoves and empty the waste-paper baskets, burning their contents in the boiler that fired the central heating. For a fee, she agreed not to burn the contents of the waste-paper baskets, but to smuggle them out of the Embassy and hand them over to Major Henry at a secret rendezvous, usually the church of Sainte-Clothilde or that of Saint-François-Xavier.

The codename given to Mme Bastian by the Statistical Section was 'Auguste', and thanks to her the traffic in waste-paper continued without a hitch along what came to be called the 'normal route' – the *voie ordinaire*. There were some dangerous moments: in 1893, a year before the arrest of Captain Dreyfus, a mistress discarded by Brücker informed the German Ambassador that both Brücker and Marie Bastian were spies. She was not taken seriously. Those responsible for security at the German Embassy reassessed the trustworthiness of their French staff, but cleared Brücker and considered it inconceivable that someone as apparently stupid as Mme Bastian could be a risk. She pretended to be illiterate and had been taken under the wing of the Ambassador's daughter who was living in the Embassy at the time. A former military attaché, Funke, who had been transferred to Madrid, took the trouble to write to his successor, Süsskind, to say that he could have complete confidence in Mme Bastian, who also cleaned the flat of the military attaché. He was not to know that Mme Bastian had just received a bonus from the Statistical Section for purloining a bundle of Süsskind's letters providing evidence of an adulterous affair.[19]

Towards the end of August 1894, Mme Bastian delivered via the 'ordinary route' a new consignment of waste-paper from the German Embassy, including the contents of Major von Schwartzkoppen's waste-paper basket. The archivist, Gribelin, entered the sum of 100 francs paid to 'Auguste' on 27 August,[20] but the consignment remained unexamined because on 25 August Major Henry, who was in charge of the *voie ordinaire*, took a month's leave to hunt in his native Péronne. He did not return to work until 25 September, and it was only some days later that he examined the contents of Schwartzkoppen's waste-paper basket.

Among the waste-paper he found a note torn into six pieces which, when pieced together, read as follows:

With no news suggesting that you would like to see me, I am sending you, in the meantime, sir, some interesting information:

1. A note on the hydraulic brake on the 120mm cannon and the way in which it performs;

2. A note on covering troops (some modification will be made in the new plan);

3. A note on a modification made to artillery formations;

4. A note relating to Madagascar;

5. The *Proposal for a Firing Manual* for the field artillery (14 March 1894).

This last document is extremely difficult to get hold of, and I can only have use of it for a very few days. The Ministry of War has sent a specific number to the various regiments, and the regiments are responsible for them. Each officer who has one must return it when the manoeuvres are over. If you want to take from it what is of interest and hold it at my disposal afterwards, I will get hold of it . . . This, unless you want me to make a copy *in extenso* and send you the copy.

    I am off on manoeuvres.

The note, or *bordereau*, as it came to be called – a term used in banking for a list or memorandum – was unsigned, but its significance was clear. Henry took it at once to his chief, Colonel Sandherr. Sandherr was appalled. The *bordereau* showed not just that there was a traitor providing secrets to the Germans but that he was an officer in the French Army – 'I am off on manoeuvres.' Most disquieting was the promise of technical details of French cannon; it indicated that the officer in question served in the artillery. But the other items offered to Schwartzkoppen – the planned deployment of covering troops, the imminent invasion of Madagascar – meant that he must have access to secrets from different *bureaux* available only to a member of the General Staff.

The 532 civil servants and 133 auxiliary employees working for the General Staff could be excluded, but this still left 220 officers seconded from different branches of the service.[21] Knowing that his reputation was on the line, Sandherr immediately ordered Gribelin to look through the archives of the Statistical Section to see if there was something written in handwriting comparable to that of the *bordereau*. Nothing was found.

At the same time Sandherr reported the discovery to his superior in the military hierarchy, the Deputy Chief of the General Staff, General Charles-Arthur Gonse, who in turn told his chief, General Raoul de Boisdeffre. Finally the Minister of War himself, General Mercier, was informed. All agreed that the traitor must be an artillery officer on the General Staff: no other possibility was considered. Mercier ordered a formal investigation. Lists were drawn up and suspects scrutinised, but none was a plausible traitor. Having gone through all the officers attached to the General Staff from the four different *bureaux*, the army chiefs were 'at the end of their tether'[22] and ready to give up.

On 5 October, the newly appointed second-in-command to the Fourth Bureau, Commandant Albert d'Aboville, turned up at the

War Ministry to take up his new duties. On the morning of the 6th his chief, Colonel Pierre-Élie Fabre, showed him a photograph of the *bordereau*. They were joined in Fabre's office by a Lieutenant-Colonel Boucher of the Third Bureau, and the three men started to speculate about who could have had access to secret information from different departments.

It was d'Aboville who came up with the idea that the traitor might be one of the interns (*stagiaires*) from the artillery: they had all done a stint in the different departments. This reasoning seemed plausible to Fabre. A list was drawn up of all artillery officers serving as interns on the General Staff. Four or five of them were known to Fabre because they had been through the Fourth Bureau in the past year. One stood out for the bad mark Fabre had given him: 'An unsatisfactory officer, very intelligent and very gifted but pretentious and with an undeveloped character . . . and a manner that would make him unsuited to the Army's General Staff.' This officer was Captain Alfred Dreyfus.

D'Aboville had also known Dreyfus: 'He had a sly character,' he was to say later, 'was little liked by his comrades and had an indiscreet curiosity which was noticed by everyone.' Fabre obtained forms filled in by Dreyfus which provided samples of his handwriting. They were all struck by its similarity to that of the *bordereau*: the word 'artillery' which was in both the *bordereau* and the sample seemed identical. They recalled that Dreyfus had gone on a tour of inspection with members of the General Staff at the end of the month of June, which would explain the reference to leaving 'on manoeuvres'.

Fabre and d'Aboville now informed General Gonse of what they had discovered, who in turn told General de Boisdeffre of this new development. When Gonse told Sandherr he slapped his forehead with the palm of his hand, saying: 'I should have realized.'[23] Sandherr did not know Dreyfus personally but he knew of his family, the Jewish textile manufacturers in his home town of Mulhouse. General Mercier, the Minister of War, was now brought up to date by Boisdeffre with the news that there was a prime suspect, a Jewish officer from Alsace. Mercier would later say that the revelation caused him 'great distress', and he also understood that they had to proceed cautiously if the only basis for the singling out of Dreyfus was an opinion on the similarity of the handwriting taken by men with no expertise in graphology.

There was an officer in the judicial division of the General Staff who was known to be an amateur graphologist – Major Ferdinand du Paty de Clam. Du Paty was a cousin of Boisdeffre and therefore someone they could trust. On the evening of 6 October du Paty was summoned by General Gonse and shown the *bordereau*. He was asked to compare the handwriting with some samples of that of a suspect, but was not given the suspect's name.

Du Paty's immediate reaction was that the *bordereau* and the samples had been written by the same person. Only now did General Gonse tell him about how the *bordereau* had come into their hands, and that the other samples had been written by Captain Alfred Dreyfus. He asked du Paty to undertake a more detailed examination and gave him the use of the office of a senior officer on the General Staff, General Renouard.

Now that he knew that the suspect was named Dreyfus, was du Paty capable of an impartial analysis, or was he inevitably affected by prejudice against Jews? Had this coloured the judgement of d'Aboville and Fabre? Historians differ on this critical question. Vincent Duclert writes that the officers 'who took charge at the beginning of October 1894 of the inquiry to identify the traitor were the same officers who, in the Fourth Bureau, had worked to exclude Jews in general and Captain Dreyfus in particular. The chance to exclude him from the General Staff was at hand.'[24] Jacqueline Rose writes that the *bordereau* was 'wilfully . . . attributed to . . . Dreyfus'.[25] Against this, Albert S. Lindemann wrote in *The Jew Accused*, 'No evidence has ever emerged of an anti-Semitic plot against Dreyfus by intelligence officers, especially not of a premeditated effort to convict someone they knew from the beginning to be innocent. Alfred Dreyfus was not the victim of a conspiracy of aristocratic officers against a Jewish outsider, as many came to believe at the time and as many historians to this day present the matter.'[26]

Robert L. Hoffman concurs that 'there is insufficient reason to believe prejudice determined the identification of Dreyfus as a suspected spy and traitor'.[27] So too Marcel Thomas, but with a proviso: 'Certainly, it did not occur to anyone, on 6 October 1894, to consider Dreyfus guilty because he was a Jew, but the fact that he was a Jew meant that they accepted more easily than they might otherwise have done the idea of his culpability.'[28] The distinction was fine but real. The 'General Staff, as a whole,' wrote Thomas, 'disapproved of the campaign against Jewish officers of *La Libre Parole*: these seemed to be in poor taste'; but many were 'prisoners, often unknowingly, of prejudices they would have been the first to deny'.[29]

Du Paty came from a family of lawyers; his grandfather had been President of the Court of Bordeaux – 'justice seemed to be a family tradition'.[30] However, he thought it unwise to put those 'who are not Frenchmen of France' in sensitive military positions.[31] Dreyfus himself came to believe that he had been condemned because he was a Jew, and that du Paty was one of those principally responsible for his misfortunes: 'The opprobrium of my death will be on Commandant du Paty,' he wrote at a time when it seemed unlikely that he would survive the tropical fevers he contracted during his incarceration. His son Pierre, writing some years later, judged du Paty 'not, perhaps, dishonest at heart' but 'naive and irresolute', and a tool of his superiors, Gonse and Boisdeffre, who 'later did not hesitate to leave him shamelessly in the lurch'.[32]

Maurice Paléologue regarded du Paty as something of a Colonel Blimp – 'pretentious, monocle in eye, well set up, abrupt in speech, and with mechanical gestures', but by no means straightforward: 'a disturbing character, with morbid mentality, a shadowy and unhinged imagination, a strange mixture of fanaticism and folly'. He was not the idiot that he was sometimes portrayed as being but 'intelligent and cultivated'[33] – fluent in German and a lover of German music who went to hear Wagner's operas at the Bayreuth Festival. Maximilian von Schwartzkoppen, who had got to know du Paty while attending manoeuvres at Toulouse in 1892, considered him an 'attractive and intelligent officer' who 'liked to talk to Germans about Germany'. Du Paty and Schwartzkoppen occasionally dined together, and the latter had been a guest at du Paty's wedding.[34]

However, Schwartzkoppen's assessment of his friend's character confirms the unsuitability of du Paty for the role to be assigned to him by Gonse and Boisdeffre. He was 'a man full of enthusiasms and exaggerated notions, a man of the study, with little sense of the realities of life. This mental myopia gave him a quality of impracticality, a touch of the blundering and erratic.'[35] Marcel Thomas talks of a 'romantic side to him' and of his 'too great a confidence in his own intuition'; he was 'the man least suited in the world to the role in which he was cast by his superiors'.

These judgements were made at a later date. In early October 1894, du Paty's role was merely that of an amateur graphologist, known and trusted by the senior officers of the General Staff. He conscientiously followed the instructions he had been given, spending the whole of the Sunday on a minute study of the different samples of handwriting, and in the evening of 7 October he delivered a report to his superiors stating that 'despite certain disparities' the resemblance was sufficient to justify further investigation.

———

General Mercier had to take great care. On the one hand, he had already been attacked by *La Libre Parole* for being a 'republican' general who protected Jews in the army such as the military doctor Schulmann; on the other, there had been the emphatic declaration in the Chamber of Deputies by the then Minister of War, Charles de Freycinet, after the death of Captain Mayer in his duel with the Marquis de Morès, that there would be zero tolerance of anti-Semitism in the army: a false accusation against a Jewish officer, or even a charge with insufficient evidence, would cause as much trouble on the left as a failure to charge a Jewish traitor would cause trouble on the right.

Mercier's next step, therefore, was to consult the Military Governor of Paris, General Saussier – the rotund bon viveur with a Jewish mistress, Mme Weil, whose husband was intermittently accused of treason in *La Libre Parole*. Saussier was in some respects a more powerful figure than General Mercier himself; for while Mercier was his superior as Minister of War, he would, should he fall from office, return to a subordinate role as a regional commander: he had no place *de jure*, as did Saussier, on the High Council of War. The two men were chalk and cheese:

Mercier dry, curt, authoritarian; Saussier indulgent but diplomatic, realistic and level-headed. These differences had led to a mutual antipathy and the likelihood that what one proposed the other would reject, and vice versa.

Saussier's immediate reaction when Mercier informed him that Captain Alfred Dreyfus was suspected of treason was to let the matter drop. He thought the prestige of the army would suffer if an officer on the General Staff was accused of selling secrets to the Germans, and that it would antagonise the Jewish community: 'you will see a hundred million francs leave France'.[36] The solution he proposed was to post Dreyfus to North Africa in the hope that he would be killed in action; but, as Mercier pointed out, he might do well and 'return with a promotion'.

Saussier also disliked Sandherr, whom he knew had a dossier on Weil and kept him under surveillance: it seemed possible that Sandherr was the source of the stories in *La Libre Parole* accusing Weil of spying. He was therefore inclined to dismiss the whole thing as 'a story invented by the Statistical Section'. As Military Governor of Paris, it was Saussier's prerogative to authorise the arrest of Captain Dreyfus should that become necessary: the thinness of the evidence made such a request unlikely.

Mercier, too, was aware that the view taken by an amateur graphologist, Commandant du Paty de Clam, would have to be confirmed by an expert and, at a meeting of the Council of Ministers held on 9 October, he asked a colleague, the Minister of Justice, Eugène Guérin, if he could recommend a professional graphologist. Guérin gave him the name of an expert at the Bank of France, Alfred Gobert.

On 10 October, Mercier went to see the President of the Republic, Jean Casimir-Perier, to tell him about the *bordereau* and the discovery of a suspect from among the officers of the General Staff; he did not give that officer's name. Like Saussier, Casimir-Perier was not unduly disturbed by what he was told: the documents listed in the *bordereau* did not seem of great importance and measures could surely be taken by the War Office to limit any damage that might be done by the leak. Mercier next told the Prime Minister (President of the Council of Ministers), Charles Dupuy: again, he did not name the suspect. Dupuy proposed a sub-committee to deal with the matter composed of himself, the Minister of War, the Minister of Justice and the Minister of Foreign Affairs.

It was this last, Gabriel Hanotaux, who when the sub-committee met on the following day, 11 October, spoke forcefully against embarking on a process that could lead to nothing but disaster. The evidence had been stolen from the German Embassy and should that become known it would lead to a diplomatic incident of a most serious kind.* Mercier stood firm. The security of the nation was in jeopardy and, anyway, it was now 'too late to turn back'. The Prime Minister, Dupuy, proposed a compromise. The investigation would proceed for now but, if no better evidence could be found against the suspect than the similarity of his handwriting to that of the *bordereau*, then it would be abandoned.

Why was Mercier so determined to pursue the inquiry? He was, as we have seen, a 'republican' officer married to an English Protestant and so free of the knee-jerk anti-Jewish prejudice found among many of his conservative Catholic colleagues. Did a stubborn trait in his character lead him to defy Hanotaux as he had Saussier – a personal prejudice exacerbated by the traditional rivalry between the Foreign Office on the Quai d'Orsay and the War Ministry on the rue Saint-Dominique? Was he afraid of losing face with Sandherr, Gonse and Boisdeffre if he was seen to back down? Or was it in the back of his mind that the prosecution of a Jewish officer would re-establish his credentials among right-wing deputies and the journalists on *La Libre Parole*?

Marcel Thomas believed that he made the decision to pursue the inquiry 'in good faith, and after having fully considered the matter'. [37] Mercier had been given prima facie evidence of treason by the Statistical Section and felt it was his duty to uncover the traitor. However, he may not have realised at this point the extent to which his hold on office

* The Franco-Prussian war had arisen out of the umbrage taken by the French over the Ems dispatch – a telegram from the secretary of Kaiser Wilhelm I, then taking a cure in Bad Ems, to the German Chancellor Otto von Bismarck describing an exchange between the Kaiser and the French Ambassador which was edited by Bismarck and released to the press.

would depend upon a successful outcome to this investigation, nor was he aware of that flaw in his character which led him to convert suspicion into a probability and probability into a certainty, and stick to that certainty through thick and thin. Having made up his own mind that Dreyfus was guilty, Mercier saw 'the legal process, though necessary, as no more than a simple formality'.[38]

The simple formality, however, required detailed preparation: nothing should be left to chance. It was important to have the police on side, and so Mercier told Sandherr, Henry and du Paty to brief the Prefect of the Paris Police, Louis Lépine. The handwriting expert from the Bank of France, Alfred Gobert, was summoned to the rue Saint-Dominique and worked throughout the day of Friday, 12 October; he was not given the name of the suspect. Lépine promised the services of his Chef du Service d'Identité Judiciare (head of the Judicial Identification Service), Alphonse Bertillon.

However, before the experts' reports were submitted, the decision was taken to prepare for the arrest of Captain Dreyfus. On the evening of 12 October, Commandant du Paty de Clam was summoned by General de Boisdeffre and told that he had been chosen to make the arrest. Du Paty, realising that he was being asked to embroil himself in a matter likely to be controversial and of uncertain outcome, did what he could to persuade Boisdeffre that he was not the right man for the job. 'You will poison my life,' he told his cousin. 'I am head of a family. It is a job for a bachelor.' He suggested a fellow officer, Georges Picquart. But Boisdeffre insisted: 'You weren't educated by the Jesuits, you have no Jewish connections.'[39] Du Paty acquiesced.

On 13 October, General Mercier left Paris to attend military manoeuvres in Limoges. In his absence, the arrangements he had made for the expeditious arrest and conviction of Captain Dreyfus hit their first obstacle. The handwriting expert from the Bank of France, Alfred Gobert, delivered his report. The samples of handwriting he had been asked to compare were certainly 'of the same graphic type', but there were 'numerous and important disparities which had to be taken into account'. The *bordereau*, 'written quite naturally and normally in a rapid hand', could have been written by 'a person other than the suspect'.

This setback was serious but not insurmountable, and certainly not sufficient to stop the momentum towards making an arrest. Gobert had not been told the name of the suspect but, on his own admission, he had quickly guessed it, and this made Gobert himself suspect in the eyes of those who had called upon his expertise. Gobert worked for the Bank of France, and the Bank of France was in the hands of the Jews. Gobert would not want to antagonise them by giving evidence that compromised one of their own.

Secondly, his opinion was contradicted by the man brought in to study the *bordereau* by the Prefect of Police, Lépine. Alphonse Bertillon was not a handwriting expert as such but the inventor of a system of criminal identification known as anthropometry. He had developed it over the fifteen years that he had worked in the Prefecture and, with the science of fingerprinting still in its infancy, had been successful in identifying multiple offenders: his system had been adopted by police forces in Britain and the United States.

Bertillon acknowledged at once that the two examples of handwriting were not identical but said it was ridiculous to suppose that a spy would write such a compromising note in his own hand. Naturally, he had taken the precaution of disguising his handwriting. The *bordereau* was an 'auto-forgery'. Subsequently Bertillon would show how, cunningly, the spy had imitated the hand of different members of his own family for different words so that, if an incriminating document was found in his home, he could show that it was a botched forgery, while if it was found outside his home, the differences would establish that it could not have been written by him.

This convoluted theory was illustrated with a drawing of a fort that might have been designed by Vauban to show how a besieged spy would defend himself against attacks coming from different directions.[40] The theory would later be dismissed as the product of an unsound mind, but at the time it was treated with respect and impressed Mercier. Bertillon was, after all, an internationally acknowledged expert on criminal identification and he was vouched for by the civilian Prefect of Police, Lépine. His opinion was also a godsend as a counterweight to that of Gobert.

Mercier ordered the arrest of Captain Dreyfus. A date was set. The Governor of the Cherche-Midi military prison, Commandant Ferdinand Forzinetti, was told to prepare a cell for a high-ranking prisoner. Commissaire Armand Cochefert, chief of the Criminal Investigation Department at the Prefecture of Police, was seconded to assist du Paty in making the arrest. On the evening of 15 October a group consisting of Generals de Boisdeffre and Gonse, Colonel Sandherr, Commandant du Paty and Commissaire Cochefert met to confirm the details of the plan. Dreyfus would be summoned to the War Ministry for a 'general inspection' by the Chief of the General Staff. He would be met by an officer who had taught him at the École Polytechnique, Commandant Georges Picquart. Picquart would escort him to the ante-room of Boisdeffre's office where they would find du Paty de Clam. Commandant Henry from the Statistical Section and Commissaire Cochefert would remain concealed behind a screen.

Feigning an injury to his finger, du Paty would ask Dreyfus to copy out a letter, and closely study him while he was writing. Du Paty would then subject him to a summary interrogation and finally charge him with treason. A service revolver with a single bullet in its chamber would be placed within reach so that Dreyfus, if a shred of honour remained in him, would be able to 'render justice to himself'.[41]

Dreyfus Accused

1: Alfred Dreyfus

While this plan for the morning of 14 October 1894 was being rehearsed at General Staff Headquarters on the rue Saint-Dominique, Captain Alfred Dreyfus was at home with his family in his apartment on the other side of the River Seine. He had by now received the order to present himself for a general inspection the next morning wearing civilian clothes, but it gave him no cause for anxiety. At ease among those he loved, that Sunday evening was, as he later told his wife Lucie, a moment of particular happiness.

> A brilliant and facile career was opened to me; the future appeared under bright auspices. After the day's labours I tasted the repose and the charms of family life. Interested in all the manifestations of the human mind, I delighted in reading during the pleasant evenings passed at my own fireside. My wife and I were perfectly happy, and our first child enlivened our home. I had no worldly anxieties; the same profound affection united me with the members of my own and my wife's family. All that renders life happy seemed to smile on me.[1]

This is how Alfred Dreyfus remembered his last moments of freedom, and aspects of this recollection are undoubtedly accurate. He and his wife did indeed have no 'worldly anxieties' – both were rich in their own right. They had a spacious and elegant apartment on the avenue du Trocadéro: when teaching at the École Supérieure de Guerre, Alfred could walk to work, crossing the Seine on the Pont de l'Alma or the Pont des Invalides. It is also true that his was a closely knit family, and that he had great intellectual curiosity which he could satisfy reading by the fireside in his home.

Less certain can have been Dreyfus's confidence in the continuance of his 'brilliant and facile career': he had already suffered, in his own view, from the prejudice felt among senior officers against Jews. There was also the possibility that a scandal might erupt which would jeopardise both his career and his happy marriage. He had always enjoyed the company of attractive women, in particular *femmes galantes* – women, we are told by Vincent Duclert, who were 'neither prostitutes nor women of the world' but 'who took lovers and liked love, sometimes profiting from it'. Duclert, one of the most recent and most hagiographic of Dreyfus's biographers, admits that his subject's 'recent marriage had not wholly persuaded him to give up these pleasures. And even his great affection for Lucie had not extinguished the desire to please and seduce.'[2]

Dreyfus had met a young woman called Suzanne Cron at the races in April 1894. She was separated from her husband and in the process of getting a divorce. He had visited her on a number of occasions in her apartment on the rue de Calais and envisaged renting a villa in which she would live as his mistress. In July, he seems to have got cold feet and brought the liaison to an end, but Suzanne Cron continued to write impassioned letters, the last ending 'Life and death'. She was not the first object of Dreyfus's extramarital dalliances. There had been an earlier liaison with a slightly older woman of Austrian origin, Marie Déry, which had ended in 1893, and another with a woman called Mme Bodson.[3] Earlier still, before his marriage, Dreyfus had befriended a widow, a Mme Dida, who was later shot dead by a Russian adventurer, Pierre Wladimiroff. Soon after the murder, Mme Dida's father had called on Dreyfus at his home on rue François 1er to tell him that he had been named by Wladimiroff as one of Mme Dida's former lovers. Dreyfus had denied this – he said that they had merely been friends; but he had subsequently been summoned to give evidence before the *juge d'instruction*. His career would undoubtedly suffer if there was another incident of this kind.

Vincent Duclert takes the view that Dreyfus's infatuations with these *femmes galantes* were not consummated – were mere *amitiés amoureuses*: 'After the serious illness of his wife, following the birth of their second child, he returned in part to a bachelor life. He was constantly drawn to beautiful women in whose company he experienced an amorous pleasure [*un plaisir amoureux*].' He takes Dreyfus at his word in stating that he 'did not cross the gap between this and consummated adultery', although it seems unlikely that Dreyfus would plan to install Suzanne Cron in a villa simply for tea and sympathy. Be that as it may, by the middle of October 1894, Dreyfus seemed to have mastered his dangerous weakness for beautiful *femmes galantes* and the risk of scandal receded. The future did indeed seem bright for this captain in the artillery, still only thirty-five years old.

———

Dreyfus's rapid rise in the military hierarchy was particularly noteworthy because his background was so different from that of most officers in the French Army. Born on 9 October 1859, he was the youngest of seven children of the textile manufacturer Raphaël Dreyfus and his wife Rachel. For the first ten years of his life he had lived with his parents in Mulhouse – first in a small apartment on the rue du Sauvage, later in a large house on the rue de la Sinne, the move reflecting the rapid rise in the fortunes of the family following Raphaël's commercial success. Alfred had three sisters and three brothers and 'as the youngest-born, he was especially petted by his parents and elder brothers and sisters'.[4] Because of his mother's ill-health, his eldest sister Henriette played a maternal role. Among his siblings, Alfred was particularly close to his brother Mathieu – as open and easy-going as Alfred was reserved and retiring.

The improvement in the family's material circumstances was only part of a metamorphosis that had taken place as a result of Jewish emancipation following the French Revolution. Raphaël's first language was

German, and his French had at times been ridiculed by French-speaking brokers at the cotton exchange because of his use of German words and his thick Alsatian accent.[5] However, by the late 1850s Raphaël had given up some of the practices of orthodox Judaism, had dropped the Germanic spelling of his name, Dreÿfuss, and had adopted a French wardrobe and way of life. Photographs show him clean-shaven with short side-whiskers – a striking contrast to the 'long, full beards of his forefathers'.[6] His children were bilingual but even Alfred, who had received a French education, 'spoke French with a distinctly German accent'.[7]

Mulhouse, formerly Mülhausen, was a predominantly Protestant city that, until the French Revolution, had been a free city within the Swiss Confederation and often a place of refuge for Jews fleeing from the intermittent pogroms in Alsace. A sense of solidarity between the two oppressed minorities led the Protestant industrial oligarchy to open up, 'if only part way', to Jewish entrepreneurs. The town's synagogue was designed by a Protestant architect. 'Not one Catholic enterprise would be established in Mulhouse in the nineteenth century.'[8] Catholicism was the religion of the mainly German workers who manned the looms. These workers had gone on strike in 1870; the *fabricant-ocratie* had called in a regiment of cavalry to restore order. 'These social protests exacerbated religious antagonism between the Protestants and Catholics.'[9] It was during these disturbances that Jean Sandherr, the father of the chief of the Statistical Section in 1894, had 'marched through Mulhouse shouting "Down with the Prussians of the Interior!" which in local parlance meant "Down with Protestants and Jews"'.[10] The Dreyfus family had kept off the streets and remained behind the closed doors of their apartment.

France's defeat in the Franco-Prussian war was a catastrophe for the Dreyfuses and had a traumatic but formative effect on the young Alfred. 'Do you remember my telling you', Alfred would later write to his wife Lucie, 'how, more than ten years ago, at Mulhouse, in the month of September, I heard a German military band go marching past our house, celebrating the victory of Sedan? My grief was so over-whelming that I swore to devote all my strength and intelligence to the service of my country . . .'[11] The Dreyfuses were ardent French patriots, but France for them was not so much a tribe with a Christian heritage or a territory studded with the monuments of its Christian past as a nation that had repudiated sectarianism and superstition to guarantee for all its citizens the Rights of Man.

Under the provisions of the 1871 Treaty of Frankfurt, residents of Alsace and Lorraine were given the choice of remaining as subjects of the Kaiser or retaining their French citizenship and going into exile. Raphaël Dreyfus, though his mother tongue was German and his mills were now in Germany, did not hesitate in choosing to remain a citizen of France. He was, as his grandson Pierre would later describe him, one of 'those Alsatian patriots who preferred exile to German domination'.[12] Raphaël therefore moved with his wife and younger children to Basel in Switzerland, only forty kilometres from Mulhouse, and left his eldest son Jacques in Mulhouse to run the factory. This meant that Jacques, who had fought in the Alsatian Legion throughout the Franco-Prussian war, was obliged to adopt German nationality. Raphaël and Rachel's eldest daughter Henriette now married a textile manufacturer, Joseph Valabrègue, and went to live with him in Carpentras, the capital of the former Papal State of the Comtat Venaissin in the south of France. Jacques, too, was married soon after the family's dispersal, to Louise Wimpheimer, the daughter of an industrialist from Philadelphia in the United States. Alfred, now thirteen, was sent as a boarder to an elite private school in Paris, the Collège Chaptal.

Although this abrupt removal of a boy of this age from a doting family to the cold corridors of a boarding school was common in England, it was not in France and may have contributed to an Anglo-Saxon reserve in the young Alfred – what the French call *le flegme anglais*. Even before leaving home, 'his sisters had noted his reserve . . . when visitors called at the home . . . Later that shyness bordering on timidity became a reserved, highly controlled manner that at times came across as arrogance. He had difficulty "opening up".'[13] However, he excelled at his studies and it quickly became clear to his teachers, to his family and to Dreyfus himself that he could legitimately aspire to enter one of France's elite Grandes Écoles. Alfred had in mind the École

Polytechnique, established at the time of the Revolution, and a military academy under Napoleon I, and now once again France's leading educational institution for scientists and engineers.

The École Polytechnique was the portal through which Dreyfus hoped to enter the officer corps of the French Army. The other acknowledged route was the military academy of Saint-Cyr, but, though 'Jews were not formally excluded [from the academy] . . . the prevailing conservatism and above all the methods of recruitment in reality prevented them from getting in. The preparations for the entry exams were in the hands of religious establishments, especially those run by the Jesuits, in particular the famous school on the rue des Postes in Versailles.'[14] The École Polytechnique, by contrast, was republican in spirit – combining 'perfectly the republican ideology with intellectual ideology to combat the obscurantist forces of the *ancien régime* and the Church'.[15]

Competition for a place was intense and, after gaining his baccalaureate at the Collège Chaptal, Dreyfus spent two years preparing for the entrance exams to the École Polytechnique at the École Saint-Barbe where the fees were 4,000 francs a year. He was intellectually able, hard working and good at exams. The results of the entrance exam taken in 1878 placed Dreyfus 182nd out of 236. He graduated two years later from the École Polytechnique, 128th out of 235. He was commissioned as a sub-lieutenant, and enrolled in the army's school of artillery at Fontainebleau.

Over the next ten years, Dreyfus applied the talents he possessed to furthering his career. He became an expert horseman and was deemed 'extremely qualified' to teach horsemanship to squadrons in Paris.[16] He was assiduous in performing his duties and even went beyond what was expected of him, seeking out difficult work and demonstrating his newly acquired scientific knowledge and his quick understanding. Some of his studies on financial resources and mobilisation in time of war were praised by his superiors but provoked jealousy in his peers. He had unconventional views on military matters, which he defended vigorously, even vehemently, in debate with senior officers. These were qualities that appealed to the modernisers in the High Command but not to the traditionalists. To apply terms that might have been used by the English equivalent of the Saint-Cyrians, Dreyfus was 'pushy', he 'tried too hard' and was 'too clever by half'.

Dreyfus saw no active service; he never served abroad. He was appreciated by his superiors for his 'very lively intelligence' and 'excellent memory' and was only marked down in routine appraisals for his awkward manner and monotonous voice. This sometimes came across as arrogance: Dreyfus did not suffer fools gladly and felt 'he had little in common with his garrison colleagues' in Paris or Le Mans.[17] He was also set apart from his fellow officers by a private income of 20,000 francs a year – ten times the basic salary for a lieutenant at that time. Two-thirds of French officers had no private income.

This substantial supplement to Dreyfus's army pay enabled him to avoid the communal life of the barracks and 'secure the finest lodgings' wherever he was posted. He made no friends. Was this because he was cold-shouldered by the Saint-Cyrians among his fellow officers? Did they feel that, as a Jew, he did not 'fit in'? Or was it because Dreyfus preferred to keep himself to himself? There were, after all, many officers who were not Saint-Cyrians but, like Dreyfus, secular-minded graduates of the École Polytechnique: not all of these can have been anti-Semites yet, even among his fellow Polytechniciens, Dreyfus did not make friends. He thought it was 'absurd to bore oneself with a society of tiresome . . . disagreeable, often spiteful and envious men'.[18] He often 'took long walks alone'[19] and spent his leave going to see an art exhibition in Amsterdam or visiting relatives at Bar-le-Duc, Carpentras and even German-occupied Alsace – on one occasion obtaining a visa from the German Embassy, on another entering the territory without one.

2: Lucie Hadamard

Dreyfus preferred the company of women to men – no doubt seeking in his liaisons with the *femmes galantes* Mmes Dida, Déry, Bodson and Cron the cosseting he had received in childhood from his affectionate elder sisters. Arthur Meyer, the director of the conservative newspaper *Le Gaulois*, grandson of a rabbi and convert to Catholicism, would later write that Jews were sentimental villains who 'spend their youth in love with women who are not their race, seduce them, often have children by them, and leave them to wed Jewesses with dowries'.[20] In Marcel Proust's *À la recherche du temps perdu*, the Jewish Charles Swann marries his mistress Odette de Crécy, but it seems unlikely that Dreyfus contemplated following his example by marrying one of the easy-going women whose company he enjoyed.*

In this Dreyfus was conforming to the conventions of his class at that time. But it also demonstrates the limits of his concept of assimilation, and his commitment to liberty, equality and fraternity as the pre-eminent ideals of the society in which he lived. Dreyfus was a secularist: he did not believe in the precepts of Judaism, nor did he live in accordance with the law of Moses. Yet there is no evidence that he contemplated looking for a wife from outside the Jewish community† any more than he had looked for friends among his gentile comrades-in-arms. The one fellow officer whom Dreyfus did befriend at the École Polytechnique – they used the familiar form *tu*[21] – was also Jewish, Paul-David Hadamard, and it was Hadamard who introduced him to his future wife.

On 12 September 1889, Dreyfus was promoted to the rank of captain and was appointed as adjutant to the army's School of Pyrotechnics in Bourges. He was now thirty-three years old – tall, already balding, wearing pince-nez glasses but with a fine moustache. Earlier that year Paul-David Hadamard had taken Dreyfus to a family gathering at the home of his cousins David and Louise Hadamard. David Hadamard, then in his late fifties, traded in diamonds, a business he had inherited from his father. His wife Louise, née Hatzfeld, was the daughter of an industrialist, director of a steel works in Ars-sur-Moselle, who was a graduate of the École Polytechnique and had served as an officer in the artillery. Although David Hadamard had been born in Paris, his

---

* Cf. Jean-Paul Sartre in *Anti-Semite and Jew*, pp. 130–1: 'The love of a Jew for a Jewess is not of the same nature as the love he may feel for an "Aryan" woman. There is a basic doubling of Jewish sensibility concealed beneath the exterior of a universal humanism.'

† His brother Jacques had married an American, but she was a Jewish American.

family, like that of his wife, came from the lost provinces of eastern
France.

David and Louise Hadamard had five children, among them three
daughters, Lucie, Marie and Alice. It was the eldest, Lucie, then aged
twenty-five, who caught Alfred's eye as a possible wife. She was 'not a
stunning beauty'[22] but she was attractive – tall and slim, with broad
shoulders, dark eyes and thick black hair 'parted in the middle and
pulled back with a bandeau to control her curls'.[23] She had been
brought up in her parents' country house in Chatou near Paris and
educated largely by tutors in the home. Lucie was a talented pianist and
music was 'her first love', but like the other members of the Hadamard
family she esteemed intellectual achievement. Her mother was related
to Adolphe Hatzfeld, who had co-authored the seminal *Dictionnaire
Général de la Langue Française*; and her father's sister, Lucie's aunt
Eugénie, was married to David Bruhl whose son-in-law, Lucien Lévy-
Bruhl, was a distinguished philosopher.

The Hadamards were, then, socially superior to the Dreyfus family
in a number of ways. The Dreyfuses were rich but the Hadamards were
richer, and while the Dreyfuses were provincials with no roots in the
metropolis, the Hadamards were part of the Jewish elite with fine apartments in Paris or the suburbs and country houses within easy reach: the
Hadamards an apartment on the rue de Châteaudun and a country
house at Chatou; the Lévy-Bruhls 'one of the finest houses in the Parc
des Ibis on the avenue des Courses at Le Vésinet'. The Hadamards were
friends of the Chief Rabbi, Zadoc Kahn; unlike the Dreyfuses, 'the
family's private culture was still marked by Jewish practice, no matter
how attenuated'.[24]

What made Alfred Dreyfus a suitable *parti* for the Hadamards' eldest
daughter was his standing as an officer in the French Army. Certainly,
'his family were more than respectable' and came 'from the same Jewish
Mosello-Alsatian background'; he was vouched for by their nephew
Paul; he seemed 'serious and responsible' and 'his wealth and his
career assured the future of their daughter'.[25] But it was the career that
singled him out and made him particularly attractive to Lucie. 'She
was a merchant's daughter, and she . . . loved him for his uniform and

his sword.'[26] Dreyfus was given the green light and, upon returning to Bourges, courted Lucie by correspondence.

The courtship was successful. Alfred Dreyfus and Lucie Hadamard were married on 21 April 1890. The religious ceremony was performed in the Jewish synagogue on the rue de la Victoire by Zadoc Kahn, the Chief Rabbi, and was followed by a reception in the Hadamards' apartment on the rue de Châteaudun. They then left for a honeymoon in Italy, staying on Lake Como and in Florence. They returned via Basel in Switzerland, and then Mulhouse, so that Lucie could meet members of her husband's family who had not been able to attend the wedding.

When they returned to Paris, Alfred and Lucie moved into an apartment at 24, rue François 1er in the 8th arrondissement. It was an area 'that had attracted significant numbers of affluent Jews whose families had first settled in central and eastern districts'[27] but was also a short walk from Les Invalides. A rich man before his marriage, Alfred Dreyfus was now richer still. Lucie's dowry had included 'a trousseau of linen, lace, jewelry, and furniture valued at 20,000 francs; interest at 3 per cent on a sum of more than 35,000 francs; and more than 160,000 francs in cash – all of which, under the Code Napoleon, had been transferred to her husband's name on the day of their wedding'.[28] Lucie could expect an inheritance of more than 500,000 francs while Alfred himself had 'a permanent facility of several hundred thousand francs'.[29]

This prosperity enabled Alfred to stable two horses which he rode in the Bois de Boulogne. He 'ordered specially tailored uniforms and indulged his taste for chocolates and small cigars'.[30] He and Lucie moved from the rue François 1er to a grander apartment at 6, avenue du Trocadéro in the 16th arrondissement, where Alfred supervised the construction of a wine cellar. On 5 April 1891, Lucie gave birth to a son, Pierre, and soon became pregnant again. After the birth of her second child, a daughter, Jeanne, on 22 February 1893, Lucie was unwell for some time and, while Alfred was anxious and dutiful as a husband, he continued with his extramarital affairs. Vincent Duclert judges that 'Lucie loved Alfred deeply. Alfred loved her probably rather less, but he admired what she represented and the family into which he had married.'[31]

There was an element of Jekyll and Hyde in Alfred's behaviour in the years between his marriage and his arrest. He would return home from his office for a quiet dinner with Lucie, prepared by their Alsatian cook, Mlle Hassler, and then go out to the theatre or a concert or visit his parents-in-law for a rubber of bridge. In summer he would spend the weekends at Houlgate in Normandy where his family were on holiday, but during the week revert to his 'bachelor life'. Even when he was with Lucie, he was subject to 'mercurial moods, the abrupt shift from light-hearted discussions to an obsession with work, and a relentless perfectionism that made him appear selfish and insensitive'.[32] He acknowledged that he found it difficult to 'open up' and agreed 'that Lucie had a right to know more about the man to whom she was entrusting her life', but he had good reason to keep some things from her and was temperamentally incapable of breaking his 'disastrous habit' of taking everything seriously. He did not have much of a sense of humour.

3: The École de Guerre

Alfred Dreyfus's obsession with work came from his ambition to rise in the hierarchy of the French Army and gain entry to its General Staff. What might hitherto have been a pipe dream for the son of a Jewish textile manufacturer with a good brain but no connections among the right people had become a practical proposition after the reforms put through by Charles de Freycinet when Minister of War in 1888.

The École de Guerre, founded in 1880 to replace the École Militaire Supérieure along the lines of the Military Academy in Berlin, admitted its pupils strictly on merit and after the most rigorous of competitive examinations.[33] This gave an advantage to graduates from the École Polytechnique whose intellectual formation was closer to that of the École de Guerre than to that of Saint-Cyr. General de Miribel, as Chief of the General Staff at the time, had pushed through the reforms initiated by Freycinet. To break the system of co-option that favoured aristocratic officers educated at Jesuit schools, he laid down that the top twelve graduates would go on to serve as interns in the four *bureaux* with a view to recruitment to the General Staff (see above, p. 31).

Though enforced less rigorously by Miribel's successor, General de Boisdeffre, this system was still in force and was the obvious path for Dreyfus to take to the top. While still teaching at the artillery school in Bourges, he had swotted for the entrance examination – 'a three-day marathon of military tactics, topography, history and German'. He was the only candidate from the artillery school in Bourges to pass. He now entered the École de Guerre, and his success showed that Miribel's strictly meritocratic criteria for entry were still in force – but it was around this time, in May 1892, that Édouard Drumont embarked upon his campaign in *La Libre Parole* against the presence of Jewish officers in the army which led to the duels between Drumont himself and Crémieu-Foa, with Count Esterhazy as the latter's second; then that of Armand Mayer – an Alsatian Jew and Polytechnicien – with the Marquis de Morès in which Mayer was killed. Dreyfus did not attend Mayer's funeral because he was not in Paris, but he was undoubtedly present in spirit among the 20,000 who attended the obsequies presided over by the Hadamards' friend Zadoc Kahn, the Chief Rabbi.

Having won a place at the École de Guerre, Dreyfus was determined to pass out top in his class. As he studied he was confident that intellectual competence had replaced martial bluster as the qualities required in the leaders of a modern army. Somewhat naively, he ignored the evidence that the French officer corps remained governed by unwritten codes.[34] He was oblivious to the 'tensions between the modernists and the traditionalists', and failed to realise that the latter's position had been strengthened by the replacement of General de Miribel as Chief of the General Staff by General de Boisdeffre.

Dreyfus was abruptly made aware that the rules of the game he had thought abolished were still in force when he received the results for his final exams at the École de Guerre. In the course of his studies, he had been commended by the Commandant, General Lebelin de Dionne, for his mastery of military theory and administrative practice, for his 'good education, work habits and quick intelligence', and for his 'very good conduct and deportment'. His horsemanship and knowledge of German were regarded as outstanding – the only drawbacks being his short-sightedness and his monotonous tone of voice.[35] These minor failings should not, and did not, prevent Dreyfus from scoring high marks in his final examinations, but his overall score was lowered by a zero given by the examiner, General Pierre de Bonnefond, in an area of appraisal called *côte d'amour* – which might be translated as team spirit, or an ability to fit in.

As a result of this zero, Dreyfus had fallen from third to ninth place in his class – still an astonishing accomplishment, given that the young Napoleon Bonaparte, whose military genius Dreyfus greatly admired, had graduated from the École Militaire forty-second out of fifty-eight; and it was sufficient to gain him an internship on the General Staff. However, Dreyfus was incensed by the zero for *côte d'amour* and many of his biographers have shared his sense of outrage and ascribe it, like Dreyfus, to General de Bonnefond's expressed dislike of Jews. Ruth Harris asserts that Bonnefond's 'outrageous "fixing" of Dreyfus's exam results showed that prejudice was still rife'.[36] Vincent Duclert states that 'Captain Dreyfus became the preferred target for those officers who wanted to thwart the modernist means of advancement and were determined to prevent, above all, the entry of Jews into the "Holy of Holies" of the General Staff.'[37]

Douglas Johnson, on the other hand, in his *France and the Dreyfus Affair*, writes that 'it is important not to exaggerate the extent or the power of anti-Semitism in the French army', and cites the career of Maurice Weil, who 'retained the protection of powerful allies, not only Saussier, but a number of other generals'.[38] And, as Albert S. Lindemann points out in *The Jew Accused*, there were 'a surprisingly large number of Jewish officers in the French army (the figure of three hundred was often mentioned by the early 1890s of whom ten were generals)'. He adds that the percentage of Jewish officers was 'consistently at around 3 per cent from the 1860s to the eve of World War I. With Jews constituting between 0.1 and 0.2 per cent of the total population in those years, that meant an overrepresentation of between thirty and sixty times . . . Many spokesmen for the Jews in France claimed that the military was unusually open and just in its treatment of Jews.'[39] Marcel Proust, who had a Jewish mother, enjoyed his life in the army. 'It's curious', he wrote to a friend later in his life, 'that you should have regarded the army as a prison, I as a paradise.'[40]

The army was one thing: the General Staff another. General de Bonnefond was known to have said that 'he didn't want a Jew in the General Staff', and another Jewish intern, Captain Picard, had also been marked down. Dreyfus therefore filed a complaint with the Commandant of the École de Guerre, General Lebelin de Dionne. His complaint was rejected.[41] That rejection has also been ascribed to a reflex anti-Semitism in Lebelin de Dionne; however, it is a judgement that might have been unaffected by prejudice, given what is known of Dreyfus's temperament – his view of his fellow officers as 'tiresome . . . disagreeable, often spiteful and envious men'; his disdain for barracks life and the officers' mess; his aloof manner, his intellectual arrogance, his inflexibility and undisguised exasperation at the inefficiencies caused by the 'old spirit' in the army, contrasting it unfavourably with the professionalism of the German Army.[42] A senior officer must have a rapport with his men and his fellow officers. Intellectual brilliance is not the sole quality, or even the most important quality, by which to judge a candidate's suitability for high command.

Even after being marked down on *côte d'amour*, Dreyfus still qualified for a place as an intern on the General Staff; and here his progress did not falter until he reached the Fourth Bureau where his immediate superior, Commandant Bertin-Mourot, criticised him for pursuing his own studies at the expense of more mundane duties. Another assessor, Colonel Roget, judged Dreyfus to be 'a very intelligent officer with many gifts, an impressive memory, a great facility for the assimilation of facts, but without a character that inspires great confidence and who therefore it would be better not to keep on the General Staff after he has completed his studies'.[43] Colonel Fabre, the chief of the Bureau, wrote in his final report that Dreyfus was 'an incomplete officer, very intelligent and very gifted but undeveloped when it comes to character, awareness and attitude required for a place on the Army General Staff'.[44]

As with the zero for *côte d'amour* in the École de Guerre, biographers such as Vincent Duclert believe that this marking down came from the determination of the chiefs of the Fourth Bureau to keep a man who was both a Jew and a moderniser out of the General Staff. However, even these senior officers had to proceed with caution. Since the death of Captain Mayer, and the War Minister de Freycinet's warning that anti-Semitism in the army would not be tolerated, a career could be jeopardised by an open expression of antipathy towards a Jew. No professional soldier would give a quote or put his name to an article in Drumont's *La Libre Parole*. There were few open expressions of anti-Semitism, and even those made in private were rare. Even du Paty de Clam thought it 'severe' when General Alfred-Louis Delanne, head of the Third Bureau of the General Staff, said 'No Jews here'. At the time, wrote du Paty, 'I was imbued with the humanitarian prejudices and had good relations with intelligent Jews who were artists or scholars . . . But there are situations when it is preferable not to have people [in sensitive posts] who are not indisputably Frenchmen from France.'[45]

Many French officers from a conservative and Catholic background shared du Paty's view that Alsatian Jews were not wholly trustworthy, but it could never be said openly that a promotion should be blocked because an officer was a Jew. Instead, what were seen as Jewish traits would be ascribed to a candidate without reference to their source: he was over-confident, his formation was incomplete, his manner was off-hand. To Vincent Duclert, these 'subtle and perverse means of discrimination' were driven by 'a visceral and dogmatic anti-Semitism';[46] but was this true in the case of Dreyfus? Joseph Reinach admitted in his history of the Affair that Dreyfus was disliked by his fellow officers, and it is not absurd to speculate that, if Alfred had had the warm and open personality of his brother Mathieu, he might have achieved his ambition of gaining entry to the General Staff.

6

Dreyfus Condemned

1: Arrest

At nine in the morning of Monday, 15 October 1894, Captain Alfred Dreyfus turned up as instructed for a general inspection at the head-quarters of the General Staff on rue Saint-Dominique; he had walked in the autumn sunshine from his flat on the other side of the Seine. He was met by Commandant Georges Picquart, whom he knew from the École de Guerre, and was escorted by him to the office of General de Boisdeffre. In the ante-room he was presented by Picquart to another uniformed officer whom he had not met before: this was Commandant du Paty de Clam. Also in the room were three other men in civil-ian clothes — Félix Gribelin, the archivist from the Statistical Section; Armand Cochefert, head of the CID at the Prefecture of Police; and Cochefert's deputy, Henri-François Boussard. Hidden behind a screen was Commandant Henry from the Statistical Section.

Commandant du Paty de Clam handed Captain Dreyfus a form and asked him to fill it in. Puzzled by the presence of the three civilians, and by the absence of General de Boisdeffre, Dreyfus nonetheless did what was asked of him: he sat down at a small table and filled in the form. Du Paty then asked him, as a favour, if he would write a letter at his dictation which was to be signed by General de Boisdeffre. He said he could not write it himself because of an injury to a finger, hold-ing up his right hand encased in a black glove to prove his point. Still more perplexed, Dreyfus took up pen and paper and du Paty started his dictation.

> Paris, 15 October 1894.
> Having the best of reasons, sir, for temporarily retrieving the documents
> I sent to you before I left on manoeuvres, I now ask for their return at
> the hands of the bearer of this letter, who is someone to be trusted.
>   I remind you that it is a matter of the utmost importance:
>   1. A note on the hydraulic brake of the 120 cannon and the way in
> which it performs—

Du Paty now broke off his dictation and asked Dreyfus aggressively: 'What is the matter? Your hands are trembling.'

Dreyfus replied that his fingers were cold.

'Pay attention,' said du Paty in the same aggressive tone of voice. 'This is a serious matter.' The dictation continued.

>   2. A note on covering troops.
>   3. A note relating to Madagascar—

Du Paty had had enough. He stood up, laid his hand on Dreyfus's shoulders and said, in a booming voice, 'In the name of the law, I arrest you. You are accused of the crime of high treason!'

As soon as du Paty had said these words, the two policemen, Cochefert and Boussard, came forward, grabbed Dreyfus and searched him. Dreyfus was dumbfounded. He made no physical resistance but loudly insisted upon the absurdity of what had just been said. 'I have never had any relations with a foreign agent. I have a wife and children. I have a private income of thirty thousand francs. Here are my keys. Take them. Search my home. You'll find nothing.' Then: 'At least show me the evidence for the crimes you say I have committed . . .'

'The evidence is overwhelming,' said Cochefert.

The search of Dreyfus's person completed, du Paty began a vigorous interrogation, hoping that the shock of his sudden arrest might induce a confession. He produced a copy of the Penal Code and read out

Article 76 which stated that the punishment due to those who 'have engaged in machinations or shared information with foreign powers' was death. He then put further questions about Dreyfus's time as an intern, trying to match the date of his departure on a tour of inspection with the 'manoeuvres' mentioned in the *bordereau*.

After du Paty came Cochefert: the interrogation continued for more than three hours. Dreyfus repeated over and over again that he had had no contact with a foreign power. Cochefert advised him to tell the truth because they had 'indisputable evidence' against him – including documents written in his own hand. 'Are you telling me that you have never given to a foreigner notes and documents of the kind we are talking about, and which could be used against our country?'

'Never,' said Dreyfus. 'I say it again. I have never done anything of the kind you are suggesting.'

Du Paty took up the refrain, repeating over and over again that Dreyfus was a traitor.

'Kill me,' Dreyfus shouted. 'I'd rather have a bullet in the head . . .'

'It is not for *us* to kill you,' said du Paty, removing the file that concealed a loaded revolver.

'Ah, no,' said Dreyfus, realising what was expected of him. 'I am not going to kill myself. I want to live to establish my innocence.'[1]

Commandant Henry, the thickset officer of peasant stock who ran the dirty tricks department of the Statistical Section, now appeared from behind the screen where he had been hiding. 'Commandant,' said du Paty to Henry. 'All you have to do is take Captain Dreyfus to the Cherche-Midi. He is already under arrest.'

Henry escorted his prisoner out into the rue Saint-Dominique where they took a horse-drawn cab to the military prison. Dreyfus, not knowing of Henry's role in his arrest, poured out a torrent of anguished thoughts. 'This is terrible, *mon commandant*. I am accused of something dreadful! I'm accused of the crime of high treason!'

'The devil, but why?' asked Henry.

'I have no idea! It's as if I've gone mad. I'd prefer a bullet in my head! I am not guilty! This charge will ruin my life . . . It's a dreadful accusation, and completely false . . . I can see that the Ministry would not have proceeded against me without some evidence; it must have seemed convincing to them and damning for me, but it must be false . . . I can't believe that I have enemies who would pursue me with such enmity . . . I don't understand it. I demand justice.'[2]

At the Cherche-Midi military prison, Dreyfus was handed over to the Governor, Commandant Ferdinand Forzinetti, and locked up in a cell. No one was informed of his detention. He was allowed no contact with the outside world. It was now that he became demented – possessed by fury and despair. He paced up and down in his cell, overturned the bed and table, hit his head against the walls, screamed with pain. Forzinetti came to try and calm this 'true madman, with eyes shot through with blood'.[3] Dreyfus would not be calmed. He wished he had shot himself when given the chance and asked Forzinetti to bring him a revolver. The Governor refused. He remained with Dreyfus until three in the morning. He had no idea why Dreyfus had been arrested but, witnessing his distress, he felt sure that his prisoner must be innocent. Before leaving the cell, Forzinetti made Dreyfus promise that he would not try to kill himself because suicide would be taken as an admission of guilt.

———

As soon as Dreyfus had left with Henry for the Cherche-Midi prison, Commandant du Paty de Clam had gone with Commissaire Cochefert and Félix Gribelin, the archivist from the Statistical Section, to the apartment of Alfred and Lucie Dreyfus on the avenue du Trocadéro. Although they had Alfred's keys, they rang the bell and were admitted by a maid. The maid informed Lucie Dreyfus of their presence. Lucie sent word that her husband would be back shortly: he had to change into his uniform to return to his regiment. Du Paty sent the maid back with the message that they had to come to see Mme Dreyfus, not her husband.

Lucie joined the three men in her living room.

'Madame,' du Paty said, 'I have a very sad task to perform.'

'My husband is dead!' cried Lucie.

'No, worse than that,' said du Paty.

'He fell off his horse?'

'No, madame. He is in prison.'

Lucie was aghast. 'Where is he? In which prison?'

Du Paty refused to expand on what he had said. He told Lucie that the whole matter must remain secret. Lucie said that she could surely inform her husband's brothers. 'One word to anyone,' said du Paty, 'one single word from you will be disastrous for him. The only way to save him is to say nothing.'

Lucie accepted what she had been told, but nonetheless protested to du Paty that her husband was undoubtedly the victim of some terrible misunderstanding, and was certainly innnocent of any wrongdoing. She told them of her husband's righteousness, his loyalty, his devotion to duty, his love of his country. This cut no ice with du Paty. He and Cochefert proceeded to search the apartment, taking anything they thought relevant – Dreyfus's private correspondence, his account books, the files he had brought home from work. They then left and went to the apartment of the Hadamards on the rue de Châteaudun, to see if their suspect had concealed incriminating material with his parents-in-law: they might even have been their son-in-law's accomplices. Du Paty and Cochefert seized Alfred's letters written to Lucie at the time of their engagement. Nothing incriminating was found in either of the two apartments, but so convinced was du Paty that Dreyfus was a traitor that he decided this merely revealed his cunning. 'We found nothing,' du Paty told Commandant Picquart when he got back to the Ministry. 'He has got rid of everything! There's nothing left!'[4]

For the two days following his arrest and imprisonment, Dreyfus was left alone in his cell. It was only on 18 October that du Paty came to continue his interrogation. Again, he was accompanied by the archivist Gribelin, who took notes. Du Paty's main objective was to obtain a confession. There was no question of torture: Forzinetti, the prison Governor, turned down a request made by du Paty for a bright light to disorientate the prisoner. However, du Paty used a number of ploys of his own invention to break down the stubborn resistance of the accused. He made Dreyfus write, over and over again, the phrase 'I am off on manoeuvres', and by repetitive questioning tried to get him to admit that he had had access to the documents mentioned in the *bordereau*. Du Paty cut up photographs of Dreyfus's letters and photographs of the memorandum, mixed them together in his cap, and had Dreyfus pick them out and identify them. Dreyfus never once made a mistake. Du Paty asked him a series of leading and, to Dreyfus nonsensical, questions but resolutely refused to tell him the precise reason for his arrest.[5]

While du Paty continued with his interrogation of Dreyfus in the Cherche-Midi prison, François Guénée, a former undercover police officer then working for the Statistical Section, was sent by Colonel Sandherr to rummage around in Dreyfus's private life to see if he could find some corroborative evidence against him. He clutched at straws. Just as du Paty had decided that the absence of any evidence found in Dreyfus's flat merely confirmed his deviousness, so Guénée interpreted everything he discovered as evidence against him: Dreyfus was said to have 'a louche manner very similar to that found among those who practise espionage'; his fluency in German and Italian was suspicious; and his courtesy betrayed 'the obsequiousness of his character, well suited to dealing with agents of foreign powers'.[6]

Guénée's mission was to find a motive for Dreyfus's crime. At first a need for money seemed unlikely because Dreyfus was rich, but Guénée picked up rumours that Dreyfus gambled and had run up huge debts. It was said that Louise Hadamard, Alfred's mother-in-law, had complained to the Chief Rabbi about his gambling,[7] but when this was put to Dreyfus in the Cherche-Midi prison, he vehemently denied that he had ever gambled outside the family circle – a few francs on a game of bridge.

More damaging was the discovery of his liaisons with *demimondaines*. At first Dreyfus had disowned the ladies in question, hoping to hide his infidelities from Lucie, but he was forced to admit that he knew the ladies in question when given their names. The uncovering of Dreyfus's past – a recent past in the case of Suzanne Cron – confirmed to the priggish du Paty that he was not a man of honour: 'anyone who commits adultery is capable of betraying his country,' du Paty would tell Dreyfus's nephew Paul. 'I would never wish to touch a woman other than my wife, anyone who does is a wretch.'[8] But it did not furnish a motive. Could something be made of the fact that the Dreyfuses employed an Alsatian cook who hardly spoke French, had never applied for French nationality and had an illegitimate child? More promising was the discovery that a Dutchwoman, a Mme van Delden, lived in the same apartment block as Dreyfus. But it turned out that she was on bad terms with the Dreyfuses, and that the soldier who visited her from time to time was not Captain Dreyfus but General de Boisdeffre.[9]

The best du Paty could come up with in his search for a motive was the admission by Lucie Dreyfus, when questioned further, that 'Dreyfus had been made ill by his disappointment at being marked down on graduating from the École de Guerre'; that he had had nightmares, and had said over and over again: 'What is the point of serving in this army when, however hard one tries, one's merit will not be rewarded?' When confronted with this, Dreyfus admitted that 'perhaps on leaving the École, I had a moment of discontent which I shared with my wife. There is nothing more natural than that.'[10] It was no doubt natural, but the idea of taking revenge on an army that had spurned him was not just the most plausible but the only motive du Paty could suggest.

Du Paty remained certain that Alfred Dreyfus was the traitor who had written the *bordereau*, but his failure to get him to admit his guilt after interminable interrogation made him see that there was insufficient evidence to gain a conviction. On 27 October the Chief of the General Staff, General de Boisdeffre, at a meeting in his office with Sandherr, Henry and du Paty, chastised his cousin for his failure to build a case against Dreyfus. 'You've got nowhere with your Dreyfus. You've got nothing. You must surely realise that all your moral certainties, all your deductions, your expertise in handwriting, don't make up for the lack of a clear confession. That's what you must get and, if you can come up with nothing more than that scrap of paper, General Saussier is quite capable of refusing to sign an order to proceed.'

According to his own account of this meeting, du Paty replied with an equal vehemence, 'Allow me to say, *mon général*, that the man you call "my Dreyfus" is also yours; and what you call "my scrap of paper" is the basis of the inquiries which you told me to pursue, and is the only material proof which you have shown me . . . I am unable to say that I have found any others in Dreyfus's home: I am unable to say that he has confessed. So, if the moral certainty is judged insufficient, if the material evidence is too weak, the solution is simple: we must let him go.'[11]

Two days later, du Paty wrote a formal letter to General de Boisdeffre confirming what he had said at the meeting. On 31 October, he wrote to the same effect to the Minister of War, General Mercier. He told him that he remained convinced of the guilt of Dreyfus but there was not enough proof to convict him. He recommended that he be released.

2: The Secret File

General Mercier faced a dilemma. He had recently been defeated in the Chamber of Deputies on a number of issues; politically his position was precarious.[12] The charge that he had been soft on the Jewish doctor, Schulmann, was repeated over and over again in the right-wing press. He had exceeded his powers in ordering the arrest of Dreyfus without the authorisation of General Saussier. Mercier had enemies both within the army and in the Chamber who were ready to pounce on any mistake he might make. It was already clear that the Prime Minister, Dupuy, would ask for his resignation if the premature arrest of a French officer was exposed by the release of Dreyfus.

But Dreyfus's arrest could not be kept secret. On the very day that Mercier received du Paty's letter, 31 October, the Havas news agency reported the arrest of 'an officer suspected of having communicated to a foreign power some unimportant but nevertheless confidential documents'. The next day, 1 November, the story was picked up by *La Libre Parole* and published under the headline 'High Treason. Arrest of a Jewish officer A. Dreyfus'. The acting editor, Adrien Papillaud, had received an anonymous letter on 28 October which read as follows:

My dear friend. You see, what I told you is quite correct. The man arrested on the 15th on a charge of espionage, and who has been imprisoned in the Cherche-Midi, is Captain Dreyfus, living at 6, avenue du

Trocadéro. It has been put about that he has gone on a journey, but that is a lie to hush up the affair. All Israel is in a state of ferment.[13]

The die was cast. If Mercier were now to free Dreyfus, he would be accused, as in the case of Schulmann, of being in the pay of the Jews. He would also lose face with his cabinet colleagues, particularly the Foreign Minister Hanotaux, who had advised him to drop the case against Dreyfus. On 3 November, at Mercier's instigation, General Saussier finally signed the order to proceed against Captain Alfred Dreyfus and appointed a Commandant Besson d'Ormescheville as the examining magistrate.

Saussier's acquiescence in Mercier's plans is puzzling. He had rebuked Forzinetti for imprisoning Dreyfus without his authorisation. 'If you weren't my friend,' Saussier had said, 'I'd send you to prison for two months for having accepted a prisoner without my orders.'[14] Could Saussier have intervened because of the irregularity of the process leading to Dreyfus's arrest? At a shooting party at Marly, he had told the French President, Jean Casimir-Perier: 'Dreyfus is not guilty. That fool Mercier has put his finger in his own eye again.' Quite possibly Saussier, frequently attacked in *La Libre Parole* for protecting the Jewish officer Maurice Weil, did not want to make things more difficult for himself by intervening in the case of another Jew, Alfred Dreyfus; or, more probably, as he suggested to Casimir-Perier, he was confident that if he let the thing run, it would lead to the fall of his adversary, General Mercier.

———

The military investigating magistrate, Commandant Besson d'Ormescheville, held twelve sessions between 7 and 23 November 1894. Although appointed by the sceptical Saussier, d'Ormescheville appears to have accepted from the start the view of the Statistical Section and the General Staff that Dreyfus was guilty and so saw it as his duty to draw up an irrefutable case against him. Perhaps, like so many officers in the French Army, he believed that espionage by a Jewish officer was an accident waiting to happen; or he had been influenced by reading a trashy novel set in the War Ministry that had been serialised in *Le Petit Journal* during the summer and featured spies, artillery officers, former Polytechniciens, bellicose journalists and devious Jewish gamblers.[15] Or perhaps he was intimidated. 'I know', wrote a correspondent in *La Libre Parole*, 'that someone has dared to offer a million francs to the investigating magistrate if he agrees, not necessarily to conclude that Dreyfus is innocent, but simply to cast doubt on his culpability.'[16]

For whatever reason, d'Ormescheville certainly did not work on the case with an open mind. He went through the police reports, interviewed witnesses and interrogated the accused, putting the same questions, often word for word, as du Paty de Clam. He looked into information gathered by Guénée about Dreyfus's life in the *demi-monde* – some of it accurate but much of it untrue. Dreyfus's accounts were examined in detail and revealed nothing irregular. A police report that Dreyfus was not known in gambling cirles was 'lost' in the Prefecture and so was never submitted to d'Ormescheville. D'Ormescheville accepted du Paty's view that Gobert, the handwriting expert of the Banque de France, could not be trusted because of the bank's links with Jewish financiers, and judged his opinion no more authoritative than that of Colonels Fabre and d'Aboville.[17]

D'Ormescheville looked into Dreyfus's two years at the École de Guerre. His failure to make friends among his fellow students was considered sinister: his companions remembered him as awkward, obsequious, indiscreet and inordinately pleased with himself. Everything for which Dreyfus was once commended by his teachers was now used against him. His eagerness to learn became an incriminating curiosity; it was remembered that he hung around in offices and asked to see documents which often went missing: 'wherever he passed, documents disappeared'.[18] His remarkable memory was a tool for espionage; so too his knowledge of German and Italian.

This same inversion was applied to the failure of the investigators to find anything incriminating among Dreyfus's private possessions.

The search of his residence yielded more or less the results that he claimed it would. But it is legitimate to suspect that if no letter, even from family members . . . and no bill, even from tradesmen, was found in the search, it was because anything that might have been in any way compromising had been hidden or already destroyed.

Assisted by du Paty in preparing his report, d'Ormescheville accepted his Alice in Wonderland logic that the absence of evidence was a sign of guilt. He also suggested that, because Dreyfus had the character and temperament that you might expect to find in a spy, he was a spy.

He is . . . of a rather supple – even obsequious – character, quite suited for relations of espionage with foreign agents. He was thus the perfect choice for the miserable and shameful mission that he either inspired or accepted and to which – quite luckily for France, perhaps – the discovery of his intrigues has put an end.

On 3 December, Commandant d'Ormescheville presented his report (*acte d'accusation*) to General Saussier, who the next day signed the order for Dreyfus's court martial.

———

Throughout November 1894, when d'Ormescheville was conducting his investigations, the right-wing press had been feasting on the leaks emanating from the War Ministry, and hounding its chief, General Mercier. On 4 November, *La Libre Parole* published a long list of Mercier's failings as Minister of War, leading up to the uncovering of a Jewish spy on the General Staff. 'We have, nevertheless, a consolation: it was not a true Frenchman who committed the crime.'[19] On 9 November the same paper published a statement from General de Bonnefond, the officer who had marked Dreyfus down at the École de Guerre: 'You know . . . we buy our information about foreign armies [from] Italian Jews, German Jews, Rumanian Jews . . . Why would a French Jew behave any differently from the others?'[20] Also on the 9th, *La Patrie* linked Dreyfus to Schwartzkoppen, the German military attaché, which led to a letter in *Le Figaro* the following day from the German Ambassador, Graf Münster von Derneburg, stating that

'Never has Lieutenant-Colonel von Schwartzkoppen received letters from Dreyfus. Never has he had any relations, either direct or indirect, with him. If this officer is found guilty of the crime of which he is accused, the German Embassy is not mixed up in the afffair.'

On 22 November, *La Libre Parole* laid into Mercier once again:

> The Dreyfus affair has taken a nasty turn for the government. We have spoken to sevcral senior officers, all of whom have replied by present-ing the following dilemma: either General Mercier has arrested Captain Dreyfus without proof, in which case his superficiality is a crime; or he has allowed evidence of his treason to be lost, in which case his negli-gence is a crime. In both cases, General Mercier is unworthy of the post he holds. In such a situation, one can be guilty of stupidity as well as of a crime.[21]

Mercier was well aware of this dilemma, and on 28 November he gave an interview to a journalist on *Le Figaro*, Charles Leser. 'It is said that Captain Dreyfus offered documents to the Italian government. This is wrong. It is impossible for me to say anything more because of the current investigation. All that I can say is that his guilt is absolute, it is certain.'[22]

By this highly irregular intervention in the judicial process, Mercier had laid down his marker and so, when it came to the court martial, nothing could be left to chance. It was now that this 'republican' general favoured by the left decided to compile a secret dossier of dubi-ous evidence that would strengthen the case against Dreyfus.[23] Colonel Sandherr was happy to co-operate. He too feared for his position and for the reputation of the Statistical Section, if it was shown that it had jumped to the wrong conclusion in a precipitate way: its methods had recently been attacked in the conservative journal, *France Militaire*.[24]

Sandherr also felt that he possessed corroborative evidence that seemed to implicate Dreyfus directly. A French agent, Richard Cuers, working in the German counter-intelligence agency, the Nachrichtenbureau, had informed the head of his network in Brussels, Laboux, that a deco-rated officer was paying visits to Colonel von Schwartzkoppen in Paris and was in in his pay. Laboux passed the information back to Sandherr. Who else could this refer to but Dreyfus?

Sandherr was no fool. He knew as well as du Paty that there was no irrefutable evidence against Dreyfus. If he had not been under pressure from Mercier to nail Dreyfus, would he have dropped the case? Probably not. There was a spy in the officer corps of the French Army; information from Cuers and Val Carlos, the agent in the Spanish Embassy, warned of this, and the *bordereau* confirmed it. It also suggested that the spy had access to secrets from the different *bureaux* of the General Staff. The interns had such access. Dreyfus was therefore a suspect, and those suspicions were confirmed by the opinion of three out of the five expert graphologists who had by now been consulted that his handwriting and that of the *bordereau* were the same.

A final and what appeared to be conclusive piece of evidence of Dreyfus's guilt came in the form of a telegram sent by Alessandro Panizzardi of the Italian Embassy to his superiors in Rome on 2 November 1894. This was intercepted by the Post Office and sent to the Bureau du Chiffre at the French Foreign Office on the Quai d'Orsay for decryption. There it became apparent that Panizzardi was using a new key for the code. On 6 November, a provisional decrypted version of the telegram was sent to Sandherr which seemed to confirm the guilt of Dreyfus: 'Captain Dreyfus has been arrested. The War Minister has proof of his relations with Germany. I have taken all precautions.'

Sandherr was delighted. However, four days later, on 10 November, the codebreakers at the Quai d'Orsay tried a new key to decipher the telegram and this gave a different meaning to the telegram – one which suggested that Panizzardi knew nothing about Dreyfus: 'If Captain Dreyfus has had no relations with you, it would be advisable to instruct the Ambassador to publish an official denial to avoid comments in the Press.'[25]

To prove to Sandherr that the new version was the more accurate, the army's liaison officer with the Quai d'Orsay, Captain Pierre Matton, had a double agent working in the Italian Embassy slip a message with recognisable names to Panizzardi who encrypted the message and sent it to Rome. The intercepted message was duly delivered to the codebreakers at the Quai d'Orsay who were unaware of Matton's experiment: the message was deciphered and demonstrated conclusively that the new key was correct.[26]

This did not suit Sandherr or those now working on the secret dossier in the Statistical Section, and the version of the telegram that went into the file read: 'Captain Dreyfus has been arrested. The War Minister has proof of his relations with Germany. I have taken all precautions.' All were now convinced that the traitor had to be convicted and the end justified any means. Commandant Henry led the team that trawled through the fragments of information in the files of the Statistical Section to see if something could be found that would link the *bordereau* to Dreyfus. There was, first of all, the letter from Schwartzkoppen to Panizzardi dating from the spring: 'Attached are 12 master plans of Nice which that scoundrel D. gave me in the hope of restoring relations.' This filching of master plans had been going on for some time, and so the 'D' was unlikely to refer to Dreyfus: moreover, as Sandherr's drunken deputy, Commandant Cordier – Father Josué – had pointed out, it was unlikely that the military attachés would refer to an agent by the initial of his real name. But it was not impossible, and certainly could be made to seem likely to the judges at a court martial. There was also a letter from Panizzardi to Schwartzkoppen dating from February 1894 which opened 'My dear Bugger', and contained a request for Schwartzkoppen 'to broach this question with your friend' – which could be taken to be a reference to Dreyfus.

This was still not enough to convince the judges of a court martial of Dreyfus's guilt. Attention now turned to the reports that Guénée had written earlier in the year on the information provided by his agent in the Spanish Embassy, Val Carlos. Could something be done with these? A couple of sentences, purporting to record the words of Val Carlos, were inserted into these reports: 'it emerges from my last conversation with Captain von Süsskind that the German attachés have in the offices of the General Staff an officer who is informing them admirably well'. And: 'Someone in the Ministry of War . . . has tipped off the German military attachés . . . That is further proof that you have one or several wolves in your sheep-pen . . .'[27]

Knowing just how feeble these scraps were as evidence against Dreyfus, the prosecution decided that they would not be shown to the defence but presented to the judges alone. Du Paty was recruited to write a 'commentary' on this additional information, explaining how they established the guilt of the accused. If the judges themselves had misgivings about the legality of what was being done, 'national security' would be invoked as a justification. Even in a court martial held in camera, the secret service could not be expected to reveal either its methods or its sources.*

3: The Court Martial

Alfred Dreyfus, still held in the Cherche-Midi prison, was confident that he would soon be released. On 29 October, du Paty had finally shown him a photograph of the *bordereau*. 'Do you recognize this letter as being in your handwriting?' he had asked. Dreyfus immediately felt 'a sense of deliverance'. The handwriting, though similar, was clearly not his.[28]

Dreyfus was now permitted to communicate with his wife Lucie, and Lucie to inform others of the catastrophe that had befallen Alfred. She immediately wired her brother-in-law, Mathieu Dreyfus, in Mulhouse; he took the night train to Paris, arriving on the morning of 1 November. Two years older than Alfred, he was not just a fond brother but his closest friend. It had never occurred to Mathieu, when he saw the newspaper headlines proclaiming the arrest of a Jewish officer on charges of espionage, that the officer might be his brother. As he would later explain, 'I was brought up with him, I lived with him in the greatest intimacy; he has no thoughts hidden from me. Nothing in his life or his character indicates the possibility of such a crime.'[29]

Although close, the two brothers were very different in a number of ways. Where Alfred was awkward and abrupt, Mathieu was suave, charming, witty, sensitive, good-natured. Alfred was balding; Mathieu

---

* The same argument was advanced, and was accepted by the courts, by the British intelligence service in the twenty-first century.

was tall with blond hair and blue eyes. Alfred's voice was monotonous and metallic, Mathieu's 'pleasant and sonorous'. Alfred's manner was gauche, Mathieu's elegant, aristocratic, debonair. It was said that 'the textile manufacturer had the strong bearing of a distinguished military officer, while the career soldier with the pince-nez had the pallid distracted look of a reserved and serious scholar'.[30]

Mathieu was intelligent and shared Alfred's intellectual curiosity. He too had thought of a military career but he had failed to get into the École Polytechnique from Sainte-Barbe and so had returned to Mulhouse, where he ran the family's factories with his brothers Jacques and Léon. Out of the office, he pursued his interest in literature and philosophy, particularly the philosophy of the Enlightenment: he had a bust of Voltaire on his mantel.[31] He had married the daughter of an Alsatian industrialist, Suzanne Schwob. Her uncle Adrien Schwob was the mayor of Héricort, and the wedding was celebrated in a garden of his estate – a civil ceremony that was not followed by a second service in the synagogue. Schwob was a Freemason, and it was probably through him, or possibly through fellow industrialists Paul Jeanmarie or Rudolph Koechlin, that Mathieu had been admitted to a Lodge. He was a member of the Mulhousian *fabricantocratie* and would go hunting with his fellow industrialists in the forests around Mulhouse.[32]

As soon as he arrived in Paris, Mathieu Dreyfus set to work to expose the absurdity of the charges brought against his brother. The only contact that Lucie had had with the prosecuting authorities was Commandant du Paty de Clam, and Mathieu at once sent his nephew Paul, the eighteen-year-old son of his brother Jacques who was in Paris at the time, to the offices of the General Staff to request an interview. Paul was received by du Paty. 'I have searched for the truth,' the monocled officer told the young man. 'Your uncle is guilty. He is a wretch, a two-faced monster leading a double life – normal and correct with his wife, secretive and mysterious with loose women.' He then raved about his own marriage and the death of his wife, spoke of the 'indignity' of treason against women, and said that a man who betrayed his wife was quite capable of betraying his country. The young Paul Dreyfus left in tears.[33]

That afternoon, du Paty called on Lucie and Mathieu Dreyfus at the apartment at 6, avenue du Trocadéro accompanied by the archivist from the Statistical Section, Félix Gribelin. 'The charges are devastating,' he told Mathieu. 'There is not one chance in a thousand that your brother is innocent. Moreover, he has already half confessed to me.' He repeated what he had said to Paul. 'Your brother was leading a double life. He was seeing women. He is a monster, a two-faced monster. He had a hole right here.' Du Paty pointed to his forehead.

Mathieu asked if he could see his brother and confront him with these charges. 'Put the witnesses that you need in the same room behind doors, or in a next-door room; conceal them in such a way that my brother believes that he is alone with me. I swear to you that I will ask him "Alfred, did you do it? Tell me whether you are guilty or not." If he says yes, I will hand him a gun with which to kill himself.'

'Never, never,' said du Paty. 'One word, a single word, could mean a European war.'[34]

It was now clear to Mathieu that Commandant du Paty de Clam was not susceptible to a reasoned argument: he felt he was talking to a lunatic and was appalled that his brother's fate lay in this man's hands.[35] The court martial would go ahead and his brother would need the very best legal representation. Who would take the brief? Lucie's cousin, the philosopher Lucien Lévy-Bruhl, knew one of France's pre-eminent lawyers, Pierre Waldeck-Rousseau. A native of Nantes, Waldeck-Rousseau had impeccable republican credentials: his father René had played a role in the revolution of 1848. Elected to the Chamber of Deputies in 1876, he promoted reforms to France's judicial system and the legal recognition of trades unions. Despite coming from a Catholic family, he had supported the laicisation of primary education enforced by Jules Ferry in 1881–2, and had voted in favour of military service for seminarians, Sunday working and divorce.

In 1889, Pierre Waldeck-Rousseau had given up politics to devote his time to the practice of law. Big money was being made at the Paris bar by lawyer-politicians such as Eugène Étienne, Georges Leygues,

Louis Barthou and Raymond Poincaré (Poincaré represented the Schneider-Creusot armaments industry).[36] The year before the arrest of Dreyfus, Waldeck-Rousseau had successfully defended Gustav Eiffel on charges of corruption following the Panama Canal scandal. Lévy-Bruhl arranged a meeting between Mathieu and this eminent lawyer, but after considering the brief for a couple of days, Waldeck-Rousseau turned it down. He claimed that he no longer took on criminal cases – but, had that been the case, he would not have agreed to look at the brief in the first place. The true reason was that he was about to return to politics, standing for the Senate in the staunchly Catholic depart-ment of the Loire. A lifelong proponent of liberty and equality before the law, he nonetheless sensed the political risks involved in defend-ing a Jewish officer accused of treason. His advice to Mathieu was to approach another eminent lawyer who had no involvement in politics and specialised in criminal law, Edgar Demange.

Edgar Demange, at the age of fifty-three, was at the summit of a successful career. Having won a national debating contest as a young man, he had made his name by taking on sensational cases, success-fully defending Prince Pierre Bonaparte – the son of Lucien Bonaparte, Napoleon's brother, charged with the murder of a twenty-two-year-old journalist, Victor Noir – and some of the anarchists arraigned after a bomb was thrown into the Chamber of Deputies. It was Demange who had secured the acquittal of the Marquis de Morès after his duel with Captain Armand Mayer. Of particular value in the case of Dreyfus were Demange's religious beliefs and links to the army: he was a devout Catholic, the son of an army officer and married to the daughter of a general.

At first, Demange proved to be as reluctant as Waldeck-Rousseau to take the case. However, Mathieu persisted and Demange agreed to consider the brief when, after d'Ormescheville had completed his inquiries, he could study the papers. The report was submitted to General Saussier on 3 December. The next day Demange was permit-ted to visit Alfred Dreyfus in the Cherche-Midi prison and there he told him bluntly that if, after studying the papers that he was to receive later that day, he felt that Dreyfus was guilty, he would not take the case. He warned both Alfred and Mathieu of the risk they ran in accepting these terms. 'If my conscience prevents me from defending your brother, my refusal will become known . . . I will be your brother's first judge.'[37] Confident that he would find no credible evidence, the two brothers asked him to go ahead.

Demange read d'Ormescheville's dossier overnight and on 5 December summoned Mathieu and Lucie Dreyfus to his chambers. He told them that he had studied the indictment and that, in his view, Alfred Dreyfus had no case to answer. The only evidence against him was a single unsigned, undated document which might or might not be in his handwriting – a matter upon which the expert graphologists failed to agree. He told them that he was appalled by 'the incoherence and hate' emanating from d'Ormescheville's report: an examining magistrate should have been impartial. 'If Captain Dreyfus were not Jewish,' he concluded, 'he would not be in prison.'[38]

The court martial opened on 19 December 1894, in a small courtroom within the Cherche-Midi military prison. Interested parties such as Mathieu Dreyfus and a large number of journalists jostled to find seats. There were seven judges, presided over by Colonel E. Maurel. None had any particular training in the law. One had been seconded from a cavalry regiment, six from the infantry. None was from a regiment of artillery. The prosecutor was Commandant André Brisset, counsel for the defence Edgar Demange.

The defendant, Alfred Dreyfus, was escorted into the court. He saluted the judges. When he gave his age as thirty-five, André Bataille, covering the trial for Le Figaro, was incredulous: he seemed more like fifty. Brisset, the prosecutor, opened the proceedings by asking that, in the interests of national security, the court martial be held in camera. Demange protested, but he was overruled: the judges agreed to a closed session. The public gallery was cleared. Only the Prefect of Police, Louis Lépine, and Commandant Georges Picquart, appointed as their official observer by the War Ministry and General Staff, were permitted to remain.

Alfred Dreyfus was called to the witness stand; he gave evidence in the same monotonous tone that had consistently been remarked upon throughout his career. His answers were clear and precise. There were no histrionics, no displays of emotion. This cerebral man with his faith in reason was confident that a dispassionate demonstration of the facts would be enough to establish his innocence.

It was only when the court started to hear the testimony of some of Dreyfus's superiors – Gonse, Fabre, d'Aboville and, above all, Commandant du Paty de Clam that it became evident that common sense might not prevail. Du Paty claimed that Dreyfus had given himself away when writing to his dictation in the office of General de Boisdeffre on 15 October: realising that the words he was writing were those of the *bordereau*, he had started to tremble. Demange, in cross-examination, pointed to the paper in question and showed that there was no change whatsoever in the handwriting. That was only to be expected, du Paty replied. Dreyfus, aware that he was under suspicion, had mastered his emotions. 'I wanted to see if he had been warned; questioned closely by me, he *should* have trembled. But he did not tremble, so he was pretending, he was warned. An innocent individual who had been brought there with nothing to hide would have trembled at the accusation, would have made a movement of some kind.'[39]

Commandant Picquart, the official observer from the War Ministry, was 'embarrassed' by du Paty's line of argument and it did not seem to convince the judges. At this stage in the trial, Picquart thought that Dreyfus would be acquitted, and so did the Prefect of Police, Louis Lépine. The lack of a clear motive was a grave weakness in the prosecution's case. Du Paty scraped the barrel in suggesting that money paid by a German insurance company after a fire in one of the Dreyfus family's factories was a covert reward for treason.[40] No reference was made in the prosecution's submission to Dreyfus's religion or race: 'the prosecution did not try to bolster it by aspersions [*sic*] about Dreyfus's racial or religious background, by asserting that Jews were naturally treacherous'.[41] But Dreyfus was nonetheless plausible in the role in which he had been cast. Lépine, who was a civilian and an experienced witness of many trials, found that the manner in which Dreyfus protested his innocence was unconvincing. 'His voice was atonal, lazy, his face white . . . Nothing in his attitude was of a kind to evoke sympathy, despite the tragic situation in which he found himself . . . Occasionally, in the course of the debates, his face twitched convulsively; sometimes a tremor came over it, but there was no expression of indignation, no *cri de coeur*, no expression of feeling . . .'[42] Picquart, too, thought that Dreyfus should have risen to the occasion and defended himself 'in the style of the times'. The clerk of the court, Vallecalle, was later to say: 'in his place, I would have yelled my head off'.[43]

Commandant Picquart reported daily on the progress of the trial to General Mercier and Colonel Sandherr; Sandherr was also kept informed by Henry and Lauth, 'who shuttled between the court room and the Ministry of War'.[44] All became worried by the prospect of an acquittal. It was time for a dramatic intervention. Henry, who was a friend of one of the judges, Commandant Gallet, sent him a note asking to be recalled to give further evidence.

Henry, the officer who had risen from the ranks, with the Légion d'Honneur pinned on his breast, returned to the witness stand. With his bluff manner he came across as the kind of honest trooper who could be relied upon to call a spade a spade. He now told the court that in his earlier testimony he had withheld evidence because of its sensitivity, but now he felt he must tell all. In February of that year, 'an honourable person' had warned the Statistical Section that an officer in the Second Bureau was selling secrets to the Germans. He had repeated his warning in June. Henry was referring to Val Carlos, the agent in the Spanish Embassy, but he then went far beyond what Val Carlos had said. Pointing at Dreyfus, Henry said in a loud, portentous voice: 'And that is the man!'

Furious, Dreyfus leaped to his feet and demanded to know the name of this 'honourable' man. Demange, equally indignant, insisted that the informant be summoned as a witness. What was his name? Slapping his head, Henry said: 'When an officer has a secret like that in his head, he keeps it even from his cap!'

'Do you affirm, on your honour,' Colonel Maurel, the President of the court, asked Henry, 'that the treasonous officer was Captain Dreyfus?'

Pointing now at the crucifix on the wall, Henry said solemnly: 'I swear to it.'

The character witnesses now called in favour of Dreyfus did not undo the impression left by Henry's testimony. The Chief Rabbi of Paris, also called Dreyfus and speaking in a Yiddish accent, told the court that it was inconceivable that Alfred would betray his country. The philosopher Lucien Lévy-Bruhl, a physician named Vaucaire and Arthur Amson, a prominent industrialist, said the same but were not the kind of people to impress the military judges. Character witnesses from the army had been hard to find: Dreyfus now paid the price for his aloofness in the officers' mess. At first Mathieu had found only one officer, Commandant Clément, willing to testify in his brother's favour. Subsequently, 'after much prodding by the family', four other officers agreed to submit depositions describing Dreyfus as a 'good and loyal soldier'.[45]

Dreyfus himself would later make excuses for the failure of his comrades to come forward to defend him. Told by General Gonse that he was guilty, and that there was proof of his guilt, it was impossible for them to believe otherwise. 'From that time on,' he was later told by a colleague at the École de Guerre, 'we forgot all your qualities, all the friendly relations we had had with you, and concentrated only on searching in our memories for any fact that might corroborate the certainty of your guilt. All was grist to that same mill.'[46]

The criminologist Bertillon took the stand to testify that, in his opinion, Dreyfus had written the *bordereau*. Certainly, there were small but clear differences between samples of Dreyfus's handwriting and the handwriting of the *bordereau* noted by the graphologists Gobert and Pelletier, but these showed only that Dreyfus had tried to disguise his own handwriting. It was an 'auto-forgery'. He had traced letters used by his brother and his wife. A spy who knew he was under suspicion would hardly write spontaneously in his own hand.

———

On 21 December, the prosecutor Brisset summed up the case against Dreyfus that followed closely the indictment prepared by d'Ormescheville. The next day, Demange made his final plea for the defence. In a three-hour oration he demonstrated that none of the evidence against Dreyfus amounted to proof. He dismissed the stories of Dreyfus's love affairs as worthless gossip and ridiculed du Paty's suggestion that Dreyfus's knowledge of foreign languages, excellent memory and curiosity about military matters meant he was a spy. Equally absurd was du Paty's inverted logic – that the failure to find any incriminating evidence in Dreyfus's flat proved that it had been either hidden or destroyed, and that the absence of any change in Dreyfus's handwriting when taking dictation showed the sangfroid of a traitor. And the prosecution had failed to come up with a credible motive. Why would an officer with substantial private means who was well known for his patriotism, and whose career in the army had been a remarkable success, sell military secrets to the Germans?

However, Demange told the judges, these were all matters of secondary importance. At the heart of the case was the torn scrap of paper filched from the waste-paper basket of the German military attaché – the *bordereau* – and there was no proof that it had been written by Dreyfus. First, as to its substance: no evidence had been presented to establish that Dreyfus had seen documents relating to the hydraulic brake on the new cannon or that he had had access to confidential information on the deployment of 'covering troops'; and no officer from the First Bureau had been found to say that Dreyfus could have obtained confidential information on artillery formations or plans for the invasion of Madagascar. No superior officer had given evidence that Dreyfus had asked to see the artillery manual of 1894, let alone asked to take it away for study. As for the final phrase, 'I am off on manoeuvres,' at no point when serving as an intern on the General Staff had Dreyfus taken part in manoeuvres.

And finally the handwriting of the *bordereau*: Demange ridiculed Demange's theory of an auto-forgery, and insisted to the judges that difference of opinion among the expert graphologists on the question of the handwriting meant that at the very least there was a reasonable doubt, and if there was a reasonable doubt Captain Dreyfus must be acquitted.

Dreyfus himself was pleased with his counsel's closing speech. 'Maître Demange, in his eloquent address, refuted the expert reports, demonstrated all the contradictions and asked how it could have erected a charge of this kind without supplying any motive. An acquittal seemed certain.'[47] Lépine, having seen Demange act for the anarchists, had a high opinion of his skills as an advocate and judged his closing speech 'very fine', but thought he laid too much emphasis on the *bordereau* and seemed to rein in his eloquence for fear it would alienate the military judges. In a civilian court, his strategy would have been correct: the *bordereau* was at the heart of the case against Dreyfus and, had he been addressing civilian judges trained in the law, he would only have had to establish that there was a reasonable doubt and the case would have collapsed. But the judges were soldiers, not lawyers, and it went against the grain of their military training to doubt the judgement of their superiors on the General Staff.

Demange himself realised that the protocols found in civilian courts had not been adhered to by the military: he had observed the comings and goings of du Paty, Sandherr, Lauth and Picquart and the exchanges these officers had had with the prosecutor, Commandant Brisset, the witnesses and even the judges.[48] What he could not know was that, when the judges retired to consider their verdict, they took with them a sealed envelope that Commandant du Paty de Clam had handed to the President of the court, Colonel Maurel, asking him to consider its contents in the name of the Minister of War. Maurel broke the seal and the seven judges now saw the different pieces of evidence compiled by the Statistical Section with du Paty's commentary, showing how they corroborated the evidence against Dreyfus. None of the judges appeared to appreciate that it was illegal to submit evidence not seen by the defence.

The manner in which this secret dossier was shown to the judges, and the forgeries it contained, were the first unambiguous acts of injustice against Alfred Dreyfus and were almost certainly unnecessary. Colonel Maurel later admitted that he looked at only one of the items and it did not affect his decision. The letter mentioning 'the scoundrel D' made some impression on another of the judges, Captain Martin

Freystaetter, but together with his colleagues on the bench his mind was already made up. After deliberating for over an hour, the judges returned to the court and pronounced their verdict. With no dissenting vote, Dreyfus was found guilty. He was sentenced to military degradation and deportation for life to a penal colony where he was to be held in a fortified enclosure. He was also ordered to pay the costs of the trial of 1,615 francs and 70 centimes.

————

When the verdict reached in the closed courtroom was announced to the wider world, it was received with universal approbation. Maurice Paléologue noted in his diary on Sunday, 23 December 1894: 'There is only one note in the comments on the verdict this morning throughout the whole of the Paris press, from the extreme right to the extreme left, from the clerical and monarchist journals to the organs of the most extreme socialism: approval, relief, satisfaction, joy – a triumphant, vindictive, ferocious joy.'[49] *La Libre Parole* announced the verdict with the words: 'Out of France with the Jews. France for the French.' But the left was as exultant as the right, and Mercier was their hero. The Socialists in the National Assembly themselves thanked the Minister of War for having resisted the enormous pressure from shady politicians and the barons of finance to secure an acquittal. *L'Intransigeant* predicted that Mercier would never be forgiven by 'the cowardly government . . . for refusing to cover up the affair'.

The main criticism was not of the verdict but of the sentence. Under Article 5 of the constitution of the Second Republic, the death penalty had been abolished for political crimes. Treason for the benefit of a foreign power had been classified as a political crime. The right saw sparing Dreyfus the guillotine as yet further proof of the power of the Jews; the left pointed out the disparity between the death sentence passed on mutinous soldiers in the time of war and life imprisonment for a treasonous officer. A law was proposed in the National Assembly to alter this anomaly and make crimes such as Dreyfus's punishable by death. The Socialist Jean Jaurès spoke in its favour on 24 December 1894, and in an article the following day – Christmas Day – Jaurès's fellow Socialist, Georges Clemenceau, made the same point. There was a scandalous disproportion between treachery on the one hand, 'unquantifiable but not punished by death, and a moment of panic in a young soldier punished by instant execution'.[50]

The number of people who thought that Alfred Dreyfus had been wrongly condemned was small; besides his family, there was the Governor of the Cherche-Midi prison, Commandant Forzinetti, persuaded by the distress he had witnessed in his prisoner, and the handwriting experts Gobert and Pelletier, who remained convinced that Dreyfus had not written the *bordereau*. There were also some doubts in high places. The eminent historian Gabriel Monod, lunching with the ailing French Foreign Minister Gabriel Hanotaux, asked him if he was sure that Dreyfus was guilty. 'I am not the one who judged him,' said Hanotaux. 'Other than that, I have nothing to say.' But as Monod was leaving, Hanotaux's secretary, Villox, followed him out into the street, took him by the arm and said: 'You know, we think that General Mercier has made a great gaffe.'

The Jewish community lay low. The Chief Rabbi of Paris had given Dreyfus a character reference but had admitted to the court that he knew nothing of the legal process that had led to his arraignment. The Jewish journalist Bernard Lazare, a vigorous opponent of anti-Semitism, wrote from Stockholm to his publisher, Pierre-Victor Stock: 'Ah! If it was just some poor devil, I would immediately worry about him, but Dreyfus and his people are very rich, they say, and they can certainly manage without me, especially if he is innocent.'[51] But the grandees of high finance – the Rothschilds, the Ephrussis, the Camondos – had no reason to believe that Dreyfus was innocent, and did not want to give credence to the charges made by Drumont and *La Libre Parole* that they would always weigh in to protect one of their own. The most widespread view was expressed in *Le Figaro* the day after the verdict had been delivered: 'Now that it is all over, let us speak as little as possible of this sad story.'

At the Ministry of War, and in the offices of the Statistical Section, there were a few loose ends to be tied up. General Mercier had received the news of Dreyfus's conviction as he waited, in full-dress uniform, to leave for a dinner at the Élysée Palace. He said nothing. The only comment came from his English wife: 'The poor man.'[52] Later, back at work at the Ministry of War, he summoned Boisdeffre, Gonse, Sandherr, du Paty and Henry and asked for assurances, on their word of honour, that they would never reveal what had occurred before and during the trial of Dreyfus. He ordered that the secret dossier, which had been returned by Colonel Maurel to Commandant du Paty de Clam, and by du Paty to Sandherr, should be disassembled – the different documents returned to their relevant files and du Paty's commentary destroyed. The order was carried out, but not before Colonel Sandherr had taken the precaution of making a copy of du Paty's commentary, to which he could refer should there be a change of government with a new Minister of War.

4: Degradation

Before Alfred Dreyfus could start his life sentence in a penal colony, he had first to suffer the ordeal of a ritual degradation. This ceremony took place on the morning of 5 January 1895 in the large courtyard of the École Militaire before contingents from different branches of the armed forces, including officers from his alma mater, the École de Guerre, and an invited group of spectators. Dreyfus was brought there early in the morning from the Cherche-Midi prison by a detachment of Republican Guards commanded by a Captain Lebrun-Renault. While waiting in a small room for Dreyfus to be summoned to play his painful role, Lebrun-Renault engaged his prisoner in conversation. 'Have you considered killing yourself?' he asked Dreyfus. Dreyfus replied that he would certainly have killed himself had he been guilty but he was not. He told Lebrun-Renault that he had even rejected a suggestion by Commandant du Paty de Clam that he should claim that he had been acting as a double agent on his own initiative, handing over some worthless documents to Colonel von Schwartzkoppen in the hope of receiving some more substantial information in return.

At 8.45 a.m. Dreyfus was handed over by Captain Lebrun-Renault to an escort of an officer and four men from the artillery. He was led out into the courtyard of the École Militaire where the serried ranks of soldiers had been drawn up to witness the spectacle. A stand had been erected for journalists and distinguished guests. The troops were silent but from beyond the gates separating the courtyard from the Place de Fontenoy came the roar of a huge crowd shouting 'Death to the traitor!', 'Dirty Jew!', 'Long live France!'; and Parisian urchins, who had climbed up into the branches of trees, shouted 'The swine!' and 'The coward!' as Dreyfus emerged from the École Militaire.

To the beat of drums, Dreyfus marched 'with an assured step' to the centre of the courtyard where General Paul Darras, mounted on a horse, and the clerk of the court martial, Vallecalle, awaited him. The drumbeat stopped. The four officers of the escort stepped back. Vallecalle saluted General Darras and read aloud the judgment pronounced on Dreyfus by the court martial. Dreyfus listened to this sentence in silence. General Darras now spoke: 'Dreyfus, you are unworthy to bear arms. In the name of the President of the Republic, you are hereby degraded.' Dreyfus cried out in his metallic voice: 'Soldiers, an innocent man is being degraded! Soldiers, an innocent man is being dishonoured![53] I am innocent, I swear that I am innocent. I remain worthy of serving in the army. Long live France! Long live the army!'[54]

Sergeant-Major Bouxin of the Republican Guard, 'a giant of a man', stepped forward. The stitching of Dreyfus's insignia of rank had been loosened the day before by a fellow inmate of the Cherche-Midi prison, and his sabre scored at its centre: now the insignia and epaulettes were torn from his tunic and the red stripes from his trousers. Next, Bouxin took Dreyfus's sword, drew it from its sheath and broke it over his knee. Again, Dreyfus shouted: 'Long live France! I am innocent! I swear it on the heads of my wife and my children.'

His uniform now in tatters, Dreyfus was paraded in front of the silent ranks of soldiers, journalists and guests. As the crowds behind the closed gates and railings caught sight of him, the cry went up: 'Coward! Judas! Dirty Jew!' To the friend of Edmond de Goncourt, Léon Daudet, this 'debris from the ghetto' was like 'an automaton on parade', his face 'the colour of treason'. 'A stubborn audacity persisted which killed all compassion. This was his last walk among men, yet he seemed to be profiting from it, so great was his self-control and his defiance of disgrace.'[55]

Another right-wing journalist, Maurice Barrès, described Dreyfus marching towards the assembled journalists 'with his cap thrust down over his forehead, his pince-nez on his ethnic nose, his eyes dry and angry, his whole face hard and defiant . . . Through some fatal power he possessed, or as a result of the ideas now associated with his name, the wretch evoked only loathing among those who watched him walk past. His foreign physiognomy, his impassive stiffness, the very atmosphere he exuded, revolted even the most self-controlled spectators.'

Dreyfus himself was in a daze. 'I asked myself what I was doing there. I seemed the victim of a hallucination, but alas my torn and sullied clothing brought me back rudely to the reality of the situation,'[56] he later wrote. 'I heard the howls of the deluded mob. I could feel the shudder with which it looked upon me in the belief that the condemned man in their presence was a traitor to his country.'[57] He was sufficiently detached to feel some sympathy for those who abused him and called for his death. 'I can well excuse the anger, the rage of this noble nation when they learned that there was a traitor among them.'[58]

More has been made of this spectacle in the courtyard of the École Militaire by subsequent historians than Dreyfus made of it himself. 'Dreyfus's degradation', wrote Vincent Duclert in 2006, 'allowed the French nation to reinvent itself as a race from which the Jews would be excluded and which would construct itself in opposition to them.'[59] To Ruth Harris, writing in 2010, it was an act of revenge taken by the French 'not only against a modern traitor but against the immemorial Jew, in punishment for his terrible deeds across the centuries'.[60] Undoubtedly, evidence for such grandiose judgements is found in the invective of journalists such as Léon Daudet and Maurice Barrès, and also in the remarks attributed to Colonel Sandherr. 'It's quite clear that you don't know the Jews,' he told the representative of the Foreign Office, Maurice Paléologue, who sat beside him during the ceremony. 'The race has neither patriotism, nor honour, nor pride. For centuries they have done nothing but betray.' Paléologue had said that if he were in Dreyfus's position and was innocent, he would be less docile. 'I would rebel, I would struggle.'[61] And Colonel Picquart, after a fellow officer, Captain Tassin, had remarked on the way Dreyfus had squinted down at the gold-braided insignia as it was torn from his uniform, had said: 'Good Lord, yes. He was thinking of the weight of the gold. So many grams for this, so many grams for that!' And when Tassin had said he felt sorry for Dreyfus's children, Picquart had replied: 'For goodness sake, there isn't a Jew who doesn't have a convict in his family.'[62]

However, the Paris correspondent of the Austrian *Neue Freie Presse*, Theodor Herzl, a Hungarian Jew, who witnessed Dreyfus's degradation, shared the general view that Dreyfus was guilty and 'in his initial reports on Dreyfus's court martial emphasised French anti-German xenophobia'.[63] Later it would be claimed that Dreyfus's degradation was a defining moment in the birth of Zionism because it convinced Herzl that Jews would never be secure in Europe and must establish a Jewish homeland in Palestine. Herzl himself did not discourage this view when, five years later, the campaign to rehabilitate Dreyfus had led to a major social and political crisis with an anti-Semitic dimension. But it has been established by the historian Shlomo Avineri[64] that Herzl hardly mentioned Dreyfus in his journals at the time, and it was rather the rise of anti-Semitism in Russia, Germany, Austria and eastern Europe that convinced him that the Jews must have a state of their own.

On the morning of 5 January 1895, Herzl accepted that Dreyfus was a traitor and that his demeanour was consistent with guilt. Others took a different view. The actress Sarah Bernhardt, herself partly Jewish, judged Dreyfus's protestations of innocence to be sincere.[65] And Edmond de Goncourt, after receiving a report from a friend, Carrière, who had been part of the crowd outside the gates, wrote that he 'was not convinced of his guilt', suspecting that 'the judgements of the journalists were the judgements of the little boys in the trees'.[66]

After the ceremony, Dreyfus, no longer a soldier, was taken by gendarmes to the civilian La Santé prison to await transportation: he was now, as *Le Petit Journal* put it, 'no longer a man, he is a number on a chain gang'. Armand Nisard, Director of Political Affairs at the French Foreign Office, was less sanguine: after hearing the report of his deputy, Maurice Paléologue, on the ceremony at the École Militaire, he said, 'We'll hear more about this Jew,' and indeed it was the name of Dreyfus, not the number of a convict, that was blazoned on the front pages of *Le Figaro* that morning.

Dreyfus had confessed! The story came from a journalist, Eugène Clisson, who, the previous evening, had joined a group of army officers at the music hall in Montmartre, the Moulin Rouge. Among the officers was Captain Lebrun-Renault, who bragged about the role he had played earlier that day. He repeated to them what he had told some fellow officers at the École Militaire – that, while awaiting his degradation, Dreyfus had told him that he had indeed given documents to the Germans but they were worthless and this was merely to obtain more significant information from them in return.

The sensational news caused dismay in the High Command. Lebrun-Renault himself who, after his mission, had told his superiors that he had 'nothing to report', was first summoned by General Gonse to explain himself, and later called to the Élysée Palace by the President of the Republic, Jean Casimir-Perier, alarmed by the reaction of the German Ambassador, Graf Münster von Derneburg, to the report stating that his military attaché had been engaged in squalid espionage. Lebrun-Renault, who had earlier been told by General Gonse to keep his mouth shut, at once retracted his story, not just before the President of the Republic but also before the press.

The damage had been done. Already the German Chancellor, Chlodwig zu Hohenlohe, had written to the French Prime Minister, Charles Dupuy, asking for 'a formal declaration' by the French government that the German Embassy was not involved in the Dreyfus Affair. Gabriel Hanotaux, the Foreign Minister, who should have handled the matter, was now a sick man convalescing in Cannes, and Dupuy was 'overwhelmed . . . by the course of events',[67] and so it was the President himself, Casimir-Perier, who undertook the task of assuaging the indignation of the German government. On 6 January 1895 he received

Graf Münster von Derneburg at the Élysée Palace, hoping to match the truth of the matter to German sensitivities. He explained that, while the incriminating document had indeed come from the German Embassy, there was nothing to suggest that it had been solicited by anyone in the Embassy, nor could the Embassy be held responsible for anonymous material received through the post. The President and the Ambassador accepted that this formula should form the basis of a joint declaration, and the President promised to ask the editors of the leading French newspapers to put an end to a press campaign that sought to poison relations between Germany and France.

At this, the very highest level of government, there was an amicable understanding that Germany was in no way responsible for the traitorous behaviour of Captain Dreyfus. The press was not so easily tamed; *Le Soleil* called the Germans 'the reptiles beyond the Rhine'. But the fear and loathing of the enemy had found a useful scapegoat in the man who had betrayed France. The public were baying for blood and Dupuy's government were keen to appease it. The law would be changed to impose capital punishment for treason, but it could not be applied retrospectively. Yet to many it was intolerable that a traitor like Dreyfus should suffer the same punishment as the Communards who had been deported to New Caledonia.

New Caledonia, a large island less than 1,300 kilometres east of Australia in the South Pacific, had been named as such by Captain Cook because it reminded him of Scotland. Seized by the French during the early years of the Second Empire, it was used as a penal colony well into the twentieth century. Many Communards had been sent there in 1871, among them the polemical journalist Henri Rochefort – the Marquis de Rochefort-Luçay – once a Socialist, later a Boulangist and now a vociferous nationalist and scourge of the Jews. After only a year in New Caledonia, he had escaped on an American boat to San Francisco.

If Rochefort could escape, why not Dreyfus with the money and influence of 'all Israel' behind him? Already *La Libre Parole* had stated that it was only because 'the Jews had had too little time' that Dreyfus had not been kidnapped in Paris. It was beyond doubt that 'an international "Jewish syndicate"' would try to arrange his escape.[68] To the government of Dupuy – to any French government – the political consequences of an abduction would be catastrophic. There was also the public lust for retribution. Dreyfus had to be sent somewhere not only more secure but also less agreeable than New Caledonia. On the very day of his degradation, 5 January, Dupuy's cabinet met to consider an alternative. General Mercier, the Minister of War, proposed that the present law be modified to enable Dreyfus to be held on Devil's Island, part of a penal colony on the Salvation Islands off the coast of French Guiana. It would be both more secure than New Caledonia and more acceptable to public opinion as a place of punishment because of its intense heat and torrid climate.

General Mercier's proposal was accepted. The law re-establishing the Salvation Islands as a place of deportation was passed without a debate by the Chamber of Deputies on 12 February 1895. Vincent Duclert believes that Mercier changed the place for Dreyfus's exile not merely to appease public opinion and ensure that Dreyfus did not escape, but also to punish him for his stubborn refusal to confess. 'The idea of a law re-establishing the Salvation Islands was his response to Dreyfus's defiance of the established truth'; and this change to the law was only one part of the 'expiatory punishment' that he planned for the guilty man. A whole raft of orders and directives particular to Dreyfus added up to a truly horrific regime.[69]

Mercier may also have borne in mind some statistics: of the 7,000 convicts sent to the Salvation Islands in 1856, some 2,500 had died before the year was out.[70] The death penalty may have been abolished for political crimes, but for a man as enfeebled as Alfred Dreyfus already was, malaria would do the work of the guillotine.

7

The Salvation Islands

1: Transportation

Awaiting deportation in a cell in the Santé prison, Dreyfus was without the modest solace of a governor who believed him innocent, as had Forzinetti at the Cherche-Midi. He could receive visits and enter into correspondence; together with an English grammar which Alfred had requested to help pass the time by learning the language, Lucie had sent into the prison 'a sturdy portable inkwell'. Her visits were severely circumscribed; they had to be in the presence of the Governor who would place himself between Dreyfus and his wife, and Dreyfus was not allowed to approach her, let alone embrace her.[1] Lucie asked if she could be allowed to kiss her husband if her hands were tied behind her back. Her request was refused.

It was therefore easier for them to express their feelings in their correspondence, and Lucie's letters, sent to Dreyfus while he was in prison both before and after his degradation, reveal a remarkable devotion unaffected by what she must have learned about Alfred's philandering in the course of his trial, and it was this devotion that saved him from despair. 'You are the single thread that attaches me to life,' he wrote to her from Cherche-Midi prison on Christmas Eve of 1894. 'I am proud of you and will try to be worthy of you.'[2] Vincent Duclert describes their exchange of letters as 'one of the most beautiful love correspondences of all time',[3] and it is notable that, even though others had not read her letters,* Lucie's devotion to her husband inspired respect in even his most vociferous detractors. Ruth Harris points out that 'as the daughter of a wealthy diamond merchant, and an Alsatian Jewess, Lucie . . . could have made an irresistible target for anti-Semitism and envy. However, despite its savagery, *La Croix* never once attacked her; she was a model of motherly and wifely virtue utterly beyond reproach . . .'[4]

'Mon trésor chéri', 'Poor dear Freddy', 'Je t'embrasse comme je t'aime', 'Bon soir et bonne nuit', 'Je t'embrasse de toutes mes forces'.[5] In the same way as a sailor fished out of a freezing ocean is revived by the warmth of another human body, so Lucie's letters, imbued with conjugal passion, sustained her husband. She was still only twenty-five, ten years younger than Dreyfus, but she now revealed a strength of character all the more remarkable given her sheltered upbringing. She made Alfred promise not to take his own life and fortified him with her own fervent belief in his rehabilitation. 'My line of conduct is clear. I will never leave you. Never. I do not want to live, I cannot live, except for you.'[6] 'God will make up to you for it all and will recompense you a hundredfold for your suffering.'[7] 'You are strong in your innocence; imagine that it is someone other than yourself who is being dishonoured; accept the unmerited punishment; do it for me, for the wife who loves you. Give this proof of affection, do it for your children; they will be grateful to you one day.'[8]

Like the wives of the Russian Decembrists who accompanied their husbands to exile in Siberia, Lucie was determined to join Alfred in New Caledonia, his presumed destination. 'The law allows the wives and children of convicts to follow them. I don't see what objection there could be to that.' When Alfred tried to deter her, she rounded on him:

Do you not wish me to join you? No, my treasure, you won't make me change my mind. By refusing me the happiness of living with you out there you are demanding a sacrifice which is beyond me. I am ready to support anything, but I want to suffer with you, at your side, I want to fight with you. I will not abandon you. Our children will be well

* The full correspondence was only published in October 2005.

The Taking of the Bastille by Jean-Pierre Houel. The storming of the Bastille by 60,000 Parisians on 14 July 1789 liberated four forgers, an Irish lunatic and an incestuous aristocrat. However, the Bastille symbolised the arbitrary powers of the absolute monarch and this was the first act of defiance against King Louis XVI.

The Tennis Court Oath (1791) by Jacques Louis David. Locked out of their usual meeting place, the delegates of the Third Estate gathered in an indoor tennis court and proclaimed themselves a National Assembly. They were joined by most members of the Fourth Estate, the Catholic clergy.

Le prêtre refractaire, engraving by Léopold Massard, based on Henri Baron. On 12 July 1790, the National Assembly passed a law demanding an oath of loyalty to a Civil Constitution for the clergy. This entailed the election of priests and bishops and a breach with the Pope in Rome. Here a priest refuses to take the oath. Most of the clergy followed suit which led to a brutal persecution of Catholics.

Napoléon le Grand rétablit le culte des Israélites, engraving, by François Louis Couché. On 21 September 1791 the National Assembly gave full civil rights to French Jews. Most, like the Dreyfus family, were from Alsace. Napoleon's conquests extended these rights throughout Europe. Here grateful Jews thank their liberator.

The Procession of the Goddess of Reason by Louis Blanc, engraved by Meyer-Heine. A woman dressed as the Goddess of Reason is carried through the streets of Paris to the cathedral of Notre Dame, converted into a Temple of Reason.

Maximilien de Robespierre (1791) by Pierre Roch Vigneron. In the place of Catholicism, French revolutionaries such as Robespierre initiated a cult of Reason.

The Drowning in the Loire During the Reign of Terror (1793) by H. de la Charlerie. An uprising of Catholics and Royalists against the Revolution in the West of France led to atrocious reprisals. Men and women are drowned off scuttled barges in the River Loire at Nantes. This persecution, 'tantamount to genocide', alienated French Catholics from republicanism.

The German nations united behind the Prussian Chancellor Otto von Bismarck to wage war against Napoleon's nephew, Napoleon III. The French were quickly defeated. Napoleon III was taken prisoner at Sedan. Here he sits looking disconsolate with his captor, Bismarck.

Under Duress (1871) by Smeeton after Janet Lange. With a knife at her breast France signs the preliminaries of the peace treaty which ceded the provinces of Alsace and Lorraine to the new German Reich.

SOUVENIR DU SIÈGE PRUSSIEN.

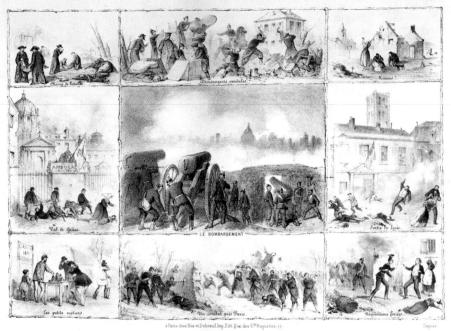

LES SOUFFRANCES DE PARIS.

The citizens of Paris, besieged by the Prussians, refused to accept the armistice negotiated by the government in Versailles and established a Commune. It was brutally repressed by French troops. In a single week in May, between twenty and thirty thousand Communards were killed.

LA RÉVOLTE DE PARIS.

Execution of the Archbishop of Paris (1871). The anti-clerical Communards executed the Archbishop of Paris, Monsignor Darboy, and fifty Catholic priests. This reinforced the association in the minds of French Catholics of radical republicanism and persecution.

Jules Ferry, French Prime Minister in 1881. His government, with six Protestant ministers, abolished Catholic primary schools in France. Catholic magistrates who resigned rather than enforce the law were often replaced by Protestants and Jews.

Édouard Drumont's *La France Juive* (*Jewish France*), which described France's Jews as 'a ruling caste' and France 'a conquered nation', sold over a million copies. Drumont's newspaper, *La Libre Parole*, exposed widespread corruption involving Jewish bankers and republican politicians in the Panama Canal Scandal. It campaigned against giving Jews commissions in the French army.

The Rothschild estate at Ferriéres. Jewish bankers and entrepreneurs amasses great fortunes and bought estates previously owned by the Catholic aristocracy. The increase of power and influence of Jews in France was widely resented

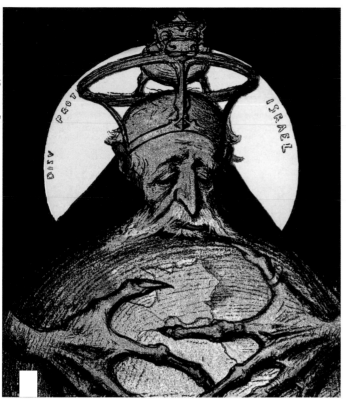

This portrait of Baron James de Rothschild, titled 'Jews Take over the World', offers a sense of the perceived threat posed by the rise of the Jews. Rothschild was said to be the model for Gunderman in Emile Zola's novel *L'Argent*.

It was widely believed by French Catholics that freemasons worked with Protestants and Jews to undermine Catholicism, France's established religion. Here the Grand Orient masonic lodge celebrates the anniversary of the 1789 revolution.

General Auguste Mercier, Minister of War in 1894. Curt, dry, authoritarian, he was mistrusted by *La Libre Parole* because of his Republican sympathies. He had an English wife and did not go to mass.

General Raoul le Mouton de Boisdeffre, Chief of the General Staff. Tall, distinguished-looking, refined, cunning and lazy, he was the architect of the French military alliance with Tsarist Russia. He and other senior army officers felt responsible for the security of France.

General Saussier. A rotund bon viveur with a Jewish mistress, the wife of Major Maurice Weil. He was subordinate to the Minister of War, General Mercier, only while Mercier held office. A mutual antipathy meant that what one proposed the other rejected.

Colonel Maximilian von Schwarzkoppen, the German military attaché in Paris. He suborned agents in co-operation with his lover, the Italian military attaché, Alessandro Panizzardi.

brought up by my parents and your brothers, until we are able to look after them ourselves. I have already said it, my darling, far from you I cannot win, I would suffer too much.[9]

Even when she learned that Alfred was to be deported not to New Caledonia but to the inhospitable Salvation Islands, Lucie was determined to join him. 'I suffer so much from being separated from you that I have made another appeal to go and share your exile. I shall at least have the happiness of living the same life as you, of being near you, and showing you how much I love you.'[10] Her family, however, knew better than she did what the living conditions were likely to be on the Salvation Islands, as did the French authorities. When the Minister for the Colonies asked the Governor of French Guiana about the possibility of Lucie joining 'the convict' in October 1895, he received the answer: 'Just returned from a tour of Devil's Island. Judge it impossible to introduce a woman convict.'[11]

Alfred himself must have realised that the Salvation Islands would be a less pleasant place to serve his sentence than New Caledonia, but this did not unduly upset him because he was confident that it would not be long before the grotesque judicial error of which he was a victim was revealed. Such was his respect for the army hierarchy, he could not conceive of any bad faith behind his prosecution; he had particular confidence in General de Boisdeffre, the Chief of the General Staff, who had once taken him aside on an army inspection and shown great interest in what he had to say. His hopes were also pinned on promises made to him by Commandant du Paty de Clam on that final visit to the Cherche-Midi prison when du Paty had tried to get Dreyfus to admit that he had given documents to the Germans in an attempt to obtain secrets from them in return.

The deal offered by du Paty was merely that, in return for a partial confession, Dreyfus would be subjected to a less rigorous regime when serving his sentence. When Dreyfus had repeated yet again that he had had no dealings with the Germans whatsoever, du Paty said: 'If you are innocent, you are the greatest martyr of all time.'[12] Dreyfus's protestations of innocence, however, were not merely to avoid martyrdom; he was as horrified as were his accusers to think that there was a traitor at the heart of the High Command. Knowing that he was not that traitor, he tried to impress upon du Paty de Clam the need to continue his investigations. He extracted from du Paty a promise that they would continue, and that he personally would keep Dreyfus informed of their progress.

Once du Paty had left, Dreyfus wrote a letter to General Mercier to make the same point as he had made to du Paty – that the traitor was still at large. 'I have been convicted, and have no special mercy or pardon to ask of you. But in the name of my honour, which I hope will be restored to me one day, I have the duty to implore you to continue your investigation. After I am gone, keep the search alive. This is the sole mercy that I request.'[13] Of course neither du Paty nor Mercier was disposed to show mercy in this or any other way. They had found the traitor. Dreyfus was guilty. The case was closed.

Mercier also had other, more important matters on his mind. On 14 January 1895, while Dreyfus was still in the Santé prison, the Prime Minister, Charles Dupuy, resigned. The next day, the President of France, Jean Casimir-Perier, followed suit. He had been elected six months before following the assassination of President Carnot. Hitherto an active politician, he had been sidelined and ignored as President by ministers, while at the same time being vilified in the press because of his wealth and privileged background. This led to a rapid disenchantment and now his resignation.

Under the constitution of the Third Republic, the president was chosen by the deputies and senators of the National Assembly. These now dismissed Casimir-Perier's resignation as the nervous tantrum of a spoiled dilettante too sensitive for the rough and tumble of political life,[14] and looked for a man to replace him who was more likely to appreciate the perks and trappings that went with being France's head of state. General Mercier's name was put forward as 'the patriot general' who had unmasked the traitor Dreyfus, but the memory of Boulanger was too fresh in the minds of the politicians for them to consider a soldier, even a republican one, as head of state. In the first round of voting, he received only three votes. The final choice was a genial businessman, the deputy for the northern port of Le Havre, Félix Faure. Once elected President, Faure asked Léon Bourgeois to form a government and, when Bourgeois had failed to secure a majority, Alexandre Ribot. Ribot disliked Mercier and chose General Émile Zurlinden as his Minister of War. General Mercier, now out of government, returned to active service as Commander of the 16th Army Corps.

On the evening of Thursday, 17 January, Dreyfus was already asleep on his bunk in his cell in the Santé prison, looking forward to a visit from Lucie the next day, when the door was opened and an official of the Ministry of the Interior, accompanied by three deputies, entered the cell. The official told Dreyfus to get dressed at once and then 'had me hurriedly handcuffed while I was scarcely dressed, and gave me no time even to pick up my eye-glasses'.[15] With no overcoat to protect him from the cold, he was taken in a closed cab to the Gare d'Orsay. There he was locked into a narrow cage in a railway compartment fitted out for the transport of prisoners; handcuffed and shackled, he had space in which to sit down but not to stretch his legs.

The train left the station for La Rochelle on the western coast of France. After frequent requests, Dreyfus was given some bread, cheese and black coffee. It was a journey of many hours in cramped conditions and, even after they had reached La Rochelle at midday on Friday the 18th, Dreyfus was not removed from his coach. A number of curious onlookers gathered to watch the prisoners taken from the train for transportation to the Île de Ré, a couple of miles off the coast, sensed from the demeanour of the guards that someone of significance was among the convicts, and then learned that that someone was the traitor Alfred Dreyfus. The word spread, and the group became a crowd. The shout went up: 'Death to the traitor! Death to the Jew!' Dreyfus remained the whole afternoon in the barred compartment of the stationary carriage, listening to the abuse of the growing crowd outside. Finally at nightfall he was taken from the coach. As soon as he was seen leaving the train, the crowd surged forward to attack him. He was struck by fists as his guards formed an inadequate cordon around him. Dreyfus, by his own account, remained impassive: 'I even felt myself alone in the middle of the crowd, and was ready to give up my body. My soul remained my own.'

Were it not for the phalanx of guards, Dreyfus would no doubt have been lynched by the crowd. He remained remarkably sanguine about the hatred he inspired. 'I heard the perfectly legitimate cries of a brave and noble people raised against a man they thought was a traitor, the lowest of wretches,' he would later write to Lucie, who had been ignorant of his ordeal; her family had removed the newspapers describing the fracas at La Rochelle before she had a chance to read them. He had an almost mystical desire to break away from his guards and offer up his body to the crowd hoping that this would somehow convince them of the purity of his soul. But the guards knew their duty: they threw him into a prison wagon and drove him, pursued by the crowd, to the port of La Palice where he embarked on a boat to take him to Saint-Martin on the Île de Ré.

It was snowing and extremely cold. From the jetty, Dreyfus was marched through the snow to the gates of the huge fortress built to the design of Vauban during the reign of Louis XIV; it replaced an earlier citadel which had held out against an English army under the Duke of Buckingham sent to raise Cardinal Richelieu's siege of the Protestants in La Rochelle. Huguenots and Jansenists had been imprisoned there and, since the Revolution of 1789, it had been used to assemble prisoners condemned to deportation to penal colonies – the *bagne*. During the Directory, several hundred Catholic priests who had refused to take the oath of loyalty to the republican regime had been held there, their deportation thwarted by the British fleet; many had died from their ill-treatment and privations.

At the gates of the fortress, the official of the Ministry of Justice handed Dreyfus over to the prison Governor. He was strip-searched, then locked up in a cell adjacent to the guard post; there was an aperture in the cell door through which, every two hours, day and night, the guards checked up on their illustrious prisoner. He remained in solitary confinement. His daily exercise was taken alone. He was searched daily. Smoking was forbidden. Twice a week, paper and pen were brought into his cell so that he could write to his wife. Other forms of writing or study were forbidden.

After two and a half weeks held incommunicado, Dreyfus was told that he was to be allowed a visit from his wife. Lucie made the arduous journey in the bitter cold to the Île de Ré on 13 February accompanied by Alfred's brother-in-law, the businessman from Carpentras, Joseph Valabrègue. Once again, the Governor had received instructions not to allow the married couple to touch one another, and sat between the two during their twenty-minute encounter. Only news of family members was permitted; they could not discuss Alfred's case or his incarceration. Nonetheless, both felt 'a great interior happiness' at seeing one another once again.

A second visit under the same conditions took place the following day. Lucie then returned to Paris but was back on the Île de Ré for two further visits on 20 and 21 February. Lucie again asked that, if her hands were tied behind her back, she might be allowed to kiss her husband; again the request was refused. This final meeting lasted an hour. Lucie then left the fortress and Alfred was taken back to his cell. They would not see one another again for more than four years.

Only hours after the departure of his wife, Dreyfus was told to put his few personal effects into a suitcase and prepare to depart. After being strip-searched yet again, he was escorted by six guards to a steam-launch which took him to the warship *Saint-Nazaire*. Once on board, he was locked into a cell beneath the bridge, with a metal grille gate that provided no protection against the cold. A hammock was thrown into the cell. He was not told where he was being taken. He was given no food. After having so recently been with his wife, knowing that he was to be cut off from her and his children in an unknown location and for an indefinite period of time, Dreyfus's morale collapsed. He threw himself on to the floor in the corner of his cell and wept.

2: Devil's Island – 1

The Îles du Salut, or Salvation Islands, lie in the Atlantic Ocean around sixteen kilometres off the coast of French Guiana and 150 kilometres north-west of its border with Brazil. Though closer to the port of Kourou at the mouth of the Kourou river, the islands were served by the larger port and regional capital, Cayenne, forty-three kilometres to the south-east. The two larger islands, the Île Royale and Île Saint-Joseph, had, since the early years of the Second Empire, housed a penal colony which had taken the name of the third and smallest of the three, Devil's Island.* Devil's Island itself, difficult to access because of the strong currents in the Passe des Grenadines which separated it from the Île Royale, had been used to isolate those convicts with leprosy. Ruins of the leper colony remained among the scrub and palm trees, the only vegetation on the island of volcanic rock.

Throughout the month of March and the first half of April 1895, Alfred Dreyfus was held in the prison on the Île Royale. This was part of a network of penal settlements in French Guiana, some on the mainland such as a centre for deportees at Saint-Jean-du-Maroni or camps deep in the jungle such as Godebert or Charvein where convicts condemned to forced labour would work in abominable conditions clearing the forests for roads and canals. Each metre of the road built linking Cayenne to Saint-Jean-du-Maroni was said to cost the life of a convict and each kilometre the life of a warden – an exaggeration, because twenty years after the construction started, the road had got no further than twenty-four kilometres and, of the 500 convicts who worked on it, 178 died.[16]

Three categories of offenders were sent to French Guiana. The first were the *transportés*, the deportees, guilty of serious crimes – armed robbers or murderers who for one reason or another had escaped the guillotine. Whatever the length of their sentence, these major criminals were forbidden ever to return to France. Even those with sentences of less than eight years were caught by the law of 1854 which imposed *le doublage*, confinement in French Guiana after their release for a period equal to their sentence.

The second category were the political prisoners, the *déportés politiques*, found guilty of espionage, treason, desertion, even counterfeiting.

---

* Because of its colourful name, the whole penitential system in French Guiana came to be called Devil's Island in books published by escaped convicts such as René Belbenoit's *Dry Guillotine* or Henri Charrière's *Papillon*.

They were sentenced either to simple deportation or, like Dreyfus, not just to deportation but to detention in 'a fortified enclosure'.

The third category of deportee were the *relégués*, recidivists who under the law of 27 May 1885 were sent to French Guiana if they had four convictions or more for theft, swindling, offences against public decency, habitual enticement of minors to debauchery, vagabondage or mendacity. Half of the deportees for life were petty criminals of this kind. They were not necessarily sentenced to forced labour; some had merely been deported and had only to report to the prison administration from time to time. They were even permitted to marry. Of the 52,000 convicts and 15,600 *relégués* transported to French Guiana, 850 were women.[17] However, the more lenient regime of the *relégués*, like that of the *libérés*, the liberated prisoners, was still harsh. The prisoners who had served their sentence, often doubled, had no money to pay for a ticket back to France. Among the *libérés*, the journalist Albert Londres counted 2,448 'whites without a roof, without clothes, without food, without work and without hope of a job. All were hungry. They are dogs without owners. Their sentence is served. They have paid. Has one the right to condemn someone for the same fault twice over?'[18]

In this nineteenth-century gulag archipelago operated by the French government in its torrid colony of Guiana, the prisons on the Salvation Islands were considered the *bagne du bagne*, the penal colony within the penal colony, and, of the three Salvation Islands, the most secure was Devil's Island.

On 14 April 1895, the preparations made for Dreyfus's transfer from the prison on the Île Royale to Devil's Island were completed with the construction of a guard-house and, some distance away, a stone hut with a corrugated-iron roof. The guard-house was surrounded by a veranda and attached to it was a look-out tower topped by a loggia from which the guards could survey the whole island and scan the sea.

The hut comprised a cell four metres square, and a small annexe for the guard, two by three metres. The cell was separated from the guards' annexe by an iron-grilled gate, and the guards' annexe from the exterior by a wooden door. Both the gate and the wooden door were locked at night. There was a change of guard every two hours so Dreyfus was woken by the jangling of keys and the turning of locks. There was a barred window to the cell with a view of the sea. The island itself measured only 1,200 by 365 metres, but when Dreyfus was released from the cabin during the day, he was confined to an unshaded area of 170 square metres between the jetty and the ruins of the leper colony. He was accompanied wherever he went by an armed guard. Conversation with the guard was forbidden. He wore the regulation clothes for a deportee: a canvas jacket and trousers, a cotton shirt, a flannel belt.

Dreyfus received the rations of a soldier which he had to cook for himself, but on arrival he was provided with no utensils. On his first morning, on 15 April, he was given a ration of bread, raw meat and green coffee beans. Wholly ill-equipped by his upbringing to fend for himself, Dreyfus had first to gather firewood, light a fire and grill the meat on some pieces of scrap metal over the embers. With no means of grinding the beans, he could not make coffee. His lunch was bread and tea, his supper bread and water.

By 19 April, Dreyfus had somewhat developed his cuisine. He made a stew in an old tin with meat, salt and a pepper that he had found growing on the island. One of the main complaints that he made in the diary which he started on his first day on Devil's Island was the way in which the wind blew the smoke into his eyes. 'My eyes suffered horribly; what misery!' On 24 April he was '*lent* four flat plates, two deep ones, and two saucepans, but nothing to put in them'. He was incensed when given tinned bacon. 'I threw it all into the sea because the tinned bacon was inedible, the rice, which was brought to me in a filthy state, was offensive, and I had nothing with which to roast the coffee beans, which, in bitter derision, were given to me raw.'[19] Instead, Dreyfus made himself a stew of dried peas 'which will be my food for the day'.

In due course, Dreyfus established a daily routine. Because the heat quickly became intolerable, he rose early.

I get up at dawn (5), light the fire to make coffee or tea. Then I put my dried vegetables on to cook, then I make my bed, tidy my room and wash. At 8 they bring me my rations. I finish cooking my vegetables; on meat days I cook that. All my cooking is done by 10, I eat what's left cold in the evening, not wanting to be in front of the fire for three more hours in the afternoon.

At 10 I eat. I read, I work and suffer until 3. Then I wash. When the heat goes, around 5, I cut wood, get water from the well, wash my clothes etc. At 6 I eat what's left of lunch. Then they lock me up. That is the longest time. I haven't been able to get a light in the hut. There is one on the guard post, but too weak to see for long. So I have to go to bed and that is when my brain begins to churn, and all my thoughts turn to the ghastly drama of which I am the victim, and I remember my wife, my children and all those who are dear to me. How they must be suffering too!

The inadequate diet gave Dreyfus stomach cramps, and he contracted a tropical fever. On 17 May, the prison doctor examined him: he prescribed forty centigrams of quinine a day and ordered twelve boxes of condensed milk for his patient and some bicarbonate of soda. 'So I shall be able to put myself on a milk diet, and shall not have to eat the food that is so repugnant to me that I have taken nothing for four days.'[20]

The lepers had cultivated tomatoes on the island and these had now grown wild and yielded a good crop. Dreyfus also received some fresh food sent to the convicts by a group of compassionate women among the wives of the prison guards; and by the summer of 1895 food parcels would arrive from Paris sent by Lucie via the Colonial Office on the rue Oudinot containing delicacies from Félix Potin and other shops in Paris – condensed milk, Vichy water, coffee, cigarettes, pipe tobacco, chocolate, biscuits and quinine – the deliveries irregular, the packages frequently delayed and sometimes pilfered en route; they nonetheless contained welcome supplements to Dreyfus's diet and were a sign that he was not forgotten. Lucie also paid 500 francs a month into an account as Dreyfus's *mass* or pocket money which he could draw on to order provisions from Cayenne.[21] He was permitted to smoke and was relieved of having to wash his own clothes: his sweat-sodden linen was sent to the laundry of the infirmary on the Île Royale but when returned to him was thrown at him as if he was a dog.

There was thus some small amelioration of the grim diet provided by the prison authorities, but there was no relief from the great heat and humidity. Around 5° north of the equator, the median temperature throughout the year in French Guiana was 30° Celsius. During the day Dreyfus would sit in the shade of his hut facing the sea hoping for a cooling breeze,[22] but by the evening when he was locked up in his cell it had become a stifling oven. Emaciated, drenched in sweat, Dreyfus had to battle with unwelcome guests.

> Vermin swarmed in my hut; mosquitoes, as soon as the rainy season began; ants, all the year round, in such large numbers that I had to isolate my table by placing the legs in old preserve boxes filled with petroleum . . . The most tiresome insect was the spider-crab; its bite is venomous. The spider-crab is a creature whose body resembles that of a crab, and its legs are long, like those of a spider. Altogether it is about as large as a man's hand. I killed many of them in my hut into which they came through the aperture between the roof and the walls.[23]

Strictly speaking, under the terms of the law, deportation should not have meant imprisonment. 'In its essence, it was simply a restriction on liberty, imposing upon the convict no other obligation than that of never leaving the territory to which he had been sent.'[24] However, Dreyfus had been sent from France with the admonition that he was 'to be treated like a hardened criminal, completely unworthy of pity'. He was never out of the sight of one of the warders. The number watching the single prisoner was increased in the course of his stay. 'At first the number of warders, exclusive of the head warder, had been five; this was raised to six and afterwards to ten warders, in the course of 1897.' At the beginning of 1898, the number was increased to thirteen.

The regime imposed on Dreyfus was posited on the assumption that at any time an attempt might be made to rescue him. It seemed possible, even likely, that under cover of night a cutter might be sent from a German cruiser; or that the power of Jewish finance might enlist help from the British navy: had not Palmerston sent gunboats to Alexandria to effect the release of the Damascene Jews? From the top of the tower attached to the guard-house, the guards scanned the horizon and the mere sight of a sail or smoke on the horizon sent them into a panic and justified in their minds the abnormal and, strictly speaking, illegal restrictions on Dreyfus's movements and keeping him, month after month, year after year, in solitary confinement.

This solitude added mental suffering to his physical ordeal. 'I never open my mouth,' he wrote in his diary. 'I am more silent than a Trappist.'[25] 'I am subject to the stupid and useless fate of the Man in the Iron Mask.'[26] 'I never see a pleasant face; I can never open my mouth to speak to any human being; night and day I must suppress heart and brain in an eternal silence.'[27] His only human contact was with the prison guards, but they were forbidden to talk to him or even to answer his questions. 'My speech was limited to asking if my letters had come or not. But I am now forbidden to ask even that; or (which is the same thing) the warders are forbidden to answer the most commonplace questions.'[28] Despite their silence, some of the guards were more sympathetic than others. 'A warder has just left, worn out by the fevers of the place. This is the second man who has been forced to leave since I have been here. I am sorry he has gone, for he was an honest man, fulfilling strictly the duties assigned to him, but loyally, with tact and moderation.'[29]

Dreyfus suspected that 'the local administration . . . feels a horror of such arbitrary and inhuman measures, but is obliged to apply them'. The prison Commandant (Dreyfus never learned his name) was a straightforward man who played things by the book; however, he was constrained by instructions from above. 'I have only to ask the chief warder for any insignificant thing of common necessity to have my request abruptly and instantly refused. Accordingly, I never repeat a request, preferring to go without everything rather than humiliate myself.'[30] Dreyfus asked for a box of tools so that he could take up carpentry; his request was refused on the grounds that he might use the tools to escape.

There came a point when Dreyfus would have preferred to work on a chain gang than to be left idle and alone. 'I have nothing to kill the terribly slow time. I asked long ago for some sort of manual labour, no matter what, with which to occupy myself a little; they have not answered me.'[31] He was allowed books, some literary and scientific reviews, and pen and paper to write letters and keep a diary. He wrote constantly to Lucie and, on 1 July 1895, an appeal to the new French President, Félix Faure, which was returned four months later: 'Rejected without comment'.

Dreyfus had with him the English grammar brought to him in the Santé prison by Lucie: 'I am going to try to study English,' he wrote in his diary. 'Perhaps the work will help me to forget for a while my sorrows.' But the climate and privations made it hard for him to concentrate. 'From time to time I try to study English, to write translations, and to forget myself in my work. But my brain is so utterly shaken that it refuses to labour; after a quarter of an hour, I am forced to give up the task.'[32]

Dreyfus was refused a lamp to enable him to read after dark. 'I have been shut up since half-past six in the evening, my hut lit only by the lantern in the guard-room. Besides, I cannot work at English all night and the few journals which reach me are quickly read.' He had a volume of Shakespeare's plays and returned again and again to the tragedies which spoke to his own. 'I never understood this great writer so well as during this tragic period; I read him over and over again; *Hamlet* and *King Lear* appealed to me with all their dramatic power.' He was particularly struck by Iago's words in *Othello*.

> Good name in man and woman, dear my lord,
> Is the immediate jewel of their souls:
> Who steals my purse steals trash; 'tis something, nothing;
> 'Twas mine, 'tis his, and has been slave to thousands;
> But he that filches from me my good name,
> Robs me of that which not enriches him,
> And makes me poor indeed.[33]

Dreyfus had the right to order twenty books every three months. Together with Shakespeare's plays, Montaigne's *Essays* were 'the most sacred texts of his exile'.[34] Besides these, in his small library, he had *Études sur la littérature contemporaine* by Edmond Scherer, *Histoire de la littérature française* by Gustave Lanson, some novels by Honoré de Balzac, Paul Barras' *Mémoires*, the *Petite Critique* by Jules Janin, a *History of Painting*, a *History of the Francs*, and volume VIII of Ernest

Lavisse's *Histoire de France*, and Arthur Rambaud's *Histoire générale du IVe siècle à nos jours*.[35] He had trouble preserving his little library from predators. 'At the end of a short time, my books were in a pitiable state; vermin got into them, gnawed them, and laid their eggs in them.'[36]

An even greater consolation for Dreyfus than his library were the letters he received from Lucie. Like his captors, Dreyfus scanned the horizon not for the sight of a boat sent to rescue him but for the mail boat from France on its way to Cayenne. His wife's letters arrived sporadically, often having taken months to arrive from France. They were read by censors at the Ministry of the Colonies and could contain no reference to his case. Lucie could do little but give news of the children, protest her great love and do what she could to sustain his morale. Initially, she still hoped that she would be able to join her husband: 'I suffer so much from being separated from you that I have made another appeal to go and share your exile. I shall at least have the happiness of living the same life as you, of being near you, and showing you how much I love you.' But even before his transfer from prison on the Île Royale to his hut on the Île du Diable, Alfred understood that her presence was out of the question. 'When I realised the rigours of my life at the Salvation Islands, I had no illusion as to the answer which would be given to my wife's requests to be permitted to come and join me. I knew they would be steadfastly refused.'[37]

Dreyfus also wrote to his children. 'I was touched to the depths of my soul', wrote Lucie, 'by the letter you wrote to our Pierre; he was enchanted, and his child's face lit up when I read your lines to him; he knows them by heart. When he speaks of you, he is all aflame.'[38] Later, she became anxious about her daughter's development.

> Jeanette is rather more difficult than she was. She is still not old enough to understand everything. She gets little fits of obstinacy, rebels against authority, and ends by shutting herself up in a silence that it is difficult for me to get her out of. But she is exceptionally kind, and makes everyone love her for her affectionate temperament. They are two good children.[39]

Dreyfus never lost interest in the way in which his children were being brought up and sent his young wife long letters of advice on their formation.

In your last letters you were telling me about Pierrot's sensitiveness, and saying that you were trying to combat it. If it is sentimentality, I say yes, a thousand times yes. But if it is a sensitiveness, don't try to deprive him of it, but try to add to it energy and determination. Let me explain: sentimentality is a weakness, a feebleness of heart expending itself upon insignificant things, or upon oneself. It makes us less able to face and bear the shocks of life. It calls upon all the energy of the soul, and ends by turning even the man who is basically good into a profound egoist.

Sensitiveness, on the other hand, so long as it is applied to things of the mind and heart, is a fine and noble quality. It is the mark of a soul capable of emotion in the presence of natural and spiritual beauties . . . In this sense it is the inspiration of all the best works of art and literature.[40]

This distinction was all-important to Dreyfus himself as he struggled to retain his sensitiveness without descending into a lugubrious, self-pitying sentimentality. While initially it was the physical privations that pre-occupied him – the intense heat and humidity, the persistent fevers, the vile food, the tormenting insects – it soon became the mental suffering that was hardest to endure. He feared for his sanity and felt he might succumb to the temptation to take his own life. 'They will certainly end up killing me by these sufferings, or forcing me to kill myself to escape madness.' 'I am in an indescribable state. I can't sleep. I am afraid of losing my sanity.'[41] 'When shall I again pass a calm and tranquil night? Perhaps not until I am in the grave when I shall sleep the sleep that is everlasting. How sweet it will be to think no longer of human vileness and cowardice!'[42]

The sound of the sea surrounding Devil's Island had a profound effect on him – both consoling but also holding out the promise of oblivion. 'The ocean, which I hear moaning beneath my little window, has always for me a strange fascination. It soothes my thoughts as it did before, and now they are very bitter and sombre. It recalls dear memories to mind, the happy days I have passed by the sea-side, with my wife and darling children.'[43] 'I feel a very strong sensation, which I felt before on the ship, of being almost irresistibly drawn to the sea, whose roaring waters seem to call to me like a great consoling power. This power the sea has over me is strong; on the ship I had to close my eyes and picture my wife so as not to give in to it.'[44] Dreyfus had promised Lucie that he would not kill himself, but it was not a promise he found easy to keep. 'What endless agony I am compelled to endure! What a sacrifice I have made in consenting to live!'[45]

Although the sudden, calamitous and incomprehensible reversal of fortune that Dreyfus had suffered brings to mind the sufferings of Job, he did not himself seek consolation in the many references to the fickleness of human fortune in the Hebrew Bible. Unlike Lucie, who referred to her husband's 'Calvary' on a number of occasions and believed that 'God, who has so sorely tried us, will give us the strength to fulfil our duty to the end,'[46] Dreyfus never lost his wholly secular outlook: even in the depths of despair, he never had recourse to any of the consolations offered by religious belief. The ideals which sustained him were secular: Truth, Justice, Honour, Courage, Loyalty, Duty. The word 'God' appears only twice in his writings and the word 'Jew' not at all.[47] The metaphors he used in describing his ordeal were Christian rather than Jewish – he too talked about his 'Calvary', his 'martyrdom' and being 'more silent than a Trappist'. One of his rare references to God was not complimentary to the deity: 'How often I am reminded of Schopenhauer's exclamation, at the sight of human iniquity: "If God created the world, I would not like to be God."'[48]

Montaigne, whom Dreyfus so much admired, envied those who 'could rest on the soft pillow of faith', but, as Édouard Drumont had noted in *La France juive*, Montaigne was a 'destroyer' who 'highlighted the vices and absurdities of humanity without proposing any better attainable ideals'.[49] The only prayers Dreyfus offered up were 'to the President of the Republic'.[50] The ideals that sustained him were those of republican France. 'Whatever may have been my sufferings,' he wrote to Lucie, 'however atrocious may have been the tortures inflicted upon me – tortures that I cannot forget, tortures that can be excused only by the passions that sometimes lead men astray, I have never forgotten that far above men, far above their passions, far above their errors, is our country. It is she who will be my final judge.'[51]

With the same belief as the French philosophers of the Enlightenment in moral progress and the perfectibility of mankind, he could not comprehend how 'in the nineteenth century, in a country like France, imbued with ideas of justice and truth, such incredible wrongs can be inflicted'. And the wrong above all wrongs that he had suffered was, in Iago's words, the 'filching of his good name'. He was a man 'who holds honour to be above everything', and he suffered not just because he was dishonoured, but because the dishonour spread to those he loved. 'If I had only my own life to struggle for,' he wrote to Lucie, 'I should certainly not struggle any longer; but it is for honour that I live, and I shall struggle inch by inch to the end.' 'I live, my loved one, because I want you to be able to bear my name, as you have done up to the present, with honour, with joy, and with love, because, in a word, I want to hand it down intact to my children.' 'It is a question of the honour of our name, of the future of our children.' With no God to see into his soul, Dreyfus's integrity existed in the eyes of others or not at all. 'Above everything else', he wrote to Lucie, 'is the worship of honour, in the strictest sense of the word. We must detach ourselves from the passions occasioned by grief and from the depression resulting from external causes. That honour which is my own possession is the patrimony and the life itself of our children.'[52]

3: Devil's Island – 2

On the night of 3 September 1896, the Governor of French Guiana received a telegram from the Colonial Ministry in Paris: 'London papers announced Dreyfus escape on American ship. Telegraph immediately prisoner's situation.' Though it was soon established by the Governor that no such escape had taken place, it exacerbated the existing paranoia of the authorities, and orders were given to the Commandant on Devil's Island to introduce new measures to ensure that such a rumour could never become true.

A double palisade was built around Dreyfus's hut. The inner wall was one and a half metres from the walls and two metres high: it impeded the circulation of air and Dreyfus lost his view of the sea. Exercise was now permitted only between the two palisades, and in his walks around his hut Dreyfus was always accompanied by a guard.

After the erection of the palisades round my hut, it became utterly uninhabitable; it was a living death. From that moment there was neither air nor light, and the heat was torrid, stifling during the dry season. In the rainy season it was a wretchedly damp lodging-place, in a country where humidity is the great scourge of the Europeans.[53]

Worse still, as an extra precaution, Dreyfus was now shackled to his bed at night. 'Two bars in the shape of a reverse U were fixed by the bottoms to the sides of the bed. Into these irons was inserted a bar to which were fastened two shackles. The prisoner's feet were placed in these shackles and pressed tightly down on the bed by the bar so that the body itself could not move.'[54] Open sores soon appeared on his ankles, which had to be dressed every morning.

The Commandant of the prison complex of the Salvation Islands, who 'always bore himself correctly', came to tell Dreyfus that putting him in irons each night 'was not a punishment but "a measure of precaution" because the prison administration had no complaint to make against me'.[55] However, soon after imposing these precautions, the Commandant was replaced by an official, Oscar Deniel, 'specially sent from Paris' to make sure there was a strict application of the new regime.

The shackling ended after two months, but the double palisades remained around the hut, and the reluctance with which the previous Commandant had imposed the inhuman regime was supplanted by the malign zeal of Deniel. The Governor of Guiana and the Director of the colony's prisons expressed 'surprise' at the new measures, and suggested that Deniel was exceeding his powers in an unjustified aggravation of the punishment of his prisoner. However, Deniel had come out from Paris with 'special instructions' from the Minister of the Colonies, André Lebon. Lebon confirmed that Deniel was acting on his orders and the objections of the Governor and Director were withdrawn.

Oscar Deniel, Dreyfus later wrote, was possessed of 'a low, hateful malice' with 'a mind that was as ill-balanced as it was full of vanity'. At times Dreyfus felt sorry for him. 'I have an immense pity for those who thus torture human beings. What remorse they are preparing for themselves, when everything shall come to light, for history unmasks all secrets.'[56] However, pity did not mean exoneration: Dreyfus, who in later life was remarkably magnanimous towards those responsible for his suffering, found it hard to forgive the unlawful excesses of Lebon and Deniel.

With hindsight, knowing that Dreyfus was innocent of the crime of which he had been convicted, his privations on Devil's Island appear abominable; but, apart from being kept in solitary confinement, his treatment was consistent with that meted out to other convicts whose crimes, in the eyes of French public opinion, were less grave. Dreyfus complained of his atrocious diet, but that of the other convicts was no better. He also complained of boredom, and asked to be given manual labour, but it seems unlikely that he would have survived for long in a chaingang on the Île Royale or in the fetid swamps on the mainland.

And how would he have been treated by his fellow convicts? The French anarchist Clément Duval had a death sentence commuted to hard labour in French Guiana in 1886 after stealing money and jewellery from a Parisian socialite and stabbing a policeman. Transported to Guiana, he was not, like Dreyfus, caged alone in a cell but thrown in with other convicts – one who had shot his mother and another his brother, later dismembering his body and feeding it to the pigs. A third had killed two old women and then raped their corpses.

The prison system in Guiana, as Duval later described it, was one of violence and depravity in which he endured forced labour, fettered ankles, rotting food, punishment cells, poisonous insects, scurvy, dysentery – a regime designed either to break or to brutalise the convicts, with petty privileges granted to informers and those who grovelled before their guards.[57] Duval's later account of his time on the Salvation Islands describes 'the scum, the murderers, the mindless brutes that people the prison'. How would the sensitive and hitherto pampered Alfred Dreyfus, with his pince-nez and love of literature, have fared in such company? Would his faith in the enlightened values of republican France – his 'beloved country' – have survived the ordeal? Forbidden to converse with his guards, Dreyfus seems to have been unaware of what went on the other side of the Passe des Grenadines: there is nothing about the penitential system in his letters, which were subject to the censor, and there is also no mention of the plight of his fellow prisoners in his memoirs. Dreyfus's outrage was at his own treatment as an innocent man: had he been guilty, he would only be getting what he deserved.

It was his sense of the injustice of his conviction that broke Dreyfus's spirit. For month after month after his arrival, he held on to the illusion that Commandant du Paty would keep his word and continue his investigation. He retained his faith in the fundamental decency of General de Boisdeffre. 'I have just written to Commandant du Paty to remind him of the two promises he made me after the sentence was pronounced,' he wrote in his diary in April 1895. '1. In the name of the Minister, to continue the investigation. 2. To inform me himself as soon as there is evidence of new leaks from the Ministry.'[58] In October he received letters from France, but the joy of hearing from Lucie was tarnished by learning that 'The guilty one is not yet discovered.'[59] By December, he had lost faith in du Paty. 'The opprobrium of my death will be on Commandant du Paty, Bertillon, and all those who have had a share in this iniquity.'

At the beginning of July 1897, he wrote again to General de Boisdeffre, as 'a cry of distress from a father who bequeaths to you all he holds most precious in the world, the life of his children, a life impossible so long as their name has not been washed clean of this horrible stain'; and on the 8th of that month he composed a second, much longer letter to the President of the Republic in which he 'opened his heart'. It is a pitiable text.

> I won't speak of my life, *Monsieur le Président.* Today, as yesterday, it belongs to my country. All that I ask, as a supreme favour, is that it be taken quickly, not slowly in atrocious agony, under so many torments that I have not deserved. What I also ask of my country is to shine a clear and bright light on this terrible drama; because my honour does not belong to the nation but it is the patrimony of my children, it is the legitimate possession of two families. And I beg you also, with all the strength of my soul, to consider the atrocious situation, intolerable, worse than death, of my wife, my family, and above all of my children, my dear children, my dear little ones who are growing up, who are pariahs; make sure that everything possible is done, everything that is compatible with the well-being of the nation, to end as soon as possible the torment of so many human beings.[60]

The form of the letter with its endless repetitions, contradictions and disjointed expressions reveals the mental state of Dreyfus at the time. His guards noted his enfeeblement, but Deniel said that he was faking. Little by little, Dreyfus abandoned the few things that had kept his mind functioning during the monotonous passing of time. He gave up his diary.

> I am so worn out, so broken in body and soul, that I am bringing my diary to a close . . . not knowing how long my strength will keep up or how soon my brain will give way under the strain of so much misery. I will close it with this last prayer to the President of the Republic in case I should succumb before seeing the curtain fall on this horrible drama. '*Monsieur le Président*, I take the liberty of asking you to allow this diary, which has been written day by day, to be sent to my wife. It may perhaps contain, *Monsieur le Président*, expressions of anger and disgust relative to the most terrible conviction that has ever been pronounced against a human being . . .'[61]

Dreyfus gave up gardening, and then reading: 'he spends much of the day sitting in the shade, a book open in his hands', reported one of his guards, 'but he does not read. One hears him sob from time to time, and sees him hide his tears.'[62]

In August 1897, Dreyfus's mental and physical condition was such that the prison doctor advised that his living conditions be improved. A new hut was built on a higher outcrop of land by convicts from the Île Royale; during the many weeks it took to construct it, Dreyfus was kept locked up. However, the new hut, once built, was 'higher, more spacious, and altogether preferable to the old one'.[63] It was divided in two by an iron grille with Dreyfus on one side and a guard on the other. Both rooms were lit by a lamp so that the prisoner could be kept under perpetual surveillance. A new stockade was erected at a greater distance from the walls of the hut so that there was more light, but Dreyfus still had no view of the sea and there was no improvement in the circulation of air; during the storms and hurricanes that came with the rainy season, pools of stagnant water formed on the floor of his hut.

As much as by the monotony and tedium of his intolerable life, Dreyfus was tormented by the lack of news from France. The letters he received from Lucie were infrequent, and suddenly, with no explanation given, he began to be given not the originals but copies made by 'an unknown hand'. Many of her letters failed to reach him, and some arrived after he had returned to France.[64] Some were, by Lucie's own admission, 'very commonplace and desperately monotonous':[65] forbidden to write about the measures she and Mathieu were taking on his behalf, she could do little but repeat time and again how much she loved him and attempt to sustain his morale.

In the autumn of 1897, there began to appear in Lucie's letters coded references to developments in Paris: on 25 September she wrote, 'I am indeed very happy to say that we are entering on the true path. I can only repeat to you to have confidence, not to grieve any more, and to be very certain that we shall attain our ends';[66] and on 6 October, 'I should like to tell you the joy I feel at seeing the horizon clearing and having come nearly to the end of our suffering.'[67] Not knowing what this signified, Dreyfus, in his replies, continued to urge her to do all that she could to secure his rehabilitation. Wholly unaware of who was responsible for his plight, he begged Lucie to see General de Boisdeffre and appeal to his sense of justice.

On Christmas Day 1897, the chief warder noted that his prisoner seemed defeated, and that he looked much older. Dreyfus's numerous appeals had been met with silence: 'silence was always the only reply that I received'. The days, the weeks, the months passed with no news. The only intimation Dreyfus gained that something might be going on in Paris came from snatches of conversation exchanged between his guards. On 28 February 1898, Dreyfus wrote an appeal directly to the Chamber of Deputies in Paris. There was no answer. Then, seven months later, on 27 October – three and a half years after arriving on Devil's Island, and four years after his arrest – Dreyfus was told by the prison authorities that a response to his petitions was on its way. He wrote ecstatically to Lucie. 'A few words to echo my immense affection for you, and an expression of all my love. I have just been told that I will receive a definitive reply to my request for a review. I await it with calmness and confidence, without any doubt that the response will lead to my rehabilitation.'[68]

Less than a month later, Deniel himself, under orders from above, delivered a telegram to his prisoner.

> Cayenne, 16 November 1898. From the Governor to the deportee Dreyfus via the senior commander of the Salvation Islands. You are hereby informed that the Criminal Chamber of the Cour de Cassation has declared admissible in the form stated an application for the review of your case, and rules that you should be informed of this and invited to present your defence.

Now that the possibility of a judicial error had been conceded by the courts, the treatment of Dreyfus improved. The letters from Lucie were no longer copies but were written in her own hand. On 28 November 1898, Dreyfus was authorised to leave the area enclosed by the palisades and take exercise from seven o'clock to eleven in the morning, and from two to five in the evening, 'within the grounds of the fortified camp'.[69] He now 'saw again, the full glare of the sun, the sea, which I had not seen for more than two years. I saw once more the stunted verdure of the island. My eyes could rest on something else than the four walls of the prison hut!'

Dreyfus would remain on Devil's Island for another six months while the Appeal Court in Paris considered his appeal; but the knowledge that his case was being reviewed brought him 'immense relief'.

> I had never despaired, I had never lost faith in the future, convinced as I was from the first that the truth would be known, that it was impossible that a crime so odious, and to which I was so utter a stranger, could remain unpunished. But, as I knew nothing of events occurring in France, and, on the other hand, saw my situation becoming daily more terrible, persecuted ceaselessly and causelessly, obliged to struggle night and day against the elements, the climate, and against mankind, I had begun to doubt that I should myself ever live to see the end of this terrible drama . . . At last, the horizon cleared; I had glimpses of the end of my own and my loved ones' martyrdom. It seemed to me that my heart was freed from an immense weight; I breathed more freely.[70]

PART THREE

The Affair

The First Dreyfusards

1: Mathieu Dreyfus

With the departure of Alfred Dreyfus from Paris, first to the Île de Ré and then to the penal settlements of French Guiana, his name ceased to appear in the press. Few outside his immediate family doubted his guilt; the great majority of Frenchmen and women felt a grim satisfaction that the traitor should be rotting on an island suitably named after the Devil, the 'Prince of Lies'. The only regret expressed by *La Libre Parole* was that he had not paid for his crime with his life, and this leniency was ascribed to the influence on the government of the Jews.

It was taken for granted, by Édouard Drumont and those of a like mind, that 'the Jews' would continue to exercise their considerable influence to come to the aid of one of their own – either to effect an escape from Devil's Island or to secure his rehabilitation by persuading public opinion that there had been a miscarriage of justice. The Jews had money, and money talks. Mathieu Dreyfus, who through contacts in Mulhouse secured an interview with his fellow citizen, Colonel Sandherr, told the chief of the Statistical Section that he would devote his 'entire life and family fortune to discovering the truth'. Sandherr, now a sick man who had received Mathieu in his home, would later claim that this was an oblique offer of a bribe. If so, Sandherr did not take it up but merely assured Mathieu that his brother's arrest came at the end of a 'long and serious inquiry'.[1]

Clearly, the most effective way to secure the release of Alfred Dreyfus would be to find the true traitor, and 'it was widely rumoured that the Dreyfus family was trying to set up a "patsy" (*un homme de paille*, a straw man), another army officer who could be blamed for the treason of which Alfred Dreyfus was guilty'.[2] The Director of the Sûreté – the criminal investigation department of the police – reported that Alfred's mother-in-law, Mme Hadamard, had promised 100,000 francs to a former policeman, Soudari, if he would find the guilty man.

The police kept Mathieu Dreyfus and other members of the family under surveillance; it seemed possible that Mathieu had been complicit in his brother's treason. They also wanted to know what they were doing to secure Alfred's release. To avoid this surveillance, Mathieu and his wife Suzanne used the alias 'Monsieur and Madame Mathieu', and had Mathieu's sister and brother-in-law, Henriette and Paul Valabrègue, sign leases and other official documents.[3] In the wake of the hysteria that arose around Alfred's trial and degradation, life became difficult for the traitor's immediate family, or indeed anyone with the name of Dreyfus. After the degradation ceremony, many of those called Dreyfus, who were no relation of the family, abandoned the name 'which had become synonymous with treason'.[4] In January 1895, Alfred's nephew was expelled from the lycée in Belfort, 'for defending his uncle's reputation and making insulting remarks about French officers; the expulsion, it was said, "is generally approved in Belfort"'. At the same time 'another nephew abandoned a place at the École Polytechnique to go instead into the family firm'.[5] In some circles the family of the traitor were treated as social pariahs: 'many honest people . . . wanted to have nothing to do with Mathieu, with Alfred's in-laws, or with anyone who was known to have contact with them. Any association with these rich and secretive Jews was assumed to be dangerous to an honest person's reputation.'[6]

Mathieu Dreyfus was to devote not just his fortune but all of his time to Alfred's rehabilitation. He gave up his position in the family firm in Mulhouse, leaving its direction to his brother Jacques, and moved to Paris. Lucie was happy to let Mathieu take charge. She had left the apartment on the avenue du Trocadéro and moved in with her parents. She told her children, Pierre and Jeanne, that their father had gone on a long journey, but she dressed in black as if a widow. The children were tutored at home, avoided playgrounds, and on trips to the country – the villa at Chatou belonging to their grandparents, or at Le Vésinet with the Lévy-Bruhls – were escorted by detectives hired by Mathieu.

Mathieu had to proceed with care. He was being watched, his mail was opened and attempts were made to suborn his servants by government agents. Since the theory was still current that the Germans had paid off Dreyfus by means of an insurance claim for a factory that was burned down in Mulhouse, it was possible that Mathieu might be charged as an accomplice. Edgar Demange, now emotionally as well as professionally engaged in the fate of his former client, warned Mathieu against keeping important documents in his home, to keep an eye on his servants and to avoid department stores where he might be arrested for shop-lifting after an item of merchandise had been surreptitiously slipped into his pocket.[7] And, when it became known that money was on offer for information that might exonerate Alfred Dreyfus, Mathieu was approached by a number of 'tricksters and fortune hunters', any one of whom might have been an *agent provocateur* from the Sûreté or the Statistical Section.

Outside the family, there were few who were prepared to jeopardise their careers or social standing by joining the campaign for Dreyfus's rehabilitation. Pierre Waldeck-Rousseau, the celebrated lawyer and champion of liberty, was a close friend of Edgar Demange and must have known from him of the weakness of the case against Dreyfus, but if he had not been prepared to court political unpopularity by taking the case himself, he was certainly not prepared to stick his neck out now.

More courageous was Forzinetti, the Governor of the Cherche-Midi military prison, who had been convinced from the start that Dreyfus was innocent and now joined the small group who assembled at the Hadamards' apartment to discuss how the campaign for his rehabilitation should proceed. Forzinetti had taken from the prison the copy of d'Ormescheville's indictment as annotated by Alfred and now gave it to Mathieu, enabling him to see more precisely how biased the military magistrate's inquiry had been. Patin, the Governor of the civilian prison of La Santé where Dreyfus had been held after his degradation, also believed that Dreyfus was innocent and offered his support to the family.

Initial approaches to potentially sympathetic journalists and politicians drew a blank. Mathieu secured interviews with senators such as Jules Siegfried and Auguste Scheurer-Kestner, Vice-President of the Senate and, as the last representative of the conquered Alsace, a senator for life. Siegfried, a former minister, promised to ensure that Alfred was well treated, while Scheurer-Kestner, after considering the matter, told Mathieu that 'the information I have received leads me to believe in his guilt'.[8] The same response came from another Mulhousian, a Monsieur Zurcher, who was a cousin of the new Minister of War, General Zurlinden: he told Mathieu that the Ministry had 'copious and clear evidence' of Alfred's guilt. Mathieu even approached Ernest Judet, a nationalist journalist on *Le Petit Journal*, who on 13 January 1895 had attacked Edgar Demange, saying that his continuing insistence on the innocence of his client led to suspicions that he was complicit in his crime.[9] Judet seemed to take on board what Mathieu had said and, when he departed, shook him by the hand.[10]

Mathieu followed every lead, however unpropitious. There was a doctor in Le Havre, a Protestant, Dr Joseph Gilbert, who thought Alfred was innocent. He took an interest in clairvoyance and invited Mathieu to Le Havre to consult a medium called Léonie. Spiritualism and clairvoyance were then in fashion, and this Norman peasant woman of around fifty impressed Mathieu with some of her inexplicable insights into his brother's case. Mathieu travelled to and fro between Le Havre and Paris. Léonie revealed that the real traitor was an officer in the Ministry of War, that he worked through a German agent called Greber and that he was a former friend of Alfred's who had turned against him when Alfred had refused to lend him money.[11]

Mathieu had such faith that Léonie would discover the name of the traitor in a hypnotic trance that he brought her to Paris and put her up in a flat on the rue de l'Arcade belonging to his sister, Louise Cahn.

Later he moved Léonie into his own home. He had been shown by Dr Gilbert how to induce these trances and thought that her second sight would enable her to 'visit' his brother on Devil's Island. In 1897 she told him that 'Monsieur Alfred can no longer see the ocean. They have built a stockade for him.' However, though the séances obsessed the whole family, they did not come up with the name of Monsieur Alfred's false friend.

———

Dr Joseph Gilbert, the physician from Le Havre who had introduced Mathieu to Léonie, had been the family doctor of Félix Faure, formerly deputy for Le Havre and now President of France. The two men remained friends, and Gilbert, at Mathieu's prompting, asked to see Faure. The request was made on 20 February 1895, but it was only on the morning of 21 October that the President received the physician at the Élysée Palace. In the face of his old friend's nagging questions about the Dreyfus case, and his insistence that the evidence of the *bordereau* was wholly inadequate as proof, Faure, exasperated, told him that there had been other evidence not shown to the defence. 'Dreyfus is guilty. He is guilty, there can be no doubt on that score. Very well, my dear friend, to put your mind at rest, I will tell you that he was not condemned on the facts that came out during the hearing, but upon the production of a document which was not shown to him, nor to M. Demange, for reasons of state.'[12]

With the President's permission, Dr Gilbert repeated this dramatic revelation to Mathieu Dreyfus, who had been waiting for him at the Hôtel de l'Athénée. Mathieu was appalled. He was appalled not just by the fact that his brother had been condemned on the basis of secret evidence, but also by the insouciance of the French President at this transgression of the most fundamental rules of justice. Worse still, he was to discover that this insouciance was shared by a handful of officers and politicians to whom the fact of this irregularity had been leaked by some of the judges at the court martial. Lieutenant-Colonel Echeman had mentioned it to a journalist on *Le Gaulois* and Commandant Freystaetter to Captain Picard, Alfred's fellow *stagiaire* at the École de

Guerre, also marked down in his final exams by General de Bonnefond who had said that he 'did not want Jews on the General Staff'. Picard had passed on the information to a friend, Léon Lévy. Another of the judges, Commandant Florentin, had told a fellow officer, a Captain Potier, about the secret dossier. All in all, around twenty officers knew of the illegality, Jews among them, but all seem to have accepted that it was justified by *raison d'état*.

Eventually Maître Demange himself was told of the perversion of the legal process by a colleague, Maître Albert Salle, who had heard about it from one of the judges. Demange demanded an immediate interview with the Minister of Justice, Ludovic Trarieux, who had already been told about the secret dossier by his colleague Gabriel Hanotaux, the Foreign Minister. It was Hanotaux who had consistently opposed the arrest and trial of Dreyfus but had been overruled by General Mercier: Mercier, in an attempt to win over Hanotaux, had shown him the letter mentioning 'the scoundrel D.'. But even Trarieux, 'a serious and scrupulous man'[13] who was worried about the rise of anti-Semitism, did not feel that this 'procedural irregularity' was enough to cast doubt on the guilt of Alfred Dreyfus. Clearly, the traitor had to be punished, and the end justified the means.

2: Bernard Lazare

Disheartened, despairing of doing anything for his brother through discreet contacts with influential politicians, Mathieu now took up a suggestion made by the Governor of the Santé prison, Patin, and endorsed by his colleague Forzinetti, that he commission a professional journalist to go over the heads of the politicians to reach the wider public through the press. 'It is before public opinion', Patin told Mathieu, 'that your brother's cause must be defended.'[14] Bizarrely, the first name suggested by Patin was that of Édouard Drumont, who, though undoubtedly a brilliant polemicist, had done much to stir up paranoid suspicion of Jewish officers in the French Army. A second name was put forward – that of the Jewish journalist Bernard Lazare.

Lazare Marcus Manassé Bernard had inverted his first and last names to produce the nom de plume of Bernard Lazare. He came from a Jewish family in Nîmes, in the south of France; like the Dreyfus family, the Bernards had established a successful textile business and, again like the Dreyfuses, were no longer strictly observant Jews but continued to keep the traditional Jewish holidays. As is apparent from his disdain for the Dreyfuses' wealth, the young Lazare rebelled against his bourgeois background, moving to Paris at the age of twenty-one, enrolling at the École Pratique des Hautes Études, writing for the theatre and newspapers and declaring himself an anarchist. He defended the anarchists Jean Grave and Félix Fénélon with his pen, and in 1896 went as a delegate to the Socialist Congress in London where he attacked his fellow Jew, Karl Marx, as 'a jealous authoritarian'.

Lazare was preoccupied with the Jewish question: he knew Theodor Herzl and also Achad Ha'am, one of the founders of the Lovers of Zion. The eruption of anti-Semitism at the time of Dreyfus's trial exasperated him because he had believed that, with the decline of Talmudic Judaism, the phenomenon should also be in decline. This was the theme of his *L'Antisémitisme, son histoire et ses causes* (*Anti-Semitism: Its History and Causes*) which was published to critical acclaim in Paris a few months before the arrest of Dreyfus in 1894. The work was in some sense a riposte to Drumont's *La France juive*, and though Lazare wrote that Drumont was 'a historian of poor documentary evidence, a mediocre sociologist and especially philosopher',[15] Drumont praised his history as 'a remarkable book, nourished with facts and dominated from end to end by a fine effort at impartiality, a discipline imposed on the mind not to yield to influences of race'.[16]

Lazare's history appealed to Drumont because, while it lacked the abusive tone, fanciful historicism, scurrilous anecdotes and pseudo-scientific theorising of *La France juive*, it accepted a number of Drumont's contentions. Why, asked Lazare, was the Jew 'ill-treated and hated alike and in turn by the Alexandrians and the Romans, by the Persians and the Arabs, by the Turks and the Christian nations? Because, everywhere up to our own days, the Jew was an unsociable being.'[17] He was more than unsociable; as a member of God's chosen race, he believed himself superior to non-Jews, and the disdain Jews showed for their gentile neighbours inevitably made them disliked by the host communities when they settled abroad. Long before they were relegated to ghettos, the Jews themselves avoided integration and assimilation by their strict adherence to the Law.

A deep-rooted animosity towards the Christian religion was equally inevitable: 'the development of the dogma of the divinity of Christ made a breach between the Church and the Synagogue. Judaism could not admit the deification of a man.'[18] 'The Gospels must be burned, says Rabbi Tarphon, for paganism is not as dangerous to the Jewish faith as the Christian sects.' The loathing of the Jews for the Christians was reciprocated by Christian loathing for the Jews: 'Thus everything concurred to make of the Jew a universal foe, and the only support he found during this terrible period of several centuries was with the popes, who wanted to preserve the Jews as witness of the excellence of the Christian faith.'

Jews were confined to ghettos, which they often accepted and even sought in their eagerness to separate themselves from the world, to live apart without mixing with the nations, to preserve intact their beliefs and their race. Protected from extinction or forced conversion by the popes, they made themselves indispensable as moneylenders, a trade forbidden to Christians. 'As possessors of the gold they became the masters of their masters, they dominated over them, and this was the only way to deploy their energy and activity.'[19] The control of the purse strings of the European nations enabled this 'energetic, vivacious nation, of infinite pride, thinking themselves superior to other nations', to indulge a 'taste for domination', a taste which persisted after their emancipation at the time of the French Revolution.

What role did the Jews play in bringing that Revolution about? The Jews, wrote Lazare, 'are not the cause of revolution', but 'the Jewish spirit is essentially a revolutionary spirit and, consciously or not, the Jew is a revolutionist'. The Jewish spirit was apparent 'throughout the period of fierce revolt against Christianity which characterised the eighteenth century [and which] repeated concerning Jesus and the Virgin the outrageous fables invented by the Pharisees of the Second Century; we find them in Voltaire and in Parney, and their rationalist satire, pellucid and mordant, lives again in Heine, in Boerne and in

Disraeli, just as the powerful logic of the ancient rabbis lives again in Karl Marx . . .'.[20] 'In labouring for the triumph of liberalism, they were looking for their own good. It is beyond a doubt that the Jews, through their wealth, their energy and their talents, supported and furthered the progress of the European revolution. During this period Jewish bankers, Jewish manufacturers, Jewish poets, journalists, and orators, stirred perhaps by quite different motives, were nevertheless all striving towards the same goal.'

Having helped to demolish the old order – the *ancien régime* – the Jews sought to dominate the new.

> As conquerors, not as guests, did they come into modern societies . . . They were not warriors . . . but they made the only conquest for which they were armed, the economic conquest for which they had been preparing for many long years. They were a race of merchants and money-dealers, perhaps degraded by mercantile practice but, thanks to this very practice, equipped with qualities that were becoming preponderant in the new economic system.[21]

This, to Lazare, was the source of the anti-Semitism that was now so virulent in France. 'So long as landed capital remained the political power, the Jew was deprived of any right; the Jew was liberated on the day when political power passed to industrial capital, and that proved fatal.' Having for so long constituted an alien and persecuted nation within other nations, the Jews were now able to dominate their former oppressors through their ascendancy in banking and trade.

Moreover, in modern society, where 'Darwin's principle of the struggle of life dominates', the Jew has an advantage over his Christian competitor – the solidarity that exists among Jews. 'In this daily struggle the Jew who, personally, as we have already seen, is better endowed than his competitors, increases his advantage by uniting with his co-religionists possessed of similar virtues, and thus augments his powers by acting in common with his brethren; the inevitable result being that they outdistance their rivals in the pursuit of any common end . . . This is the secret of their success.'

Jewish solidarity is all the stronger in that it goes so far back. 'Its very existence is denied, yet it is undeniable. The links in the chain have been forged in the course of ages until the flight of centuries has made many unconscious of their existence.' 'The Jew, even though he may have departed from the synagogue, is still a member of the Jewish free-masonry, of the Jewish clique, if you will'; and 'even the reformed Jew, who has broken away from the narrow restrictions of the synagogue . . . has not forgotten the spirit of solidarity'.[22]

What is notable about Lazare's *Anti-Semitism: Its History and Causes*, given the role that the author was to play in the Dreyfus Affair, is the support it implicitly offers to those French generals such as Bonnefond and Lebelin de Dionne who thought that Jews should be excluded from the General Staff. If Lazare's analysis is correct, they would form a clique whose first loyalty would not be to the nation state of France. 'Though often exceedingly chauvinist,' wrote Lazare, 'the Jews are essentially cosmopolitan in character; they are the cosmopolitan element in mankind . . . and with the aid of their instinct of solidarity, they have remained internationalists.'[23]

Lazare's analysis would also seem to support the views expressed in the Jesuit journal *Civiltà Cattolica* in 1889. The Jews, wrote Lazare, might not be 'solely responsible for the destruction of religious doctrine and the decay of faith', but 'they may at least be counted among those who helped to bring about such a state of desuetude and the changes which followed'. And it is also true 'that there were Jews connected with Free Masonry from its birth, students of the Kabala, as is shown by certain rites which survive. It is very probable, too, that in the years preceding the outbreak of the French Revolution, they entered in greater numbers than ever, into the councils of the secret societies, becoming, indeed, themselves the founders of secret associations.'[24]

To Lazare, the decline of religious belief was all to the good, and would lead in time to the Jewish assimilation and therefore to an end to anti-Semitism. 'The Christian religion is disappearing like the Jewish religion, like all religions, which we may now observe in their slow agony. It is passing away under the blows of reason and science. It is dying a natural death . . .'[25] So too Judaism: 'the Jews are not as yet assimilated; that is to say, they have not yet given up their belief in their own nationality. By the practice of circumcision, by the observation of their special rules of prayer, and their dietary regulations, they still continue to differentiate themselves from those around them; they persist in being Jews.'[26] But 'the time will come when they shall be completely eliminated; when they shall be merged into the body of the nations, after the same manner as the Phoenicians who, having planted their trading stations all over Europe, disappeared without leaving a trace behind them. By that time anti-Semitism will have run its course.'

At the time of Dreyfus's conviction, Lazare had written to his publisher, P.-V. Stock, that so far as he was concerned, 'Dreyfus and his family are very rich . . . they'll be able to take care of themselves without me . . .' However, he had been riled by the venomous rhetoric directed against Jews at the time of Dreyfus's arrest and trial; the case seemed to show that anti-Semitism in France, far from running its course, was on the increase and should be energetically opposed. In an article published in *L'Écho de Paris* on 31 December 1894, Lazare castigated those who were using the treason of Alfred Dreyfus as a pretext for a blanket attack on the Jews. Was Dreyfus innocent or guilty? When he met with Mathieu Dreyfus in the spring of 1895, Lazare had an open mind, but after seeing Commandant d'Ormescheville's indictment with Alfred's annotations he was persuaded that the prosecution itself was the product of prejudice.

It would later be said by the anti-Dreyfusards that Lazare, the champion of anarchists and socialists, was 'bought' by the syndicate – that he was won over to the cause of the bourgeois army officer by the retainer offered by Mathieu in exchange for his efforts on Alfred's behalf. Daniel Halévy would describe Lazare as 'a skilful business agent, an intermediary between the intellectuals and Jewish money', and Louis Lucien Klotz would accuse him of ascribing Dreyfus's conviction to anti-Semitism without evidence (both Halévy and Klotz were Jews);[27] but to Léon Blum, the Jewish writer and politician who would one day become Prime Minister of France, Lazare's commitment to the cause of

Alfred Dreyfus was akin to a conversion. The scales fell from his eyes. Dreyfus had been convicted because he was a Jew and thus became for him the incarnation of the Jew oppressed throughout the ages.

The Jew was no longer, for Lazare, the arrogant and anti-social anomaly of his history of anti-Semitism but the aboriginal victim who must now abandon his 'ancient tradition of humility' and 'ancestral pusil-lanimity' and vigorously attack the anti-Semites who attacked him.[28] This was not a struggle for the pre-eminence of his race or nation, but a pursuit of justice. 'Just as science is the religion of the positivists,' wrote Blum, 'justice is the religion of the Jew.'[29]

Lazare now joined the lawyer Maître Demange, the two prison governors, Forzinetti and Patin, and the Protestant doctor from Le Havre, Dr Gilbert, in the ranks of the Dreyfusards. Lazare also recruited, in August 1896, Joseph Reinach, Deputy for the Basse-Alpes in the National Assembly, whose brother Salomon, an eminent archaeologist, was a friend from his days in the École Normale Supérieure of Lucien Lévy-Bruhl, the son-in-law of Lucie Dreyfus's aunt Eugénie. They were the sons of a German banker, Hermann-Joseph Reinach, and nephews of the notorious Baron Jacques de Reinach of the Panama Canal scandal. Joseph was also the baron's son-in-law: he had fallen in love with an English girl, but family pressure prevented him from taking a gentile wife and so he had married his cousin.

The Reinachs were immensely rich and academically brilliant. Salomon was a curator of the Musée des Antiquités and a member of the Institut de France, and the youngest brother Théodore was also a member of the Institut and a professor of Ancient Greek history at the Collège de France. Joseph had served as private secretary to Léon Gambetta, taking over as editor of Gambetta's *La République Française*, and although his political career had faltered because of the Panama Canal scandal, he retained strong links among the Opportunist republicans.

Joseph Reinach and his brothers exemplified the opportunities open to Jews in the Third Republic. As Ruth Harris puts it, they 'epitomized a particular kind of Republican social ascent'. Their father had left Germany to live in France and take French nationality precisely because of the equality guaranteed by the Republic. As a young man, thanks to his father's fortune, Joseph 'lived like a princeling'[30] in a large house in Paris with liveried servants and private secretaries. He pursued women 'in plunging necklines', wrote Léon Daudet, 'with the gallantries of a satisfied gorilla'.[31] Inevitably, because he was a rich Jew of German extraction, and the nephew of a corrupt uncle, he was vilified by Drumont as the principal agent of the Jewish syndicate. For this reason, Reinach wanted a gentile to front the campaign for a review, but subsequently he became one of the most prominent and fearless Dreyfusards, writing polemics, fighting duels and writing a seven-volume history of the Affair.

Bernard Lazare, thanks to the funds provided by Mathieu and possibly Reinach, was now free to turn down other journalistic assignments and devote all his time and energy to a polemical essay exposing the *prima facie* miscarriage of justice – the lack of conclusive proof against Dreyfus, the naked partiality of the examining magistrate, d'Ormescheville, and the procedural irregularities of the court martial itself. He was a talented writer – precise but also impassioned – and the early drafts of his pamphlet were considered too intemperate by Mathieu and Demange. Demange felt it would be impolitic to provoke with abusive rhetoric the very people whose help they would need. He still believed that discreet lobbying was the most effective way to help Alfred. Lazare felt frustrated, 'waiting in a state of impatience, feverish to enter into action'.[32] The press had lost interest in Alfred Dreyfus but not in the Jews. In May 1895, it was proposed in the National Assembly that Jews be resettled in the interior of France, 'where treason is less dangerous'. Alfred Naquet spoke in the debate to denounce the proposal, but as the Jew who had pushed through the law permitting divorce he was howled down by the deputies on the right.

This fracas provoked a denunciation of anti-Semitism by France's most successful novelist, Émile Zola. His defence of the Jews, in an article entitled 'Pour les Juifs', was doubled-edged:

the Jews have their faults, their vices: they are accused of being a nation in the nation, of being ... a kind of international sect without real homeland; above all, of carrying in their blood a need for lucre, a love for money, a prodigious intelligence for business which, in less than a century, has led to the accumulation of enormous fortunes in their hands. But these separatist Jews, so poorly absorbed into the nation, overly avid, obsessed with the conquest of gold, are in fact the creation of Christians, the work of our eighteen hundred years of imbecilic persecution. They have been restricted to deplorable neighbourhoods, like lepers; why be surprised, then, that in the prison of their ghetto, they have tightened their family bonds![33]

Zola was not yet a Dreyfusard, and his intervention in defence of France's Jews may have seemed to some problematic. Like Lazare, he did not appear to dispute the anti-Semitic stereotype but merely blamed it on the eighteen hundred years of 'imbecilic persecution'. Stereotypical Jews crop up as characters in his novels, such as the Jewish bankers Steiner in *Nana* (1880) and Gunderman in *L'Argent* (1891). In *L'Argent*, Zola describes a group of brokers trading in the shares of defunct companies as 'an unclean Jewry' with 'fat, shining faces, withered profiles like those of voracious birds, an extraordinary assemblage of typical noses . . .' The Jewish debt-collector Busch in the same novel is quite as odious as Fagin in Dickens's *Oliver Twist*. In *La Débâcle* (1892), Zola describes 'a whole crowd of low, preying Jews' pillaging the bodies of dead soldiers after the Battle of Sedan.

At this stage, however, Zola was not speaking out against a miscarriage of justice but simply deploring a return of 'the savage war of species against species'. Drumont responded in *La Libre Parole*, accusing Zola of championing the Jews to win support for his candidacy for the Académie Française and get some publicity at a time when the sales of his novels were in decline. It was certainly the case, as Ruth Harris has pointed out, that 'his star had already passed its zenith by the early 1890s',[34] and, since he was not a man to eschew self-promotion, there may have been something behind Drumont's charge: more than twenty years before he had told Edmond de Goncourt that 'his greatest pleasure, his greatest satisfaction, consisted in feeling the power and influence that he exerted over Paris through the medium of his prose'.[35] However, the immediate result of the polemic between Zola and Drumont was to give the thwarted Lazare a pretext to enter into the fray. In a number of articles published in *Le Voltaire* in May and June of 1896, he declared war on Drumont, warning him that the Jewish worm had turned. The Jews 'have had enough of anti-Semitism; they are tired of the insults, the slander, the lies . . . and no longer satis-fied with defending themselves, they would attack you; and you are not invulnerable, neither you nor your friends'.

Lazare was as good as his word: it was a case of 'pistols at dawn'. Drumont, the passionate duellist, fired a shot at Lazare and Lazare fired a shot at Drumont. Both missed their target. Honour was satisfied. They would fight on with their pens.

3: The Cook Detective Agency

While Bernard Lazare was engaged in this polemic over anti-Semitism, but was restrained by Mathieu Dreyfus on the advice of Edgar Demange from extending that polemic into the question of Alfred's wrongful conviction, Mathieu set up a complex and expensive operation to discover who it was who had committed the crime attributed to his brother. Still kept under surveillance because suspected of complicity in Alfred's crime, and also – rightly – of devoting all his time and money to secure his brother's release, Mathieu was aware that any French citi-zen would regard it as a patriotic duty to report any approach he might make to the police. He therefore sought assistance abroad. On 15 April 1896, Mathieu and his American brother-in-law, Sam Wimpheimer, shook off the plain-clothes policemen who were following them and made for the Gare Saint-Lazare. There they took the boat-train to London via Dieppe and Newhaven.

In London, with Wimpheimer acting as an interpreter, he engaged the services of the Cook Detective Agency. It was agreed that two of their operatives would move to Paris. A young Oxford-educated 'perfect gentleman' who spoke fluent French and German would attempt to get to know diplomats from the German Embassy; the other, 'an intelligent and clever woman with a respectable air', would move to Paris and befriend the English wife of one of the security personnel at the German Embassy who was thought to have contacts with French intelligence. She would be set up in a furnished flat in the same building as her compatriot, purporting to be in Paris to further her daughter's education. The considerable cost of this operation was paid for by Mathieu from funds provided by the Dreyfus and Hadamard families.[36]

After six months, this expensive exercise had produced no results and Alfred Dreyfus, incarcerated on Devil's Island, seemed forgotten. The proprietor of Cook's Detective Agency in London felt that something should be done to revive public interest and put Mathieu in touch with the Paris correspondent of the London *Daily Chronicle*, Clifford Millage. It was agreed that, to bring Alfred back to the attention of the French public, a story should be placed in a British newspaper saying that he had escaped from Devil's Island. In return for a fee and disbursements down the line, Millage arranged for the story to appear in an obscure provincial paper, the *South Wales Argus*. It was picked up by the French press and caused the desired sensation. The imposture extended to interviews which appeared in *La Libre Parole* with the editor of the *South Wales Argus* and the captain of the SS *Nonpareil*, the ship which had supposedly taken Alfred Dreyfus to freedom.[37] However, while the name of Alfred Dreyfus may have reappeared in the pages of French newspapers, the only concrete result was to alarm officials in the Colonial Office in Paris and the prison administration in French Guiana. It was as a direct result of Mathieu's well-meant stunt that his brother had the palisade built around his hut and was shackled to his bedstead each night.[38]

Colonel Picquart

1: The Petit Bleu

In July 1895, Colonel Jean Sandherr resigned as head of the Statistical Section on grounds of ill-health. His deputy, the drunken Cordier, was not thought competent to replace him and Commandant Henry, who had run the department in the absence of his ailing chief, was not considered, as an officer who had risen from the ranks, of sufficient stature to take command. Sandherr was therefore replaced by a fellow Alsatian, Commandant Georges Picquart, who had played a peripheral role in the arrest and trial of Alfred Dreyfus. It was Picquart who had met Dreyfus when he arrived at the War Office to be first questioned and then arrested by Commandant du Paty de Clam on 13 October 1894. He had acted as official observer for the Minister of War and Chief of the General Staff at Dreyfus's court martial and it was Picquart who, at Dreyfus's degradation, had observed to a colleague, Captain Tassin, that Dreyfus seemed to be assessing the weight and value of the gold braid in his insignia of rank as it was torn from his uniform.

Picquart, born in Strasbourg in September 1854, came from a family of magistrates, civil servants and soldiers. He had an aptitude for languages, speaking French, German, English, Spanish and Italian fluently, and some Russian.[1] He was handsome, described by Paléologue as 'tall and slim, with a rather stiff manner, high forehead, eyes rather difficult to catch between his close eyebrows'.[2] He did not suffer fools gladly. The historian Marcel Thomas observed that Picquart 'had a high opinion of his own judgement and abilities with a contempt for those who disagreed'. He was also somewhat solitary and a man of few words: Joseph Reinach remarked that Picquart was 'content to be alone once his work was done, and had a horror of vulgarity'.[3] Picquart remained unmarried. He had told his sister Anna in 1883 that he would only marry a wife who was pretty, a talented musician and intellectually stimulating, and had a large enough dowry for him to sustain his present standard of living.[4] Clearly, ten years later, such a woman had yet to be found.

Picquart was a Catholic, coached by the Jesuits in their school on the rue des Postes for entry to the military academy at Saint-Cyr. He had passed out fifth in his year from Saint-Cyr and second from the École de Guerre. He saw action in Africa and the Far East, was decorated with the Légion d'Honneur, promoted to the rank of captain by the age of twenty-four and to the rank of major by the age of thirty-three.[5] His detractors ascribed this rapid promotion to his close relationship in Tonking with General Nismes, also a bachelor: gossip about his possible homosexuality pursued him throughout his career.[6]

Upon returning to France Picquart had taught at the École de Guerre, where Alfred Dreyfus had been one of his pupils. He had given him poor marks in topography and, when referring him to another officer, apologised 'for having given him the Jew Dreyfus'.[7] He accepted the post as head of the Statistical Section with some reluctance, but General de Boisdeffre had insisted and, upon his appointment on 1 July 1895, Picquart was promoted to the rank of lieutenant-colonel – the youngest in the French Army.

In his briefing by Boisdeffre, Picquart was warned that 'the Dreyfus Affair is not over. It is only beginning. A new offensive by the Jews is to be feared.' And when he went to visit the semi-paralysed Sandherr in his home, Picquart was advised to prepare himself by 'fattening' the secret file shown to the judges at the court martial. Picquart authorised Henry to re-employ François Guénée, the former undercover police officer, to see if he could dig up any more dirt,[8] but nothing was found.

Upon taking command, Picquart instituted certain changes in procedure in the Statistical Section: he ruled that, while Henry should continue to receive the contents of the waste-paper baskets of the German Embassy delivered by Mme Bastian via the 'ordinary route', Picquart should be the first to see them. Captain Lauth was given the job of pasting the scraps of paper together. Whether or not Henry observed these instructions is unclear, but in early March, with his mother gravely ill at Pogny on the Somme, he had no time to take a close look at a heavy consignment he received from Mme Bastian at the Chapel of Sainte-Clothilde and deposited at the office. It was therefore Lauth who pasted together, and Picquart who was the first to see, a document which suggested that there was another traitor selling secrets to Maximilian von Schwartzkoppen.

There was at the time (and well into the twentieth century), a network of pneumatic tubes under the streets of Paris through which letter-telegrams were sent to and from post offices in the different arrondissements, thereby ensuring delivery within a few hours. The message had to be written on a form printed on blue paper – the *petit bleu* or 'little blue'. The piece of paper retrieved from Schwartzkoppen's waste-paper basket and pieced together by Lauth was the draft of such a letter-telegram that had never been sent.

Monsieur,
Above all I await a more detailed explanation than the one you gave me the other day of the matter in hand. I suggest that you give it to me in writing so I can decide whether to continue my connection with the house of R. or not. C.

The initial C. was known to be used by Schwartzkoppen, and the Statistical Section was also familiar with his handwriting from the many letters they had intercepted, and the handwriting of the *petit bleu* was not his. Nor was the handwriting of a second note on ordinary paper, written in pencil and also signed 'C', which – though partly illegible because the tear ran through some of the words – confirmed that a transaction was taking place between Schwartzkoppen and the person to whom the note was addressed. And the name of that person was spelled out in the appropriate box on the *petit bleu*: Monsieur le Commandant Esterhazy, 27, rue de la Bienfaisance, Paris.

This was the same Marie-Charles-Ferdinand Walsin-Esterhazy who had acted as second for the Jewish Captain André Crémieu-Foa in the duel he had fought with Édouard Drumont in June 1892. It was also the same Esterhazy who had served in the Statistical Section as a German translator sixteen years earlier. Henry, when he returned to the office and was told of the *petit bleu*, was incredulous that this 'old friend', whom he remembered with fondness, could be a spy. Moreover, Esterhazy was now a protégé of the suspect Jewish officer Maurice Weil, and because Weil himself was a friend of General Saussier, the Military Governor of Paris – his wife was the General's mistress and Weil himself a *mari complaisant* – any investigation had to proceed with caution. It was perhaps for this reason, or because he was distracted by the death of his mother, or because he had a low opinion of General Gonse, responsible for the Statistical Section to the General Staff, or simply because he wanted to keep this interesting new card close to his chest, that Picquart did not immediately report the discovery of the *petit bleu* to his superiors. He instituted an inquiry under his own direction. Esterhazy was placed under surveillance and discreet inquiries were made by a police agent, whom Picquart met outside his office in front of the Louvre. Esterhazy was observed visiting the German Embassy, but it was to obtain a visa to visit Alsace for a superior officer, Colonel Abria. Picquart asked an officer he knew from his days at Saint-Cyr, Commandant Curé, who was serving in the same regiment as Esterhazy, what he thought of Esterhazy. Curé told him that Esterhazy led a dissolute life and was perennially short of money. When Picquart asked if he would obtain a specimen of Esterhazy's handwriting, Curé refused, considering it dishonourable to spy on a fellow officer.

It was only in July, almost five months after the *petit bleu* had been filched from the German Embassy, that Picquart decided to report the matter to his superiors, going over the head of General Gonse to the Chief of the General Staff, General de Boisdeffre. Picquart's urgent request led to a meeting in the General's private railway coach in the

Gare de Lyon when he arrived back from taking the waters at Vichy on the evening of 5 August 1896. Picquart told Boisdeffre about the *petit bleu* addressed to Commandant Esterhazy. The General had never heard of him, and received the news of a second traitor with apparent indifference. Feeling, perhaps, that too much had been made of the *bordereau*, and too quickly, he did not want to repeat the same mistake. He, too, had other things on his mind: the Franco-Russian alliance which he had helped to negotiate as military attaché in St Petersburg had come to fruition. There was to be a state visit by Tsar Nicholas II and his Tsarina Alexandra in a couple of months' time in which he, as Chief of the General Staff, would play a prominent role. A new scandal arising from another document stolen from their Embassy risked a fracas with the Germans at a particularly inopportune time.

Boisdeffre did not seem concerned that Picquart had yet to inform Gonse of what he had discovered. He suggested that he should tell the Minister of War, General Jean-Baptiste Billot, and Picquart went to see him the following day, 6 August. Billot approved the way in which Picquart had conducted his investigation to date, but would not as yet issue an order for a sample of Esterhazy's handwriting to be sent to the Statistical Section. As a result, when Picquart again met Boisdeffre during the month of August, they discussed the matter on the assumption that there was no link between Esterhazy and Dreyfus. Dreyfus's name came up only in the context of the dangers of proceeding prematurely against Esterhazy. 'I don't want a new Dreyfus Affair,' Boisdeffre told Picquart.[9]

By the end of the month, however, Esterhazy had brought himself to the attention of the Minister, Billot, by writing to an officer serving in Billot's cabinet, Commandant Theveney, and also to Billot's *chef de cabinet*, Calmon-Maison, lobbying for a post at the Ministry of War. His application was supported by Maurice Weil, a friend of Theveney's, and also by a deputy, Jules Roche, who was Vice-President of the Army Commission in the National Assembly. With these samples of Esterhazy's handwriting actually in his office, Billot authorised Calmon-Maison to show them to Picquart. Studying them at his desk at the Statistical Section, Picquart was immediately struck by the similarity of the hand to that of the *bordereau* which had been so thoroughly scrutinised so many times.

Picquart went to the files and took out a photograph of the *bordereau*. He compared it to the letters written by Esterhazy. The handwriting seemed to him identical. But Picquart was no expert. He therefore told Lauth to take photographs of Esterhazy's letters after blocking out the names. He summoned du Paty de Clam and asked him to compare the writing of the letters with that of the *bordereau*. 'It's the writing of Mathieu Dreyfus,' said du Paty. Alphonse Bertillon, the prosecution's favoured expert in the court martial of Dreyfus, was then asked for his opinion on the handwriting of Esterhazy's letters. 'Why, that's the handwriting of the *bordereau*.'

'And what if it were written quite recently?' Picquart asked.

'Then the Jews have trained someone in the course of a year to imitate his handwriting.'[10]

Picquart was unconvinced. He next asked the archivist, Gribelin, to reassemble the secret file shown to the judges at Dreyfus's court martial so that he could familiarise himself with its contents, as Sandherr had suggested, to fend off any moves towards Dreyfus's rehabilitation. He studied the different papers and the copy of du Paty's commentary made by Sandherr and realised at once that they proved nothing. Clearly, Dreyfus had been convicted of Esterhazy's crime.

On 1 September 1896, Picquart completed a report for General de Boisdeffre which made clear that Esterhazy was guilty of selling secrets to the Germans but merely noting in a footnote that the *bordereau* had been 'the occasion of other legal action'. To conceal the length of time during which he had kept his dramatic discovery to himself, Picquart wrote that he had received the *petit bleu* only at the end of April of that year. He delivered his report in person. When he came to mention du Paty's commentary on the secret dossier, Boisdeffre looked surprised. 'Why was it not burned as agreed?' That look of surprise was his only reaction. The General was otherwise non-committal. When Picquart saw him again the following day, he admitted that this new information had led to a sleepless night, but said that he wanted the opinion of General Gonse before making a decision.

Gonse was on sick leave at Cormeilles-en-Parisis. This 'nullity made man'[11] was certainly aware of Picquart's low opinion of him, shown by the way in which Picquart had gone over his head to Boisdeffre. The 'climate of mutual mistrust that existed between the two men complicated things from the outset',[12] with Picquart's disdain for those he regarded as his intellectual inferiors coming up against Gonse's skills at 'administrative infighting'.[13] During a two-hour briefing by Picquart, Gonse, like Boisdeffre, did not react to what he had been told, saying only at one point: 'So we must have been wrong.' And then, when the briefing on the two cases – those of Esterhazy and of Dreyfus – was completed: 'Keep them separate.'

Neither Generals Gonse and de Boisdeffre nor the Minister Billot had yet decided what line they should take on Picquart's revelations: their positions 'were not yet set'. If Picquart had shown some tact, the historian Marcel Thomas believes, he might have coaxed them into accepting that there had been a miscarriage of justice. But 'diplomacy had always been . . . the weakest quality of this stubborn Alsatian'.[14] Moreover, inadvertently, Mathieu Dreyfus had made Picquart's task more difficult by planting the story of his brother's escape. On the same day as Picquart briefed Gonse in Cormeilles-en-Parisis, the story appeared in the *Daily Chronicle* and was picked up by the French press. Reassured by the Governor of French Guiana, the government issued a denial; but Dreyfus was back in the news, and on 8 September *Figaro* published an account of the pitiable condition of the prisoner on Devil's Island which in turn provoked a rejoinder in *La Libre Parole* which declared that, quite to the contrary, Dreyfus was living 'like a brute. He could read, but prefers to eat. He guzzles, he eats, and he drinks . . .' Dreyfus remained a political hot potato.

On 10 September, an article appeared in *L'Éclair* which for the first time brought into the public domain the existence of the secret dossier. It purported to be an attack on those who were insisting upon the innocence of Alfred Dreyfus, and in so doing suggested that it might be appropriate to 'reveal on what irrefutable grounds the court martial based its decision to brand as a traitor to the country the man who seems to be benefiting excessively from an inexplicable sense of pity and a feeling of doubt which seems more generous than perspica-cious'. Four days later, a second article revealed unambiguously that an incriminating letter 'was not included in the official dossier and that it was only in secret, in the deliberation room, out of the presence of the accused, that it was transmitted to the judges of the court martial'.[15]

It never became clear who leaked this information to *L'Éclair*. The existence of the secret dossier was well known, but the list of its contents, if not wholly accurate, was sufficiently detailed to suggest an insider. Picquart believed that Dreyfus's supporters were behind the article and, in a letter to General Gonse enclosing a copy of the article, warned him of the danger of their being 'overwhelmed, locked into an inextricable position', if they did not act at once to arrest Esterhazy and rehabili-tate Dreyfus. But Gonse prevaricated. He urged caution and calm. No irrevocable decisions should be taken. With Boisdeffre's permission, Picquart went over the head of Gonse to Billot, the Minister of War.

At first Billot seemed open to Picquart's line of thought; but at a second meeting, after Billot had talked with Boisdeffre, his attitude had changed. He talked of 'military solidarity' and said that Picquart's discov-eries were 'military secrets' that could not be shared with other members of the government. Picquart returned to Gonse in an attempt to persuade him either to arrest Esterhazy or at the very least to entrap him. Gonse refused. 'What does it matter to you if that Jew stays on Devil's Island?'

'But since he's innocent . . .' said Picquart.

'So what?' said Gonse. 'That is not something that should enter into our calculations. If you keep quiet, no one will know.'

'What you're saying is vile. I don't know what I will do, but of one thing I am certain – I will not take this secret to the grave.'*

2: The Fall of Picquart

Both Gonse and Picquart had lost their tempers. The following day the two men met in calmer frames of mind. Picquart proposed send-ing a telegram, purporting to come from Schwartzkoppen, summoning

---

* Gonse would later deny that this exchange had taken place.

Esterhazy to a secret meeting. Gonse demurred. Billot, on Boisdeffre's advice, rejected the idea: 'as chief of the Army, I have no right to subject a high officer to such a thing'. Clearly, the horror at the thought of a treasonous officer which had possessed the Minister of War and the two men at the apex of the army High Command upon the discovery of the *bordereau* was not felt upon the discovery of the *petit bleu*. No one at this stage doubted its authenticity, but it was, after all, no more than 'an unsigned communication in an unknown or disguised hand, with an unclear meaning and of uncertain provenance' which, if produced as evidence in court, would lead to protests from the Germans; and the fact that Esterhazy, who on the whole was held in high regard by his superiors, had shown an unusual curiosity about artillery proved nothing.

However, it was the thought of reopening the Dreyfus case that led the three men who felt themselves responsible for the security of the state – Boisdeffre, Gonse and Billot – to impede Picquart's proceedings against Esterhazy. Was this the moment when, like the High Priest Caiaphas, they decided that 'it is better for one man to die for the people, than for the whole nation to be destroyed'?[16] History would judge them severely for a decision which left an innocent man rotting on Devil's Island; and, as Gonse's outburst to Picquart suggests, it might have been different had Dreyfus not been a Jew. But, as Marcel Thomas points out in his dispassionate account of these events, the three men 'were neither madmen nor criminals' and 'the gravity of what was at stake makes it important to try and understand the motives for their decisions'.[17] To them the choice was between injustice and disorder. With the body politic corrupt and enfeebled by social and cultural fissures, the army embodied the unity and integrity of the nation. To make public the fact that the trial of Dreyfus had been fraudulent and its verdict unsound would so discredit the High Command that the army would be fatally weakened. Furthermore, the conviction of Esterhazy would open a new can of worms, because Esterhazy might implicate Weil and Weil the 'generalissimo', Saussier.

'There will always be men', wrote Thomas, 'who will prefer injustice to disorder. It is here a matter of temperament.'[18] Had not Goethe expressed such a preference at the siege of Mainz during the French Revolutionary wars? 'The position of a Boisdeffre, of a Billot, will always be opportunistic . . . but to make the choice requires a lucid appreciation of what is involved. In this case, Gonse's decision, warmly approved by his superiors, only managed to create disorder and perpetuate injustice' and 'plunge the whole country in a dreadful struggle whose wounds took a long time to heal'.[19]

A period of 'phoney war' now started between Picquart and his superiors in which Picquart stood alone. None of his subordinates in the Statistical Section would support him because all were implicated in preparing the false evidence against Dreyfus. Moreover, all knew that their future prospects depended more on Gonse and Boisdeffre than they did on Picquart. Henry tried to convey to Picquart the folly of crossing one's superiors by telling how, when he was in the French North African light infantry, the Zouaves, the son of a colonel serving in the ranks was caught stealing from another soldier. His platoon commander wanted to prosecute him, but the influence of the culprit's father, the colonel, ensured that it was the officer, not the criminal, who was sacked.[20]

Picquart did not take the hint; he proceeded with the investigation of Esterhazy. He was well aware that this annoyed Gonse and Boisdeffre but persisted all the same. Gonse made critical comments to the effect that Picquart's obsession with Esterhazy was distracting him from his other responsibilities, but, much as they might have liked to, Gonse and Boisdeffre did not dare dismiss Picquart as chief of the Statistical Section: there was no suitable candidate to take his place. Henry, who kept them informed of what Picquart was up to, was still not considered a plausible replacement. However, it was thought possible to remove Picquart from operational control by sending him off on some special mission; and on 27 October 1896 Billot, on Gonse's advice, signed an order dispatching Picquart to reorganise the intelligence networks on the eastern borders of France. He was given only two weeks' notice.

Picquart was quite aware of what was going on. Before leaving for Châlons, he handed over to General Gonse the fruits of his investigations to date of Esterhazy and to Henry the original of the *petit bleu*. The secret dossier used to convict Dreyfus was also back in their hands and was studied for any annotations that may have been made by Picquart. François Guénée, the former agent of the Sûreté whose reports on his contacts with the Spanish diplomat, Val Carlos, had been 'nourished' to implicate Dreyfus, sent a memo to General Gonse warning him that Picquart had questioned him closely on these reports, and seemed to doubt the inferences in du Paty's commentary.

Clearly, should the case against Dreyfus be reopened, some incontrovertible piece of evidence against him had to be found in the dossier of whose existence the Dreyfus family were now aware. On 1 November – the feast of All Saints and a public holiday – Commandant Henry worked at home to manufacture a document that would put the guilt of Dreyfus beyond doubt. He had brought back from the office a short letter from the Italian military attaché, Panizzardi, to his German counterpart (and lover) Maximilian von Schwartzkoppen and an envelope on which was written Schwartzkoppen's name and address in Panizzardi's handwriting. 'My dear friend,' the letter began. 'Here is the manual. I paid for you as agreed. Wednesday, eight in the evening, at Larent's place is fine. I have invited three from my embassy, including one Jew. Don't miss it. Alexandrine.'

Henry had also obtained a sheet of the same lined paper used by Panizzardi for his letter. With the help of his wife, and possibly of an expert forger, Henry wrote an extra paragraph in Panizzardi's hand in the same blue pencil. He cut out the innocuous message from the genuine letter and glued the top with the opening 'My dear friend' and the bottom with the signature 'Alexandrine' to the forged text. The letter now read: 'My dear friend. I have read that a deputy is to ask questions about Dreyfus. If someone in Rome asks for new explanations, I will say that I have never had any dealings with the Jew. If someone asks you, say the same for no one must ever know what happened with him. Alexandrine.'

The 'deputy who is to ask questions about Dreyfus' was a reference to André Castelin, Deputy for the Aisne, who had announced his intention of putting questions about Dreyfus to Billot in the Chamber of Deputies; the undercover policeman Guénée believed Castelin, though ostensibly anti-Dreyfus, to be on a retainer from the Dreyfus family. Billot could now feel confident in confirming the soundness of Dreyfus's conviction because on 2 January 1897 Gonse and Boisdeffre showed him a photograph of the forged letter that they said had reached Henry by Mme Bastian's 'ordinary way'. Gonse and Boisdeffre had seen the original of Henry's forgery, the Minister only a photograph; and because the photograph was not altogether clear, Gribelin, the archivist, made a copy of the original in his own hand which was authenticated by the signatures of Gonse, Henry, Lauth and Gribelin himself. Though Picquart had not yet left for Châlons, and was still nominally in charge of the Statistical Section, it was thought best by the Minister to keep him in the dark.

This was not only because Picquart might have realised that the timing of this new proof of Dreyfus's guilt was rather too convenient to be plausible, but also because Picquart was suspected of being the source of leaks to the Dreyfusard camp – first of the existence of the secret dossier revealed in the article in *L'Éclair* (something that was in fact widely known); and then of the far more detailed revelations that appeared in a pamphlet that on 7 and 8 November had been sent to every member of the National Assembly, all journalists of note and other figures in public life.

———

This was *Une Erreur judiciaire: la vérité sur l'Affaire Dreyfus* by Bernard Lazare. At last, after eighteen months of preparation, Lazare had been let off the leash by Mathieu Dreyfus and Edgar Demange. The article in *L'Éclair* had already provided Lucie with a reason to petition the Chamber of Deputies for a review of her husband's case; but now Lazare presented in great detail, and in a tone shorn of bombast and abuse, the reasons why the conviction of Alfred Dreyfus should be deemed unsound. It printed the text of the *bordereau* in full and revealed that among the papers in the secret dossier shown to the judges but not to the defence was the letter mentioning 'the scoundrel D.' – with no evidence to suggest that the letter D stood for Dreyfus. Three thousand copies of the pamphlet were secretly printed in Brussels and sent to France in plain envelopes. Picquart, who on the brink of his departure conducted a hasty investigation, learned that it had cost the Dreyfus family 25,000 francs. However, its impact on public opinion was minimal: only two newspapers, *Le Temps* and *Les Débats*, mentioned its publication and discussed its contents. In the rest of the press, it was ignored.

Its greatest impact was on Gonse. The fact that Picquart had discovered only the cost of Lazare's pamphlet, not the source of the leaks, increased his suspicions that Picquart himself was that source. Worse was to come. Only two days after the publication of Lazare's pamphlet, a photograph of the *bordereau* appeared in *Le Matin*. Picquart confounded Gonse's suspicions by first denying that he had a photograph of the *bordereau* in his files, then admitting that he had been mistaken. The fear was that others would recognise the handwriting of the *bordereau* as being that of Esterhazy. Mathieu Dreyfus had the photograph from *Le Matin* copied on to posters flanked by photographs of letters written by his brother, demonstrating the difference between the two hands: the posters were put up on boards all over Paris.

The plan of the High Command to bury any doubts anyone might have about Esterhazy by sending Picquart into exile was put into effect too late. Unknown to Gonse and Billot, Picquart had been intercepting Esterhazy's correspondence with Maurice Weil which, though it revealed nothing treasonous, informed Picquart of Esterhazy's mercurial personality, and his links with Drumont and *La Libre Parole*. Billot, when he learned of this, was outraged, partly because he was afraid Weil might say something to compromise Billot's friend, General Saussier. On 12 November 1896, Billot learned that Weil had received an anonymous letter warning him that André Castelin, the Deputy for the Aisne, was going to name him and Esterhazy as accomplices of Dreyfus. It was signed 'Commandant Pierre'. The fear now was that Weil would warn Esterhazy who, seeing his handwriting on posters all over Paris, would do something foolish – flee abroad, confess, kill himself – implicit admissions of guilt that would establish the innocence of Dreyfus and therefore discredit the army High Command.

On 18 November, Jean-Baptiste Billot mounted the podium of the National Assembly to answer the questions that had been put by André Castelin. In the event, the questions were anodyne and Billot had no need to reveal the existence of the new evidence that established the guilt of Dreyfus beyond any doubt. Castelin's complaints were not about a possible miscarriage of justice but about the activities of the Dreyfusards. He wanted Lazare to be prosecuted and measures to be taken against 'the civilian accomplices' of the traitor Dreyfus. Billot reassured him that there was no question of reopening the matter of Dreyfus's conviction: 'That matter was brought to trial, and no one has the right to question the results.'[21]

3: Picquart in Exile

When Georges Picquart left Paris in mid-November 1896 to reorganise the intelligence networks in eastern France, he remained notionally chief of the Statistical Section and on good terms with both General Gonse, his immediate superior, and Henry who, in his absence and under Gonse's supervision, took on the day-to-day running of the department. Picquart was aware that on the question of Esterhazy and Dreyfus he had been at cross-purposes with Gonse and Boisdeffre, and that the first loyalties of his subordinates were not to him, but he was as yet unaware of the enmity he inspired. His loyalty to the army was paramount: he had not told anyone outside the service of his suspicions and misgivings. He had, however, from the start of his tenure as commander of the Statistical Section, consulted a childhood friend from Strasbourg, Louis Leblois – formerly a magistrate and now a lawyer practising in Paris – on the legality of certain aspects of his work that had not troubled his predecessor, Sandherr.[22]

What Picquart in his innocence did not yet realise was that Henry, with his propensity to ingratiate himself with his superiors either by anticipating their instructions or by obeying what was merely conveyed with a nod and a wink, was already at work with the help of his colleagues at setting him up as a covert accomplice of the Dreyfusards. Gribelin had learned from a journalist on *Le Matin* that the paper had obtained a photograph of the *bordereau* from an official and let it be thought that the official was Picquart (in fact it was one of the handwriting experts, Pierre Teyssonières). Letters addressed to Picquart were opened and read and one, a strange note in Spanish from a former soldier who now worked as private secretary to the Comtesse de Comminges, whose salon Picquart frequented, was presented as a coded message from the Dreyfusards, and embellished with a second and more compromising letter forged by Henry.

The letters were shown to Billot and successfully persuaded him that Picquart should not be allowed to return to Paris. Thus on Christmas Eve 1896, Picquart was told by Gonse that the mission he had undertaken to reorganise the intelligence service in eastern France was to be extended to the French North African possessions. He was to go forthwith to Marseille and on 29 December take ship for the port of Philippeville on the north-eastern coast of Algeria.

General Gonse sent his greetings to Picquart for the New Year of 1897, wishing him 'good health on your splendid trip' and signing his name 'affectionately yours'. He assured Picquart that the army would meet all his expenses and care for the horse he had left behind in Paris. Picquart responded in the same tone but, since it was clear that his mission was merely a pretext to keep him out of France, he sent in a request to be returned to regular duty – a request which was refused. It was not until March that Picquart was given permission to return to Paris, and then only for a few days. It was time enough for him to see that his position was more perilous than he had realised; and upon his return to his base in Sousse, on the eastern coast of Tunisia, he added a codicil to his will in which he described how he had uncovered the guilt of Esterhazy and the innocence of Dreyfus. He left instructions that, in the event of his death, the sealed envelope containing this codicil was to be delivered into the hands of the President of the Republic.

In May, in a curt note to Henry, Picquart castigated him for 'the lies and mysteries' used to hide the fact that he had effectively been relieved of his functions. The mask of affability was now dropped by Henry, who in his reply turned the tables on Picquart, accusing him of irregularities and falsifications. 'As to the word "lies" . . . our inquiry has not yet been able to determine where, how, and to whom the word should be applied.' On 10 June, Picquart wrote again to Henry protesting 'in the most formal manner [against] the insinuations . . . and the manner in which the facts are presented'. Knowing of Henry's contacts in the criminal underworld, and the skills of the Statistical Section when it came to disinformation and dirty tricks, Picquart became alarmed and eleven days later, on leave in Paris, went to see his friend, the lawyer Louis Leblois, and told him what he had discovered about Esterhazy and Dreyfus.[23]

Leblois, who had hitherto had no doubts whatsoever about the guilt of Dreyfus, was now persuaded of his innocence. He was a new and important recruit to the Dreyfusard cause, but his hands were tied because Picquart, before returning to Tunisia, though giving his friend power of attorney, made him promise not to repeat what he had been told to anyone in the Dreyfusard camp. As Picquart had told Gonse, he did not intend to take what he knew about Dreyfus to the grave should some 'accident' befall him while abroad, but he had confided in Leblois not to aid Dreyfus but as a precautionary measure in his own interest. Leblois, in the meetings they had each evening during Picquart's leave, tried to persuade him to speak out – to 'go public' – with what he knew. But Picquart knew that this would mean the end of his career in the army.[24] His residual feelings of loyalty to the army – his sense of honour – prevented him from betraying its *esprit de corps*, even when faced with a self-serving conspiracy to keep an innocent man on Devil's Island.

4: The Senator for Life

General Gonse, unwilling to rely on anything as insubstantial as Picquart's sense of honour to silence him, persuaded Billot to extend Picquart's mission from Tunisia to the French possessions in Indo-China. Many thousands of kilometres away, on the other side of the world, with all his communications with Metropolitan France scrutinised by the Statistical Section, Picquart was effectively neutralised and disarmed.

However, this was not the case with Leblois. His friendship with Picquart went across the tribal divide because, while both were Alsatians from Strasbourg, Picquart came from a Catholic family while Leblois's family were Protestant. Indeed Leblois was the son of a Protestant pastor and, in the words of Ruth Harris, was inspired by 'the *petite musique huguenote*, the soft but persistent melody of conscience'.[25] In her view Picquart, raised with the imprint of a hierarchical authoritarian religion, found it hard to disobey his superior officers, while Leblois, who answered only to God, was tormented by the thought that his silence was contributing to the unrelieved suffering of an innocent man.

Leblois was a member of the Alsace-Lorraine Committee, which held a dinner at Ville-d'Avray just outside Paris in early July 1897. Among those present was the sixty-three-year-old Auguste Scheurer-Kestner, once Deputy for Haut-Rhin in the National Assembly, the last elected representative of the lost province of Alsace, and now Vice-President of the Senate and Senator for Life. He too was a Protestant and part of the republican establishment: he was the brother-in-law of one former Prime Minister, Charles Floquet, and uncle of another, Jules Ferry; and he had been a friend of Gambetta. His nephew, Charles Risler, was the mayor of the 7th arrondissement in Paris where Leblois was his deputy. He had already been approached by Mathieu Dreyfus on the question of Alfred's rehabilitation but had told him he was convinced of his guilt.

By now, however, Scheurer-Kestner was not so sure, and over dinner he told Leblois of his doubts. At this point Leblois felt bound by his oath to Picquart not to divulge what he knew; but when, some days later, Charles Risler, Scheurer-Kestner's nephew, told Leblois of his uncle's preoccupation with the Dreyfus Affair, Leblois asked his colleague to arrange a meeting with the distinguished Senator, which duly took place on 13 July. After extracting the same promise from Scheurer-Kestner that Picquart had got from him – that everything he said would be in the strictest confidence – Leblois described how Picquart had uncovered the guilt of Esterhazy, the innocence of Dreyfus and the determination of the chiefs of the General Staff to do nothing to remedy this miscarriage of justice.

Scheurer-Kestner was dumbfounded but, since what he was told confirmed his suspicions, quickly convinced. He drew up a private memorandum in which he outlined the situation as he saw it: at the time of Dreyfus's conviction, no one doubted his guilt, but now the contrary was the case. The army chiefs knew that Dreyfus was innocent and Esterhazy guilty – the same Esterhazy who 'was Mayer's second in his duel with Morès* and he has flaunted it ever since in order to ask all of Jewry for money'. Scheurer-Kestner then went on to say that Esterhazy had an accomplice, Maurice Weil, a commandant in the territorial army, 'a stockbroker . . . a former horse trader', whose wife is 'on excellent terms' with General Saussier. Scheurer-Kestner next outlined the difficulties of the situation in which he found himself:

1. M. Picquard [sic] must remain out of it.
2. The Ministry defended Dreyfus's conviction in November 1896, while knowing that he was innocent.
3. Weil's relations with Saussier.
4. Any mention of the matter would expose Picquard, since General Gonse would guess at the 'source' of the indiscretion.

Commandant Henry knows everything.[26]

Attempts made by Scheurer-Kestner to get both Leblois and, through Leblois, Picquart to release him from his vow of confidentiality failed. The most he could do was let it be known to two friends among his fellow politicians, Arthur Ranc and Joseph Reinach, that he now *knew* that Dreyfus was innocent; and he authorised Reinach to pass this on to the Dreyfus family. The news of Scheurer-Kestner's conversion to the Dreyfusard cause spread quickly. When the subject came up at a dinner at the Élysée Palace, Scheurer-Kestner told one of President Faure's daughters, Lucie, how wretched he felt about the whole business: 'My heart is heavy, my conscience is racked. It's a terrible business. Captain Dreyfus is innocent. But don't say anything to your father because I

* In fact, he was Crémieu-Foa's second.

can't as yet tell him much. I am not free to do so . . .'²⁷ Lucie Faure at once told her father what Scheurer-Kestner had said. Two days later she wrote to say that he should speak to the President himself as soon as he could.

The meeting, held on 29 October 1897, was a disaster. Faure had been got at on the question of Dreyfus some time before by his former doctor from Le Havre, Dr Gilbert. Scheurer-Kestner found that his old friend Faure, once so companionable, friendly and high-spirited, had become pompous and self-important – no doubt the result of hobnobbing with kings, emperors and other heads of state. Faure made it clear to Scheurer-Kestner that, in his view, his constitutional position as President of France precluded any intervention in matters such as the Dreyfus Affair. The most that Scheurer-Kestner could get out of him was a promise that he would preserve a 'benevolent neutrality'.

The next day Scheurer-Kestner had lunch with another old friend, who *did* have the power to intervene in the Dreyfus Affair, the Minister of War, Jean-Baptiste Billot. This interview went no better. Billot had been briefed by du Paty de Clam: he quoted from the letter forged by Henry, which had been shown to him by 'a man of valour', General Gonse. He reassured Scheurer-Kestner that he was not a pawn of the clericalists: 'I find myself in a den of Jesuits here . . . The only one who is *not* a Jesuit is Jean-Baptiste Billot!' He promised to make further inquiries about Dreyfus's conviction in return for a promise from Scheurer-Kestner to hold back from any further action for the next two weeks.

That Billot should have felt it necessary to reassure Scheurer-Kestner that he was not 'a Jesuit' reveals how partisan the Dreyfus Affair had already become. Scheurer-Kestner came from a Protestant family, but he was not a Christian: he had lost his faith at the age of twenty-two and his children had not been baptised. He was a sceptical Positivist but openly proclaimed that his old religion, Protestantism, was superior to Catholicism, a religion not of morality and ethics but of blind superstition. Protestants represented progress and were natural republicans, while Catholics were reactionary and naturally authoritarian. He considered that the industrial unrest in Alsace at the time of the Franco-Prussian war was not a revolt against poverty by the Catholic workers but 'a Jesuit-led attempt to nullify economic and social progress'.[28]

Scheurer-Kestner also defended France's Jews, considering the precepts of Judaism and the Enlightenment to be expressions of the same universal values. It was therefore hardly surprising that, when it became known that he was lobbying in favour of Dreyfus, he came under attack in the nationalist press. *La Patrie* called him a naive old man who had been 'duped by scum'. Gaston Méry, in *La Libre Parole*, identified Scheurer-Kestner as a key figure in the 'Jew-loving, Huguenot cabal'.[29] *L'Intransigeant* called him 'the *éminence grise* of treason' and 'slime that had to be washed into the sewer'. The symbol of resistance to Germany was dubbed a 'Kraut' and 'a Prussian' and 'a valet of the Germans'.

Unquestionably affected by this abuse, Scheurer-Kestner nonetheless persisted in his crusade. He went to see the Prime Minister, Jules Méline, but was told by Méline that it was a matter for Billot, the Minister of War. Scheurer-Kestner took Leblois to the War Ministry to see Billot, but Leblois lost his nerve at the last minute and refused to go in. Jean-Baptiste Darlan, the Minister of Justice, whom Scheurer-Kestner went to see on 5 November, said that his office precluded any premature intervention. Scheurer-Kestner's enormous prestige was being dissipated by the day; his conviction that Dreyfus was innocent had proved insufficient to change anyone's mind.

Then, on 7 November, a fortuitous occurrence altered the course of events. Jacques de Castro, a Parisian stockbroker of South American origin, walking down a Parisian boulevard, stopped to look at the enlarged photograph of the *bordereau* which appeared on one of the posters put up by Mathieu Dreyfus. Castro recognised the handwriting: it was that of one of his former clients, Commandant Esterhazy. Through a common acquaintance, Castro arranged to see Mathieu Dreyfus. He brought with him some of the letters he had received from Esterhazy. The hand of the letters and that of the *bordereau* were identical.

Mathieu at once asked to see Scheurer-Kestner. A meeting was arranged for 11 November. When face to face with the venerable

Senator, Mathieu exclaimed: 'I can now tell you the name of the traitor. It is Commandant Charles Walsin-Esterhazy!'

'Yes,' said Scheurer-Kestner, the burden of his promise finally lifted.
'He's the one.'

———

More than a year had passed since Georges Picquart had told General
Gonse of the clear evidence he had uncovered that Alfred Dreyfus was
innocent. The determination of the army's High Command to ignore
this evidence, Picquart's reluctance to jeopardise his career by openly
defying his superiors and the sense of honour of both the lawyer Leblois
and the statesman Scheurer-Kestner that prevented them from disclos-
ing what they had been told meant that the Dreyfus family and their
friends had been denied the means with which to prise open a case
which most in France considered closed. There were no recriminations.
On 12 November, the day after Mathieu had learned the name of the
man who had committed the crime for which his brother had been
condemned, a council of war was held by the high command of the
Dreyfusard campaign: Mathieu Dreyfus, Edgar Demange, Auguste
Scheurer-Kestner and Louis Leblois, with the editor of *Le Figaro*,
Emmanuel Arène, in attendance. Arène suggested that, rather than
an immediate and outright denunciation of Esterhazy, public opinion
should be prepared for such a dramatic revelation. Under the byline
Vixi, Arène published a story on 14 November announcing that 'a well-
known officer, frequently seen around Paris, who has a title, is married
and is quite well connected', had been revealed as the true author of the
bordereau.

The article provoked a furious reaction the next day in *La Libre
Parole* under the byline Dixi. The officer identified in *Le Figaro* was
wholly innocent, the stooge that the Jews had long been seeking to
carry the can for Dreyfus's crimes. Lieutenant-Colonel Picquart was
their tool in this infamous conspiracy.

The time had come to drop the innuendo and name names.
Counselled by Demange, Mathieu composed a letter to Jean-Baptiste
Billot, the Minister of War.

Monsieur le Ministre,

The sole basis for the charge brought in 1894 against my unfortunate brother is an unsigned, undated letter showing that confidential military documents were delivered to the agent of a foreign military power.

I have the honour of informing you that the author of that document is M. le Comte Walsin-Esterhazy, an Infantry Commandant, withdrawn from active duty last spring for reason of temporary infirmities.

Commandant Esterhazy's handwriting is identical to that of the document in question. It will be quite easy for you to produce a specimen of the handwriting of the officer.

I am prepared, moreover, to indicate to you where you may find letters of his, whose authenticity cannot be contested and which date from before my brother's arrest.

I cannot doubt, *Monsieur le Ministre*, that knowing the author of the treason for which my brother was convicted, you will act swiftly to see that justice is done.

On receipt of this letter, Billot asked General Saussier to investigate the charges made against Esterhazy. The government 'owes it to justice,' he told the Chamber of Deputies, 'to the honour of the accused, to insist that the author of the denunciations produce his justification': the accused whose honour was in question was, of course, Esterhazy, not Dreyfus. To chair the inquiry, Saussier appointed the military commander of the Department of the Seine, General Georges de Pellieux. Pellieux started proceedings on 26 November. On the same day, Georges Picquart was recalled to Paris.

Commandant Esterhazy

1: Early Years

The Comte Marie-Charles-Ferdinand Walsin-Esterhazy was descended from one of the most illustrious families in Europe – the Hungarian Esterhazys. When the Russian Tsar Alexander I and the Prussian King Frederick William made their ceremonial entry into the city with Emperor Francis of Austria for the Congress of Vienna, the guard of honour 'resplendent in its lavishly embroidered hussar uniforms' was commanded by a Prince Esterhazy, 'whose jewelled aigrette and pearl-adorned boots were the source of universal admiration'.[1]

Charles Walsin-Esterhazy was a very remote descendant of this scion of the Austro-Hungarian nobility, and he was equally far from being able to afford a jewelled aigrette or pair of pearl-adorned boots. The name Esterhazy had come to him from his paternal great-grandmother, Anne-Marie Esterhazy, who had given birth to an illegitimate son in 1767. She was the granddaughter of a Comte Antoine Esterhazy who had fled to France after the abortive rising of Rakosy in the seventeenth century and had taken service under King Louis XIV. She gave her son her family name of Esterhazy but appended to it the name of a romantic hero then in fashion – Walsin.

In due course Anne-Marie Esterhazy's son married a Mlle Cartier and went to live in Nîmes. Two of their three sons joined the French Army and both reached, under Napoleon III, the rank of general.

The younger of the two distinguished himself during the Crimean war, notably in the battle of Eupatoria. He married Zélie Dequeux de Beauval, by whom he had a daughter and a son, the son being Charles-Marie-Ferdinand, born on 26 December 1847.

The younger General died in July 1857, and his widow, in her turn, in December 1865. Soon after her death, the orphaned Charles took on the title of count to which he had no right and dropped the first part of his family name to call himself Esterhazy, though others continued to use Walsin. He was only a sixteenth part Hungarian and did not speak the language, and his knowledge of German came from his studies at the Lycée Condorcet. In March 1863, at the age of sixteen, he left the Lycée Condorcet and there follows a four-year gap in his curriculum vitae: he may have been recovering from tuberculosis in the country with relatives, or travelling abroad with his mother's brother, Beauval, who was a French consul. At some point he passed his baccalaureate and applied for the military academy of Saint-Cyr, but was turned down.

Thwarted in this attempt to take the fast track to a commission, Esterhazy enlisted in May 1869 in the Pontifical Legion formed to protect the Pope in Rome from the Italian nationalists under Cavour. He resigned that commission in March 1870 and, thanks to the pulling of strings by his Esterhazy and Beauval uncles, was commissioned as a second lieutenant in the French Foreign Legion. At the outbreak of the Franco-Prussian war, before he had had a chance to serve in Africa, he was transferred to the 1st Regiment of Zouaves in the Army of the Loire. Chaotic conditions led to fast promotion – first to lieutenant, then captain, but after France's defeat there was a revision of grades which reduced him back to the rank of second lieutenant.

Esterhazy saw this demotion as a grave injustice and it left him with a lasting grudge against the army High Command. He was still only a lieutenant when serving with the 54th Regiment of the Line garrisoned at Beauvais in 1875. His talents, such as they were, seemed more suited to the intellectual aspects of the military life. He was an assiduous researcher and fluent writer, and worked for a time for the *Journal des Réunions des Officiers* in its office on the rue de Bellechasse in Paris.

In February 1877, he was posted to the Service des Renseignements as a German translator. In 1880, he was transferred to active service with the 135th Regiment of the Line stationed at Cholet.

Esterhazy was also a diligent networker, and sought to further his career less by heroics than by exploiting the contacts he made during the different stages of his career. Through the *Journal des Réunions des Officiers* he met Maurice Weil, and was thereby introduced to a circle of writers on military affairs, mostly retired officers, who published a small magazine called *L'Épée et la Plume*. A high civil servant, Gaston Grenier, whose father had been a friend of Esterhazy's, was himself a friend of Esterhazy's superior officer, Commandant Paul Saglio, whose wife was a Crémieu-Foa. It was Saglio who introduced Esterhazy to his brothers-in-law, Captain André Crémieu-Foa, and Ernest, a stockbroker.

Esterhazy had no money and this, together with the sense that he had not been promoted to a rank that his talents and pedigree deserved, led to an angry, rancorous attitude towards France and the French. Photographs of Esterhazy show him balding, with a wide moustache, and an expression of irascible indignation on his face. He was contemptuous of the army he served, described it as no more than 'a beautiful theatrical set behind which there was nothing'. He had more respect for the German Army, admiring its discipline and Junker tradition. Esterhazy was aware of the inner complexities and contradictions of his character: he was, he wrote to Mme de Boulancy, his mistress in the 1880s, 'a being of a species completely different' from her friends, capable of 'great things given the opportunity', or of great crimes. He was a Raskolnikov, an outsider like Dostoevsky's anti-hero, 'exasperated, embittered, furious', with spasms of loathing for the country that had failed to give him his due. 'If someone were to come to tell me this evening that I would be killed tomorrow as an Uhlan captain running through Frenchmen with my sabre, I would certainly be perfectly happy . . . Paris taken by storm and given over to the pillage of 100,000 drunken soldiers! That is a celebration I dream of!'[2]

Having cheated Mme de Boulancy out of what money she had, Esterhazy left her and, it being not uncommon at the time to trade a title and pedigree for a dowry, looked to marry an heiress. He applied to the agencies who arranged such marriages, hoping to find 'a young girl with five million',[3] but in fact settled for one with 200,000 francs. This was Anne de Nettancourt-Vaubécourt, the daughter of the Marquis de Nettancourt-Vaubécourt, a member of the ancient nobility of Lorraine. The marquis had no money but his bourgeois wife, from whom he was separated, provided the dowry. It is possible that her parents' separation was sufficiently *mal vu* to make it difficult to find a husband for Anne which is why the family settled for Esterhazy. The marriage took place on 6 February 1886, and was regarded by the groom from the outset as a disaster.

On their honeymoon in Venice, Esterhazy was stupefied when, 'with a bored air', Anne told him that she disliked the city 'because there was no sound of traffic'.[4] Sex was a success – 'Esterhazy recognised that his wife felt a strong sensual attraction towards him' – but that did not compensate in his mind for her other failings, particularly her extravagance when they returned to Paris and set up house. 'Concerning financial matters, my wife never for a moment realized, never even tried to understand, that when people as poor as we marry . . . they have to be thrifty and not buy themselves dresses, coats, and hats at the slightest whim, not travel first class, not pay their maids 60 francs a month.'[5] It was very much a case of the pot calling the kettle black: the real drain on Esterhazy's finances came from his own extravagances and speculation on the Paris stock exchange. The birth of two daughters bound him closer to his family because, for all his other failings, 'Esterhazy felt great affection for his children' and they for him. But this family feeling did not deter him from taking up with a young girl he met while on army manoeuvres in Touraine in 1893, and continuing to see her when she moved to Paris to give singing lessons; nor from using and losing his wife's money on his financial speculations.

There was one source of income that Esterhazy had yet to exploit and that was his Jewish friends. Soon after the duel in which he had acted as second to Captain André Crémieu-Foa (see p. 47 above), he wrote three similar begging letters – one to Maurice Weil, another to Baron Alphonse de Rothschild and the third to Baron Edmond de Rothschild, who had been his schoolmate at the Lycée Condorcet. He told them that he was destitute and that his poverty had now led to the ill-health of his wife and children. It was humiliating for him, a French officer, to beg for help but 'I will go to such lengths rather than see my family die of hunger.'

Esterhazy's misfortunes, he said, sprang directly from his perceived friendship with the Jews. 'I did not hesitate', he wrote to Baron Edmond de Rothschild, using the familiar *tu*, 'when Captain Crémieu-Foa could find no Christian officer to act as his second,'[6] but he had paid dearly for this generous impulse. Accusing him of being 'Jewified', his own family had refused to help, and as evidence of this fact Esterhazy enclosed a copy of a letter from his uncle, the diplomat Beauval: 'For me as a Christian, who believes that God punishes and compensates, I see in your misfortunes a blow from his hand. You have defended the Jews and you are brought down by money. It is the hand of God.'[7]

The letter from Beauval had been forged by Esterhazy, but it had the desired effect. Edmond de Rothschild instructed his bank to draw 2,000 francs from an account he kept for charitable donations to 'the poor' and send it to Esterhazy. Maurice Weil forwarded his letter from Esterhazy to the Chief Rabbi, Zadoc Kahn, who elicited further donations from the Jewish community.[8]

At the same time as Esterhazy was making the most of his pro-Semitic credentials, he was also making contacts with the anti-Semites of *La Libre Parole*. Indeed, on the day after the duel between Drumont and Crémieu-Foa, he had left his card at Drumont's home, and soon afterwards started a friendly correspondence with Morès. 'My dear Captain,' Morès wrote to him, 'your note pleased us both. I won't hide from you that I am happy that this affair is over and please accept an assurance of my very best wishes, etc.'[9] Esterhazy began to feed information to the military correspondent of *La Libre Parole*, Commandant Octave Biot, picked up from his contacts on the *Bulletin*, *La Revue du Cercle Militaire* and *L'Épée et la Plume*. He acted as an intermediary between the 'Israelites' and *La Libre Parole*, persuading Drumont to abandon his campaign against the incompetent, doddery General Édon, whose wife was Saussier's standby mistress. 'It is thanks to me', he wrote to the Deputy Jules Roche, 'that this scandal never saw the light of day.'[10]

Esterhazy's interest in ingratiating himself through Weil with Saussier was not to extract money but to further his career. A promotion to battalion commander meant a posting to Dunkirk, but he found life so far from Paris intolerable. After approaching the deputy Joseph Reinach and the Minister of War himself, Charles de Freycinet, he was transferred to the 74th Infantry Regiment in Rouen. But though Rouen was closer to Paris, he was bored there too, found garrison life insufferable and asked for a post at military headquarters on the rue Saint-Dominique in Paris. His request was refused.

With his career in the doldrums, Esterhazy's financial plight remained acute. The only solution seemed to be a successful punt on the stock market. There was such political turbulence in the summer of 1894 that a fall in stocks seemed certain: President Carnot had been assassinated, France was poised to invade Madagascar, there was cholera in St Petersburg and war was likely between the Chinese and Japanese. Esterhazy bet heavily on a fall in Russian bonds and in the shares of the Ottoman Bank. But the shares in the Ottoman Bank remained static and the Russian bonds rose in value. As the settlement date at the end of July 1894 approached, it looked as if finally, for Esterhazy, the game was up.

2: Schwartzkoppen

Between three and four in the afternoon of 20 July 1894, Colonel Maximilian von Schwartzkoppen, the military attaché of the German Embassy at 78, rue de Lille, was told that a Frenchman had come to ask for his help in obtaining a visa to visit Alsace-Lorraine. Schwartzkoppen agreed to see him:

> there entered a gentleman whom I recognized at once as a French officer in mufti. He seemed some 42 to 45 years old, and was of medium height and slightly built; he had drawn features, deep-set black eyes, a

good head of greyish hair, and a strong moustache with streaks of grey in it. He had on a black overcoat, and was wearing the red stripe of the Legion of Honour in its buttonhole. As he came in he showed some embarrassment and nervousness; he looked gloomily around the room to make sure I was alone.

I asked him what he wanted, and he represented himself to me as a French staff officer on active service, compelled by necessity to take a step which, he said, would make him contemptible in my eyes, but which he had carefully considered and had simply got to take, in order to save his wife and children from certain downfall and destruction. He had been unfortunate, had made some unlucky speculations, and had been reduced to financial difficulties through his wife's illness. He had a small property near Châlons, and if he was to be able to keep this for his family he had to get money in some way. He had tried every possible way to do this by straightforward and honourable means, but without success, and he had no resource left but to offer his services to the German General Staff, in the hope that in this way he would before long be put in a position to meet his manifold obligations. He had given careful thought to it, and this was absolutely the only way left to him; if it failed he must blow his brains out. The thought of his wife and children had kept him so far from doing this, although he could see perfectly well that it was really the right thing to do. He was in a very good position to render valuable service, as he had been for a considerable time in Algiers and was thoroughly familiar with military conditions there; he had also been stationed for a considerable time on the Italian frontier and had an exact knowledge of the frontier defences; in 1881 and 1882 he had served in the Intelligence Department at the Ministry of War. He was a friend of Colonel Sandherr, Head of the Intelligence Department, and had been at school with President Casimir-Perier. He was also a friend of the Deputy Jules Roche, who had promised to make him an Assistant Chief of Staff if he, Roche, became Minister of War. At the moment he was on regimental service outside Paris, but he would soon be returning to Paris and would then resume his many connections with the Ministry of War. In a few days he would be attending an important military exercise in camp at Châlons.[11]

Maximilian von Schwartzkoppen, in the memoir written eight years after the event and only published after his death, said that he was both astonished and shocked by Esterhazy's offer. 'A French staff officer on the active list unashamedly proposing to betray his country, and coolly asking a brother officer to arrange it for him!' To establish his credentials, Esterhazy took from his breast-pocket a document which Schwartzkoppen claims to have returned to him unread saying it was out of the question that he should be party to treason, and advising him to leave and forget the whole thing.

Schwartzkoppen's description of his disgust at Esterhazy's proposition may be an accurate description of his true feelings, or it may have been a precaution in case Esterhazy had been sent to entrap him. It should also be seen in the light of his assurances to his Ambassador, Graf Münster von Derneburg, that he would not indulge in anything as dishonourable as espionage. However, Schwartzkoppen had a direct line to German Army intelligence and he reported Esterhazy's offer to Major Müller, chief of the Nachrichtenbureau in Berlin. Müller told him to open negotiations with the officer who, on a subsequent unannounced visit on 27 July, introduced himself as Major the Comte Walsin-Esterhazy, battalion commander of the 74th Infantry Regiment stationed in Rouen. On 3 August, Schwartzkoppen went to Germany to see Major Müller, then on holiday at Michelstadt in the Odenwald, who suggested that he treat with Esterhazy, see what information was to be got from him and pay him according to results.

Schwartzkoppen returned to Paris on 6 August and saw Esterhazy at the Embassy on 13 and 15 August. On the first of these two visits, Schwartzkoppen returned the mobilisation instructions that Esterhazy had left with him, saying that they were valueless, but on the second visit Esterhazy produced a document outlining the General Instructions for the artillery on mobilisation which Schwartzkoppen realised would be of considerable interest to the German General Staff, and so he made his first payment to Esterhazy of 1,000 francs.

In his memoirs, Schwartzkoppen wanted to convey both the extreme reluctance with which he, a Prussian officer, took advantage of the treason of a French officer and the danger this posed, should the transaction be exposed, not just to his honour but to his position as military attaché in Paris. He also wanted to exculpate himself from the charge of negligence and so insisted that he had never received the list of documents offered by Esterhazy, the infamous *bordereau*. In his view it had been filched from the porter's lodge at the German Embassy, presumably by Mme Bastian. He claimed that he learned of its existence only when he saw it reproduced in *Le Matin* in 1896.

Qui s'excuse, s'accuse. It is difficult to understand why Mme Bastian, as Schwartzkoppen suggested, should have torn up the *bordereau* 'to make it appear that it had come out of my waste-paper basket'.[12] Schwartzkoppen was an able and intelligent officer but, with his complex love-life involving the Italian military attaché Panizzardi and the wife of the Dutch Counsellor, Hermance de Weede, it seems probable that he did indeed throw the compromising document into his waste-paper basket, and that both the *bordereau* and the *petit bleu* did reach the Statistical Section by the 'ordinary route'.

In his memoirs, Schwartzkoppen acknowledged that the final sentence of the *bordereau* – 'I am off on manoeuvres' – which the Statistical Section had such difficulty in linking to Dreyfus, referred to Esterhazy's leaving for artillery exercise in Châlons. The documents listed in the *bordereau* were indeed provided by Esterhazy, and from 13 October onwards he made fortnightly visits to the German Embassy, bringing secret documents, some with commentaries, including one which revealed the contempt Esterhazy felt for the French Army – 'a fine bit of stage scenery, charming and deceptive; one imagines that there is something behind; one pricks it; there is nothing!'[13]

Reassured that Esterhazy was what he seemed, and not a French agent sent to entrap him, Schwartzkoppen still had to guard against being duped. Esterhazy had initially asked for a monthly retainer of 2,000 francs but Schwartzkoppen, on Müller's instructions, paid only what he thought a particular item was worth. It was difficult to see how the battalion commander of an infantry regiment stationed in Rouen, even if sent on training sessions to the French military base at Châlons, could have access to any particularly valuable information; yet it was precisely because of the secret nature of the documents itemised in the *bordereau* that Colonel Sandherr and his colleagues at the Statistical Section felt sure that its author must be on the General Staff. What they failed to appreciate was just how much of this supposedly secret information was in fact in the public domain. As Marcel Thomas has established, the documents promised by the *bordereau* 'were not of capital importance' and Esterhazy could have had access to them without belonging to the General Staff.[14]

There was, then, an element of double bluff in the traffic of secret documents between Esterhazy and Schwartzkoppen. As Thomas points out, Esterhazy's real talent was as a journalist, and the material he supplied to Schwartzkoppen was much the same as he provided for Commandant Biot, the military correspondent of *La Libre Parole*. Esterhazy's talent lay not in furnishing secret documents which he was in fact in no position to obtain, but in collating details gleaned from technical journals and matching them with stories he had picked up from other journalists or fellow officers whom he met through Weil, or who belonged to the circle around *L'Épée et la Plume*, on proposed reforms to the army, plans for changes in the military hierarchy and the founding of a separate army in North Africa.

No doubt Esterhazy would have been quite prepared to sell vital secrets to the Germans, but, in Thomas's view, because he had no access to these vital secrets, 'it is less certain that he was a traitor in the juridical sense of the term'.[15] It is therefore possible that, when he came to be named as a traitor, his outrage was not wholly feigned.

Nor, it would seem, was Schwartzkoppen duped by Esterhazy because it was clear from the start – despite Esterhazy's boast of useful contacts in the High Command – that he was not himself in a position to get hold of secret documents of major importance. However, the information he did provide was useful to Schwartzkoppen as pieces of a jigsaw which, when pieced together with what he learned from other sources – from other agents; from studying specialist military magazines or articles in the press for which he employed a secretary to assist him; from the weekly briefings of Colonel de Sancy, the War Ministry's liaison officer with foreign military attachés; and even from snatches of conversation with friends and acquaintances among French officers such as Major du Paty de Clam – formed a comprehensive picture of France's military capability.[16]

––––––––––

When Dreyfus was arrested in October 1894 and subsequently tried, condemned, degraded and deported, it does not seem to have occurred to Schwartzkoppen that it was a case of mistaken identity, and that Dreyfus was paying for Esterhazy's crime. The court martial was held in camera and so, though there were stories in the press that the evidence against Dreyfus emanated from the German Embassy, no one outside the court saw the *bordereau*. Schwartzkoppen was therefore able to assure his Ambassador, Graf Münster von Derneburg, with complete sincerity, that he had never had any contact with any Captain Dreyfus and that the allegations made against the German Embassy in the French press were false.

On 25 December 1894, Münster had issued a statement to that effect: 'The German Embassy has never had the slightest dealing, whether direct or indirect, with Captain Dreyfus. No document originating with him has been stolen from the Embassy, and no demand was made for the trial to be held behind closed doors.' Schwartzkoppen had gone to Berlin and on 27 December was summoned to a meeting with the Imperial Chancellor, Prince Hohenlohe, the Chief of the Army's General Staff, and the Kaiser himself at which he repeated how baffled he was by the whole affair. However, the attacks on Germany in the French press increased in virulence and on 6 January Münster held a meeting at his request with the French President, Casimir-Perier, at which they arrived at a formula for a joint statement which, if it did not deny the fact that evidence of treason had emanated from the German Embassy, exonerated that Embassy from any responsibility for what may have arrived through the post (see p. 116–7 above).

Nor does it seem to have occurred to Esterhazy that Dreyfus had been mistaken for him. Throughout the period when the French were being driven to hysteria by the nationalist press as a result of the discovery of a spy in the French officer corps, Esterhazy continued his delivery of secret information to Schwartzkoppen. He cashed in on the

hysteria, writing an article for *La Libre Parole*, in July 1895, denouncing German espionage.[17] The material he provided for Schwartzkoppen
was often just gossip he had picked up in military circles – for example,
that the new Minister of War, Godefroy Cavaignac, intended to replace
General Saussier, and was planning to form an autonomous army in
Algeria with its own High Command.

Schwartzkoppen used this information in a report he sent to his
superiors in Berlin in January 1896 which was intercepted and studied
by Georges Picquart. But by this time Schwartzkoppen had decided
that Esterhazy was no longer providing value for money. A final test
was to ask Esterhazy for information on a matter of genuine interest
to the Nachrichtenbureau, the design of a new rifle that was to replace
the old Lebel rifle of 1886. Esterhazy plagiarised an article written by
a Colonel Ortus of the circle around *L'Épée et la Plume* on 'The Rifle
of the Future' but also made inquiries at the army base in Châlons and
had a subordinate make sketches of its design which he delivered to
Schwartzkoppen. This was 'the matter in hand' mentioned in the *petit
bleu*, and the reason the letter was never sent was that Schwartzkoppen
had decided that 'further explanations' would be pointless and so had
returned the drawings to Esterhazy with a note instead. In March 1896,
Schwartzkoppen's relations with Esterhazy finally came to an end.[18]

3: The Powerful Protectors

The loss of the fees paid by Schwartzkoppen was not as catastrophic for
Esterhazy as it would have been the year before: he had developed some
other sources of income to supplement his army pay. Under the alias of
Rohan-Chabot, he went into partnership with a madame in a brothel
at 43, rue du Rocher, supplying 1,500 names of potential clients and
investing 2,000 francs.[19] He was also paid for the research he did for the
Deputy, Jules Roche, and his friend Biot on *La Libre Parole*. Another
friend on *La Libre Parole*, Ponchon de Saint-André, who wrote under
the byline Boisandré, commissioned Esterhazy's article denouncing
German espionage. Esterhazy had also taken over from Boisandré as
his mistress a young *demi-mondaine*, Marguerite Pays, whom he had

met on a train in 1895. Devoted to Esterhazy, she too was a source of funds, provided by other lovers. Both she and Esterhazy remained on good terms with Boisandré, who was dazzled by Esterhazy's gift of the gab. 'This circle . . . on the fringes of gallantry, journalism and politics was, between 1895 and 1897, the world in which Esterhazy swam like a fish in water.'[20]

Esterhazy received a fortuitous windfall in October 1896 on the death of a cousin, Paul Esterhazy. The heirs of Paul Esterhazy were the deceased's widow, his daughters and a son Christian who were persuaded to accept the advice of their worldly cousin Charles on what to do with their money. Christian sent Esterhazy 40,000 francs on the understanding that it would be invested by the Rothschilds, Esterhazy's friends. By the end of 1897, the entire sum had been dissipated, either spent by Esterhazy himself or lost in speculations on the Bourse.[21]

Esterhazy also had high hopes, as he had told Schwartzkoppen, that the influence of his friend Maurice Weil on General Saussier, and that of the Deputy Jules Roche, would secure him a post in the cabinet of the Minister of War. However on 11 November 1896, the day after *Le Matin* had published a photograph of the *bordereau*, Maurice Weil received the anonymous letter signed 'Commandant Pierre' warning him that he was to be named by the Deputy Castelin, together with Esterhazy, as an accomplice in the Dreyfus Affair. Weil told Esterhazy about what was said in the letter, and he also told a member of the Armed Services Commission who in turn passed it on to the Minister of War, Jean-Baptiste Billot. In the event, Castelin did not mention Weil or Esterhazy in the National Assembly: his questions to Billot were innocuous, and the crisis passed (see p. 174 above).

However, Weil was shaken by both the anonymous letter and the picture of the *bordereau*. He had had many letters from Esterhazy and so must have recognised the similarity of his handwriting. Certainly, from that moment on he began to distance himself from Esterhazy and finally broke off relations altogether. This put Esterhazy into a rage. He persuaded his friends on *La Libre Parole* and *L'Intransigeant* to mount a campaign against Saussier and Billot, and even threatened, should his reasonable expectations of promotion not be met, to leave the army and 'tell a story that will create a scandal throughout the world'.[22]

———

After the scare of Castelin's questioning of Billot in the Chamber of Deputies in November 1896, the immediate danger that Esterhazy might be named as the traitor had receded but, because the handwriting of the *bordereau* was in the public domain, it could only be a matter of time before someone other than Picquart made the connection, as was to be the case with the South American stockbroker Jacques de Castro. Therefore Commandant Henry continued to manufacture evidence against both Picquart and Dreyfus: the Statistical Section became, in the words of Hannah Arendt, 'a common fake factory'.[23] He tampered with the *petit bleu* to make it seem that Picquart had altered its contents; and, encouraged by the success of his first forgery, a letter was sent to Dreyfus on Devil's Island from a certain 'Weiss' with a cryptic message written in invisible ink between the lines.[24] This was intercepted by the prison authorities and stimulated their suspicions that Dreyfus's friends were planning an escape. Henry also forged a letter to Picquart from the private secretary of his friend the Comtesse de Comminges that seemed to suggest that he was in cahoots with the Dreyfusards. This was 'inadvertently opened' at the War Ministry and shown to Billot to convince him that Picquart's mission abroad should be extended. Faked telegrams were sent to Picquart to compromise him, and Picquart himself indulged in subterfuge in his correspondence – not to conceal any contacts with the Dreyfusards but to protect the reputation of a married woman, the wife of a diplomat, Pauline Monnier, with whom, before leaving Paris, he had embarked upon an affair.[25]

With Picquart out of the way and the Minister of War, Billot, reassured of Dreyfus's guilt by the letter forged by Henry, Generals Gonse and de Boisdeffre felt they had matters under control. It was only in the summer of 1897, when Auguste Scheurer-Kestner began lobbying ministers and the President himself, that they again became alarmed. Esterhazy was being named as the real traitor and all the precautions taken to protect him would prove futile if Esterhazy himself was to panic and do something rash.

On 16 October 1897, after consulting Boisdeffre, Gonse called in the chief architect of the original case against Dreyfus, the monocled, moustachioed Major du Paty de Clam, to take charge. It was difficult to know how to proceed. Esterhazy was under surveillance and so any meeting would be noted by the police. A letter from an identifiable correspondent, even if not intercepted, would be compromising, so du Paty, with Henry's help, composed an anonymous letter to Esterhazy warning him that the Dreyfus family in collusion with Colonel Picquart intended to make him the scapegoat for Dreyfus's crime. 'You are hereby forewarned of what these scoundrels plan to do to ruin you. It is now up to you to defend your name and the honour of your children. Act quickly, for the family is about to act to assure your doom.'[26] The letter, signed 'Espérance', was sent to Esterhazy at his country house, the Château de Dommartin near Sainte-Ménehould in the Marne.

On reading the letter, Esterhazy was appalled. He immediately left for Paris and for three days lay low in the flat of his mistress, Marguerite Pays. 'I am dishonoured,' he told her. 'I will have to leave the country. I will have to kill myself.' He felt isolated and abandoned, not knowing as yet of his guardian angels in the Statistical Section and on the General Staff. On 22 October, the archivist from the Statistical Section, Félix Gribelin, called at the flat of Marguerite Pays wearing blue-tinted spectacles and a fake beard. He left a note inviting Esterhazy to meet with 'powerful protectors who wanted to save him and to whom he would well advised to listen' at the corner of the Vanne reservoir in the Parc Montsouris.

Before keeping the rendezvous, Esterhazy went first to the Crédit Lyonnais Bank, then to the offices of the newspaper *La Patrie* and finally to the German Embassy to see Schwartzkoppen. The two men had not met for more than a year. Once alone with his former paymaster, and the door closed, Esterhazy told him that their traffic in military secrets had been discovered, and that if something was not done, Schwartzkoppen would be disgraced and Esterhazy sent to replace

Dreyfus on Devil's Island. Esterhazy's solution: Schwartzkoppen must write to Lucie Dreyfus to confirm her husband's guilt. Schwartzkoppen's response: 'Major, I think you are quite mad!'

Esterhazy sobbed, raved and at one point threatened Schwartzkoppen with a pistol, but eventually calmed down and was persuaded to leave. After calling on a senator on the rue de Médicis, a 'friend' of Marguerite Pays, he went to keep his appointment in the Parc Montsouris to the south of the city. He waited at the designated spot on the corner of the Vanne reservoir. Eventually a carriage drew up and two men got out. One was Gribelin wearing his blue-tinted spectacles and false beard. The other, also with a false black beard, was Commandant du Paty de Clam. A third man, Commandant Henry, who might have been recognised by Esterhazy, remained in the carriage.

Du Paty told Esterhazy what he already knew from the 'Espérance letter' – that he was being set up as the patsy, the *homme de paille*, for the crimes of Alfred Dreyfus. Esterhazy protested that he was innocent: du Paty assured him that they knew that only too well. He produced a photograph of the *bordereau*. Esterhazy acknowledged the similarity of the handwriting and started to say that this might be his because Colonel Sandherr had in fact employed him as a double agent, but he was cut short by Gribelin. The handwriting on the *bordereau* was that of Dreyfus. That was not to be questioned.[27]

From the Parc Montsouris, Esterhazy returned to the German Embassy on the rue de Lille where he told Schwartzkoppen about his meeting 'with two representatives of the Ministry of War'. It would seem that they were both off the hook. The two men parted for the last time. A week later, Schwartzkoppen was recalled to Germany to take up an elite appointment as the commanding officer of the 2nd Kaiser Franz Ferdinand Regiment of Grenadiers in Berlin. He was also awarded the Knight's Cross of the Légion d'Honneur by the French government.

Schwartzkoppen's recall was no doubt caused by fear that he might be caught up in the growing furore around the Dreyfus Affair. The German Ambassador, Graf Münster von Derneburg, still trusting in Schwartzkoppen's assurances that he did not engage in espionage, was sorry to see him go. 'I sincerely regret that you are no longer here,' he wrote to him soon after his departure.

> The fact that the newspapers have been connecting your departure with Dreyfus astonishes me, but hardly worries me. We both well know that poor Dreyfus, as far as we were concerned, was absolutely innocent . . . Esterhazy is defending himself quite poorly and appears to be a man of rather dubious honour.
>
> All of Paris thinks of nothing but Dreyfus . . . We miss you here a great deal. Very amicably yours, Münster

Others were equally unhappy to see Schwartzkoppen leave Paris – the beautiful Hermance de Weede, no doubt, and the Italian military attaché, Alessandro Panizzardi. Writing to Schwartzkoppen on 11 December 1897, Panizzardi told him how much he missed him, adding: 'I cannot sleep at night.'[28]

––––––

Esterhazy's encounter with du Paty and Gribelin in the Parc Montsouris was followed up with regular meetings at which his protectors dropped their disguise. Marguerite Pays and Esterhazy's nephew, Christian Esterhazy, acted as intermediaries, and Esterhazy would work on a common strategy to thwart the Dreyfusards with either du Paty, Gribelin or Henry by concocting further evidence against both Dreyfus and Picquart – in Picquart's case to establish that he was in league with the Dreyfusards – with letters and telegrams that would be intercepted either by the police or by the Statistical Section itself, and shown to the ministers concerned.

There were leaks in the press which fed the furore referred to by Münster von Derneburg. Esterhazy, with his journalistic flair, was adept at dramatising his plight. He wrote to the President, Félix Faure, describing the anonymous letter from 'Espérance' that had alerted him to the conspiracy against him, assuring him that 'An Esterhazy fears no one but God' and warning him that 'my House is sufficiently illustrious in the glories of the history of France and the histories of the great

European courts for the government of my country to be concerned lest that name be dragged through the mud'. In a second letter, he said that 'Espérance', the author of the letter in question, was a 'generous woman who warned me of the horrible plot hatched against me by Dreyfus's friends with the assistance of Colonel Picquart'. She had stolen a letter from Colonel Picquart who in turn had taken it from a foreign legation – a letter 'most compromising for certain important diplomats. If I do not obtain either support or justice . . . this photograph, which is at this moment in a safe place abroad, will be immediately published.' For many weeks, the true identity of this mysterious lady titillated the readers of the national press.

4: General de Pellieux

General Georges de Pellieux's inquiry into Mathieu Dreyfus's allegations against Esterhazy, ordered by General Saussier, opened on 17 November 1897. Mathieu Dreyfus was the first witness. He pointed out not just that Esterhazy's handwriting was identical to that of the *bordereau* – a judgement confirmed by a number of graphologists – but also that Esterhazy had been in a position to deliver what was promised on the list. He also referred to Esterhazy's notoriously bad character. General de Pellieux next took evidence from Scheurer-Kestner, who referred him to Leblois and Picquart. On the morning of 18 November, Esterhazy gave evidence. He admitted the similarity of his handwriting to that of the *bordereau*, but this was because Dreyfus had received samples of his handwriting from a Colonel Bro and had no doubt copied it to divert suspicion on to an innocent man.

On 19 November, Pellieux heard the evidence of Leblois, who conceded that he had occasionally been consulted by Picquart on questions that arose in the course of his duties. It was a dangerous admission. General de Boisdeffre, whom Pellieux consulted in the course of his inquiry, showed him some of the forged telegrams which suggested collusion between Picquart and the Dreyfusards. As a result, Pellieux concluded in his preliminary report delivered on 20 November that Esterhazy, despite irregularities in his private life, 'cannot, in my opinion, be accused of treason', whereas Picquart 'seems guilty'.[29] After reading this report, the Council of Ministers ordered him to proceed with a full inquiry.

On 26 and 27 November Pellieux questioned Picquart for the first time; his tone, 'paternalistic and familiar' with Esterhazy, was cold and brutal with Picquart. Everything appeared to be going as Esterhazy's protectors had wished when there came a bolt from the blue. Mme de Boulancy, the woman who had been Esterhazy's mistress in the 1880s, still aggrieved that he had cheated her out of all her money, had shown her lawyer the letters she had received from her lover, among them the one which stated that 'If someone were to come to tell me this evening that I would be killed tomorrow as an Uhlan captain running through Frenchmen with my sabre, I would certainly be perfectly happy . . . Paris taken by storm and given over to the pillage of 100,000 drunken soldiers! That is a celebration I dream of!' (see p. 185 above).

Mme de Boulancy's lawyer gave facsimiles of some of the letters to Scheurer-Kestner who in turn showed them to General de Pellieux, urging him to seize Esterhazy's full correspondence with Mme de Boulancy. Pellieux was unsure of his powers and so consulted a young examining magistrate recommended by Commandant Henry, Paul Bertulus. This move did not seem significant at the time, but it was the first time that a civilian legal officer had been drawn into the Dreyfus Affair. Bertulus, with authorisation from the Ministry of Justice, sent the police to Mme de Boulancy's flat where she happily handed over all the letters she had received from Esterhazy.

On 27 November, *Le Figaro* published the infamous 'Uhlan' letter which the editor had received from Mathieu Dreyfus and Joseph Reinach. For a second time (the first was when he had received the anonymous letter from 'Espérance') Esterhazy panicked and thought of fleeing abroad. His only recourse was to claim that the letters were forgeries, an explanation which the right-wing papers readily accepted: 'The letters are fake,' Henri Rochefort assured the readers of *L'Intransigeant*. They had been forged by the Jew Reinach, 'the dispenser of the syndicate's millions'. However, when faced with Mme de Boulancy, Esterhazy had to admit that the letters had indeed been written by him: it was only the 'Uhlan' letter that he said had been touched up. But even if that were not the case – even if the 'Uhlan' letter was genuine – Esterhazy's supporters refused to be dismayed. What had the letters to do with the Dreyfus Affair? They revealed 'an embittered or an exalted man', but not a traitor. Don't we all have black moods? Wasn't the culprit here not Esterhazy but Mathieu Dreyfus who had dug up dirt from thirteen years before to disparage Esterhazy in the hope that this might some-how distract the world from his brother's guilt?

The main danger posed to Esterhazy and his protectors was that Pellieux might ask for a handwriting expert to study the letters to Mme de Boulancy and compare the handwriting to that of the *bordereau*. Pellieux also had in his possession the file of fake telegrams that they knew would not bear close scrutiny. To compound this danger, the Italian Foreign Minister now wrote to his French counterpart, Hanotaux, to say that the Italian military attaché, Alessandro Panizzardi, was prepared to appear as a witness and attest that the sentences alleged to have been written by him mentioning Dreyfus either by name or initial 'were inauthentic'.

General de Boisdeffre quickly wrote to the Council of Ministers pointing out that Panizzardi's evidence, if heard, would be 'necessar-ily suspect' and therefore of no value. He also asserted, on his own authority, that the documents referred to *were* authentic. He attached three letters, the first two of which referred only to 'D.' but the third – the Henry forgery – spelt out the name Dreyfus 'letter by letter'. These convinced the ministers who then rejected the offer made by the Italians. The letters were returned to their file in the Ministry of War.

As Pellieux prepared his report, Boisdeffre and Gonse could feel that they had manipulated him to their satisfaction: Pellieux would exoner-ate Esterhazy. The only remaining danger was that such an exonera-tion would mean a prima facie libel of Esterhazy by Mathieu Dreyfus. Should Esterhazy sue? A civil action, out of the control of the army, with lay judges able to subpoena documents and subject them to scru-tiny and a lay jury to deliver a verdict, was too hazardous to be allowed.

But what reason could be given for Esterhazy to desist? A court martial. Esterhazy himself would demand a full court martial to re-establish his honour. He would be acquitted and through his acquittal the guilt of Dreyfus would be established once and for all.

After some initial hesitation, Esterhazy fell in with the plan. On 2 December, Pellieux received a letter from Esterhazy – a letter he had already seen in draft, and which he himself had amended – demanding to be tried by court martial. 'As an innocent man, the torture I have been enduring for fifteen days is superhuman . . . Neither a refusal to prosecute, nor a dismissal of charges, is enough to assure me the reparation I feel is my due. As an officer accused of high treason, I have a right to a court martial, which is the highest form of military justice. Only a decision reached there will refute . . . the most cowardly of slanders.'

The next day, General de Pellieux delivered his final report to General Saussier. It exonerated Esterhazy, finding no evidence for a prosecution, but found that Picquart had come 'very close to dishonour' and should be subject to an inquiry into his 'infringements against honour and grave errors committed while in service'. General Saussier, with the concurrence of the Minister of War, General Billot, and the Chief of the General Staff, General de Boisdeffre, rejected General de Pellieux's recommendation that Esterhazy should not be prosecuted. Acceding to the request of Esterhazy himself, they ruled that he should be tried by court martial on a charge of treason. Esterhazy was arrested and sent to the Cherche-Midi prison.

5: Comte Albert de Mun

On 3 December 1897, a debate on the Dreyfus Affair was scheduled in the Chamber of Deputies. The Deputy for the Aisne, André Castelin – the same man whose proposed questions to General Billot had caused so much alarm the previous year – had tabled questions for the Prime Minister, Jules Méline. Also scheduled to speak was the Deputy for Morbihan department, the distinguished Catholic statesman Comte Albert de Mun.

De Mun's intervention was of some significance because, although a royalist, he had accepted the *ralliement* – the advice of Pope Leo XIII to

French Catholics that they should dissociate themselves from the royal-ist cause and rally to the Republic. He had founded a Catholic work-ers' association, L'Oeuvre des Cercles Catholiques d'Ouvriers, which had shunned the Congress of Christian Democracy held in Lyon the year before because of its anti-Semitic tone.[30] So too had Monsignor Coullié, the Archbishop of Lyon, 'because of the part played in it by anti-Semitism and leading anti-Semites'.[31] De Mun had also founded a youth movement, L'Association Catholique de la Jeunesse Française, and on social questions was to the left of the Radical government. 'The Church', he said, 'is not a policeman in the service of bourgeois society.'[32]

Those such as Joseph Reinach who saw a Jesuit conspiracy behind the anti-Dreyfusard campaign noted that de Mun was a friend of the Jesuit priest Père du Lac, who in turn knew General de Boisdeffre and had brought Édouard Drumont back to the practice of his faith. But many of de Mun's writings and public statements had made clear his distaste for radical anti-Semitism. At the time of Dreyfus's arrest, he had written a letter condemning the Assumptionist paper *La Croix* for attacking 'Jews *en bloc*, simply to flatter the taste of the Drumontists and go one better than *La Libre Parole*.'[33] The contempt he expressed for Drumont had led to attacks on de Mun in *La Libre Parole*. 'Anti-Semitism, in practice,' he wrote to Père du Lac, 'leads to violent acts and injustices with which the Catholics cannot be associated, and which would gravely compromise them.'[34]

Was the case of Alfred Dreyfus just such an act of injustice? De Mun's speech was awaited with a certain trepidation by the government, but first the Prime Minister, Jules Méline, had to answer the question of the Deputy from the Aisne, André Castelin. What could the Prime Minister say to reassure the army, public opinion and the Chamber in the light of recent events?

'I will say at once what matters in this debate,' said Méline. 'This is not about Dreyfus. At this moment, there is not and cannot be a Dreyfus Affair. A charge of treason has been made against an army officer, and this question bears no relation to the other.'

Now the tall, aristocratic former cavalry officer, Comte Albert de Mun, mounted the podium. The deputies gathered to listen to him, not just to hear what he had to say, but to appreciate the manner in which he would say it: he was considered, after Jean Jaurès, the most eloquent speaker in the Chamber. De Mun opened by professing his love of his country, and of its army, and asserting his determination to defend both, *coûte que coûte*. And what was the threat facing the army now? The Jewish syndicate that was 'working for German wages'. He called upon the Minister of War, General Billot, to come before the Chamber because 'it is to the Minister that my question is addressed, for it is he, the head of the War department, whom I want to come here to avenge, in a solemn address, the chiefs of the Army and, in particular, the chief of the General Staff'. He went on:

> We must know whether it is true that there is, in this country, a myste-
> rious and hidden power strong enough to be able to cast suspicion at
> will on those who command our Army, those who, on the day when
> great duties will befall it, will have the task of leading our Army against
> the enemy and waging a war. We must know whether such a hidden
> power is strong enough to overwhelm the entire country, as it has been
> for more than fifteen days, putting doubts and suspicions in our minds
> about certain officers . . .

Interrupted by rapturous applause from the right, centre and also the left of the Chamber, de Mun declared:

> Ah, you asked that there be no political questions raised here! No, there
> are none. There are assembled here neither friends, nor adversaries,
> neither ministers nor enemies of the cabinet; there are only representa-
> tives of the country; there are only Frenchmen concerned to preserve
> intact what is most precious to us all, what remains, in the midst of our
> partisan discord and struggles, the common domain of our invincible
> homes – the honour of the Army![35]

Almost the entire Chamber now rose to applaud de Mun. Ferocious glances were directed at Joseph Reinach who sat, his arms folded, not saying a word – afraid that were he to open his mouth he would be set upon by the incensed deputies.

The Minister of War, Jean-Baptiste Billot, who had not been present
to hear de Mun's speech, was found in another part of the building
and brought to the Chamber. 'The case of Alfred Dreyfus', he told the
deputies, 'was judged fairly and without any judicial irregularity. For
my part, in my soul and conscience, I consider the verdict to have been
just, and Dreyfus to be guilty.'

Again, there was applause from the deputies. The Socialist Alexandre
Millerand mounted the podium and laid into the government for its
pusillanimity in the face of those who were advocating a reopening of
the case against Dreyfus. He also singled out Joseph Reinach 'who is
conducting his own campaign right here, whereas . . . he should be
better advised to rehabilitate members of his own family'. The reference was to Reinach's uncle, Baron Jacques de Reinach, implicated in
the Panama Canal scandal, an issue on which both the left and right
could unite.

A motion was now put before the Chamber which supported the
Minister's 'homage' to the army and his respect for the verdict on
Dreyfus, and condemned 'the leaders of the odious campaign under-
taken to trouble the public conscience'. It was carried by a large majority.

———————

Two days later, it was the turn of Scheurer-Kestner to face the Senate.
Castigated in the anti-Dreyfusard press as 'the general agent of the
Dreyfus syndicate' and 'a filthy Huguenot', he was heard out in polite
silence by his peers. His friend the author Romain Rolland, who
watched from the gallery, described Scheurer-Kestner – 'tall, erect
and pale, his beard white with yellow locks and the austere air of a
Huguenot of the sixteenth century' – mounting the podium 'as if he
were climbing the scaffold' and stepping down 'as though he were stepping into the grave'.[36] Scheurer-Kestner, too, had made the expected
protestations of love for the army and faith in its leaders, but in his
'slow, heavy, glacial voice' had appealed for reason and justice to prevail.
Only the former Minister of Justice, Ludovic Trarieux, supported him,
saying that serious errors had been made during his tenure of office and
measures should now be taken to rectify them.

The Minister of War, Jean-Baptiste Billot, answering for the government, repeated what he had said in the Chamber of Deputies: that 'in his soul and conscience, as a soldier and as chief of the Army', he was sure that Dreyfus was guilty. The Prime Minister, Jules Méline, said once again: 'There is no Dreyfus Affair.' A motion supporting the government's stance was then passed by the Senate with no dissenting vote.

6: The Court Martial of Esterhazy

With the guilt of Dreyfus and the innocence of Esterhazy the settled opinion of France's National Assembly and of the army's High Command, it was unlikely that Esterhazy would be found guilty of treason. Nonetheless, his court martial was staged with meticulous care. First a retired officer, Commandant Alexandre-Alfred Ravary, was appointed as investigating magistrate: he held daily consultations with General Gonse. Three supposed experts were asked to compare Esterhazy's handwriting with that of the *bordereau*: one was a retired architect, the second a palaeographer and the third a former school inspector. They were all agreed that the *bordereau* was not written by Esterhazy: some of the letters were similar, which suggested that his hand might have been copied by the traitor. And would Esterhazy, had he been the traitor, not have taken more trouble to disguise his hand? Thus both the similarities and the differences exonerated Esterhazy.

Commandant Ravary concluded that Esterhazy had no case to answer, but his recommendation was rejected and the court martial went ahead on 10 January 1898. The Dreyfus family were represented in court – Mathieu by his brother's lawyer, Maître Demange, and Lucie by a bright young advocate who had made his name defending the anarchist Vaillant, Fernand Labori. Seats were reserved for them, and for the first time Mathieu and Lucie Dreyfus set eyes on the man they held responsible for Alfred's suffering – Charles Walsin-Esterhazy. As he was led into court, he came so close to Mathieu that he almost brushed against him; he seemed to Mathieu like some great bird of prey with his aquiline nose and dark, restless, hooded, piercing eyes. Indeed, all the players in the drama were present except for Generals Mercier and de Boisdeffre: Commandants Henry and du Paty de Clam, Captain Lauth and General Gonse.

It was also the first time that Mathieu and Lucie Dreyfus had seen Georges Picquart, set apart from the other officers around him by the sky-blue uniform of a lieutenant-colonel in the Algerian *francs-tireurs*. Mathieu introduced himself to Picquart, who was seated next to Scheurer-Kestner. Later, after Picquart had given his evidence, Mathieu thanked him. 'You have no reason to thank me,' Picquart replied curtly. 'I was only obeying my conscience.'[37]

Auguste Scheurer-Kestner, like Mathieu Dreyfus, was able to make his deposition in open court: both were heckled by the large body of army officers following the proceedings. The court also heard from Marguerite Pays and Maurice Weil, but it ruled that Picquart's testimony, for the sake of national security, should be held in camera. The President of the court martial, General Henri-Désiré Luxer, was not just antagonistic in his questioning but, when Picquart brought up the names of Billot, Mercier and Boisdeffre, he allowed General de Pellieux to interrupt saying that he forbade Picquart to pronounce such glorious names in such a context. Picquart's evidence was followed by that of Gonse, Lauth and Henry. Henry said that he had seen Picquart show Leblois the secret dossier. Gribelin also swore on oath that he had seen the officer show the dossier to his civilian friend.

Shortly after eight in the evening of the second day of Esterhazy's court martial, the public were readmitted to hear the verdict. By a unanimous decision of the seven judges, Commandant Charles Walsin-Esterhazy was found not guilty. From the majority of those present came rapturous cries of 'Long live the army!', 'Death to the Syndicate!' and 'Death to the Jews!' Georges Picquart and Mathieu Dreyfus were jeered at and insulted as they left the courtroom. Esterhazy, by contrast, found it hard to make his way through the throng of well-wishers – those in the court, but also the crowd of over a thousand people waiting outside the prison who, when seeing him leave the Cherche-Midi prison with his escort of friends and fellow officers, shouted 'Long live the army!', 'Long live Esterhazy!', 'Long live the martyr of the Jews!'

The day after the acquittal of Esterhazy, the Senate voted to remove Auguste Scheurer-Kestner from his position as Vice-President; and on the other side of Paris, Georges Picquart was arrested on suspicion of imparting official secrets to a civilian and sent to the Mont-Valérien prison.

Émile Zola

1: A Letter to France

The acquittal of Esterhazy, and the confirmation by both the government and the National Assembly that the guilt of Alfred Dreyfus was not to be questioned, left the Dreyfus family and their supporters baffled and dismayed. It was clear that, whatever the evidence and however clear the reasoning, the French were unwilling to accept that they were being deceived by the leaders of the one institution that retained their respect – the army. It was a time of intense rivalry among the European powers, particularly in Africa. A force of 150 French riflemen under Major Jean-Baptiste Marchand was hacking its way through the jungles of central Africa from Senegal to the Sudan to establish a French presence on the Nile at Fashoda to thwart Britain's ambition of establishing its rule from the Cape to Cairo.

In France, there was little respect for the state as such. Charles Péguy, an ardent Dreyfusard, felt that the republican 'mystique' had died at the time of General Boulanger. The middle-class ascendancy that had existed since the Restoration – whether under kings, an emperor or a republic – with bankers and leading industrialists firmly in charge was now being challenged by anarchists, socialists and trades unions. France was a democracy; there were periodic elections. But there was a widespread belief, confirmed by the Panama Canal scandal, that the politicians were corrupt, manipulated by secretive and unaccountable agencies – the Jesuits, claimed the left; the Freemasons, claimed the right – and, in the case of Dreyfus, the Jewish syndicate.

Not that all the members of a particular group were necessarily of a like mind. There were some Catholic Dreyfusards and Jewish anti-Dreyfusards, but on the whole the different 'tribes' closed ranks. Jews, Protestants and free-thinkers thought the worst of the Jesuit-educated officers on the General Staff while the Catholic, conservative, aristo-cratic elements in society had a blind faith in the integrity of the High Command.

At the time of Esterhazy's acquittal, the centrist republican politi-cians were mostly concerned to establish their patriotic credentials by lauding the army: they had yet to see that the Affair could be used as a stick with which to belabour the right. A difference of opinion, however, had appeared on the left with Alexandre Millerand, as we have seen, vilifying the Dreyfusards and castigating in particular the Dreyfusard Deputy Joseph Reinach, Jean Jaurès wavering and Georges Clemenceau now a convinced Dreyfusard.

Clemenceau's political career had faltered because of his involvement in the Panama Canal scandal, and his identification with British inter-ests: 'aoh yes'! After losing his seat in 1893, he had concentrated on journalism and, even though back in the Chamber by 1897, he still saw the press as a powerful 'fourth estate'. As Pierre Miquel noted in his *L'Affaire Dreyfus*, 'the Clemenceaus, the Rocheforts, knew how to use the press and to inflate it with their faith and their passion . . . The Dreyfus Affair is above all about the manipulation of public opinion. At every stage, as it unfolds, one finds the press – not a press faith-fully reporting on what was taking place, but an aggressive, provocative partisan press . . . a "gutter press".'[1]

Newspaper proprietors were as partisan as the journalists who wrote for their papers – Drumont on the right, of course, but also members of the syndicate: Edmond de Goncourt was told that 'the money behind *L'Autorité*, that conservative paper, is supplied by a Jew, by a certain Fould, and there's a clause in his agreement by which Cassagnac [the editor] undertakes not to attack the Jews'.[2] Readers of the Parisian press did not expect detachment or objectivity. 'French people don't think for themselves any more,' wrote Drumont, 'they don't have the time, they no longer know how to, they let their newspapers do their thinking for them, their brains are made out of paper.'[3]

In order to help French people to think along the same lines as he did, Clemenceau founded a new newspaper, *L'Aurore*, in 1897, with an old leftist, Ernest Vaughan – a former Communard and follower of the anarchist Pierre-Joseph Proudhon. Sharing Clemenceau's conviction that Dreyfus was innocent, *L'Aurore* called for a review, and this backing was particularly welcome for the Dreyfusards because on 13 December, when the controversy over Esterhazy was at its height, *Le Figaro*, long an ally of the Dreyfusards, was forced by the large number of cancelled subscriptions to withdraw its support; its director, Fernand de Rodays, said that the paper would henceforth remain neutral.

It was now that France's best-selling novelist and polemical journalist, Émile Zola, entered the lists as the champion of Alfred Dreyfus. Zola would later admit that his initial interest in the Affair was as a novelist, and was focused on the dramatic possibilities in the story. 'The novelist was above all seduced and exalted by such a drama,' he wrote, 'and pity, faith, the passion for truth and justice all came later.'[4] However, rather than write a novel based on the Dreyfus Affair, Zola had joined the fray as a journalist and in articles for *Le Figaro* had gone beyond his denunciation of anti-Semitism in 'Pour les Juifs' to an unambiguous support for the Dreyfusard cause. Zola had an acute understanding of the power, but also the amorality, of the French press – not just 'the gutter press in heat, making its money out of pathological curiosity, perverting the masses in order to sell its blackened paper' but also those 'so-called serious and honest' papers which content themselves 'with recording all with scrupulous care, whether it be true or false'.[5]

On 6 January 1898, Zola published a pamphlet, *Lettre à la France*, in which he appealed to France's 'good-hearted and commonsensical people' not to believe all they read in the papers about Esterhazy and Dreyfus. 'A hundred papers repeat every day that it is unacceptable to public opinion that Dreyfus should be innocent, that his guilt is

necessary for the salvation of the nation.' This was perfect idiocy –
une parfaite bêtise. He poured scorn on Commandant Ravary, General
de Pellieux and 'the three experts who did not see at first glance the
complete identity of Esterhazy's handwriting and that of the *bordereau.*
Take from the street a passing child and show him the two samples:
"It's the same gentleman who wrote the two." He doesn't need experts
– the fact that the two are identical is obvious for all to see!'[6]

The time had come, wrote Zola, to call to account a press that shamed
France in the eyes of the whole world – 'papers such as *L'Écho de Paris,*
a literary journal, so often in the avant-garde when it comes to ideas,
and which has made such trouble over the Dreyfus Affair with vitriolic
and partisan columns that are unsigned'. And *'le Petit Journal* with its
circulation of a million, directed at the humble, reaching everywhere,
spreading error, misleading opinion, this is a serious matter. When one
has charge of so many souls, when one is the pastor of a whole people,
one must act with a scrupulous intellectual probity, or risk committing
a civic crime.'[7]

2: 'J'accuse'

Even as his *Lettre à la France* appeared in the bookshops, Zola was
working furiously on another pamphlet which went much further than
ridiculing Commandant Ravary and General de Pellieux, or the three
handwriting experts who had given evidence at Pellieux's inquiry. It was
clear that these men were just pawns, as were the judges who would
acquit Esterhazy. The time had come, Zola judged, to be done with
the sniping in the press and lob a mortar bomb into the debate. He
would write an open letter to the President of the Republic, Félix Faure,
naming names. Ravary and Pellieux were puppets: he would charge
the puppet-masters who were conspiring to protect a traitor and let an
innocent man rot on Devil's Island.

It was a dangerous venture. The press in Paris was partisan and unruly,
but there were laws against defamation that were enforced: Morès had
been imprisoned for libel and Zola had no proof to back up what he
said. He might be France's best-selling author with an international

reputation but that did not mean that he was immune from prosecution. Zola knew the risks he ran; indeed he compounded those risks by
writing in a deliberately provocative and intemperate style. Scheurer-
Kestner, Picquart, Leblois and Demange had tried a soft approach and
it had made no impression on public opinion whatsoever. Zola knew
his audience; they wanted heroes and villains, not a nuanced analysis
of legal procedures.[8]

'*Monsieur le Président*,' Zola began,

> Permit me, as a gesture of gratitude for the kind welcome you once
> extended to me, to express my concern for your well-deserved glory,
> and to tell you that your star, so happy until now, is threatened by the
> most shameful and the most ineradicable of stains ... This stain of
> mud on your name – I was going to say on your reign – is this abomi-
> nable Dreyfus Affair! A Court Martial is about to dare to acquit, under
> orders, an Esterhazy, flying in the face of all truth and justice ... and
> history will state that it was under your presidency that such a crime
> was committed. Because they have dared, I will dare too. I will speak
> the truth because I have promised to speak the truth if justice ... is not
> done in its entirety. My duty is to speak, I do not want to be complicit.
> My nights would be haunted by the spectre of an innocent man who
> is dying out there, from the most atrocious tortures, for a crime he did
> not commit.

Zola then outlined his understanding of what had occurred. He
named as the chief conspirator *un homme néfaste* – an ill-omened man
– Commandant du Paty de Clam. It was he who took advantage of
the 'mediocre intelligence' of the Minister of War, General Mercier, of
the Chief of the General Staff, General de Boisdeffre, 'who appears to
have given in to his religious bigotry', and of the Deputy Chief of the
General Staff, General Gonse, 'whose conscience seems to adapt to a
number of things'.

> But in the final analysis it was Commandant du Paty de Clam who
> first led them all on, who hypnotised them because he was involved in

spiritualism, occultism, he converses with spirits. One cannot conceive of the ordeal he put the unfortunate Dreyfus through, the traps into which he hoped he would fall, the mad inquiries, the monstrous fantasies . . .[9]

Having established the flimsiness of the case against Dreyfus, Zola outlined the cast-iron case against Esterhazy – his name on the *petit bleu*, his handwriting not similar to that of the *bordereau* but identical. Since 'a conviction of Esterhazy would inevitably lead to a retrial of Dreyfus', du Paty de Clam and the General Staff had moved to protect him. There had been a moment when the Minister of War, General Billot, seeing the evidence against Esterhazy, might have intervened. 'He hesitated for a brief moment between his conscience and what he believed to be in the interest of the Army.' He chose the army and from that moment 'he became as guilty as the others'. 'Can you grasp this?' Zola asks the President. 'For the last year, General Billot, Generals Gonse and de Boisdeffre, have known that Dreyfus is innocent, and they have kept this terrible thing to themselves. And these people sleep at night, and have wives and children they love!'

If these were the villains, Zola's heroes were Lieutenant-Colonel Georges Picquart and the Senator for Life Auguste Scheurer-Kestner. Both had warned how the case could

degenerate into a public disaster. But no. The crime had been committed and the General Staff could no longer admit it. And so Lieutenant-Colonel Picquart was sent away on official duty. He was sent further and further away until he found himself in Tunisia, where they tried eventually to reward his courage with an assignment that would certainly have got him massacred, in the very same area where the Marquis de Morès had been killed. He was not in disgrace, indeed General Gonse even maintained a friendly correspondence with him. It is just that there are certain secrets that are better left alone.

But Picquart would not leave the secrets alone so he,

the one decent man involved . . . who, alone, had done his duty, was to become the victim of truth, the one who got ridiculed and punished. Oh Justice, what horrible despair grips our hearts! It was even claimed that he himself was the forger, that he had fabricated the *petit bleu* in order to destroy Esterhazy. But, good God, why? To what end? Find a motive? Was he, too, on the Jews' payroll? The best part of it is that Picquart was himself an anti-Semite. Yes! We have before us the ignoble spectacle of men who are sunken in debts and crimes being hailed as innocent whereas the honour of a man whose life is spotless is being vilely attacked: a society that sinks to that level has fallen into decay.

By his own admission, Zola's letter was long but he ended it with a ringing denunciation of those who had conspired to see that the innocent Dreyfus was punished for the crimes of the guilty Esterhazy.

I accuse Lieutenant-Colonel du Paty de Clam of being the diabolical creator of this miscarriage of justice – unwittingly, I would like to believe – and of defending this sorry deed, over the last three years, by all manner of ludicrous and evil machinations.

I accuse General Mercier of complicity, at least by mental weakness, in one of the greatest iniquities of the century.

I accuse General Billot of having held in his hands absolute proof of Dreyfus's innocence and covering it up, and making himself guilty of this crime against mankind and justice, as a political expedient and a way for the compromised General Staff to save face.

I accuse General de Boisdeffre and General Gonse of complicity in the same crime, the former, no doubt, out of religious prejudice, the latter perhaps out of that *esprit de corps* that has transformed the War Office into an unassailable holy ark.

I accuse General de Pellieux and Major Ravary of conducting a villainous inquiry, by which I mean a monstrously biased one, as attested by the latter in a report that is an imperishable monument to naive impudence.

I accuse the three handwriting experts, Messrs Belhomme, Varinard and Couard, of submitting reports that were deceitful and fraudulent, unless a medical examination finds them to be suffering from a condition that impairs their eyesight and judgement.

I accuse the War Office of using the press, particularly *L'Éclair* and *L'Écho de Paris*, to conduct an abominable campaign to mislead the general public and cover up their own wrongdoing.

Finally, I accuse the first court martial of violating the law by convicting the accused on the basis of a document that was kept secret, and I accuse the second court martial of covering up this illegality, on orders, thus committing the judicial crime of knowingly acquitting a guilty man.

In making these accusations I am aware that I am making myself liable to articles 30 and 31 of the law of 29 July 1881 regarding the press, which makes libel a punishable offence. I expose myself to that risk voluntarily.

As for the people I am accusing, I do not know them, I have never seen them, and I bear them neither ill-will nor hatred. To me they are mere entities, agents of harm to society. The action I am taking is no more than a radical measure to hasten the explosion of truth and justice.

I have but one passion: to enlighten those who have been kept in the dark, in the name of humanity which has suffered so much and is entitled to happiness. My fiery protest is simply the cry of my very soul. Let them dare, then, to bring me before a court of law and let the inquiry take place in broad daylight! I am waiting.

With my deepest respect, Sir.

Émile Zola, 13 January 1898

Having written his letter, Zola decided that it would have a greater impact if it was published not as a pamphlet but in a newspaper. He showed it to Clemenceau and Ernest Vaughan who thought it superb; so too did the staff of *L'Aurore* to whom Zola read his polemic aloud. It was Clemenceau who came up with the idea of calling the piece 'J'accuse' the title to be printed as a banner headline on the front page.

The paper went to town on its scoop: 300,000 copies were printed; posters put up all over Paris; and several hundred extra paper-boys recruited to sell the paper in the streets. On the morning of 13 January 1898, more than 200,000 copies were sold in a few hours. To some, this was 'the greatest day of the Affair'. The Socialist Jules Guesde called it 'the greatest revolutionary act of the century'.[10] To Léon Blum it was 'a masterpiece', a piece of writing 'of imperishable beauty', and Zola's act 'was that of a hero'.[11] It was certainly a defining moment in the history of journalism; it has been often imitated, and is frequently remembered when its inspiration is forgotten.

———

'J'accuse' has been criticised for being too emotive, too melodramatic; the word 'crime' appears ten times in the course of twenty lines. But, given that much of what he wrote was inevitably conjecture, Zola's pamphlet was a remarkably accurate summary of the Dreyfus Affair. It laid too much responsibility on du Paty de Clam and not enough on Mercier, Boisdeffre and Gonse. Colonel Sandherr was left out of the frame altogether, as were his minions from the Statistical Section, Henry, Gribelin and Lauth. He was hard on General Billot: he was not to know that the letter the Minister had been shown naming Dreyfus, supposedly from Panizzardi to Schwartzkoppen, was a forgery, though clearly Billot had his suspicions. 'We are in the shit,' he told a cabinet colleague, Ernest Monis, 'but it hasn't come from my arse.'[12]

Zola's sensational intervention has also had its critics, both subsequently and at the time. Albert S. Lindemann concedes that 'J'accuse' put 'life back into the campaign to free Dreyfus', but 'even more powerfully revived the previously unsuccessful anti-Semitic movement of the late 1880s and 1890s'.[13] Scheurer-Kestner was shocked by Zola's tract. 'Zola took the revolutionary path,' he wrote. 'What a mistake! The era of stupidities began.' Scheurer-Kestner 'was not wrong', wrote Marcel Thomas, 'that the terrible misfortunes which the country was to know for many years were caused by these new tactics adopted by the revisionists'.[14]

The problem was not just the content of 'J'accuse' but also the reputation of its author, Émile Zola. His status as France's best-selling author certainly ensured public attention, but to the conservative

Catholic element in French public opinion his name acted as a red rag to a bull. Four years before, in 1894, Zola had published a novel called *Lourdes* – a story set in the shrine in the Pyrenees where the Virgin Mary was said to have appeared to a young shepherdess, Bernadette Soubirous. Miraculous cures were believed to have occurred when the incurably ill were bathed in the waters of a spring on the site of the apparition. These miracles were seen by Catholics as a divine refutation of the Positivist, atheist ideology of the Third Republic. The annual pilgrimages to Lourdes, largely organised by the Assumptionist Order, promoted 'an alternative image of France . . . one that bound spirituality to politics, and France to the ancient traditions of rural, aristocratic Catholicism'.[15]

Lourdes was particularly significant to the women of France, and the influence of women on the unfolding Dreyfus Affair should not be underestimated. They did not have the vote: the male champions of Liberty, Equality and Fraternity were afraid that their wives would vote for Catholic candidates. But their influence, in alliance with priests, was considerable – particularly when it came to Lourdes. The social mix among the pilgrims to Lourdes – the duchess and the peasant united in their care of the sick and in their Eucharistic devotions – offered a paradigm of unity that eluded the 'fraternal' republicans. There were 'hundreds of thousands of Catholic women in religious orders, mainly working in nursing and teaching and . . . untold legions of lay women active in fundraising and charity', revealing 'how comparatively small were the republican initiatives in such fields'.[16] And if they had saints to look up to such as St Vincent de Paul or St John Vianney (the Curé d'Ars), they also had devils to look down upon – among them, Émile Zola.

Already a *bête noire* for the graphic portrayal of sex in his novels, Zola had outraged Catholic opinion by fictionalising the case of Marie Lebranchu in his novel *Lourdes*, suggesting that after a miraculous cure she had had a relapse, which was untrue.[17] Zola had not denied that cures took place but said they were brought about by hysteria in suggestible neurotics. To Catholics, Zola became 'an emblem of the satanic nature of anti-clericalism', and the Assumptionists' magazine

Le Pèlerin (The Pilgrim), alongside illustrations of miraculous cures, had caricatures of Zola, depicted as a Freemason 'angered that his . . . novel had not undermined the shrine's success'.[18]

There were other reasons to dislike Zola. He was not a fully fledged Frenchman. His father, originally Francesco Zolla, was an Italian engineer who had settled in Aix-en-Provence. Émile's private life was unwholesome: he had two concurrent families, one legitimate, the other by his wife's chambermaid, Jeanne Rozerot. Mme Zola 'apparently had a previous chambermaid', noted Edmond de Goncourt, 'whom the good Zola started pawing about. She dismissed her and stupidly filled her place with another very beautiful girl . . . this was the girl whom Zola has made his hetaera for his second home.'[19]

Even Zola's fellow authors had misgivings about their friend. Goncourt described how, at a dinner with Ivan Turgenev and Alphonse Daudet, 'Zola, with his coarse hair falling straight down over his forehead, and looking like a brutish Venetian, a Tintoretto turned house-painter . . . suddenly complained of being haunted by the desire to go to bed with a young girl – not a child, but a girl who was not yet a woman. "Yes," he said, "it frightens me sometimes. I see the Assize Court and all the rest of it."'

Goncourt thought Zola mean-minded: 'Poor Zola . . . found it impossible to hide the spiteful envy which a colleague's success always inspires in him'; and Daudet, after hearing Zola belittle Goncourt, 'felt that the veil which had hidden the man's worst side from him had suddenly been torn aside, and that he had found himself in the presence of a false, shifty, hypocritical creature, "an Italian, yes, an Italian", he kept saying'.[20]

A competitive spirit in authors often leads them to an exaggerated disparagement of their *confrères*, and there was a widespread envy in the Goncourt circle of Zola's immense success. However, the facts of Zola's private life, the pornography of his novels and his dishonest portrayal of Lourdes led the very people whom the Dreyfusards should have tried to win over to decide that everything Zola wrote in 'J'accuse' must be lies.

The anger ignited by 'J'accuse', however, was deeper and more wide-spread than that felt by envious authors or devout ladies who believed in the miracles at Lourdes. For days after its publication, 3,000 youths went on the rampage in the streets of Nantes, smashing the windows of shops owned by Jews and assaulting the synagogue. In Rennes, the capital of Brittany, 2,000 rioters attacked the home of two Jewish academics. In Bordeaux, demonstrators shouted 'Death to Zola!', 'Death to Dreyfus!' and 'Death to the Jews!' There were demonstrations in Moulins, Montpellier, Poitiers, Tours, Angoulême and Toulouse. The army was called in to restore order in Angers and Rouen. In Saint-Malo, Dreyfus was burned in effigy. In Nancy, in eastern France, Jewish shops and the synagogue were attacked by demonstrators; and towards the end of January 1898 there were similar outbreaks in other cities in Lorraine. In Dijon and Châlons, police were called out to protect syna-gogues and shops owned by Jews.

By and large, anti-Semitic agitation was found in the larger towns and cities – notably in the west of France where there were few Jews but where there remained folk memories of the persecution of Catholics during the French Revolution; and in the east where there were substantial Jewish communities, and age-old conflicts and commercial rivalries came into play. There were rural communes in which anti-Semitic sentiment intruded on traditional festivities: at Chapareillan in the Isère, a stuffed model representing Zola, 'the impudent defender of the traitor Dreyfus', was burned in the bonfire; and in Saint-Jean-de-Maurienne in Savoy, a mannequin representing Zola and Judas was carried in the Mardi-Gras procession.[21] Even in the intimacy of an *haut-bourgeois* household in the Landes, outrage could be expressed with small, symbolic gestures: the French Catholic novelist François Mauriac, then a child, was told by his parents to call his chamber-pot 'Zola'.[22]

The worst riots set off by Zola's 'J'accuse' were in Algeria, where there remained a deep-seated resentment of the Crémieux decrees of 1871 which had given French citizenship to the entire Jewish community – seen 'as an act of favouritism on the part of the nascent Republic'.[23] Between 18 and 24 January 1898, there was

rioting in almost all Algeria's towns and cities. In Algiers itself, rioting that started on 18 January went on for several days. The Jewish
bazaar was destroyed and every day Zola was burned in effigy. In
some cases, the Jewish proprietors defended their shops, and in the
ensuing conflict there were casualties. A number of policemen were
wounded and a demonstrator killed. 'The Jews have dared to raise
their heads,' said a lawyer called Langlois. 'We must crush them.'
During the funeral of the demonstrator, Jews were stoned and one
beaten to death. There were more than 100 casualties and over 600
arrests. A young student, Max Régis Milano – like Zola, of Italian
extraction, who dropped the Milano to become Max Régis and
was described as 'tall, handsome, strong and energetic' – was the
most charismatic of the street-fighters' leaders. His adoring followers roamed the streets singing anti-Semitic songs and subscribed to
the newspaper he founded, *L'Antijuif*. Anti-Semitic demonstrations
continued for months after the publication of 'J'accuse', and in May
Édouard Drumont, invited to stand by Régis, was elected as one
of the six deputies from Algiers to the National Assembly with a
majority of 13,000 votes.

———————

In January 1898, there remained five months until a general election,
but the centrist government of Jules Méline could still be brought
down by defections in the Chamber of Deputies. It therefore had to
move with caution on the Dreyfus Affair. Méline and Billot understood
only too well that Zola, in writing 'J'accuse', meant not only to shift
public opinion in favour of a review but also to provoke the government to sue him for criminal libel – a legal process that would mean
examining the Affair in a civilian court. Both were keen to avoid this
and hoped that if they ignored 'J'accuse' it would soon become yester-
day's news. However, opposition politicians from both left and right
were not going to let the government off the hook. In the Chamber of
Deputies, on 13 January the Comte de Mun demanded that steps be
taken to punish 'the bloody outrage' of Zola's attack on the army's High
Command; and the Radical Godefroy Cavaignac, the former Minister

of War, assured the Chamber that support for the army came from the left as well as the right. He rebuked the government for not making public the conclusive evidence proving Dreyfus's guilt, in particular evidence of the confession that Dreyfus had made at the time of his degradation.

Present in the Chamber was Charles Dupuy, Prime Minister at the time of Dreyfus's court martial, who was well aware that Dreyfus had not confessed to his crime; but neither he nor the other statesmen who knew that this was a canard said anything to contradict Cavaignac. Méline repeated the government's position – that Dreyfus's guilt had been established by due process of law: it was a *chose jugé*, an established verdict. However, General Billot, speaking before him, and buoyed up by the applause he received when praising the army, assured the Chamber that legal action would be taken against Zola, and Méline was obliged to give the same assurance.

At a second debate, on 22 January, Méline, pressed by Cavaignac, confirmed that Dreyfus had confessed to his crime to his escort at his degradation, Captain Lebrun-Renault. He made clear that to attack the verdict on Dreyfus was to attack the nation. 'What we are defending are the permanent interests of the country: our military power and the renown of France abroad . . . Like soldiers, we will remain at our posts.'[24] His words were vigorously applauded by most of the deputies, but it was all too much for the Socialist leader, Jean Jaurès. Now, for the first time, he came off the fence on the Dreyfus Affair, denouncing the 'Jesuit-spawned generals protected by the Republic' and the pusillanimity of the government. 'Do you know what we are suffering from? What we are all dying from? I say so assuming full responsibility: ever since this affair began, we have all been dying from half-measures, reticence, equivocations, lies, and cowardice! Yes, equivocations, lies, and cowardice!'

Tumult and uproar. A deputy from the Gard, the Comte de Bernis, denounced Jaurès as 'the syndicate's lawyer'; Jaurès shot back that Bernis was 'a wretch and a coward'. More tumult. More insults. Bernis hit Jaurès. Soldiers were called in to clear the Chamber.

3: The Trial of Émile Zola

On 7 February, Émile Zola, and the managing editor of *L'Aurore*, Alexandre Perrenx, were put on trial on a charge of defaming not Commandant du Paty de Clam, or Generals de Boisdeffre and Gonse, but the judges who had acquitted Major Esterhazy. The libel was Zola's accusation that they had acquitted Esterhazy 'under orders'. This narrow definition of the libel would be a handicap, but it did not deter the Dreyfusards from preparing a case which, they hoped, would establish the criminality behind Dreyfus's continued detention. A committee was formed to work on Zola's and Perrenx's defence which included among its members the former Minister of Justice Ludovic Trarieux, Louis Leblois, Joseph Reinach and Mathieu Dreyfus. On Leblois' recommendation, Zola retained the lawyer Fernand Labori who had represented Lucie Dreyfus at Esterhazy's court martial.[25] Léon Blum assisted Labori. Perrenx was defended by Albert Clemenceau, the brother of Georges.

The presiding judge, Albert Delegorgue, was described by Joseph Reinach as 'a big and rotund man who was neither mean nor lacking in wit'; but the prosecuting attorney, the Advocate General Edmond Van Cassel, was 'surly and brutal', and both had a clear brief to keep the proceedings within the narrow limits of the charge. The jury was made up of merchants and artisans. When the trial opened, the courtroom at the Palais de Justice was packed with army officers, journalists, society ladies, government officials – among them Maurice Paléologue from the Foreign Office – and foreign diplomats, including military attachés such as Panizzardi. The only protagonist to stay away was Mathieu Dreyfus, who felt that his presence might cause a riot.

Lucie Dreyfus attended the first session – pale, nervous and dressed, as she had dressed since her husband's conviction, in black. She was inevitably a figure of pathos but also of curiosity and admiration: only three weeks before, on 19 January, the Dreyfusard paper *Le Siècle* had published some of the letters written by Alfred Dreyfus to Lucie from prison which successfully added poignancy to the case. She took the stand as the first witness, but when Fernand Labori asked her 'What is

your view of Émile Zola's good faith?' the presiding judge would not
allow her to answer. 'The question will not be put!' It was a phrase that
was to be repeated interminably throughout the trial.

After Lucie's mute presence on the witness stand came the evidence
of Leblois, then that of Scheurer-Kestner, but again the judge pre-
empted any attempt to widen the scope of the trial. 'The question will
not be put!' On the second day, General de Boisdeffre was called to the
stand. Marcel Proust, then a young novelist and ardent Dreyfusard,
described the arrival of Boisdeffre at the Palais de Justice in his novel
Jean Santeuil.

> A cab drew up. An officer got out accompanied by a gentleman in
> civilian clothes. 'That's not him.' – 'Yes, it is.' – 'Nonsense, that's not
> Boisdeffre.' – 'It is, I tell you.' The gentleman in civilian clothes was
> very tall. The most noticeable thing about him was a very high top-hat
> tilted at an angle. Listening apparently to the officer beside him with
> close attention, he moved forward slowly with a stiff motion of the legs,
> as though he were very tired. Every now and again he came to a halt.
> Though he still gave the impression of youthfulness his cheeks were
> covered by a delicate red and purple mottling such as one sees on garden
> walls in autumn when they are clothed in Virginia Creeper. There was
> a look of concentrated attention in his eyes but from time to time they
> blinked with a sort of nervous tic and now and again he plucked at
> his moustache with an ungloved hand . . . He seemed very calm and
> completely unhurried. As he passed, the onlookers raised their hats and
> he returned the salutation politely like a man of very high rank, some
> Prince of the church, who, knowing that he may excite envy, is at pains
> to disarm it by the perfection of his manners.[26]

If not a Prince of the Church, Boisdeffre was, as his bearing suggested,
a man of great importance in the French Republic – not just the Chief
of the General Staff of the French Army, but one of the principal archi-
tects of the Russian alliance which Zola himself had told Félix Faure
was one of the glories of his presidency. He did not seem to be someone
whose integrity could be put in doubt, and when he asserted from the

witness stand that 'Dreyfus's guilt has always been certain' it undoubtedly carried great weight in the minds of the jurors. When Boisdeffre
was cross-examined by Labori, he avoided answering any difficult questions by saying either that they would risk the security of the state or
that they put into question matters that had been settled once and for
all at the time of Dreyfus's court martial – the *chose jugé*.

After Boisdeffre, General Gonse confirmed what Boisdeffre had said.
General Mercier was then called to the stand – also 'a man of very high
rank' – serene, precise, speaking as though confident that no sane man
or woman could question what he said. He refused to answer questions
about the secret dossier and told the court that, while he had no reason
to reconsider the court martial of Dreyfus, if he did he would confirm,
on 'his word as a soldier . . . that Dreyfus was a traitor who has been
justly and lawfully convicted'.[27]

Commandant du Paty de Clam provoked derision among the
Dreyfusards in the courtroom by marching in and saluting the President
as if on parade. He too refused to answer most of the questions put
to him on grounds of national security. Henry, now promoted to the
rank of lieutenant-colonel, followed du Paty into the witness box. He
resorted to a different means of evasion: he was sick; he had a doctor's
certificate to prove it; and the effect of the medicine he had taken, and
insomnia, made it hard for him to understand the questions put to
him. At the request of General Gonse, he was excused. 'Colonel Henry
is extremely ill,' said Gonse. 'He has made a great effort to be here; I ask
the Court to excuse him.'

Alphonse Bertillon gave his evidence with the help of a blackboard
which he used to illustrate his theory of auto-forgery. It was ridiculed
by Labori and Albert Clemenceau, and he stood down amid derisive
laughter. 'Here is the sum total of the charge of 1894,' said Labori. 'The
bordereau! And there is the principal expert!'

Esterhazy was grilled by Albert Clemenceau with over sixty questions
about his private life, all of which he declined to answer. He looked
furtive, hunted, acutely uncomfortable, but was saved by the presiding
judge from answering the crucial question put by Clemenceau: had
he had any dealings with Colonel von Schwartzkoppen? The question

was inadmissible, ruled Judge Delegorgue, because it impinged on 'the honour and the security of the nation'.

'From which one may conclude', asked Albert Clemenceau, 'that the honour of the nation allows an officer to do these things but not to talk about them?'

Esterhazy, in a state of near-collapse, returned to his seat among the spectators to the cheers of the officers around him.

———

Colonel Picquart, also in uniform – the gold-braided sky-blue uniform of a *franc-tireur* – had been released from detention to attend the hearing. As described by Proust, his bearing as he entered the courtroom was in contrast to du Paty's. It was as if

> he had only just dismounted, and still retained even on his feet the quick, light movements of a Spahi, walking quickly straight ahead, with that free and easy carriage of the body which a man might show who had just dropped his reins and unbuckled his sword, and with a look of mild bewilderment upon his face advanced to the President's seat, where he came to a stop and saluted, not in military fashion, but with a mingled air of timidity and frankness, as though his every gesture was free of all formality or merely external significance but was overflowing like his walk, the sideways carriage of his head as would soon be apparent, his well-bred voice, with all the elegance and warmth of his personality.[28]

Youthful in appearance, sometimes abstracted 'as if an artist as much as a soldier', his face still red from the North African sun, Picquart described to the court how he had uncovered the evidence of Esterhazy's guilt; and how his report to his superiors had been ignored. Maurice Paléologue found Picquart's manner in the witness stand hesitant, unhappily caught between his duty to the army and his duty to the truth. Some of the Dreyfusards were disappointed by his detachment: 'more warmth would not hurt', said Reinach. The anti-Dreyfusards saw in the controlled way in which he gave his evidence a duplicitous cunning. If so, it was a cunning that paid off: his evidence so impressed his audience that there were shouts of 'Long live Picquart!'

Henry, who was considered well enough to be called back to rebut Picquart, admitted that his claim to have seen Picquart show Leblois the secret dossier was to be taken 'figuratively', not literally, but he insisted that 'Colonel Picquart has lied' – a charge that would later lead to a duel. Pressed with awkward questions by Albert Clemenceau, he pleaded a relapse and was permitted to leave the stand.

The defence now produced an array of expert witnesses to refute the 'insane' hypothesis of Bertillon and show that it was beyond doubt that the *bordereau* and Esterhazy's letters were written by the same hand. General de Pellieux came to the defence of the man his inquiry had exonerated. He insisted that, unlike Dreyfus, Esterhazy had no access to the documents named in the *bordereau*. He appealed to the patriotism of the jurors: 'What do you want this Army to become on the day of danger, which may be closer than you think? What do you want for the poor soldiers, who will be led into fire by leaders that have been demeaned in their eyes? It is to the slaughterhouse that your sons would be led, gentlemen of the jury!' The army would have been happy, he insisted, 'had the court martial of 1894 acquitted Dreyfus; it would have proved that there was not a traitor in the army, and we are still in mourning over that fact. But what the court martial of 1898 [of Esterhazy] would not admit, the chasm it would not cross, was this: that an innocent man should take the place of Dreyfus, whether he be guilty or not. I have finished.'[29]

But Pellieux had not finished. After Picquart had returned to the stand to demonstrate that Esterhazy could easily have had access to the documents listed in the *bordereau*, he was provoked to break 'the pact of silence' that until then had restrained him to tell the court the whole truth. There was a document – a document that had nothing to do with Dreyfus's court martial – that proved without doubt the guilt of Dreyfus. 'And that proof I saw . . . There came to the Ministry of War a paper whose origin cannot be doubted and which says – I will tell you what it says: "I have read that a deputy is to ask questions about Dreyfus. If someone in Rome asks for new explanations, I will say that

I have never had any dealings with the Jew. If someone asks you, say the same for no one must ever know what happened with him . . ." And, gentlemen, the note is signed . . . That is what I have been anxious to say.'

Pellieux was referring to the letter forged by Henry which had been used to reassure men like Billot and Pellieux behind the scenes but was never intended to be brought out into the open. 'The honest General Pellieux', wrote Marcel Thomas, 'made the gaffe which in the long term produced the key to Henry's machinations.'[30] The Dreyfusards already suspected the existence of such a letter; Billot had referred to it when lobbied by Scheurer-Kestner. But now with feigned astonishment Labori asked for the document he referred to to be produced in evidence. 'Whatever respect I may have for General de Pellieux's word as a soldier, I cannot accord the slightest importance to this document. So long as we do not see it, so long as we have not discussed it, so long as it has not been made public, it counts for nothing.'

General Gonse stepped in to undo the damage done by Pellieux's revelation. 'The Army is not afraid of the light. It is not afraid to say where the truth is to be found to save its honour. But discretion is required; and I do not see how, in the interests of national security, one can bring a document of that kind into open court.' But Pellieux was not to be restrained. 'And there are other documents,' he assured the court, 'which will be outlined by General de Boisdeffre!'

'What Pellieux has done is idiotic,' Henry told Paléologue; but any hope among the Dreyfusards that the cat might get out of the bag was demolished by the superlative gamesmanship of General de Boisdeffre. Recalled the day after General de Pellieux's triumphant assertion that he would tell all, this man of very high rank – indeed, of the highest rank in the hierarchy of France's most respected institution – addressed the court in a calm, emphatic and above all authoritative tone of voice. 'I will be brief. I confirm that, on all points, General de Pellieux's evidence is correct and authentic. I have not a single word more to say. I don't have that right; I repeat, gentlemen, *I do not have that right.*' To make further disclosures would put at risk relations with Germany, and might even lead to war. He emphasised the words, 'I do not have that right,' and concluded his short address with an appeal to the jury. 'And now, gentlemen, let me conclude by saying one thing. You are the jury, you are the Nation. If the Nation does not have confidence in the leaders of its Army, in those who bear the responsibility for its defence, they are ready to hand over that onerous task to others. You have only to speak. I will say nothing more.'

General de Boisdeffre left the stand, applauded by the anti-Dreyfusards in the well of the court. Maître Labori protested that he had not had an opportunity to cross-examine him about 'the document that offered no semblance of value or authenticity', but the presiding judge refused to recall the august Chief of the General Staff. His had been a triumphant tour de force, giving the shopkeepers and artisans on the jury the choice of either accepting the existence of secret but incontrovertible proof against Dreyfus or disarming the nation by precipitating the resignation of the chiefs of the General Staff.

They had no choice. Despite a dreary summing up by the Advocate General, Edmond Van Cassel, described by *La Libre Parole* as 'like drizzle from a grey sky', and despite three days of argument by Labori, an emotional plea by Zola and an irrefutable case made by Albert Clemenceau on behalf of Alexandre Perrenx – all, in fact, bundling the innocence of Dreyfus with that of their clients, and all heckled by jeers and catcalls from the public gallery – the jury returned a verdict of guilty. Zola was sentenced to a year in prison, Perrenx to four months, and each was fined 3,000 francs. They were released pending an appeal.

There was jubilation among the anti-Dreyfusards, with shouts of 'Long live the army!', 'Death to Zola!' and 'Death to the Jews!' Zola was escorted from the Palais de Justice through a hostile crowd by a phalanx of friends: had he been acquitted, said Georges Clemenceau, 'none of them would have emerged alive'. The celebration of the verdict extended beyond the Palais de Justice to other parts of Paris and continued throughout the night. As the news spread to the provinces, groups gathered in bars and bistros to pass motions of support for the army. Crowds marched through the streets shouting 'Long live the army!' and 'Down with the Jews!' 'I will not attempt to describe', wrote one of the brightest of the anti-Dreyfusard intellectuals, Maurice Barrès, 'the excitement, sense of brotherhood, the joy at the way things had turned out.' He wrote this in *Le Figaro*, the paper that had once supported the Dreyfusard cause.

Zola and Perrenx were not the only ones to be punished for defying the army's High Command. The day after the verdict was delivered, the Prime Minister, Jules Méline, told the Chamber of Deputies that 'There is no longer either a Zola trial or a Dreyfus trial; there is no trial at all . . . all this has to stop . . . And from now on, all those who would continue the struggle will no longer be arguing in good faith . . . We will apply to them the full severity of the laws, and if the arms at our disposal are insufficient, we will ask you for others.'

On 26 February, Colonel Georges Picquart was dismissed from the army for 'grave misdeeds while in service'. He was also deprived of his pension. Louis Leblois was dismissed as deputy mayor of the 7th arrondissement in Paris by the Minister of the Interior, Louis Barthou; he was later suspended from the Paris bar for six months 'for having consulted outside his office' and broken the professional confidence of his client, Picquart, to Scheurer-Kestner. Scheurer-Kestner, when he stood for re-election to the post of Vice-President of the Senate, suffered a decisive defeat. The eminent chemist Professor Édouard Grimaux, who had given evidence in favour of Zola, was dismissed from his post at the École Polytechnique.[31] Both Joseph Reinach and Jean Jaurès lost their seats in the general election in May.

The Pen versus the Sword

1: The Intellectuals

The presence of Édouard Grimaux on the list of those who suffered for their support of Dreyfus is evidence of a social phenomenon that is now common but had its genesis in the Dreyfus Affair – the rise as a power in moulding public opinion of 'the intellectuals'. Just as Zola's 'J'accuse' was the first intervention of an author in the affairs of state since Voltaire's championing of the case of Jean Calas, a Protestant wrongly accused of murdering his son, so the recruitment in the Dreyfusard cause of writers, artists and academics set an example which was frequently to be followed by later generations. 'I was the first Dreyfusard,' Proust would claim ('with pardonable exaggeration and pride', adds his biographer George D. Painter), 'for it was I who went to ask Anatole France for his signature.'[1]

The petition to which Proust referred was for a review of the verdict on Dreyfus, issued the day after the publication of 'J'accuse'. It was drawn up by Zola himself and Émile Duclaux, head of the Institut Pasteur. Duclaux, and Lucien Herr, the librarian at the École Normale Supérieure, circulated the petition among the scientists and scholars at their institutions. The net was extended by younger writers such as Marcel Proust who went around Paris collecting signatures. A second petition was organised by Professor Grimaux on 15 January. Among the signatories whose names remain familiar in the twenty-first century were the poet Charles Péguy and the painter Claude Monet.

The first petition was published on 14 January 1898 in *L'Aurore* under the headline 'Manifesto of the Intellectuals': the term 'intellectual' had been used before by Guy de Maupassant and by Maurice Barrès, but it was here that its trajectory into the contemporary consciousness began. The term was ridiculed – Barrès referred to the signatories in *Le Journal* as the 'demi-intellectuals', and the literary critic Ferdinand Brunetière, a convert to Catholicism, questioned the very idea that authors and academics should possess some superior wisdom when it came to the law. 'The intervention of a novelist,' he wrote, 'even a famous one, in a matter of military justice seems to me as out of place as the intervention, in a question concerning the origins of Romanticism, of a colonel in the police force.'[2]

Brunetière's anti-Dreyfusard stance went beyond questioning the qualification of a novelist to judge judicial questions; he had been critical of Zola as a writer long before the Dreyfus Affair.[3] His misgivings about intellectuals, which he expressed in a book entitled *After the Trial*, were part and parcel of his misgivings about academics as such, with their arrogant assumption that their insights into the working of the material world somehow placed them on the moral high ground. He did not understand, he wrote, 'what entitles a professor of Tibetan to govern his equals, nor what rights to obedience and respect are conferred by a knowledge of the properties of quinine or cinchonine'. To Brunetière, the Dreyfusard impugning of the integrity of the French High Command was symptomatic of the wider takeover of France by 'arrivistes' – 'Freemasons, Protestants and Jews', who all had 'the great advantage of not being tied by any commitment to the past'.[4]

Barrès was even more specific in associating the Dreyfusards with those 'foreign' elements in French society – the sons of immigrants like Zola, rootless cosmopolitans, Germanised philosophers and of course the academics at the École Normale where 'many students and the most respected masters were Jewish'.[5] His stance surprised and disappointed Léon Blum, who had tried to win him to the Dreyfusard cause.[6] Some of the antagonisms that came to the surface during the Dreyfus Affair harked back to past conflicts; Brunetière had attacked Zola in his *Le Roman naturaliste* of 1883, for example, and a similar antagonism was felt by another young right-wing intellectual, Charles Maurras, for the eminent and influential historian, Gabriel Monod. Monod was one of the earliest Dreyfusards, sceptical since the time of Dreyfus's conviction, who before Zola's 'J'accuse', on 6 November 1897, had published an open letter in *Le Temps* calling for a review.

Monod and Maurras had crossed swords long before the Affair over the Latin versus Germanic influences on Merovingian France – Maurras seeing Monod's historicism as part and parcel of an affinity for all things German. Monod was a Protestant from an extended family of Franco-Swiss-Danish industrialists whose choice of wives from the Protestant nations of northern Europe showed, said Maurras, that they were not true Frenchmen. As a boy, while studying in Paris, Gabriel Monod had lodged with the Protestant pastor Edmond de Pressené. Later, he had married Olga Herzen, the daughter of the exiled half-Russian, half-German revolutionary writer Alexander Herzen. It was only to be expected, then, said Maurras, that Monod should join the Dreyfusards' attack on the French Army.

Gabriel Monod had taught Bernard Lazare; Lazare was a friend of Léon Blum and Charles Péguy. Péguy, then a Socialist, was a militant Dreyfusard – 'the military leader' of a 'little army of Justice and Truth' formed by the students from the École Normale who congregated in a bookshop, the Librairie Bellas, that Péguy had bought with his wife's dowry. Léon Blum spent most mornings there. The little army would protect Dreyfusard professors from attacks by anti-Semitic gangs. They were heady days for the young, feeling themselves to be the protagonists of righteousness in these great events – a defining moment, as Péguy was to say, in the histories of France, of Christianity and of Israel.[7]

———

Moving in a rather different milieu, Marcel Proust was also an active Dreyfusard. His father, Adrien Proust, a distinguished doctor, originally from Illiers in Normandy, had considered the Catholic priesthood before turning to medicine. At one time *chef de clinique* at the Charité Hospital in Paris, he had been admitted to the Légion d'Honneur for his pioneering work on the spread of cholera.

In 1870, Adrien Proust had married Jeanne Weil, the Jewish daughter of a rich stockbroker – at twenty-one, fifteen years younger than her husband. Her family came originally from Metz in Lorraine. Marcel was thus half-Jewish, something he felt ashamed of, like his homosexuality. In the view of his biographer George D. Painter, Proust sought 'to palliate the guilt of his Jewish blood' and 'his awakening perversion' by assiduous social climbing.[8] Thanks to his father's high reputation and the money that came from the Weils, Marcel was raised in a privileged *haut-bourgeois* circle; he used to play with Antoinette and Lucie Faure, the daughters of the future President, in the gardens on the Champs-Élysées. However, as a young man his ambition was to be received in the drawing rooms of the aristocracy on the Faubourg Saint-Honoré, and by December 1893, the year before Dreyfus's court martial, Proust had gained an entrée into the salons of the Princesse de Wagram and her sister, the Duchesse de Gramont. Both these ladies were born Rothschilds, which meant that Proust had not yet reached the top because 'it was felt that their husbands had been declassed by marrying outside the nobility into non-Aryan money'.[9]

Some of France's most illustrious aristocrats had restored the fortune of their houses by marrying Jewish or American heiresses. 'It is interesting to note', wrote Proust's friend Boni de Castellane, 'that the great wealth of some Americans gives them a particular allure . . .'[10] De Castellane himself married an American, Anna Gould. Édouard Drumont, in *La France juive*, raged against the rich Jews who had bought the ancestral estates of the French nobility, and also against those French aristocrats who had 'tainted' their blood by marrying Jewish heiresses. Jules Guérin complained that the arrogant aristocrats ousted from their chateaux by the Revolution of 1789 had merely been replaced by 'our Jewish financiers and their friends, new *seigneurs*, insolent and without pity'.[11]

Anti-Semitism among the aristocracy itself had been exacerbated by their financial losses with the collapse of the Union Générale, and the first major anti-Semitic rally in France, in January 1880, was held at the Jockey Club. However, nothing was clear-cut. Boni de Castellane, ostensibly anti-Semitic, mixed socially with the Rothschilds and was keen to get the half-Jewish Sarah Bernhardt to dine with him. The editor of the main society newspaper, *Le Gaulois*, Arthur Meyer, was a Jewish convert to Catholicism married to a Turenne. The Comtesse Rosa de Fitz-James was a Viennese Jew with the maiden name of Gutman: she 'was said to keep a secret weapon in her desk: a list of all the Jewish marriages in the noble families of Europe'.[12] In fact they were published in the *Almanach de Gotha* and were widely known.

There were French Jews who preferred not to be identified as such. Both Proust and his mother sought to avoid a hotel in Évian filled with Jews, and did not want to be counted among them;[13] but when Marcel came to champion Dreyfus his Jewish connections could be neither concealed nor denied. 'What's the good old syndicate doing now, eh?' he was asked by the Prince de Polignac. Polignac was a friend of Charles Haas, the model for Swann in Proust's *À la recherche du temps perdu*; but he did not, like Swann, 'turn from those friends who became anti-Dreyfusards'. Proust's friend Marie Finlay also adopted the anti-Dreyfus cause, despite her Jewish parentage, 'in the name of good taste'.[14]

Proust's Dreyfusism was nurtured in the salon of Mme Straus, the daughter of Fromental Halévy and widow of the composer Georges Bizet: half Spanish through her mother, she was said to be the model for Carmen. Unlike the fickle Carmen, however, Geneviève Straus was 'notoriously' faithful to her second husband, the Rothschilds' lawyer Émile Straus, who happily spent his money on the entertainment of the writers, painters and politicians who came to her salon.

The influence of such society women on French politics was considerable in disseminating information and organising networks. It was in Mme Straus's salon in October 1897 that Joseph Reinach first declared that Dreyfus was innocent, and under his influence 'it became the G.H.Q. of Dreyfusism' where her son Jacques Bizet, her Halévy nephews and Marcel Proust organised the first petition of the intellectuals that was published in *L'Aurore*.[15]

When Dr Adrien Proust learned that his two sons, Marcel and Robert, had come out as Dreyfusards he refused to speak to them for a week.[16] He would not sign his son's petition: he was an example of an upright man with no trace of anti-Semitic sentiment who accepted the judgement on the question of Dreyfus's guilt by those he felt were in a position to know. He was a personal friend of many of the members of Méline's government, particularly of the Foreign Minister, Gabriel Hanotaux, who had used his influence to get Marcel a job at the Mazarine Library.

Hanotaux, it will be recalled, had advised against prosecuting Dreyfus in November 1894, not because he thought Dreyfus innocent, but because he feared the diplomatic consequences should it become known that documents had been stolen from the German Embassy. Along with other members of the Council of Ministers at the time, he was aware of the haste with which General Mercier had proceeded against Dreyfus, but this did not lead him to cast doubt on the *res judicata* in 1898. The only former minister to do so was Ludovic Trarieux, Minister of Justice at the time. Appalled by the anti-Semitic demonstrations at the Palais de Justice during Zola's trial, he decided to form an association to protect the rights of individual citizens. On 20 February 1898, Trarieux invited a number of lawyers and academics to his home for the first meeting of this League of the Rights of Man (Ligue des Droits de l'Homme). Though open to men and women of all religions and political persuasions, the reference in its name to the 1789 Declaration of the Rights of Man was unlikely to attract those who saw that Declaration as the source of the evils that came with the French Revolution. Its initial membership of around 800 grew, by September 1899, to 12,000: it was organised into 'sections', 'a term that evoked the radical activism of the Parisian *sans culottes* during the Revolution'.[17]

To counter the influence of the League of the Rights of Man, the poet, playwright and veteran politician of the right, Paul Déroulède, revived an association he had formed back in 1882 with Félix Faure, the League of Patriots (Ligue des Patriotes). Its original aim was to stiffen the resolve of the French to recover the lost provinces of Alsace and Lorraine, but when Déroulède had backed General Boulanger, he had lost the support of many of its republican members, and the League was dissolved by the government in 1889.

Now, nine years later, Déroulède sought to revive it, and exploit the political turbulence caused by the Dreyfus Affair to promote his ideas for constitutional reform – an executive presidency on the American model rather than a parliamentary democracy of the kind established in France and Britain. He had a considerable following: he was liked for his open nature and admired for his patriotic poems. The revived League of Patriots recruited 18,000 members, 10,000 of them in Paris.

Numerically, then, at their inception, the two leagues – one Dreyfusard, the other anti-Dreyfusard – were mismatched; and there was an even greater disparity when it came to the press. *L'Aurore*, despite the momentary boost to its circulation with the publication of 'J'accuse', sold around 200,000 copies each day as against 500,000 copies of Édouard Drumont's *La Libre Parole* and one and a half million of Ernest Judet's anti-Dreyfusard *Petit Journal*. On top of that, there was the enormous circulation of the Assumptionists' *La Croix* which, unlike the Parisian titles, reached deep into rural France with its many regional editions.

2: The Good Name of France Abroad

Jules Méline had said that his government would preserve France's good name abroad: the opposite turned out to be the case. The verdict on Zola, and the anti-Semitic riots which followed, shocked the world. In Belgium there was dismay, in the United States outrage. In Victorian Britain, Zola would not have been the nation's first choice as a champion of liberty: his novels dealt with sex with a frankness unimaginable in those of Dickens, Hardy or Trollope – or, for that matter, in those of Turgenev or Tolstoy – and so he was not, in the eyes of *The Times*, 'a novelist whom one would allow one's wife or servant to read'.[18] Nevertheless, his conviction was considered a disgrace. 'Zola's true crime has been in daring to rise to defend the truth and civil liberty,' said *The Times*. 'For that courageous defence of the primordial rights of the citizen, he will be honoured wherever men have souls that are free.'[19]

London's *Daily Mail* took the same line: 'France is disappearing from the list of civilised nations.' The British Ambassador in Paris,

Sir Edward Monson, though not yet convinced of Dreyfus's innocence, wrote in his dispatches to London of 'discreditable proceedings', a 'diabolical conspiracy' involving senior officers and 'a very great probability that justice has not been done'.[20] Even in Russia, where anti-Semitism was quite as powerful and prevalent as it was in France, the verdict on Zola received a bad press.

The German government in Berlin was in two minds about the Dreyfus Affair because, in a very real sense, the left hand of the government – the German Foreign Office – had not known what the right – the General Staff's intelligence service – had been up to. From the very start, Graf Münster von Derneburg, the German Ambassador, assured by Schwartzkoppen that he was not involved in espionage of any kind, had repeatedly and indignantly rebutted the charges made in the French press that the *bordereau* had come from the German Embassy. It was now clear to Münster that he had been deceived.

The theft of documents from the German Embassy by agents of French intelligence was now an open secret, but Henry, with the tacit encouragement of Gonse and Boisdeffre, now went beyond the genuine *bordereau* and Henry's forged letter from Panizzardi to Schwartzkoppen to draw the Kaiser himself into the Dreyfus Affair. An adjutant of General de Boisdeffre, Major Pauffin de Saint-Morel, briefed Henri Rochefort, the former Communard who had escaped from the penal colony in New Caledonia and was now editor of the right-wing *L'Intransigeant*, that Dreyfus had been named in a letter written by the Kaiser. On 13 December 1897, Rochefort published a story entitled 'The Truth about the Traitor'. In it he asserted that Dreyfus, realising that anti-Semitic prejudice would thwart his ambitions in the French Army, had written to Kaiser Wilhelm to ask him if he could transfer his allegiance to him and enter the German Army with the same rank. The Kaiser had replied to Dreyfus through the German Embassy in Paris accepting his offer of a switched allegiance, but asking him to remain 'as an officer on a special mission in France'. The Kaiser had promised that in the event of war he would 'at once assume his proper rank in the German army'. Dreyfus had accepted this condition 'and his treason then began, and continued up to the day of the arrest of the traitor'.[21] The French, Rochefort asserted, had photographs of the letters from the Kaiser to the German Ambassador – in one of which Alfred Dreyfus is mentioned by name. The originals had been returned to Münster von Derneburg after the Ambassador, learning of the theft, had threatened a diplomatic rupture between Germany and France.

This story of a letter mentioning Dreyfus, annotated by the Kaiser himself, was one of Henry's inventions: he had mentioned it to Maurice Paléologue who, knowing that it was out of the question that the Kaiser would communicate with a spy, realised that such a letter, if it existed, must have been forged. This was the moment when Paléologue, a mild anti-Semite, changed his mind about the guilt of Dreyfus.

However, the letter's existence was accepted in anti-Dreyfusard circles. The anti-Dreyfusard Princesse Mathilde Bonaparte, the daughter of Jérôme, Napoleon's brother, a *salonnière* during both the Second Empire and the Third Republic, told her fellow *salonnière* Geneviève Straus – a convinced anti-Dreyfusard – that she should know that 'there is irrefutable evidence' against Dreyfus. 'I have it from General de Boisdeffre himself that the General Staff has managed to lay its hands on some letters written to Dreyfus by the Kaiser; and there is no doubt about their authenticity.'[22]

Paradoxically, the only expression of sympathy for the position taken by the French General Staff and its Statistical Section came from their opposite numbers in Berlin. 'I feel convinced that the French Government has no choice but to hold out to the very last against any rehearing of the case,' Major Dame of the Nachrichtenbureau wrote to Maximilian von Schwartzkoppen. 'They will be made absolute fools of if the truth comes to light.' 'One would be very glad', he added, 'to see poor Dreyfus rehabilitated . . . But if the whole thing comes to public knowledge it will become difficult for the Government to prevent the Press and public from attacking the Embassy.'[23]

Maximilian von Schwartzkoppen, now back in Germany as Colonel of the 2nd Kaiser Franz Ferdinand Regiment of the Grenadier Guards, protested later in life that he too would like to have seen Dreyfus rehabilitated. 'My situation became extraordinarily painful,' he wrote.

I was now faced with the question of whether I should come forward with an explanation of the lamentable and terrible mistake and so secure the liberation of the innocent man who had been condemned. If I had been able to do as I wanted to, I should certainly have taken that step! But on reflection I came to the conclusion that I would not interfere in the matter, since as matters now stood, I should not have been believed; and also, since from considerations of diplomacy, such a step would have been inexpedient.[24]

Schwartzkoppen insisted that he was ordered to say nothing about the Dreyfus Affair; however, there were other reasons for lying low. Graf Münster was clearly fond of him, and it would be painful for him to discover how thoroughly he had been deceived by his military attaché. And there was Schwartzkoppen's reputation as a competent officer: how would it look if he admitted that he had thrown top-secret and highly compromising documents – the *bordereau* and the *petit bleu* – into his waste-paper basket?

Pressure was to build up on Schwartzkoppen as the Affair progressed in the course of 1899, but at least he was no longer in Paris. This was not the case with his friend Alessandro Panizzardi, the Italian military attaché, who had been dragged into the frame by mention in *L'Éclair* of the 'Canaille de D.' letter used as evidence against Dreyfus in his court martial. In bad French and an illegible hand, Panizzardi wrote to Schwartzkoppen complaining that his name had been brought into the affair by Esterhazy – something he considered outrageous 'considering that I have done nothing to him and did not even know him'. Panizzardi said he knew '*for certain*' that his letters to Schwartzkoppen had been stolen from Schwartzkoppen's flat in the rue de Lille by the porter's wife, and

are being made use of to condemn an innocent man, and all because these papers were not burnt. There is no knowing how it will all end . . . I have had plenty of hard work in sticking up for you, but that was my duty as a friend. But it must not be assumed that they know nothing here in Paris. The Scheurer-Kestner syndicate has passed round information in every direction, and many people now know all about what went on between you and E. But as they are eager to see the condemnation of Dreyfus confirmed, they all say nothing.[25]

Throughout these letters from Panizzardi to Schwartzkoppen, there is a mix of the misery of an abandoned lover and plaintive rebuke at being left to carry the can. To prevent their being opened by the French, Panizzardi's letters were posted in Turin; and Schwartzkoppen's replies have not survived. But it is clear from Panizzardi's further letters that Schwartzkoppen had rebuked him in turn. 'You know well', wrote Panizzardi, 'that if anything upsets me I am very free in my language, and you must bear in mind that what I have told you and what is being said here about me cannot be exactly pleasant for me . . .'

Panizzardi reported to Schwartzkoppen that 'the Syndicate' were attempting to blackmail him. He had been visited by

> two people who had declared that they had knowledge that I had in my possession all the receipts for the money that E. received from you; they then demanded that I should produce all these documents, or else they would start a campaign against me in the Press! I showed these two persons the door and threatened to set the public prosecutor on to them for blackmailing. You see that I am being allowed no peace, and they are trying to take advantage of my friendship with you to get further information.[26]

It is clear from Panizzardi's letters to Schwartzkoppen that the German and Italian governments understood quite well what was going on in Paris. The main objective of the German and Italian diplomatic missions was to avoid being contaminated by the seedy business of espionage. 'My relations with your Embassy had become intolerable,' wrote Panizzardi. 'Every time the Ambassador saw me he always asked me one and the same question, whether you had had any relations with E. . . . I always declared that I had no knowledge of it, and in the end I put long distances between my visits, in order to evade these questions.'

The Italian Ambassador, the Conte Giuseppe Tornielli, who, like Graf Münster von Derneburg, had been kept in the dark about the secret activities of his military attaché, had belatedly learned some of the facts and made contact with Auguste Scheurer-Kestner to impress upon him that the initial 'D' in the letter to Panizzardi from Schwartzkoppen used as evidence against Dreyfus could not refer to Dreyfus because Panizzardi had had no contact with Dreyfus. Nor, of course, had Panizzardi had any contact with Esterhazy, and the Italians objected strongly to being linked to such a 'scoundrel' in any way.

The friendship between Panizzardi and Schwartzkoppen was put to the test when an Italian publicist living in Paris, Enrico Casella di Collato, arrived in Berlin at the end of December 1897 with an introduction to Schwartzkoppen from Panizzardi: Panizzardi had written on his visiting card that Casella was a personal friend and 'a thorough gentleman'. Schwartzkoppen called on Casella on 1 January 1898 at the Kaiserhof Hotel where he was staying. When their conversation turned to the Dreyfus Affair, Casella asked him if he was personally convinced that Dreyfus was innocent. 'Yes,' Schwartzkoppen replied, 'I know that he is not guilty.' And when asked for his opinion of Esterhazy, Schwartzkoppen said: 'I believe he's capable of anything' ('Je le crois capable de tout').

The two men got on well. They dined together at the Kaiserhof on 3 and 5 January, and Schwartzkoppen escorted Casella to the Friedrichstrasse Station when he returned to Paris on 5 January. What neither Schwartzkoppen nor Panizzardi knew at the time was that Enrico Casella had been sent to Berlin by Mathieu Dreyfus. He offered to give evidence at Zola's trial but his offer was turned down. He then published an account of his conversation with Schwartzkoppen in the *Réforme de Bruxelles* and the *Siècle* in Paris. Panizzardi – instructed by his Ambassador the Conte Tornielli to distance himself from the Dreyfus Affair – blamed Schwartzkoppen for this indiscretion, while Schwartzkoppen felt he had been misled as to the trustworthiness of Casella by Panizzardi's introducing him as a personal friend and thorough gentleman.

3: Cavaignac

At the time of the general election, held in France in May 1898, there was a brief lull in the agitation surrounding the Dreyfus Affair. Zola had appealed against his conviction and once again Generals Gonse and de Boisdeffre faced the danger of allowing the Affair to escape from military jurisdiction. To prepare an examination of the evidence by civilians, General Billot, in his last months in office, instructed his son-in-law, a magistrate, Adolphe Wattine, assisted by a young officer, Captain Louis Cuignet, to assemble all the 365 documents relating to the Dreyfus Affair into one dossier. Their work was supervised by General Gonse, who made sure that genuine documents were mixed with forgeries, and even genuine documents altered to fit in with the narrative put forward by the General Staff.

The wisdom of this ordering of the evidence became clear when, in the course of the proceedings in the Court of Appeal considering Zola's request, the eighty-year-old Attorney General, Jean-Pierre Manau, made an impassioned speech, insisting that those who called for a review of the case against Dreyfus 'were neither traitors nor sell-outs, but guardians of the honour of the country'.[27] The judges allowed Zola's appeal on a technicality: the Minister of War had brought the case against Zola, but the Minister of War had not been defamed. It was for the judges at Esterhazy's court martial to bring the charges. On 8 April 1898, by a vote of five to two, the officers duly decided to sue Zola, and a second trial was scheduled for after the election.

During the election campaign that spring, the innocence or guilt of Alfred Dreyfus was not an issue because so few of the candidates had championed his cause. The Radical leader, Léon Bourgeois, and the Radical newspaper, *La Dépêche de Toulouse*, both took the line of *res judicata*, and the Socialists declined to become involved in this 'bourgeois civil war'. Even Jean Jaurès, now a proponent of review, did not mention Dreyfus in his election manifesto, but that did not save him from losing his seat in Carmaux.

The plight of the innocent man languishing on Devil's Island was not thought on the left to be something that would interest their voters; on the right, on the other hand, anti-Semitic rhetoric went down well. The Assumptionist Order organised support for 'nationalist' candidates through *La Croix*, *La Bonne Presse* and Justice-Equality Committees – Comités Justice-Égalité. In the Assumptionist periodicals, caricatures depicted 'bespectacled, hook-nosed Dreyfusards' as 'the cerebral degenerates' who sustained republicanism and Zola as a fat man obsessed with his own faeces.[28] With or without the help of the Assumptionists, the anti-Dreyfusards did well. Édouard Drumont was elected by a large majority in Algiers; the anti-Dreyfusards Paul Déroulède and Paul de Cassagnac also won seats. However, these conservative gains were mostly at the expense of the Radicals and Socialists and did not affect the final outcome. A majority of moderate republicans in the old chamber was replaced by a similar majority of moderate republicans in the new one.

The government of Jules Méline seemed safe, but this was an illusion. The left-leaning deputies in his centrist block were alarmed by the clericalist and anti-Semitic belligerence of the nationalists on the right and would not permit Méline to govern with their support. His government fell on 15 June 1898 and, after two false starts, the President, Félix Faure, asked the Radical, Henri Brisson, to form a government. The right – Drumont and his friends – had voted to bring down Méline because of his perceived weakness in the face of Dreyfusard agitation. Brisson, to spike their guns, appointed as Minister of War in his cabinet Godefroy Cavaignac – a Radical and republican with an impeccable pedigree: his grandfather had been a prominent revolutionary in 1789, voting for the execution of King Louis XVI; his father was the general who had restored order in Paris in the 1848 revolution and stood for president against Louis Napoleon; and Cavaignac himself, as a student at the Sorbonne, had established his republican credentials by refusing to accept a prize from the hands of the Prince Imperial.

Cavaignac had already served under Brisson as Under-Secretary for War in the mid-1880s, and under Léon Bourgeois as Minister of War two years before his present appointment. He was therefore no novice when it came to the exercise of power and became the 'preponderant personality' in the new government.[29] He had gained a reputation for integrity and incorruptibility at the time of the Panama Canal scandal, and was held in high regard for his commitment to social justice.

Cavaignac was also a patriot and convinced anti-Dreyfusard. This should have made his appointment as Minister of War welcome to Boisdeffre and Gonse, but in fact his inflexible sense of mission and famous integrity were not as reassuring to the conspirators when it came to Dreyfus as the shifty inertia of Méline and Billot. Cavaignac was anything but inert, and was determined upon taking office to settle the Dreyfus Affair once and for all. He would cut loose the seedy Esterhazy and nail the treacherous Picquart. On 28 June 1898, he instructed Colonel Gaudérique Roget, chief of the Fourth Bureau of the General Staff, and Captain Louis Cuignet, who had worked with Gonse and Wattine on the file, to extract those documents, so often referred to but not yet brought into the public domain, that established definitively the guilt of Dreyfus.

Boisdeffre and Gonse had hoped that the size of the dossier would deter anyone from looking too closely at its contents, but Cavaignac was not to be put off. Boisdeffre, as a precaution, told Cavaignac that he himself had not authenticated every item in the dossier but his 'unlimited trust in Lieutenant-Colonel Henry had seemed to him a sufficient guarantee'. He also advised Cavaignac of the dangers of referring to those documents which implicated the military attachés of foreign powers. Cavaignac ignored his advice.

———

A debate in the Chamber of Deputies was scheduled for 7 July 1898. Cavaignac decided he would make this debate the occasion of a major speech on the Dreyfus Affair. He equipped himself with the pertinent documents, among them a copy of notes supposedly made by Captain Lebrun-Renault at the time of Dreyfus's 'confession' in 1898. Two days before the debate, he showed sixty of the most pertinent documents to the Prime Minister, Henri Brisson, and the Minister of Justice, Ferdinand Sarrien. Captain Cuignet was there to point out their signif-icance. Brisson and Sarrien were predictably impressed by the letter from Panizzardi to Schwartzkoppen which mentioned Dreyfus by name. Cavaignac was authorised to proceed with his plan to 'pulverize' the syndicate.[30]

Cavaignac's sense of mission was invigorated by a move made by the Dreyfusards that same day: Lucie Dreyfus applied to the Minister of Justice, Sarrien, to have her husband's conviction annulled on the grounds that secret documents had been unlawfully shown to the judges at his court martial and not to the defence. Such audacity enraged the anti-Dreyfusards, and when the debate opened on 7 July the terrier-like Deputy for the Aisne, André Castelin, demanded that punitive measures be taken against the leaders of the Dreyfusards – Mathieu Dreyfus, Georges Picquart, Joseph Reinach and Edgar Demange.

Cavaignac then mounted the rostrum and in his 'dry and harsh' tone of voice began his peroration. He spoke caustically of Esterhazy, 'an officer who tomorrow will receive the punishment he deserves', and gently of the Dreyfusards who through 'a misunderstanding' had come into conflict with the army 'whose sacred mission is to defend the patrimony of France, not only her material patrimony, but her intellectual and moral patrimony as well'. 'Never', Cavaignac insisted, 'could any consideration of public welfare, whatever it be, lead me to keep an innocent man in prison,' but the proofs of Dreyfus's guilt were overwhelming. It sufficed to produce three 'out of thousands'. The first was the letter from Alessandro Panizzardi to Maximilian von Schwartzkoppen mentioning 'that scoundrel D.'. The second was a letter which actually mentioned Dreyfus by name. And the third was evidence that, at the time of his degradation, Dreyfus had confessed his guilt to Captain Lebrun-Renault. In the face of these incontrovertible proofs, it was surely time for all Frenchmen to accept the verdict and 'proclaim that the Army which is their pride and their hope . . . is not only strong with the nation's trust, but strong as well in the justice of the acts that it has accomplished'.

The overwhelming majority of deputies rose to applaud Cavaignac, who, as he descended from the rostrum, basked in the euphoria of his admirers on both left and right. The Prime Minister, Henri Brisson, hoping to share in Cavaignac's glory, declared that he had spoken for the government, not just for himself. A motion that Cavaignac's speech should be posted in every commune in France was carried unanimously with sixteen abstentions: fifteen Socialists and the former Prime Minister, Jules Méline.

The Dreyfusards were shocked and dismayed that Cavaignac should have decided so emphatically in favour of documents which they knew must have been forged. His reputation for integrity and a commitment to justice led the press to accept what he had said. Only Jaurès realised that Cavaignac's speech had in fact furthered the Dreyfusard cause. The new Minister of War had conceded that the anti-Dreyfusards had acted in good faith; that diplomatic embarrassment or a fear of war was an insufficient reason to conceal the roles of the German and Italian military attachés; that *res judicata* should not block an examination of the evidence against Dreyfus; that secret documents had indeed been shown to the judges; that Esterhazy was a scoundrel who would be thrown out of the army. And the *bordereau*, the only real evidence against Dreyfus, had not been mentioned by Cavaignac at all.

If all this was clear to Jaurès, it was also evident to Gonse and his friends in the Statistical Section. 'The Minister would have done well not to have read the letters,' remarked Lieutenant-Colonel Henry, whose forgeries, quoted by Cavaignac, were now posted in all the 36,000 communes in France. And what would be made of Méline's abstention? Gonse agreed with Henry. The apparent triumph was in fact a disaster. Things would not end well.[31]

In the other camp, because the forged letters were now in the public domain, Georges Picquart felt able to write to the Prime Minister, Henri Brisson, to tell him that he was 'in a position to establish before any competent jurisdiction that the two documents dated 1894 cannot be applied to Dreyfus and that the one dated 1896 has every appearance of being a forgery'.[32] This letter, sent on by Brisson to Cavaignac, so enraged the Minister of War that he initiated legal proceedings against Picquart.

Picquart, meanwhile, was involved in legal proceedings of his own: he had filed a complaint against persons unknown for sending him telegrams in Tunisia, one signed 'Speranza', the other 'Blanche', intended to prove that he was in league with the Dreyfusards. The examining magistrate in charge of the case was Paul Bertulus, first drawn into the Dreyfus Affair over Esterhazy's compromising letters to Mme de Boulancy (the 'Uhlan' letter: see p. 201 above). It was clear to Picquart that the fake telegrams were the work of his former subordinates in the Statistical Section, but which of them could be charged with the crime?

Then, at the beginning of July 1898, a witness came forward to say that he knew all about the provenance of the false telegrams and more besides. This witness was Christian Esterhazy, the nephew of Charles, who had finally discovered that the money he had inherited from his father Paul, and which he had thought was invested with the Rothschilds, had in fact been spent by his uncle on high living and stock-market speculations. To punish his uncle Christian had made contact with the Dreyfusards and presented them with documentary proof of the contacts between Esterhazy and du Paty de Clam. He said that one of the telegrams under investigation had been written by Esterhazy's mistress, Marguerite Pays. To gain a sample of her hand-writing, Mathieu Dreyfus had flowers sent to her by an intermediary which elicited a polite note of thanks in a hand identical to that of the 'Speranza' telegram.

There was now a race between the military and civilian branches of justice to arrest Esterhazy. Bertulus got there first. Esterhazy and Marguerite Pays were both arrested on 12 July. On the same day, the order was signed to proceed against Picquart, and on 14 July Picquart joined Esterhazy in the Santé prison. Du Paty de Clam had been named by Christian Esterhazy as the officer who had colluded with his uncle, and both the archivist of the Statistical Section, Gribelin, and General Gonse – summoned by Cavaignac for an explanation – were happy to make du Paty the scapegoat. Henry realised that things were unravelling: he 'could feel the ground quaking' and, when confronted by his old friend Bertulus, he broke down and wept, shouting: 'Save us, save us . . . you must save the honour of the Army.'[33]

However, Henry had recovered sufficient composure when giving evidence against Picquart before the military investigating magistrate, Colonel Pierre-Élie Fabre. Henry, together with Lauth and Gribelin, insisted that they had seen Picquart showing top-secret documents to Picquart's lawyer Leblois. Fabre therefore ordered the arrest of Leblois; but could Leblois, as a civilian, be brought before a military court?

On 18 July, these two legal processes provoked by the Dreyfus Affair were supplemented by a third – the opening at Versailles of the second trial of Émile Zola on the charge of defamation. His lawyer, Maître Labori, had objected to the trial being held outside Paris, and had tried to get the scope of the charge extended beyond Zola's claim that the military judges in Esterhazy's court martial had acquitted him 'under orders'. All these judicial moves failed. In protest, and on the advice of Labori, Zola withdrew from his own trial, leaving the courtroom to cries of 'Coward!', 'Traitor!', 'Go back to the Jews!' and, from Paul Déroulède, 'Get out of France! Go back to Venice!'

Along with Alexandre Perrenx, the managing editor of *L'Aurore*, Zola was sentenced *in absentia* to a year's imprisonment. But by then Zola had taken the advice of his detractors: he had left France for England, where he would remain under an assumed name for the next eleven months.

———

Zola had eluded Cavaignac's fanatical attempt to punish the Dreyfusards, but the Minister of War had others besides Zola in his sights. He now elaborated a plan to bring before the Senate, constituted as a High Court, all the leading Dreyfusards on a charge of treason. The Prime Minister, Henri Brisson, and the other ministers turned it down flat. Cavaignac was frustrated by his colleagues' pusillanimity; he would have to bring charges of defamation instead. But he was consoled by developments in the courts. The Court of Appeal ruled that Commandant du Paty de Clam, as an officer, did not fall under the jurisdiction of the civilian examining magistrate Bertulus; and on 12 August a grand jury dismissed the charges against Esterhazy and Marguerite Pays. Both were released from gaol. The only person now in prison and facing criminal charges of revealing state secrets to Leblois was Georges Picquart.

The Road to Rennes

1: Lieutenant-Colonel Henry

Captain Louis Cuignet, the young officer asked by General Billot, when he was still Minister of War, to assist his son-in-law, the magistrate Adolphe Wattine, in examining and ordering the dossier on Dreyfus at the War Office, had been told to continue his work, without the help of Wattine, by the new Minister, Godefroy Cavaignac. Cavaignac would need all the evidence at his fingertips for the actions he planned to bring against the Dreyfusards.

On 13 August 1898, the day after charges of forgery had been dropped against Charles Esterhazy and Marguerite Pays, Cuignet was working late at the War Office. He was taking a closer look at the critical 1896 letter from Panizzardi to Schwartzkoppen, mentioning Dreyfus by name, which his boss, Cavaignac, had quoted in his powerful speech in the Chamber of Deputies on 7 July, and which was now posted outside the *mairie* of every commune in France. The letter had been written on a piece of paper with faint coloured lines. Holding it up to the light of the lamp on his desk, Cuignet noticed that the colour of these lines at the top and bottom of the letter differed slightly in hue from those in the middle: all were blue but the former were a blue-grey whereas the latter were a blue tinged with mauve. Clearly, the central section had been inserted between the opening and closing sections of the letter. This crucial piece of evidence in the case against Alfred Dreyfus had been forged.

The next morning, Cuignet reported his discovery to General Roget, Cavaignac's *chef de cabinet*. In daylight, the forgery was less apparent, but, with curtains drawn and the letter held up to the light, Roget was forced to acknowledge that Cuignet was right. The two officers took the letter to the Minister, Cavaignac. He too had to accept the evidence of forgery. His thoughts and feelings at that moment are not on record but can be imagined. Cavaignac's absolute certainty that Dreyfus was guilty had come up against the fact that a critical piece of evidence that had been used to convince him had been fabricated by someone in the Statistical Section. Should he, like General Gonse when told about the *petit bleu* by Picquart, tell Cuignet and Roget to ignore this inconvenient discovery?

Countering this temptation was Cavaignac's self-image as a man of unimpeachable integrity. To cover up a crime, whatever the motives of the criminal, and however justifiable it might seem in terms of *raison d'état*, went against everything Cavaignac had stood for since the time of the Panama Canal scandal. Should he sacrifice this reputation because of the imbecile antics of the Statistical Section, and no doubt some senior officers in the General Staff?

Cavaignac pondered these questions over the next two weeks. Roget and Cuignet were ordered to keep what had transpired to themselves. When the time came, it would be Cavaignac who would inform the Prime Minister and his cabinet colleagues of Cuignet's discovery. On 15 August Cavaignac went to Mâcon in Burgundy with the Minister of Justice, Ferdinand Sarrien: he said nothing about the forgery to Sarrien. Eight days later he was in Le Mans, in the north-west of France, and made speeches, as he had done in Mâcon, professing his love and admiration for the army.[1]

Back in Paris, while Cavaignac was on his tour of the provinces, Charles Esterhazy was summoned before a board convened by the Military Governor of Paris, General Émile Zurlinden, at Cavaignac's request, to judge whether Esterhazy should remain an officer in the army. Esterhazy was not prepared to go down without a fight: on 23 August he persuaded Drumont to publish an article in *La Libre Parole* suggesting that Cavaignac's vendetta against Esterhazy was at the behest of the Jewish syndicate which, when it had disposed of Esterhazy, would move on to bring down du Paty de Clam, Lauth, Henry, Boisdeffre and General Mercier himself. To discharge Esterhazy would be to betray the army.

Esterhazy defended himself aggressively before the board. He claimed that he had turned down an offer from the syndicate of 600,000 francs to admit to being the author of the *bordereau*; and that the 'dirty tricks' he had played to thwart Picquart had been the idea of Commandant du Paty de Clam, acting in the name of the General Staff. Called as a witness, du Paty found it difficult to deny this: Esterhazy had kept a compromising letter in his handwriting. Esterhazy threatened to say more and so the board, while it recommended discharging Esterhazy for 'habitual misconduct', acquitted him of having done anything dishonourable. General Zurlinden suggested to Cavaignac that he extend 'a certain indulgence towards Commandant Esterhazy', not because Esterhazy merited it, but because the inquiry had turned up 'grave revelations about the role of certain officers in the Army General Staff' in the Esterhazy affair. Cavaignac ignored this tacit warning that Esterhazy, if pushed too hard, might spill more beans: he at once signed the order for Esterhazy's discharge from the army. But it no doubt brought home to him the high probability that news of the forgery would eventually leak out, and that it could only enhance his reputation for honesty and integrity if he were to be the one who made it known.

There could be no real doubt about whom the forger could be. On 30 August Generals de Boisdeffre and Gonse were summoned to the War Office to attend the questioning by the Minister of Lieutenant-Colonel Hubert Joseph Henry. Before the interrogation began, Boisdeffre was shown the evidence of forgery by Cavaignac and appeared astonished. At 2.30 p.m. Henry appeared, accompanied by Gonse. Colonel Roget took the minutes of the meeting but the questioning was undertaken by Cavaignac himself. He pointed out the different coloured lines in the Panizzardi letter and asked Henry for an explanation. Henry blustered. Cavaignac persisted. 'Given the facts, no explanation would be as serious as an inadequate one. When and how did you reassemble this document?' At first Henry denied that he had fabricated anything, but little by little Cavaignac's persistent questioning wore him down. He admitted that he had 'arranged a few sentences'.

'Which of the words did you invent?'

'I don't remember.'

'Who gave you the idea of doing what you did?'

'No one.'

Generals Gonse and de Boisdeffre said nothing.

'My superior officers were very worried,' Henry went on. 'I wanted to reassure them, give them some serenity. I told myself: Let's add a sentence: if we only had definitive proof . . . No one knew about it. I acted solely in the interests of my country.'

'Now, Henry,' said Cavaignac. 'I appeal to your honour as a soldier. Tell me the truth.' In that dry, rasping voice that had so impressed the Chamber of Deputies, the Minister continued with his interrogation. Eventually, the truth emerged which Cavaignac summarised as follows: 'In 1896, you received an envelope with a letter inside, an insignificant letter; you suppressed the letter and fabricated another one?'

'Yes.'

Colonel Roget took Henry into another room. Boisdeffre, who had said nothing throughout the interrogation, now went to Cavaignac's desk, took pen and paper, and wrote:

> *Monsieur le Ministre.* It has just been proved to me that my trust in Colonel Henry, Chief of the Intelligence Service, was not justified. That trust, which was absolute, has led me to be deceived, and declare a document genuine when it was not, and to present it to you as such. As a result of these developments, *Monsieur le Ministre*, I have the honour of asking you to accept my resignation.

Cavaignac tried to persuade Boisdeffre to change his mind: he was unable to see, as clearly as the Chief of the General Staff, that the game was up – that, 'like a sandcastle before a wave, the fragile evidence which the General Staff had taken four years to build' was about to collapse.[2]

'Anyone can make a mistake,' said Boisdeffre, 'but not everyone has sworn before a jury that a document is genuine when it is not . . . When one finds oneself in such a situation, the only thing to do is to leave.'

The news of the forgery was made public in a terse communiqué issued by the Agence Havas that same day. 'Today in the office of the Minister of War, Lieutenant-Colonel Henry was acknowledged to be, and acknowledged himself to be, the author of the letter dated October 1896 in which Dreyfus is named. The Minister of War has immediately ordered the arrest of Lieutenant-Colonel Henry, who has been taken to the Fortress of Mont-Valérien.'[3]

Henry had had a premonition of disaster when he had broken down in tears before Judge Paul Bertulus and begged him to save the honour of the army. That crisis had passed and he had had good reason to suppose that the revisionists had been thwarted. Revisionist sentiment was still confined, on the whole, to Jewish *salonnières* and Parisian 'intellectuals'. Sentiment in rural France, if it was aware of the Dreyfus Affair, was firmly anti-Dreyfusard. In Henry's home village of Pogny, a commune of 589 citizens, a young man was charged with abuse for calling another 'a no-good bastard, a liar, a Zola, a Dreyfus'.[4] Henry had planned to return to Pogny that August, as he did every year, for the opening of the hunting season.[5]

Now – a concession not granted to Alfred Dreyfus in October 1894 – Henry was allowed by his escort, Colonel Ferry, an adjutant from the fortress of Mont-Valérien, to call in on his wife and child in their small flat on the avenue Duquesne and pick up a set of civilian clothes, clean linen and some personal belongings. He told his wife Berthe what had happened, but added that all would be well. 'My conscience is clear.' In the coach taking him to Mont-Valérien to the west of Paris he was less sanguine. 'My poor wife, my poor little boy,' he said to Colonel Ferry. 'Everything has collapsed in an instant. I will not be there for the opening of the hunt. What will they think?'[6] The son of the soil who had risen from the ranks to be the de facto chief of French military intelligence, one-time mayor of Pogny, now faced criminal charges, imprisonment and degradation.

At the Mont-Valérien fortress he was put in a room in the officers'
wing – the same room in which Colonel Picquart had been confined
the previous winter. He was treated courteously, but solitude did not
alleviate his agitated condition. On the morning of 31 August, he asked
for paper, pen, ink and a bottle of rum. He wrote to General Gonse.
'General, I have the honour of requesting that you agree to come and
see me here. I absolutely must speak to you.' He sent off the letter but
clearly did not expect his request to be met. Drinking the rum from a
tumbler, he next he wrote to his wife.

My adored Berthe, I see that I am abandoned by everyone except you,
and yet you know in whose interests I acted. My letter is a copy and
contains nothing, absolutely nothing, that is forged. It merely confirms
what I had learned verbally a few days earlier. I am completely innocent,
they know it, and it will become clear to all later on; but right now, I
can't speak. Take good care of our adored little Joseph, and go on loving
him, as I love him and as I love you.

Goodbye, my darling; I hope you will be able to come and see me
soon. I embrace you both from the very bottom of my heart.

It was hot in the cell. Henry drank more rum and started another
letter to his wife: 'My beloved Berthe. I am like a madman; a frighten-
ing pain has grasped my brain. I am going for a swim in the Seine . . .'
He put down his pen. The heat was intolerable. Henry took off his
outer clothes and lay down on the bed.

Soon after six that evening, the orderly bringing supper to Henry's
cell received no answer when he knocked on the door. The door was
locked. The Lieutenant on duty forced it open and found Henry
stretched out on his bed. His body was stiff, the sheets soaked with
blood. In Henry's hand was the razor with which he had cut his throat.

After his body had been laid out by the doctor on duty at Mont-
Valérien, it was placed on a makeshift catafalque in the officers' mess.
Friends and fellow officers came to pay their last respects – among
them colleagues from the Statistical Section, including the archivist
Félix Gribelin and Henry's close friend and collaborator Jules Lauth.

Later Henry's corpse was transferred to Pogny for burial. Because he had taken his own life, there were no religious rites. Nonetheless, he was buried in style – a procession of villagers, firemen, a local band and many of his fellow officers following the bier down the village street. The coffin was draped with Henry's uniform, and his decorations, among them the Légion d'Honneur, were placed on a cushion. His superior officers in the army to which he had devoted his life, Generals Gonse and de Boisdeffre, were not present among the mourners.

As a result of Henry's suicide, many of those who had until then been convinced of the guilt of Dreyfus began to have doubts.[7] Among them was the Prime Minister, Henri Brisson. On 3 September he let it be known to Mathieu Dreyfus that the moment had come for Lucie to make a formal request for a review. The request was duly made, but it came up against the inflexible opposition of Cavaignac. For Cavaignac, the Henry forgery and Henry's suicide changed nothing. The very fact that he, Cavaignac, had exposed the forgery gave him the authority to pursue his plan for the prosecution of leading Dreyfusards. If the government agreed to a review, he would resign.

Brisson called his bluff. He accepted Cavaignac's resignation and replaced him as Minister of War with General Émile Zurlinden, the Military Governor of Paris. Zurlinden had held the post before, succeeding General Mercier in January 1895. At first he seemed prepared to go along with the review, but he was persuaded by the officers intimately acquainted with the case – General Roget and Captain Cuignet – that Henry's forgery had no bearing whatsoever on the guilt or innocence of Dreyfus; the bogus letter from Panizzardi to Schwartzkoppen was dated over a year after Dreyfus's conviction, and so had no bearing on the *res judicata*; and it had been assembled by Henry only to counteract Picquart's forgery of the *petit bleu*. Henry had been guilty of nothing but an excess of zeal. The real criminal was Picquart, and on 4 September Zurlinden announced that Picquart was to be tried by court martial for 'forgery and traffic in forgeries'.

On 17 September, at a meeting of the Council of Ministers, Brisson refused Zurlinden's request to put the prosecution of Picquart on the agenda, and instead carried a motion to accept Lucie Dreyfus's request for a review: the politicians were beginning to distance themselves from the army. Zurlinden promptly resigned and was replaced as Minister of War by General Charles Chanoine, a man with a good military record and known sympathies with the left. But Chanoine proved no less amenable to a review than had Zurlinden. He reappointed Zurlinden as Military Governor of Paris, which meant that the plan to court-martial Picquart could proceed. Faced with the prospect of being removed from the civilian prison of La Santé where he was then held to the military prison, the Cherche-Midi, Picquart made an open statement at a preliminary hearing to the effect that if he, like Henry, was found with his throat cut 'I would like it to be known . . . that it will have been murder, for a man of my kind would never for an instant consider committing suicide.'

The Review Commission, asked to decide whether Dreyfus should be allowed to appeal against his conviction or not, met on 21 September 1898, but failed to agree. Brisson persuaded a majority of his colleagues in the Council of Ministers to allow the appeal to proceed all the same. The Foreign Minister, Théophile Delcassé, was particularly keen to remove this divisive issue from the political arena by placing it *sub judice* because of the confrontation with Britain over Fashoda. The motion was carried by six votes to four: General Chanoine abstained.

The move enraged the nationalists. Against a background of industrial unrest, rumours circulated of an impending coup led by Generals de Pellieux or Zurlinden. The diplomatic defeat of France in its face-off with Britain over Fashoda fuelled the nationalist hysteria. Brisson and his government were perceived to be weak and, before a mob of protesters outside the National Assembly on 25 October, General Chanoine resigned. This precipitated a collapse of Brisson's government: a vote of confidence was lost by 286 votes to 254. However, the permission to allow an appeal could not be rescinded. On 27 October, two days after the fall of the government, proceedings opened at the Cour de Cassation – France's highest appeal court – with a request by the *rapporteur*,* Alphonse Bard, that the judges should 'bring the truth to

* An official appointed by the court to look into a case.

light': 'Removed from every other consideration than that of justice, invulnerable to any suggestion, insensitive to threats and to outrage, you have before you a great task. You will appreciate what it requires and you will do what your conscience dictates.'[8]

On 29 October, after two days of deliberation, the presiding judge of the Criminal Chamber of the Cour de Cassation, Judge Louis Loew, declared the request by Lucie Dreyfus 'admissible in its present form'. The appeal would be heard.

2: Sub Judice

Three Ministers of War had resigned, and now a government had fallen, as a result of the Dreyfus Affair. A new government was formed by Charles Dupuy, the Opportunist republican who had been Prime Minister at the time of Dreyfus's conviction. He was in a better position than most to know the truth or falsity of many of the stories circulated by the anti-Dreyfusards – for example, that Dreyfus had confessed his guilt to Captain Lebrun-Renault. However, for all the courage he had shown five years before when the anarchist Vaillant had thrown a bomb into the Chamber of Deputies, he was aware that there was something more explosive and potentially destructive in the Dreyfus Affair. To placate the Dreyfusards he chose a Protestant civilian, Charles de Freycinet, as Minister of War, while to reassure the right he appointed as Minister of Justice Georges Lebret, a professor of law from Caen in Normandy, who was approved of by Drumont and *La Libre Parole* for his anti-Dreyfusard views.

The sympathies of the new ministers were of less significance now that Dreyfus's appeal was being heard by the judges of the Criminal Chamber of the Cour de Cassation. What the anti-Dreyfusard officers had always feared had come to pass: the case had been transferred from a military to a civilian jurisdiction; and the tears of the old Attorney General Jean-Pierre Manau and the elevated language of the *rapporteur* Alphonse Barr revealed where their sympathies lay. There was a barrage of abusive rhetoric from the anti-Dreyfusard press. The presiding judge, Louis Loew, who was a Protestant from Alsace, was called 'the Jew Lévy' by Henri Rochefort in *L'Intransigeant*. Rochefort said that the judges had been bought by the syndicate like 'bar girls', and that they should have their eyelids cut off by 'a duly trained torturer', and

> large spiders of the most poisonous variety placed on their eyes to gnaw away the pupils and crystalline lenses until there were nothing left in the cavities now devoid of sight. Then, all the hideous blind men would be brought to a pillory erected before the Palais de Justice in which the crime was committed and a sign would be placed on their chests: 'This is how France punishes traitors who try to sell her to the enemy!'[9]

Less fantastical anti-Dreyfusards, such as the Catholic convert from Judaism Arthur Meyer, the editor of *Le Gaulois*, also wrote that the judges had been bought and were out to undermine the army 'out of hatred for the sabre'. Once they had destroyed France's defences, they would retire from the fray with 'their fortunes made'. Even 'so comparatively sagacious and so generous a man as Albert de Mun', wrote Denis Brogan, 'saw in the agitation for reopening the Dreyfus case merely a conspiracy to make the French soldier distrust his officers, to cast doubts and suspicions on his leaders'.[10] Each side saw the case of Dreyfus as a proxy for a more momentous struggle: for science, progress, liberty, democracy and above all justice for the Dreyfusards; for the anti-Dreyfusards, the survival of France as an ordered, wholesome, moral, Catholic nation, secure against its Protestant enemies across the Channel and the Rhine, imbued with a true fraternity that acknowledged spiritual truths and transcendental values, not subject to plunder and manipulation by an anonymous and self-interested plutocracy.

Each side had its bogeymen. For the anti-Dreyfusards, it was the syndicate – the secretive, transnational network of world Jewry with its allies, or stooges, the Protestants and Freemasons. For the Dreyfusards it was the Catholic Church, in particular the Society of Jesus with its sinister and secretive power exercised through the confessional and its schools; its members taking oaths of blind obedience to their General in Rome – the 'black pope' – and the Pope himself. Unlike the amorphous nature of the Jewish syndicate, here was an enemy for all to see

– subversives in black soutanes who despite the patriotic rhetoric of their pupils, the Postards* and Saint-Cyrians, owed their first obedience to an Italian and taught that the end justified any means so long as it was *ad maiorem Dei gloria*, for the greater glory of God.

As Michael Burleigh has pointed out, the creation of these bogeymen was exacerbated as a convenience by the popular press in which cartoonists could reduce 'complex issues to crude and sometimes vicious stereotypes, for it was far easier to depict a freemason or a Jew than a liberal, or a Jesuit rather than a moderate lay Catholic'.[11] The term 'Jesuitical' proliferates in the anti-clerical and Dreyfusard invective – in the speeches of Clemenceau and Jaurès – particularly in relation to the French officer corps and the army's High Command. Dupuy, in his first speech as Prime Minister to the National Assembly, referred to 'clerical influences' within the army. For the Reinachs, wrote Ruth Harris, their 'Franco-Judaism was inseparable from their anti-clericalism'. Joseph Reinach in a letter to his brother rebukes him for being 'more dirty-minded than the Catholic priests who screw chickens and goats'.[12]

The particular *bête noire* of the anti-Dreyfusards was the Jesuit Père Stanislas du Lac de Fugères. Joseph Reinach claimed he was 'astir in every intrigue'.[13] This suave and intelligent priest came from a family of the lesser French nobility that traced its pedigree back to the thirteenth century. Though born in Paris, he had served his novitiate in the Jesuit house at Issenheim in Alsace. In October 1871, at the age of thirty-six, he had succeeded Père Léon Ducoudray, who had been shot by the Communards, as rector of the École Sainte-Geneviève on the rue des Postes where pupils were coached for the entry exams for Saint-Cyr. When the Jesuits were expelled from France by the government of Jules Ferry in 1880, he had founded a school in Canterbury in England.

Joseph Reinach's contention that the Jesuits in general, and Père du Lac in particular, directed the anti-Dreyfusard campaign as part of a wider plan to foster a *coup d'état* and replace the anti-clerical Republic with a pro-Catholic authoritarian regime is found in a number of commentaries on the Affair. Hannah Arendt in *The Origins*

* Graduates of the Jesuit school in Paris on the rue des Postes.

of Totalitarianism wrote that 'the Jesuits were not prepared to tolerate the existence of officers immune to the influence of the Confessional'[14] and had a 'coup d'état policy' that they 'and certain anti-Semites were trying to introduce with the help of the army'.[15] One contemporary historian, Robert Tombs, regards the charge that 'the Jesuits through their influence over Catholic army officers were running the anti-Dreyfus plot in order to destroy the Republic' a 'more plausible accusation' than some of the wilder charges against the order;[16] another, Ralph Gibson, calls the idea 'demonstrably a total delusion'.[17] None of the Dreyfusard conspiracy theories explain why the Prefect of Police, Louis Lépine, or Commissaire Armand Cochefert, should have been susceptible to the influence of Jesuits.

Ruth Harris writes of Père du Lac that 'there is no hard evidence that he was responsible for directing the military cover-up, as the Dreyfusards claim',[18] but she does not enumerate the soft evidence. She tells her readers that Père du Lac was asked by the husband of Picquart's mistress, Pauline Monnier, to guide her conscience; that 'she was said to have accused du Lac of breaking the seal of the confessional, though what confidence he broke, if any, has never been determined'; and that, after temporarily breaking with her lover, Mme Monnier rejected du Lac's spiritual direction and resumed her affair with Picquart. Christian Vigouroux suggests that du Lac told Boisdeffre about Picquart's adulterous affair, though he concedes that his source 'is not necessarily an expert on religious matters'.[19] Ruth Harris also tells us that it is 'impossible to know' whether Père du Lac was the model for the Jesuit schoolteacher in Octave Mirbeau's novel *Sébastien Roch*, Père de Kern, who grooms and eventually rapes one of his pupils, but mentions the speculation as an example of how 'clerical, spiritual and sexual violation became a central theme of Dreyfusards wishing to demonize their opponents'.[20]

It is likely that some in the Society of Jesus accepted the hypothesis of a Judaeo-Masonic conspiracy to de-Catholicise France as outlined in *Civiltà Cattolica* in Rome in 1889. The statutes which excluded Jews from the Society opened it to the charge of institutionalised anti-Semitism.[21] There are also connections to be made between Père du

Lac and some of the anti-Dreyfusards. He brought Drumont back to the practice of the Catholic faith, and was a friend of the Comte de Mun, who presided over the Administrative Council that ran the École Sainte-Geneviève, and was said to be Boisdeffre's confessor, though he told Reinach that he knew him 'only in passing'.[22]

In an attempt to link the Jesuits to *La Libre Parole*, the anti-Dreyfusards pointed out not just the pastoral link between du Lac and Drumont but also the fact that a M. Odelin, who had administered the École Sainte-Geneviève for the Jesuits until 1890, had invested money in *La Libre Parole* when it was founded two years later. However, it would seem that Odelin parted company with the Jesuits because of a difference of opinion, and pulled out of *La Libre Parole* for the same reason. Thus the link between the Jesuits and *La Libre Parole* is a tenuous one. It was Père du Lac, after all, who upbraided Jules Guérin for attacking a Jewish convert to Catholicism called Dreyfus (see p. 36 above).

Was Père du Lac an *éminence grise* who, through his influence on Boisdeffre, controlled the army through its General Staff? A Dreyfusard journalist described how 'in his cell there is a crucifix on the wall and permanently open on the writing table, an annotated copy of the Army List'.[23] During du Lac's tenure as Rector of the École Sainte-Geneviève between 1872 and 1880, a total of 213 of his pupils won a place at the École Centrale, 328 at the École Polytechnique and 830 at Saint-Cyr. It is likely that a number of these former pupils looked back on their Rector with affection. However, of the 180 officers in the General Staff in 1898, only a dozen had been educated at Jesuit schools,[24] or, by a count provided in a letter to *The Times* by Comte Albert de Mun, 'nine or ten'. 'Moreover,' as de Mun pointed out to the readers of the English newspaper,

> these officers are chosen exclusively from among the first twelve in the École Supérieure de Guerre, admission to which school is by competitive examination. I might also reveal . . . that of the officers concerned in the Dreyfus case not one has been brought up by the Jesuits, neither General Mercier any more than General Gonse or General Pellieux, nor

Colonel Henry any more than Lieutenant-Colonel du Paty de Clam, nor Lieutenant Picquart any more than Commandant Esterhazy.[25]

Certainly, General de Boisdeffre had spent two years in the Jesuit school of Vaugirard, in Paris, but he spent eight years at the secular lycée in Alençon from which he gained entry to Saint-Cyr. Neither Billot, Cavaignac, Zurlinden nor Chanoine had been educated by the Jesuits. The only general known to be a devout Catholic was Boisdeffre. 'I have known General de Boisdeffre for nearly twenty years,' Maurice Paléologue told the Prime Minister, Charles Dupuy, on 29 December 1898. 'Henry's suicide was a terrible blow to him. Since then he has shut himself up in the country, in silence, prayer and poverty. If tomorrow I were told that he had become a Carthusian or a Trappist, I should not be in the least surprised.'[26]

Those unacquainted with the relation of penitent to confessor may find it difficult to accept that General de Boisdeffre had not consulted Père du Lac, his spiritual director, on the question of Dreyfus. But as the editor of the journal of the English Jesuits, the *Month*, wrote on this point:

Anyone who will take the slightest pains to ascertain from his Catholic acquaintances what kind of relations a Catholic public man can have with his priest-friends, or even with his confessor, will learn that such relations do not include subjecting his own judgement to theirs in regard to the matters, secret or otherwise, of his public employment. We can imagine what a Catholic Postmaster General would reply to a priest who should have the impudence, which none could have, to strive through him to direct the administration of the General Post Office. And the same may be said of General de Boisdeffre and Père du Lac. Père du Lac would be the last man in the world to pry into the official secrets of a Commander-in-Chief, and General de Boisdeffre would have been the last to permit such an intrusion – for, let us take this opportunity of saying it, those who know General de Boisdeffre, know him to be a man of conspicuously high and honourable character, and absolutely incapable of the iniquities imputed to him by reckless partisans . . .[27]

With hindsight it may be wondered whether this judgement of General de Boisdeffre's character is sound; but it remains unlikely, though not impossible, that he would have consulted his confessor – whether it be Père du Lac or any other – on matters of state.

With the exception of the Assumptionists and their Comités Justice-Égalité formed to support nationalist and anti-Dreyfusard candidates in the election of May 1898, there would seem to have been no direct intervention by the institutional Church in the Dreyfus Affair. Anti-Semitism is found in some bishops and a number of priests, but broadly speaking the Catholic bishops took the line that the case of Alfred Dreyfus was a judicial matter in which, by the terms of the Concordat, they were not permitted to intervene: it was a reticence that was to cost the Church dear. Edward H. Flannery, in his *The Anguish of the Jews*, dismisses Hannah Arendt's claim that the Jesuits masterminded the anti-Dreyfusard campaign but concurs with her view that the staunch-est anti-Dreyfusards were tribal Catholics – 'Catholics without faith' – who regarded Catholicism as integral to French identity and saw the Dreyfusard campaign to discredit the army as part of a long-term 'de-Christianisation' of society by 'Talmudic Judaism'.[28]

The most significant exponent of this view was Charles Maurras, a writer and journalist from a monarchist family in Provence and the adversary of Gabriel Monod. He had lost his faith in his youth but wrote that 'the interests of Roman Catholicism and those of France' were 'nearly always identical and nowhere contradictory'.[29] He regarded French Jews, and more particularly French Protestants, as alien entities within the nation.

> Nationalist writers observe that our Jews, thus naturalized, have not ceased for this reason to form a community of their own, a state quite distinct from the French State: their practice of marrying either among themselves, or with their kind from the North or the South of Europe, accentuates this difference between Jewish society and the rest of French society. A similar complaint . . . has been raised against the Huguenots.

Though they were originally of irreproachable French blood, they are
intellectual and moral dissidents, and have special affinities with our
most redoubtable foreign rivals. It is to be regretted that . . . Protestant
society has come to have a mentality quite different from the traditional
French mentality; and between the two there has developed, more and
more, a state of secret war, not a war of race, or even of religion, but,
rather, of culture, of thought and of taste.[30]

Jews, but particularly Protestants, were therefore a cultural Fifth
Column that sapped the strength of France in its struggle with its
'redoubtable enemies', Protestant Germany, Britain and the United
States (the US at that moment was wresting Cuba and the Philippines
from Catholic Spain). The crime of the Dreyfusards, in Maurras's view,
was to exalt 'a vague and unrealistic ideal of "Justice" above the concrete
conditions within which the human race alone could attain as much
justice as possible. It was folly to put justice before the state: there had
been states without justice but no justice without the state.'[31]

Maurras did not simply reject the claims of Christianity, he thought
Jesus of Nazareth 'essentially a charlatan'[32] whose exaltation of the meek
and poor over the 'mighty' was a 'recipe for disaster' at a time of a
Darwinian struggle for survival by Europe's nation states. He applied
this Nietzschean ruthlessness to the case of Dreyfus. 'Was France to be
weakened because of some artificial doubts about the guilt of one man?'
It was not surprising that those who sought to discredit the French
Army by calling for a review of Dreyfus's conviction were almost all
from the Jewish and Protestant communities, who felt a greater affinity for their co-religionists in other countries than they did for their
fellow citizens in France: he referred to them as *métèques*, a term used
in ancient Greece for resident foreigners with limited rights.

Maurras had a fertile and flexible mind. Faced with the suicide of
Henry, he did not support the idea put forward in some provincial
editions of *La Croix* that he had been murdered by agents of the syndicate to keep him quiet but, quite to the contrary, wrote that Henry had
forged the letter from Panizzardi and then taken his own life to save the
nation from war. In two articles published in *La Gazette de France* on

5 and 6 September, Maurras described how this 'energetic plebeian'* had taken upon himself to counteract Picquart's forgery of the *petit bleu* with a forgery of his own. To reveal the real source of his certainty of the guilt of Dreyfus – by implication, the *bordereau* annotated by Kaiser Wilhelm II – would lead to war. A court martial might lead to damaging disclosures about his superior officers. 'Our poor half-Protestant upbringing', wrote Maurras, 'is incapable of appreciating so much moral and intellectual nobility.' He went on: 'Colonel, there is not a drop of your precious blood which does not steam still wherever the heart of the Nation beats . . . Before long from the country's soil, in Paris, in your little village, there will arise monuments to expiate our cowardice . . . In life as in death, you marched forward. Your unhappy forgery will be counted among the best acts of war.'[33]

This idea of Henry as a martyr was taken up by the other anti-Dreyfusard newspapers – *La Libre Parole*, *Le Petit Journal*, *L'Éclair* and of course *La Croix*, which dropped the idea that Henry had been murdered. It reinvigorated the anti-Dreyfusards who had been demoralised by Henry's suicide. It led to a surge of sympathy throughout the nation for Henry's pretty widow, Berthe, and her little son Joseph. Always on the lookout for something to boost circulation, *La Libre Parole* published an article about the plight of 'the widow Henry' by the proto-feminist writer Marie-Anne de Bovet (the Marquise de Bois-Hébert) entitled 'To Good People' – 'Aux braves gens'. In it she revealed the plight of Mme Henry, a woman whose noble husband had been calumniated by Joseph Reinach: Reinach had accused Henry of being Esterhazy's partner in treason. How could an impoverished widow seek redress for such an insult in the courts? *La Libre Parole* would open a subscription list to raise money for legal action. It would be a memorial to 'the brave French officer killed, murdered by Jews . . . However small the contribution, it will be a slap in the obscene face of the ignoble Reinach.'

The appeal was an astounding success. In the space of a month, 25,000 contributions raised 131,000 francs. A list of subscribers was

* Maurras had just returned from the Olympic Games in Athens, which may be why he used categories such as 'plebeian' and '*métèque*'.

published in *La Libre Parole* which allows a dissection of the social forces arraigned against Dreyfus, and the vituperative comments that accompanied some of the contributions gives an insight into the deep loathing found in some circles for Jews. Few contributions came from white-collar workers, domestic servants, industrialists or professionals in the countryside. A high proportion came from manual workers, artisans, students and the liberal professions in the big cities. The largest number of contributors were serving members of the armed forces – 4,500, of whom 3,000 were officers on active service, among them nine colonels and lieutenant-colonels and five generals – one of them General Mercier; and, from the army reserve, thirty generals and fifty-five colonels or lieutenant-colonels.[34] Out of 55,000 priests in France, 300 subscribed to the Henry memorial – approximately one-half of 1 per cent.[35] No Catholic bishop sent a contribution, something which disappointed some of their clergy – 'A poor priest, sickened to realize that no bishop in France has sent in his offering'; and 'M. . . . heartbroken to see that not a single bishop has participated in the subscription.'[36]

Incongruously, there were few contributions from Brittany and the Vendée – the most Catholic French regions and also politically the most royalist and right wing: Stephen Wilson ascribes this to the fact that the population was too backward and illiterate to be susceptible to a press campaign, or that in those areas 'Jewish minorities were unimportant or unknown', but it might also be explained by the disapproval by devout Catholics of Henry's suicide – a mortal sin.

Some of the subscribers were not Catholic at all: one came from 'a freethinker who is opposed to Jewish or Protestant clericalism as to any other', another from 'a freethinker' who feared that 'the Jews will turn us all into church-goers'. Many of the workers and artisans felt that they had been exploited or badly treated by Jewish employers and they expressed the common complaints against the amorality of the money economy: 'In contrast to honour which is embodied in the army and the family, the Jew is identified with money which is liquid and unstable, and associated with social change, uncertainty and possible disaster'; 'For France, against the triple alliance of Freemasons, Jews and Protestants . . .'.[37] Some of the donations were accompanied by the kind of crude anti-Semitic abuse found in Drumont's *La France juive*. Jews were 'unclean'. One contributor 'would like to eat some Jew, so that he could defecate it'; another said he would like 'a bedside rug made with Yid skins so that he could tread on it night and morning'. There was 'a military doctor . . . who wishes that vivisection were practised on Jews rather than on harmless rabbits'.[38]

There was 'a definite social cachet in contributing to the cause'.[39] The pre-revolutionary aristocracy was strongly represented with seven dukes and duchesses, two princes, fifty marquises and over two hundred counts, viscounts and barons, among them Comte Albert de Mun who sent in fifty francs 'to defend our beloved army'. The Duc d'Orléans, on the other hand, made a contribution, 'not actually under his own name, but yet transparently'; there was a measure of opportunism in this because 'some of the Orléans princes knew, through their relations with Queen Victoria, that the Kaiser had told his grandmother that Dreyfus was innocent'.[40] So too the Empress Eugénie, living in exile in Britain, which may be why the Bonapartists were largely absent from the subscription list.

There were a large number of doctors and lawyers: analysts of the list have suggested that the competition of Jews within these professions had fostered anti-Semitism, just as perceived exploitation by Jewish employers accounts for contributions from 'three embroiderers from Bains-les-Bains, Vosges, who in working for a Jew make 14 sous in 15 hours'. There were many women among the subscribers, and a strain of sexual phobia is discernible in some comments that accompanied their contributions: 'a working woman seduced and deceived by her Jewish boss' and 'a man of Roubaix who wants to contribute his modest share to snatch a French woman out of the hands of a Jew'.[41]

Mme Henry, 'veiled in mourning, epitomizing pure and fragile womanhood',[42] became an icon for the anti-Dreyfusards to match the Dreyfusards' Lucie: one a real widow, the other a grass widow who had worn black since her husband's incarceration. The many thousands of letters of support that Lucie received from well-wishers provide a snapshot of Dreyfusards comparable to the list of contributors to the 'Henry monument'. Here too there were Catholics and aristocrats, but there were often personal reasons for acting contrary to type. Monseigneur de Schad, the Private Chamberlain to Pope Leo XIII, was a German; Lady Stanley, the wife of the explorer, was English; Père Hyacinthe was a defrocked priest married to an Englishwoman; Prince Albert of Monaco, who sent a message to Lucie inviting her and her husband to his chateau at Marchais in Champagne after 'the holy work of justice was done',[43] was married to Alice Heine, the daughter of a German-Jewish financier, widow of Duc Armand de Richelieu and distant cousin of the poet Heinrich Heine.[44] Prince Albert rewarded the first Dreyfusard from outside the Dreyfus family, Major Forzinetti, by giving him a job in the government of Monaco.[45]

This is not to suggest that all the Dreyfusards had ulterior motives for supporting the case for a review, but it is notable how tribal loyalties affected judgements on both sides of the divide. As the Affair progressed, one finds fewer and fewer atypical partisans in either camp. Abbé Pichot was a Dreyfusard – one of 'the rare priests who had the courage to take up the defence of justice and truth';[46] the Abbé Brugerette was another; and the Abbé Augustin Serres a third. The Catholic historian Paul Viollet, Professor of Law at the École des Chartes, initially joined the League of the Rights of Man but, finding it too anti-clerical, resigned and founded a Comité Catholique pour la Défense du Droit – a Catholic Committee for the Defence of the Law. However, the anti-Dreyfusard press did not want to let their readers know that there were Catholic Dreyfusards any more than the anti-clerical Dreyfusards. 'By this reciprocal reticence,' writes Pierre Miquel, 'they were often unknown and underestimated.'[47]

———

The most notable exception to this rule that tribal loyalties affected the judgement of Frenchmen and women during the Dreyfus Affair was Georges Picquart. Though clearly not a devout Catholic, as his adulterous liaison with Pauline Monnier makes evident, he came from a Catholic family in Alsace and had in him all the reflex anti-Semitism of his fellow Alsatian and predecessor as chief of the Statistical Section, Colonel Jean Sandherr. Captain Tassin had put about the remarks made by Picquart during Dreyfus's degradation about him evaluating the gold braid as it was torn from his uniform and 'For goodness sake, there isn't a Jew who doesn't have a convict in the family!' But such reflex anti-Semitism is found in many of the Dreyfusards – in Zola, Jaurès, Scheurer-Kestner, Loew – and like them, faced with the obscene and murderous abuse of Jews triggered by the Dreyfus Affair, Picquart had reflected on his own prejudices and tried to suppress them. During his stay in prison, he took up the study of art and, in a letter to a friend, wrote that he had 'ignored the fact that Rembrandt was Jewish and saw for what they are – these stupid prejudices'.[48]

Picquart let it be known, however, that his belief in the innocence of Dreyfus had nothing to do with Dreyfus being a Jew. In exonerating Dreyfus and exposing Esterhazy, he was merely doing his duty. 'I don't understand why I am being exalted by some and insulted by others,' he wrote to a friend. 'I did nothing but my duty.'[49] This distancing of himself from the Dreyfusards which he had kept up for so long after discovering the *petit bleu* could not be sustained. He had become the hero of the Dreyfusards and the *bête noire* of the anti-Dreyfusards, particularly his fellow officers in the French Army. 'Dreyfus is not an object of hatred among army officers,' wrote Maurice Paléologue. 'They talk about him with stern coldness or contempt, but without anger, and sometimes even pity. But the mere mention of the name of Picquart rouses them; they hate, loathe and execrate the renegade to the point of fury.'[50]

General de Pellieux put out disinformation to the effect that Picquart was a neurotic who indulged in hypnotism, occultism and spiritualism; and rumours of his homosexuality were revived. Several right-wing papers described Picquart's female characteristics, his 'smooth, almost feminine manner'. At the second Zola trial, Esterhazy shouted at Picquart 'Have you no shame?' in a high-pitched, woman's voice. The prolific novelist Gyp (Sibylle Aimée Marie Antoinette Gabrielle de Riquetti de Mirabeau, Comtesse de Martel de Janville), who, when summoned as a witness, gave her profession as 'Anti-Semite', wrote a *roman-à-clef* in which Picquart is portrayed as a man with a 'complicated' love life. Dreyfusard women write passionate love letters to their imprisoned hero, but their love provokes only indifference from the 'deranged and unhealthy' officer, whose desires are 'the most rascally and repugnant of all'.[51] This image of an effeminate decadent was compounded by stories in the press, such as that in Rochefort's *L'Intransigeant* on 16 March 1899, describing how Picquart received up to forty visitors every day in his cell in the Cherche-Midi prison – 'ecstatic fifty-something-year-old *demi-vierges*' who brought him embroidered slippers, pâtés, sausages, pastries, fine wines and jam.

The attempts to portray Picquart as homosexual suggest that the General Staff, if they were indeed informed of his affair with Pauline Monnier by Père du Lac, thought that information would be less damaging and so kept it to themselves. Though it was still widely believed that Picquart had been bought by the syndicate, they hoped to convict him on the two specific charges of forging the *petit bleu* and conveying official secrets to his lawyer Leblois. On 24 November 1898, the Military Governor of Paris, General Zurlinden, ordered the court martial to take place on 12 December.

On 28 November, the socialist Alexandre Millerand, converted by Henry's suicide to the Dreyfusard cause, proposed a motion in the Chamber of Deputies to order a postponement of Picquart's court martial. Raymond Poincaré, the Minister of Finance at the time of Dreyfus's conviction who had hitherto said nothing about the review, rose to speak. 'The time has come', he said, 'when to remain silent would be an act of cowardice.' He called upon his friends Barthou, Leygues and Dupuy, who had been Prime Minister at the time, to accept that, if it was possible that a miscarriage of justice had taken place when they were in power in 1894, then they were under 'an imperious obligation' not to do anything to prevent it being discovered and redressed. It was a cautious double-negative that followed years of silence.

Why, Poincaré was asked, had he waited until now to speak up in favour of review? His answer was plausible and straightforward. At the time he had been told it was the *bordereau* that proved the guilt of Dreyfus. There was no mention of a secret dossier or a confession. Now the adventitious introduction into the polemic of new evidence suggested that the original conviction may have been unsound. 'I am well aware that today, in breaking my silence, I am exposing myself to attacks, insults and slander. That does not matter to me. I am happy to have taken the opportunity in speaking from this podium of doing what my conscience dictates.'

Poincaré was an experienced advocate; he had made his fortune representing the armaments industry in the courts, and his 'confessional' tone was staged to reclaim the moral high ground for the centrist republicans. In this he was backed by his former colleague and fellow lawyer Louis Barthou. Millerand's motion was lost by 338 to 83; the Chamber was still overwhelmingly anti-Dreyfusard. But in the Senate another lawyer and republican heavyweight, Pierre Waldeck-Rousseau, proposed a change to the law that would permit the Cour de Cassation to suspend Picquart's court martial.

Waldeck-Rousseau had been in at the very start of the Dreyfus Affair when Mathieu had asked him in 1894 to defend his brother. Political considerations had led him to decline (see pp. 102–3 above); he had recommended his friend Edgar Demange, and most certainly knew from Demange of the irregularity of the proceedings that sent Alfred Dreyfus to Devil's Island. Had he suffered from a bad conscience like Poincaré? Or had considerations of political advantage changed? His motion was defeated but only by the deciding vote of the President of the Senate. Half the senators had been persuaded by the sagacious Waldeck-Rousseau, not only by the eloquence of the most able lawyer of his generation, but by the fact that this most cautious and reserved of politicians had chosen this moment to come off the fence.

———

In the event, the failure of the motions in both houses of the National Assembly was circumvented by a legal manoeuvre. On 8 December 1898, after a submission by Picquart's lawyers, the Cour de Cassation called for the dossier to be retrieved for its perusal from the military prosecutors, which effectively postponed the court martial *sine die*. This, to the anti-Dreyfusards, was a further proof that the judiciary were in the pay of the syndicate. In fact, as Jean-Louis Bredin, himself a lawyer, wrote in his book *The Affair*, 'most of the Court's judges had behind them a long past devoted to the study of legal theory and practice. The juridical spirit had formed them.' Most were by disposition conservative, a number anti-Semitic. However, the great majority were committed to the secular republic. At the time of Jules Ferry's anti-clerical laws in the early 1880s, some 200 Catholic magistrates had resigned, and in 1897 the republican government had dismissed 609 sitting magistrates deemed to have Bonapartist, royalist or clericalist sympathies; a further 300 magistrates had resigned in protest. This purge, 'as brutal as it was arbitrary . . . showed little respect for judicial independence'.[52]

As a result, many of the judges, even if predisposed to reject a review on the grounds of *res judicata*, were also trying to make out which way the wind was blowing and were prepared to become Dreyfusards if the government changed its mind. Most kept their opinions to themselves; however, Judge Loew, like the Attorney General Manau and the *rapporteur* Alphonse Bard, made no secret of the fact that he favoured a review, while Judge Sevestre, who had family links with the army, was among those who were against it. However, a decisive intervention by the anti-Dreyfusards came from a judge in the Civil Chamber of the Cour de Cassation, Judge Jules Quesnay de Beaurepaire. He claimed that when Colonel Picquart had been summoned from prison to give evidence to the court's Criminal Chamber, he had been held in his office for want of space anywhere else in the Palais de Justice; and while he was there the *rapporteur* Bard had chatted to Picquart in the most friendly manner, addressing him as 'My dear Picquart', asking for his view on the statements of other witnesses, and saying 'Take a look at Gonse's testimony. I think we've got him.' Bard had even arranged for Picquart to receive a hot drink.

Beaurepaire's disclosures were picked up by the nationalist press and quickly became an affair of state. On 8 January 1899, in protest at the government's failure to deal satisfactorily with his charges of partiality, Beaurepaire resigned as presiding judge of the Civil Chamber. He was replaced by Judge Alexis Ballot-Beaupré, but the Minister of Justice Georges Lebret also instructed the presiding judge of the Cour de Cassation, Charles Mazeau, to supervise Judge Loew, and choose his own *rapporteur* to inquire into the charges brought by Beaurepaire. The inquiry concluded that there were no grounds for suspecting any of the judges of the Criminal Chamber of any wrongdoing, but that the charges had undermined the public's confidence in the court's impartiality and therefore the case should now be heard by the Combined Chambers of the Cour de Cassation – the Criminal and Civil Chambers, and the Chambre des Requêtes. The government accepted this recommendation, and on 28 January introduced legislation transferring the competence of the Criminal Chamber to the Combined Chambers.

The Criminal Chamber was only days away from delivering its verdict; the government therefore had to act quickly. The proposed intervention – the executive tampering with the judiciary – was, wrote Bredin, 'without precedent and in defiance of the law',[53] and, in the view of Maurice Paléologue, was an 'arbitrary incursion by the political power into the realm of justice'.[54] However, a law 'dispossessing' the Criminal Chamber of the Dreyfus case was passed by the Chamber of Deputies by 324 votes to 207, with the centrist republicans and two-thirds of the Radicals voting with the right. On 27 January, the debate moved to the Senate, but there too, despite a magisterial speech by Pierre Waldeck-Rousseau opposing the law, it was passed by 155 votes to 125.

3: Grand Guignol

On 16 February 1899 – the day on which the debate on the law of dispossession was held in the Senate – the President of France, Félix Faure, held a number of meetings at the Élysée Palace, one with Prince Albert of Monaco, another with Cardinal Richard, the Archbishop of Paris. When the serious business of the day was completed, the President withdrew to his private quarters. Beyond his study was a small boudoir – the *salon bleu* – where at 5.30 p.m. he received Marguerite Steinheil, the beautiful twenty-nine-year-old daughter of a Jewish industrialist in Metz and now the wife of the painter Adolphe Steinheil.

An hour and a quarter later, the President's private secretary heard screams coming from the *salon bleu*. At the secretary's behest, the locked door was forced open by an officer of the guard to find Faure comatose, his clothes in disarray, and a naked Mme Steinheil caught by his fingers entwined in her hair. The hysterical young woman was freed and, once dressed, was hurried out of the Élysée Palace. The two doctors summoned to attend to the President found that he had suffered a cerebral haemorrhage. Mme Faure was informed. A priest arrived from La Madeleine and performed the last rites of the Catholic Church. Faure died a few hours later.*

Faure's death was a setback for the anti-Dreyfusards. He had set his mind against a review from the time back in 1895 when his friend Dr Gilbert had raised the question of a possible miscarriage of justice; and had confirmed this stance when another old friend, Auguste Scheurer-Kestner, had asked him to intervene in October 1897. Concomitantly, it was an opportunity for the Dreyfusards. Under the constitution of the Third Republic, the President was chosen not by a popular vote but by the deputies and senators in the National Assembly. Some republicans in the centre favoured Jules Méline as the new President; others, supported by the left, put forward the President of the Senate, Émile Loubet. The left liked Loubet because he had ruled in favour of the Carmaux strikers in 1892; to the right, he was a scoundrel who had tried to cover up corruption during the Panama Canal scandal.

Loubet was elected on the first round of voting with 483 votes against 279 for Méline. Already the nationalist press were claiming that Félix Faure, 'the great friend of the army', had been murdered by 'some Judith or Delilah' at the behest of the Jews. Now the election of Loubet, a known Dreyfusard and so 'the elect of the synagogue', was regarded as 'an insult to France', 'a challenge to the army' and 'a victory for Jewish treason'. On his way to the Élysée to pay his respects to his dead predecessor, the sound of the military band playing the 'Marseillaise' was drowned out by the boos, whistles and abuse of the crowds lining the route.[55]

For the nationalist opponents of the republican regime, the election by a clique of corrupt politicians of the Panamist 'candidate from Devil's

---

* Marguerite Steinheil went on to have affairs with a number of famous men. She was charged with perjury, married an English peer and died in Hove in 1954.

Island', and the evidence of popular fury at their choice, convinced them that the time was ripe for a *coup d'état*. Paul Déroulède alerted the members of his League of Patriots and Jules Guérin mobilised his Anti-Semitic League. The aim of the coup, in Déroulède's words, was 'to kick out of France a foreign constitution – just as Joan of Arc had kicked out the English' and 'leave it to the people to choose the President of the Republic'.[56] While the militant members of the two Leagues were ready for action, and Déroulède felt he could count on the sympathy of the Parisian crowd, it would be the army that would overthrow the rotten Republic at the state funeral of Félix Faure.

To enlist the support of the army, a general of some standing would have to be brought onside. The first candidate was General de Pellieux who, since holding the inquiry into Esterhazy, had become Esterhazy's champion and an implacable anti-Dreyfusard. Pellieux gave vague assurances. The funeral took place on 23 February 1899 starting with a Requiem Mass at the Cathedral of Notre Dame. Learning that the cavalcade accompanying the catafalque would end at the Place de la Nation, Déroulède summoned his supporters by posters and *petits bleus* to gather to intercept the column of soldiers at the Place de la Bastille. At his side were his deputy, Marcel Habert, and the right-wing ideologue, Charles Maurras. When the troops approached, however, they were led not by General de Pellieux but by General Roget – formerly chief of the Fourth Bureau of the General Staff, subsequently Cavaignac's *chef de cabinet*, and a convinced anti-Dreyfusard, but not privy to the plans for a coup. Pellieux, it turned out, had lost his nerve and persuaded General Zurlinden, still Military Governor of Paris, to replace him with General Roget.

Déroulède tried to make the best of this unexpected turn of events. The number of supporters who had gathered at the Place de la Bastille was smaller than he had hoped for, but many more lined the route to the Élysée. Déroulède therefore stepped forward and took hold of the bridle of General Roget's horse. 'Follow us, General! Take pity on the nation! Save France and the Republic! To the Élysée!' Roget refused. Trying to shake off the importunate Déroulède, he pointed his sabre towards the Boulevard Diderot which led to the barracks. Déroulède would not give up. He ran beside the General's horse and, when the column reached the gates to the Reuilly barracks, once again took hold of the bridle and repeated his plea. Roget ignored him. Clinging to the horse's reins, Déroulède and Habert were dragged through the gates of the barracks while Guérin, Maurras and his other supporters remained outside.

Déroulède now harangued both General Roget and his junior officers, chastising them for betraying their own cause: 'You are no longer soldiers, you are parliamentarians!' Roget tried to get his uninvited guests to leave. They refused. At midnight, the police commissioner Armand Cochefert arrived at the barracks and arrested Déroulède and Habert – the same Cochefert who had taken part in the interrogation and arrest of Alfred Dreyfus in October 1894, telling him that 'the evidence is overwhelming' (see p. 87 above). He took his prisoners back to the central police station where, to Déroulède's disgust, they were merely charged with riotous trespass. He persuaded Cochefert to insert in the charge-sheet that he 'had gone to the Place de la Nation to persuade soldiers to overthrow the Republic'.[57] On 29 May 1899, Déroulède and Habert were put on trial for sedition. After a cursory deliberation by the jury, they were acquitted and Déroulède was carried from the Palais de Justice on the shoulders of his cheering supporters.

4: Review

On the same day as Déroulède and Habert were set free, the Combined Chambers of the Cour de Cassation assembled in the *grande-chambre* of the Palais de Justice to consider their verdict on the case of Alfred Dreyfus. The building was suitably grandiose for this gathering of fifty judges in their splendid robes. It had been built on the site of the palace of the saintly King of France, Louis IX; the only part that survived was the exquisite Sainte-Chapelle, built by the King to house a most precious relic that he had purchased from the Byzantine Emperor in the thirteenth century, Christ's Crown of Thorns. The relic had disappeared at the time of the Revolution of 1789 and the chapel was now dwarfed by the grandiose monument to the high ideal of that Revolution – the Palais de Justice.

Maurice Paléologue, who claimed descent from the emperors of Byzantium, describes the *grande-chambre* as 'sumptuously decorated in the glittering Roman *palazzo* style; there are too many accessories, too many mouldings, too much foliage, too many garlands, too many allegorical scenes. Among all this richness all the charm of the clear harmonies of Paul Baudry's glorious ceiling, *The Apotheosis of Law*, is lost.'[58]

Paléologue had been called twice to give evidence before the Combined Chambers. As representative of the Foreign Office, he was asked about the crucial telegram of 2 November 1894 from the Italian military attaché, Alessandro Panizzardi, to his superiors in Rome (see p. 98 above). Document No. 44 in the Dreyfus file was the first version of the telegram which implicated Dreyfus: 'Captain Dreyfus has been arrested . . . I have taken all precautions.' Paléologue attested before the court that both his conscience and his instructions from his superiors obliged him to say that this document 'is not just a wrong translation; it is a falsification'.[59] This had caused consternation in the court: among the fifty judges there were passionate anti-Dreyfusards who believed that anyone who gave evidence in Dreyfus's favour was, as the nationalist press termed Paléologue, a traitor, liar, forger and German spy.

On 27 April 1899, Paléologue had been recalled to the court to have the original telegram decrypted in the presence of Captain Cuignet, now an energetic opponent of review, and of General Eugène Chamoin, an impartial observer sent by the Minister of War. The telegram was deciphered and proved that the text Paléologue had shown to the court was correct and Document No. 44 a forgery. General Chamoin signed the report which established this with 'a good grace'; Cuignet also signed, 'quivering with rage'.[60]

A few days later, at a dinner with the Romanian Minister, Grégoire Ghika, Maurice Paléologue found himself sitting next to Hermance de Weede, the wife of the Counsellor of the Netherlands Legation. Paléologue, who was himself conducting an affair that was to last a lifetime with the actress Julia Bartet, took a certain pleasure in discussing the Dreyfus Affair with this woman who had been Schwartzkoppen's mistress: Paléologue had seen the file of more than eighty of their love letters. He told her that he still had doubts about the innocence of

Dreyfus; Hermance de Weede was indignant but admitted that her husband, too, had the same doubts. Paléologue was tempted to point out that she had been in a better position than either of the two diplomats to 'extract from Schwartzkoppen the truth about the Dreyfus case'.

————

On Saturday, 3 June, after four days of intense and sometimes acrimonious disputation, the fifty judges of the Combined Chambers gathered to deliver their judgment. The Cour de Cassation could not declare Dreyfus innocent or guilty; it had the power, as its name suggests, to 'break' (or quash) a verdict but not to reverse it. It could have ruled that he had no case to answer; but such a judgment was not what Dreyfus or his family or his supporters wanted. They were determined that he should be exonerated by his fellow officers in a second court martial. Lucie Dreyfus's lawyer, Maître Henri Mornard, made this clear to the court: it was for 'military judges' to admit the error 'with joy in their hearts'. He looked forward to that moment when 'the blessed dawn of the day will allow the great light of concord and truth to shine over the nation'.

Mathieu Dreyfus, Bernard Lazare, Jean Jaurès, Georges Clemenceau and Louis Leblois were among the lawyers, journalists and politicians packed into the ornate *grande-chambre* to hear the verdict. This was not like the snakepit of the National Assembly with its seedy politicians: here they were in the Holy of Holies of the secular Republic committed to Liberty, Equality and Fraternity. And just as the army had its glittering gold-braided uniforms, and the Church its dazzling vestments, so these fifty high priests of the Republic, with the Cour de Cassation's chief presiding judge Charles Mazeau as their primate, had their ermine-edged robes in scarlet and black, and black hats to match the *képis* and mitres.

In solemn tones, Mazeau now went through the evidence against Dreyfus. It had been established to his satisfaction that the supposed confession had not taken place and that the *bordereau*, 'the principal basis for the accusation and the conviction of Dreyfus', 'was not written

Captain Alfred Dreyfus. The youngest son of a Jewish textile manufacturer in Mulhouse, Dreyfus graduated with high marks from the École Polytechnique and the École de Guerre. He was shy, awkward and spoke in a monotonous voice. Serving as an intern on the General Staff, he was marked down for his awkward bearing which he ascribed to the anti-Semitism of senior officers.

Lucie Dreyfus, née Hadamard, with her husband and two children, Pierre and Jeanne. The youngest daughter of a diamond merchant, she married Alfred Dreyfus at the age of twenty-five. Despite learning of his infidelities in the course of his court-martial, she remained totally loyal to her husband and wanted to follow him to Devil's Island.

Mathieu Dreyfus, Alfred's older brother, was as open and easy-going as Alfred was reserved and retiring. He co-ordinated and financed the campaign for a re-trial.

Colonel Georges Picquart. From a Catholic background, he had a meteoric career in the French army and was appointed Chief of the Statistical Section on the death of Colonel Sandherr. The draft of a letter-telegram filched from Schwarzkoppen's waste-paper basket led him to realise that Dreyfus was innocent. His discovery was ignored by his superiors who posted him abroad.

Commandant Charles-Ferdinand Walsin-Esterhazy, the man to whom the letter-telegram from Schwarzkoppen was addressed. A degenerate and embittered man, perennially short of money, it was believed on the Right that he had been chosen to replace Dreyfus by the Jewish 'syndicate'. Picquart was said to be in its pay.

Major Armand du Paty de Clam. An officer on the General Staff, an amateur hand-writing expert, and a cousin of General de Boisdeffre, he was given the task of gathering evidence against Dreyfus. He was convinced of his guilt and hoped to extract a confession.

Commandant Joseph Henry, the son of a farmer who had risen from the ranks to be third in command at the Statistical Section, recruited agents from the Parisian low life and was adept in the dirty tricks department. He revered his superiors and liked to anticipate their unspoken orders.

Le Petit Journal

Le Petit Journal
CHAQUE JOUR 5 CENTIMES
Le Supplément illustré
CHAQUE SEMAINE 5 CENTIMES

SUPPLÉMENT ILLUSTRÉ
Huit pages : CINQ centimes

ABONNEMENTS

	TROIS MOIS	SIX MOIS	UN AN
PARIS	1 fr.	2 fr.	3 fr. 50
DÉPARTEMENTS	1 fr.	2 fr.	4 fr.
ÉTRANGER	1 50	2 50	5 fr.

Sixième année — DIMANCHE 13 JANVIER 1895 — Numéro 217

LE TRAITRE
Dégradation d'Alfred Dreyfus

Ritual degradation in front of serried ranks of soldiers at the École Militaire was part of the sentence handed down after the judges of his court-martial had unanimously found Dreyfus guilty of betraying military secrets to a foreign power.

Alfred Dreyfus at the time of his conviction and deportation from France.

Devil's Island. When he first arrived in French Guiana, Dreyfus was held in the prison on the Île Royale while a hut and guard house were built on the smallest of the Salvation Islands, Devil's Island. Until then it had housed convicts with leprosy. He would remain there in solitary confinement for more than four years.

Comte Albert de Mun. A great orator and liberal Catholic who abhorred anti-Semitism and accepted France's republican form of government, he believed that the agitation to re-open the case against Dreyfus was the work of 'a mysterious and hidden power strong enough to be able to cast suspicion at will on those who command our Army'.

Henri Marquis de Rochefort. A Communard who had escaped from the penal settlement in New Caledonia, he had become an extreme nationalist and fanatic anti-Semite, convinced that the judges who re-opened the case against Dreyfus had been bought by the Jewish 'syndicate'.

Jules Guérin, founder of the Anti-Semitic League, joined Déroulède in his attempted coup and named his League after a Masonic Lodge to avoid legal restrictions imposed on unauthorised associations.

Maurice Barrès. An erudite journalist, essayist and politician, he believed that France was threatened by a coalition of Protestants and Jews whose first loyalties lay with their co-religionists abroad.

Émile Zola. One of France's leading
novelists, he exposed the conspiracy against
Dreyfus in his polemical article, *J'Accuse*. It
led to anti-Semitic riots throughout France.

Edgar Demange, the eminent lawyer
who was convinced of Dreyfus's
innocence and undertook his defence.
He was a devout Catholic and married
to the daughter of a general.

Marcel Proust described himself as 'the first
Dreyfusard' because he persuaded the writer
Anatole France to sign a petition in favour of
Dreyfus. Proust's mother was Jewish: his father,
Dr Adrian Proust, when he learned that his two
sons had become Dreyfusards, would not speak
to them for a week.

Jean Jaurès. Socialist firebrand and the finest orator in the National Assembly, he was a late convert to the Dreyfusard cause. He blamed the conspiracy on 'Jesuit-spawned generals' and exploited the Affair for an anti-clerical agenda.

Georges Clemenceau. A Socialist politician tarnished by the Panama Canal Scandal, he became a leading Dreyfusard and fought duels with both Edouard Drumont and Paul Déroulède.

Pierre Waldeck-Rousseau, French prime minister in 1899. He persuaded President Loubet, after Dreyfus's second conviction, to grant him a pardon. Dreyfus was freed but many of his supporters thought he ought to have returned to prison to fight on. Waldeck-Rousseau used the Affair to close down Catholic schools and disband religious orders.

Alfred Dreyfus leaving the courthouse during his second court martial, at Rennes in 1899. The soldiers have their backs turned – considered by the Dreyfusards to be a calculated insult.

The anticlerical governments of Waldeck-Rousseau and Émile Combes closed all Catholic schools in France and dissolved Catholic religious orders. Dreyfus believed that his Affair had prepared public opinion for this legislation. Here Carthusian monks are evicted from their mother house, La Grande Chartreuse.

In 1906, Dreyfus was declared innocent by the joint Courts of Appeal and reinstated in the army with the rank of Major. Here he receives the cross of the Legion of Honour at a ceremony at the École Militaire where he had suffered ritual degradation eleven years before.

by Dreyfus but by Esterhazy'. This judgment in no way impugned the honour of the army which, 'thank God, transcends these proceedings which cannot affect it, and does not require to defend its honour that an innocent convict be kept on Devil's Island'. It was not for the court to pronounce Dreyfus innocent; it merely had to rule that 'a new element had emerged' which might lead to a different verdict.

Mazeau now read out the court's conclusion. The verdict against Alfred Dreyfus delivered on 22 December 1894 was rescinded and annulled. The accused was ordered to appear before a second court martial in the city of Rennes which would decide solely whether or not Dreyfus was guilty of having entered into correspondence with a foreign power or one of its agents in order to assist it in hostilities against France; and whether he had assisted its ability to do so by procuring the notes and documents mentioned in the *bordereau*.

For Mathieu Dreyfus, this was a moment of unalloyed triumph. So too for Lucie who, though not present at the hearing, was immediately informed of the court's decision. Their battle was won. What was clear to a majority of France's best legal minds would be equally clear to seven officers conducting a court martial and through them the army and all honest Frenchmen and women. Who could doubt the innocence of Alfred Dreyfus after this decision, and when, on the very day that the judgment was given, *Le Matin* published an interview with Charles Esterhazy in which he admitted that he had written the *bordereau*? 'Yes, I wrote the *bordereau*, at the request of my superior and friend, Colonel Sandherr.' It was the explanation that he had tried to put to du Paty de Clam but had been cut short. He went further: Generals de Boisdeffre, Gonse and Billot had all known that the *bordereau* had been written by him.

A hard core of sceptics remained on the far right, but this extra-parliamentary opposition was paying out the rope with which to hang itself. The decision of the Combined Chambers enraged them: the judges had 'bled the cash boxes of the syndicate dry'. The acquittal of Déroulède and Habert led them to think that the public were behind them: Barrès talked of civil war.[61] President Loubet, at the races at Auteuil, was hissed and booed by the *haut monde* and finally attacked by the young Baron Fernand Chevreau de Christiani, the President's top hat being knocked off his head by the baron's cane. A fight broke out between the racegoers and the police; most of the fifty men arrested wore white carnations in their buttonholes and had titles dating from the *ancien régime*.

Fifty was a paltry number, however, when compared with the 100,000 who turned out to demonstrate in favour of the Republic and acclaim President Loubet, or even when compared with the majority of deputies who voted to have the verdict of the Combined Chambers on the Dreyfus Affair posted in all the communes of France, thereby effacing the shame of the forgeries embedded in Cavaignac's proclamation. This shift of opinion in the Chamber doomed the dithering Dupuy. He was voted out of office. Poincaré, Loubet's first choice to succeed him, failed to form a government; Loubet's next choice, the inscrutable Waldeck-Rousseau, succeeded. Both President and Prime Minister were now Dreyfusards: it had become a necessary qualification for their jobs.

———

On 6 June 1899 all charges against Georges Picquart and Louis Leblois were dismissed; after 384 days in prison, Picquart was set free. Hundreds came to lionise him; thousands sent telegrams to congratulate him. Ludovic Trarieux, the former Minister of Justice and founder of the League of the Rights of Man, held a dinner to celebrate the great event. A motion was carried by the League acclaiming the achievements of 'Dreyfus's champions – Picquart, Scheurer-Kestner and Zola'. But what of the first Dreyfusards? In an article in *L'Aurore*, Bernard Lazare protested that they had been forgotten: the lawyer Edgar Demange, the prison Governor Ferdinand Forzinetti, Picquart's lawyer Louis Leblois and, of course, Lazare himself. He had been asked by Mathieu Dreyfus to keep a low profile because he was 'too committed, too Jewish', too proud of being a Jew.[62] Even at this, their moment of triumph, fissures had started to appear in the Dreyfusard camp.

Rennes

1: The Return from Devil's Island

On 5 June 1899, at 12.30 p.m., the chief warder on Devil's Island entered the hut in which Alfred Dreyfus had been living for more than four years and handed him a note. It stated that the verdict imposed on him on 22 December 1894 had been annulled, and that he was to be retried by a court martial to be held in Rennes. Dreyfus was no longer a convict but a prisoner on remand. He was to be allowed to wear the uniform of an officer in the French Army with the rank of captain. The military guard was to be withdrawn and replaced by civilian gendarmes. A cruiser of the French navy, the *Sfax*, had been dispatched to bring the prisoner back to France.

'My joy was boundless, unutterable. At last, I was escaping from the rack to which I had been bound for five years . . .'[1] Dreyfus records this in his memoirs with a certain sadness because, as he later realised, he was under a misapprehension. He assumed that the annulment of the verdict meant that he had been proclaimed innocent. 'I thought everything was going to be terminated speedily; that there was no further question of anything but a mere formality.' It had taken seven months for his appeal to be heard, first by the Criminal Chamber of the Cour de Cassation, then by the Combined Chambers, and only in the last of those seven months had some scraps of information about his own case got through to him – the existence of Esterhazy, Henry's forgery and suicide, Zola's intervention and Picquart's travails. The 'grand struggle undertaken by a few great minds, full of the love of truth, was utterly unknown to me'.

A squad of gendarmes arrived from Cayenne to replace the military warders, as did civilian clothes and a hat sent by the mayor of Cayenne. While waiting for the *Sfax*, Dreyfus wrote a note to be telegraphed to his wife: 'My heart and soul are with you, with my children, with all of you. I leave Friday. I await with immense joy the moment of supreme happiness to hold you in my arms. A thousand kisses.'

On the evening of Thursday, 8 June, Dreyfus saw the smoke of a steamer on the horizon: it was the *Sfax*. At seven the next morning, the prison launch came to take him to the cruiser and, after more than four years of solitary confinement on the inhospitable outcrop of rock, he left Devil's Island. A heavy swell prevented him from making the transfer on to the *Sfax*. Dreyfus was sea-sick. At ten, the sea was sufficiently calm for the launch to come alongside the warship. Dreyfus was received on deck by the second officer and taken to a cabin of a non-commissioned officer; a metal grating had been placed over the porthole. During the long voyage back to France, Dreyfus was allowed an hour's exercise on deck in the morning and another in the evening. For the rest of the day, and during the night, he was locked in his cabin. When the ship stopped in the Caribbean, an officer gave him some books and a copy of *The Times* in which he read that Commandant du Paty de Clam had been arrested and taken to the Cherche-Midi prison. When the *Sfax* called at the Cape Verde Islands to take on coal, Dreyfus asked to send a telegram to General de Boisdeffre to thank him for all he had done.[2]

The *Sfax* reached France in the early morning of 30 June 1899. That night, in heavy rain and with a gale-force wind, Dreyfus was transferred first into a small dinghy, then into a steam-launch, which took him to the quay at Port-Haliguen on the coast of Brittany. A line of soldiers surrounded the dock. From there, with an escort of three gendarmes, a carriage took him to the railway station at Quiberon; here again, soldiers were posted on the platform. From Quiberon, they took a train to Rennes. After a journey of more than two hours, and another ride in a coach from the station through the streets of Rennes, Dreyfus arrived at the military prison.

It was six in the morning. Dreyfus was locked in a cell. At nine he was led to an adjacent cell that had been furnished with a table and two chairs. He was told that his wife had arrived to see him. Dreyfus was seized by 'a violent trembling'; 'my tears flowed, tears which I had not known for so long a time . . .' Lucie was shown in. 'It is impossible for words to describe the deep emotion which my wife and I both felt at seeing each other once more. In our meeting were mingled feelings of joy and grief . . .' Inhibited by the presence of an army lieutenant, they could do little more than look into one another's eyes, 'concentrating in this interchange of looks all the strength of our affection and of our determination'.

Over the following days, Dreyfus received in this furnished cell further visits from Lucie, from Mathieu and from his lawyers, Edgar Demange and Fernand Labori. In his weakened condition, both physical and mental, it took a great effort for Dreyfus to absorb and understand what he was now told. He had always been sure that in the end justice would prevail, but he had had no inkling of what tortuous dramas had culminated in the decision of the Combined Chambers.

Only now did Dreyfus learn from his brother and his lawyers about the heroes and villains of his Affair: the upright Picquart, the anguished Lazare; of Zola, Trarieux, Mornard, Clemenceau, Jaurès; and of those who had stopped at nothing to keep him on Devil's Island – the Ministers Billot and Cavaignac, the Generals de Pellieux, Roget, Gonse and – most wounding of all – the man in whom Dreyfus had placed so much faith, de Boisdeffre. 'My illusions with regard to some of my former chiefs faded away, one by one; my soul was filled with anguish. I was moved with profound pity and sorrow for that Army which I so loved.'[3] Dreyfus also learned that the sudden and baffling change in the conditions in which he had been held on Devil's Island at the beginning of September 1896 – the shackles and the palisade – was a response to the story of his escape that Mathieu had planted in the English papers.

───────

The new court martial was scheduled to start on 9 August 1899. Dreyfus had little more than a month to study the documentary evidence of the complex conspiracy that had started with the single secret file containing the few forgeries shown by General Mercier to the judges at his first court martial, and now consisted of 1,500 documents in 'ten boxes of files'[4] assembled by Captain Cuignet under the tutelage of General Gonse. He had to read the transcripts of the trial of Zola with General de Boisdeffre's sworn testimony as to the authenticity of Henry's forgery, the report prepared for the Cour de Cassation by Maître Mornard, and the record of the hearings of the Court's Criminal Chamber, and then of its Combined Chambers.

Dreyfus's health deteriorated. The sudden transfer from a tropical to a temperate climate meant that he constantly shivered with cold. There was a recurrence of the fever he had contracted on Devil's Island. Concentration was difficult; for a while he was confined to his bed and fed on a diet of milk and eggs. But all this suffering was now bearable because he was confident that, after passing through the formality of the second court martial, his ordeal would finally end and he would be able, 'restored to my wife and little ones, tranquilly to forget all the sorrows of the past, and live again once more'.[5]

2: The Second Court Martial – 1

Rennes, the capital of Brittany, had been chosen as a venue for the second court martial by Charles Dupuy before leaving office. The reason given was its proximity to the west coast of France. It was hardly a neutral city: Brittany was the most profoundly Catholic part of France. There had been anti-Semitic riots at the time of Zola's trial. Folk memories of the brutal suppression of the Catholic royalists by the revolutionaries of 1789 remained strong. 'Thus Dreyfus and Judas were the same thing, as were the English and the Germans, both Protestants.'[6] As Joseph Reinach was to point out, 'Mercier himself could not have chosen a better place for the re-condemnation of his victim.'

The court martial was held not in Rennes's Palais de Justice nor in an army barracks but in a lycée adjacent to the military prison. This enabled Dreyfus to pass from the prison to the lycée protected from the public. The school had been built in the 1860s on the site of the Jesuit college where Chateaubriand had been a pupil, and his name was inscribed together with other great Breton writers such as Lammenais and Renan in the school's auditorium, the *salle des fêtes*, which had been converted into a courtroom. Maurice Paléologue, who attended the trial as the official representative of the Foreign Office, and whose diary is a prime source for what took place behind the scenes, feared that the theatrical setting of the *salle des fêtes* would 'exaggerate still further the dramatic elements in the case which ought to be decided in cool and calm surroundings'.[7]

It was a forlorn hope. Both in France and abroad, the second court martial of Alfred Dreyfus promised to be one of the great trials of the century. Lawyers, generals, witnesses, politicians, official observers and journalists came to Rennes from all over France. There were a large number of foreigners, noted Paléologue: 'British, German, Italian, Russian, Belgian, Dutch, Scandinavian, Swiss and American – most of whom are of the Jewish type'.[8] All had to find somewhere to stay. The Prefect had reserved rooms for Paléologue and the representative of the Ministry of War, General Chamoin, at the Hôtel Moderne. General Mercier lodged with an old friend who lived in Rennes, General de Saint-Germain: this house became the headquarters of the anti-Dreyfusards, among them Cavaignac, Barrès, Drumont, and also members of the local clergy and gentry.

The Dreyfus family rented a house belonging to a widow, Mme Godard, found for them by a Protestant pastor. Dreyfus's lawyer, Maître Labori, took lodgings in a house on the Place Laënnec. For safety's sake, the Dreyfusard headquarters was set up at an inn outside Rennes, the Auberge des Trois Marches; here Colonel Picquart's former batman helped serve the food prepared by the proprietors for the diverse collection of journalists, intellectuals and politicians. Reinach, Clemenceau and Zola remained in Paris, judging that their presence might provoke the anti-Dreyfusards. Scheurer-Kestner was too ill to attend.

The seven judges appointed to conduct the court martial all held the rank of colonel or below. They were not trained lawyers. The presiding judge, Colonel Albert Jouaust, was Director of Engineering in the

10th Army Corps. The other six officers were all, like Dreyfus, artillery officers – Lieutenant-Colonel François Brogniart and Commandant Julien Profillet from the 10th Artillery Regiment; Commandant Lancrau de Bréon, Commandant Émile Merle, Captain Albert Parfait and Captain Charles Beauvais from the 7th. All had passed through the egalitarian École Polytechnique; none had attended the 'clericalist' military academy at Saint-Cyr. Merle and Profillet had known Godefroy Cavaignac at the École Polytechnique, but the only officer who had shown his hand in any way was Commandant Lancrau de Bréon: with his wife, he had contributed five francs to the Henry Monument. Paléologue's Breton secretary, the Vicomte du Halgouët, who was with him in Rennes, knew the Bréons. They were all devout Catholics; the Commandant's brother was a priest but one of that rare species, a Dreyfusard priest,[9] while his cousin and fellow officer Colonel de Villebois-Mareuil was a convinced anti-Dreyfusard.*

The military prosecutor, Commandant Louis-Norbert Carrière, a graduate of Saint-Cyr and former infantry officer, had retrained as a military prosecutor after his retirement from active service; he was now sixty-six years old. He came to Rennes with his dog and a tame crow. 'He and his crow must get on well together,' judged Paléologue, who watched them in the courtyard outside the lycée, 'for, having the same-shaped head, the same facial angle, the same brain structure, why should there be any difference in their mentality?'[10]

To assist him Carrière enlisted a civilian lawyer, Jules Auffray, who was a friend of General Mercier and had acted for *La Libre Parole*. Just as Gonse had hoped to establish the guilt of Dreyfus by the sheer number of documents in his dossier, so Carrière's tactic was to overwhelm the judges with testimony: he summoned eighty[11] witnesses, four times the number called by the defence. A key witness was notable for his absence: Charles Esterhazy had written to Carrière from London saying that he could not afford to travel to Rennes, and that anyway he knew that the judges were determined to acquit Dreyfus.

---

* Colonel de Villebois loathed the British because of Fashoda and died fighting for the Boers.

He repeated that he was the author of the *bordereau* but 'before God and the sacred memory of my father, I swear that I entered into relations with Schwartzkoppen only on orders from Sandherr'.[12] This letter was leaked to *Le Matin* and published on 7 August 1899, the first day of the court martial.

On that first day, Rennes was like a city under martial law. Soldiers and gendarmes lined the streets. Cavalry were posted at junctions. A number of roadblocks were set up in the streets leading to the lycée and only those with tickets for the trial were allowed through. It was a show of force to impose order but also, perhaps, to intimidate the Dreyfusards. 'There was a great clamour from the movement of the horses,' wrote Mathieu Dreyfus, 'the rattling of sabres, the noises of rifle butts.'[13] The short path his brother would take from the military prison to the lycée was lined by soldiers, their backs to the prisoner, which the Dreyfusards considered a calculated insult.

Inside the *salle des fêtes*, on the stage beneath a crucifix, was an oblong table and behind it chairs for the seven judges. Behind them were seats for the official representatives of the Ministry of War and Ministry of Foreign Affairs, General Eugène Chamoin and Maurice Paléologue. To the right of the stage sat counsel for the defence, and there were two chairs for the prisoner and his guard. To the left sat the military prosecutor, Commandant Carrière, with his assistant Auffray and the clerk of the court. Behind the lawyers on both sides of the room were benches for the press; and facing the stage, taking up the bulk of the auditorium, were rows of seats for the witnesses who would be called to give evidence, and those who through connections or their innate distinction had managed to obtain tickets to watch the show.

A barrier separated this audience from the witnesses, and a voluntary segregation separated the witnesses into two camps. Here, after all, was a group of men – and one woman, Mme Henry – whose mutual antagonism had brought France close to civil war. Here, in the front row, was Jean Casimir-Perier, President of the Republic at the time of Dreyfus's arrest in 1894, and next to him General Mercier. Here, among the many officers with their clanking sabres and clinking spurs, were the former Ministers of War General Billot, General Zurlinden

and Godefroy Cavaignac. Here was General Roget – the man who had
once asked the Statistical Section to help him dispose of a troublesome mistress, who had been Dreyfus's assessor at the École de Guerre
and judged him unsuitable for the General Staff, and who, six months
before, had refused to join Déroulède's attempted coup. Here were
Generals de Boisdeffre and Gonse, and Captains Cuignet and Lauth
– Lauth present both as a witness in his own right and as an escort for
Mme Henry.

There was little glitter of uniforms in the opposing camp on the
left of the auditorium. There were two officers prepared to give
evidence that exonerated Dreyfus, Commandants Ducros and
Hartman; and Captain Martin Freystaetter, one of the judges in
the first court martial, now convinced that its judgment had been
wrong. The key witness for the defence and hero of the Dreyfusards,
Georges Picquart, who in all the previous hearings had appeared in
the blue and gold uniform of his regiment, had been thrown out
of the army and so now wore civilian clothes. He sat next to the
Socialist politicians Jean Jaurès and René Viviani, with whom he
chatted as the room filled up. Paléologue feared that the three men
grouped together would be seen by the anti-Dreyfusards as a *tableau
vivant* of treason – the alliance between 'the defenders of the Jew and
the destroyers of our national traditions. I fear that the Jew will pay
for this edifying spectacle.'[14] A finding that Dreyfus was innocent
would prove Picquart right.

————

At seven in the morning, all stood as the seven military judges wearing full-dress uniform filed into the school hall. The guards saluted.
The judges acknowledged their salute and took their seats. The presiding judge, Colonel Albert Jouaust, declared the session open and, in a
sharp, dry voice, summoned the accused. The room was silent. All eyes
turned towards the door through which the principal protagonist of
the national drama would appear. As 'the whole hall seemed to hold
its breath', the door opened and Dreyfus marched into the room. He
reached the podium, saluted the judges, went to his place beside his

lawyers and, with Colonel Jouaust's permission, removed his *képi* and sat down.

The effect Dreyfus produced on the thousand or so spectators packed into the courtroom was both dramatic and confused. Here, finally, in flesh and blood was the man who for years had been talked of almost as a symbol, an abstraction. And what flesh and blood. He wore the gold-braided uniform of a captain in the Artillery, together with boots and spurs, but 'his arms were withered, his knees so thin that they seemed to pierce the cloth of his trousers. There were just a few white hairs on his bald pate. Only the staring eyes behind his pince-nez gave some slight animation to his cadaverous face.'[15] Even Maurice Barrès, looking on from the benches reserved for the press, wrote of how 'the whole court-room swayed with combined horror and pity when Dreyfus appeared'. Here was the traitor, but 'at that moment we felt nothing but a thin wave of pain breaking over the auditorium. A miserable human rag was being thrown into the glaring light.'[16]

The clerk of the court read out the indictment – the same that Dreyfus had heard in 1894. Hearing the allegations for a second time, Dreyfus momentarily lost control of his feelings: a few tears ran down his cheeks. He then regained his composure and 'resumed his impassive mask, his poor worn-out mask, lined with pain'.[17] Jouaust asked Dreyfus to respond to the charges; his tone was abrupt and unfriendly. Dreyfus answered 'in a dry, monotonous, jerky voice'. He denied the charges. 'I affirm again that I am innocent. I have put up with so much for five years, *mon colonel*, but yet again, for the sake of my honour and that of my children, I declare that I am innocent.' He swayed with dizziness; his face had grown pale. Jouaust persisted: 'So you deny the charges?' 'Yes, *mon colonel*.' His protestations of innocence were repeated over and over again in a monotonous voice and, in exactly the same way as his dreary delivery had alienated those who had been present at his first court martial, so now his audience felt he was failing to fulfil the dramatic potential of his role.

Paléologue had not been present at the first trial, but he had witnessed Dreyfus's degradation before the École Militaire and remembered that there too his protestations of innocence had been unconvincing. At that time he had thought Dreyfus guilty; subsequently he had reached a near-certainty that he was not. But now, once again, Dreyfus's protestations of innocence revived his misgivings. 'Why, now I *knew* that they were true, did they still sound so false to my ear? Why is this man incapable of putting any warmth into his words? Why in his most vigorous protestations can nothing of his soul emerge through his strangled throat?'[18]

Clearly, since there had been no drama school on Devil's Island, it was perhaps expecting too much of Dreyfus that he should have learned how to play the innocent victim to the public's satisfaction. Not only was he debilitated by disease and the years of mistreatment, he also retained his inhibited personality, and the same faith in reason and common sense. He had expected the court martial to be a formality, yet here he was being asked to repudiate the same smears and insinuations about his womanising, his gambling, his curiosity about military matters, his trips to Alsace. Only new falsehoods roused him from this tedium: no, he had not dined with the German military attaché with his mistress, Suzanne Cron; no, he had not confessed to his crime to Captain Lebrun-Renault at the time of his degradation. 'I have always declared my innocence; I have always defended my honour. By the head of my wife and children, I swear that I am innocent!'

The same bafflement at the sheer irrelevance of so much of the material presented in court was evident when, on Tuesday, 8 August, General Chamoin submitted to the court, sitting in camera, the Dreyfus dossier from the Ministry of War. Dreyfus appeared bemused. 'His attitude', wrote Paléologue, 'seemed to say: "What have those piles of paper got to do with me?"' And it was a proper question: among all the mass of documents, 'there are not twenty lines', Paléologue realised,

> that really apply to him. The whole secret file of the intelligence department consists of nothing but apocryphal or adulterated documents; inaccurate translations, distorted evidence, fragments of foolish or fabricated gossip; scraps of paper arbitrarily fitted together, to which any meaning whatever can be attached, like the sibylline leaves; and insignificant jottings into which profound and cabalistic meanings are read.[19]

After General Chamoin it was Paléologue's turn to present the Dreyfus dossier from the Ministry of Foreign Affairs. He managed to persuade the court that 'the packet of sixty-four charming and intimate letters' written by Hermance de Weede to Maximilian von Schwartzkoppen had no relevance to the Dreyfus case and could therefore be removed from the dossier. Of utmost importance to the case, however, was the telegram in the file from Panizzardi to his superiors in Rome sent shortly after Dreyfus's arrest. Paléologue was able to demonstrate that it was not merely inaccurately deciphered but an outright forgery. There was also the question of a copy of the *bordereau*, annotated by the Kaiser himself and mentioning Dreyfus by name, that had supposedly come into the possession of the Statistical Section by the 'usual route'. Learning of the theft of this document back in January 1895, it was claimed, the German Ambassador, Graf Münster von Derneburg, had threatened war if it was not returned. It was returned, so the prosecution claimed, but not before it had been photographed.

Henry had alluded to the existence of such a document to Paléologue before his suicide and Paléologue realised that, if it existed, it must be a forgery because the Kaiser would never have direct relations with a spy. In court Paléologue, who was scrupulous to separate his opinions from the facts, told the military judges that the file from the Quai d'Orsay contained no reference to this 'fantastic episode' whatsoever. Did the judges believe him? During a recess, Paléologue was questioned by three of them – Profillet, Beauvais and Parfait. 'If you would only tell us everything you know,' said Beauvais. Paléologue assured him that he was telling them everything he knew. Clearly, they thought he was holding something back. 'Don't insist, Beauvais,' said Commandant Profillet. 'Monsieur Paléologue's task is difficult enough as it is.'[20]

In the absence of this annotated *bordereau*, or any piece of new evidence, the court now went over yet again the evidence that had been produced at the first court martial and that had been exhaustively investigated in repeated hearings ever since. Was the handwriting on the *bordereau* that of Dreyfus? Was Dreyfus's possession of the keys to all the cupboards in the offices of the Fourth Bureau incriminating when it was in fact Commandant Bertin-Mourot who had given him the keys so that he could make a methodical study of the dossiers the cupboards contained?[21] Even the definitive conclusions reached by the Combined Chambers of the Cour de Cassation – for example, that Dreyfus had not confessed his guilt to Captain Lebrun-Renault – did not prevent the prosecution from bringing such matters up once again.

Two crucial witnesses were unavailable – Esterhazy because he was in England, Henry because he was dead. Without Henry to give evidence, his widow Berthe was called to the stand – 'tall, slender, dark, with fine eyes that shone beneath her long crêpe veils'.[22] Barrès reported that she had several times shouted 'Judas!' at Dreyfus from the well of court. She was asked what she knew about the way in which her late husband had obtained the *bordereau*, and then what, in her opinion, Henry had meant, in his last letter to her from the fortress of Mont-Valérien, by the phrase 'you know in whose interests I acted'. Briefly, she closed her eyes. Then, 'in a hesitating, sing-song voice, like a little girl reciting her catechism, she said: "It was in the interest of the army . . . the army that my dear husband . . . committed . . . committed his crime. It was the interest of the army that always guided . . . guided his conduct. And in the interest of whom else, gentlemen, could you believe that he would act?"'[23]

When Mme Henry stepped down from the witness stand, Captain Lauth rose to give her his arm and escort her out of the room.

———

After Mme Henry, General Roget was called to the stand. By his military stance and commanding manner, he had an air of authority that inevitably impressed the seven junior officers acting as judges. It was, wrote Paléologue, as if he had been 'ordering them to carry out a manoeuvre'. He said that Esterhazy could not be the traitor because he had no access to the secret documents mentioned in the *bordereau*. He insisted that Esterhazy's louche character and disordered private life, while regrettable, had no bearing on the case before them. It was the same when Generals Billot and Zurlinden gave evidence: here were the great military leaders of France assuring their subordinates that Esterhazy was innocent and Dreyfus guilty. Cavaignac, too, though not a soldier, was indubitably a man of great intelligence and high distinction who put the case of the General Staff with lucidity and precision.

General de Boisdeffre gave evidence on 19 August. For Dreyfus, this was perhaps the most painful session of all because for so long he had believed that his former chief wished him well. Now he heard his hero, old before his time, repeat in a weary tone of voice his conviction that Dreyfus was guilty, that Esterhazy was the *homme de paille* – the patsy – put up by the Dreyfus family. When asked if he had any questions to put to Boisdeffre, Dreyfus simply replied: 'I do not wish to respond to General de Boisdeffre.'

Just as Dreyfus had had faith in General de Boisdeffre, so too had Commandant Henry; it was in *his* interest that he had acted. During Henry's interrogation by Cavaignac, Boisdeffre had said nothing. Had he been ignorant of what this over-zealous subordinate had done for his sake? 'Why did Henry', Boisdeffre asked Paléologue after giving evidence, slumped in a chair in Paléologue's office in the lycée, 'Why did Henry . . . and others as well, perhaps, commit all these aberrations, since there is no doubt about Dreyfus's guilt?'

Paléologue reversed the question. 'Why should Henry and *certainly* others as well have committed all these aberrations if they had not felt that you and General Gonse were going to be forced to acknowledge Dreyfus's innocence?' It was, he believed, to cover the tracks of Esterhazy, and not just Esterhazy: Paléologue believed that Henry was in fact complicit in Esterhazy's treason, together with Maurice Weil and a fourth and as yet unidentified officer in the army's High Command.

'I understand less and less,' said Boisdeffre, 'for I can neither accept what you say nor refute it . . . There's nothing left for me but to disappear. I'm finished, finished!'[24]

Gonse did no better than de Boisdeffre. Only a week or two before the opening of the court martial, he had been dismissed as Deputy Chief of the General Staff. In giving his evidence, he 'stumbled, lost the thread of his thought, and retracted what he had said'. The witnesses from the Statistical Section gave conflicting evidence. Lauth, Henry's friend and the *cavaliere servente* of his widow, told the court of a secret war waged against the Germans by his former chief, Colonel Sandherr, through 'intoxification' – passing false information to the enemy via double agents – evidence which showed that forging documents was part of the everyday work of the Section. Commandant Cordier, Sandherr's deputy, on the other hand, broke ranks with his former colleagues and told the court of his doubts about Dreyfus's guilt: the anti-Dreyfusard press dismissed this as the unreliable testimony of an alcoholic.[25]

Félix Gribelin, the archivist from the Statistical Section who had witnessed the arrest of Dreyfus by du Paty de Clam, told the court that Dreyfus's shiftiness about his extramarital affairs confirmed his guilt.[26] Alphonse Bertillon, the Chef du Service d'Identité Judiciare, took the stand once again to expound his theory of auto-forgery – a theory which the experts appointed by the Combined Chambers had unanimously judged to be 'devoid of all scientific value'.[27]

The irrelevance of much of the evidence, the admission of hearsay, the mix of opinion with fact and the mingling of judges, witnesses and prosecutors during the court's recesses appalled observers from outside France. A drink offered to Picquart during a recess of the Criminal Chamber, and a judge calling him 'my dear Picquart', had been sufficient to have the case removed from that court's jurisdiction. Now, there were regular friendly exchanges between the army officers involved in the court martial. General Mercier discussed the trial with General Chamoin, the representative of the Ministry of War; while Maurice Paléologue, representing the Foreign Office and, like Chamoin, supposedly impartial, was asked by one of the judges, Lieutenant-Colonel Brogniart, 'as a private individual', whether he thought Dreyfus innocent or guilty. Paléologue repeated his theory that it was not Dreyfus who was the traitor but Esterhazy in cahoots with Henry and Maurice Weil. 'Maurice Weil? Who is this Maurice Weil?' Brogniart had never heard of him, and 'his surprise turned to astonishment when I told him the improbable story of this Jew'.[28]

3: The Second Court Martial – 2

The two lawyers defending Dreyfus might have been more effective had they not disagreed, acrimoniously, about how to proceed. Edgar

Demange, Dreyfus's first counsel and loyal supporter, wanted to avoid any kind of confrontation with the army and its General Staff and persuade the judges to acquit Dreyfus on the grounds of reasonable doubt. Fernand Labori, on the other hand, wanted to expose the monstrous conspiracy that had first led to Dreyfus's conviction and subsequently kept him on Devil's Island.

The two men differed in style as well as tactics. Whereas Demange spoke courteously to the judges, putting his questions 'with the solemnity of a head waiter passing the turbot',[29] Labori was pugnacious and argumentative, more than willing to confront the presiding judge, Colonel Jouaust. 'Maître Labori, I would ask you to speak with moderation,' Jouaust said to Labori after one of his flamboyant outbursts.

'I have not uttered a single immoderate word.'

'But your tone is immoderate.'

'I am not in control of my tone.'

'Well, you should be. Everyone is in control of his person.'

'I am in control of my person but not my tone.'

'I shall withdraw your right to speak.'

'Go ahead and withdraw it.'

'Sit down.'

'I will sit down, but only because I choose to.'

The antipathy between the two defence lawyers was all too apparent. Labori undermined Demange by revealing that the Statistical Section had a file on him because he specialised in the defence of foreign agents.* Labori himself was considered suspect after defending the anarchist Vaillant who had thrown a bomb into the Chamber of Deputies. However, Labori was the *bête noire* of the nationalists not for acting for Vaillant but for defending Zola. On 14 August 1899, at six in the morning, while he was walking with Picquart from his lodgings on the Place Laënnec towards the court along the banks of the River Vilaine, Labori was shot in the back at a distance of three metres. The

* Sandherr had told Paléologue that Demange 'was an unpleasant, very unpleasant character, who had made a speciality of defending spies; he was in the hands of the Jews. At the intelligence department we have a file about him which might take him a long way.'

young man who had fired the shot fled; Picquart pursued him but he escaped. Labori was taken to the house of Rennes's leading Dreyfusard, Professor Victor Basch, where it was found that the bullet lodged in his back had missed his spine and done no serious damage.

Despite the deployment of hundreds of soldiers and gendarmes to search for the would-be assassin, he was never found. Paléologue's secretary, the Breton Vicomte du Halgouët, predicted correctly that 'the gendarmes and the police will come back empty-handed for the attempted murderer will have the whole population on his side. I know our peasants. They never denounce each other any more than they ever agree to give evidence against each other. They have remained exactly as they were at the time of the *chouannerie*' – the uprising of the Catholic royalists in 1793.

Barrès wrote cynically that the defence would be better off with-out 'the impetuous lawyer'. Colonel Jouaust refused to suspend the proceedings and so Henri Mornard was brought in to replace Labori; but, after only eight days, Labori returned to his place in court. The week of recuperation had exacerbated his paranoia: he suspected that what Barrès had said was true – that the Dreyfus family felt that Alfred's cause would be better served without him. Conspiracy theories entered his head. Hearing that Joseph Reinach had met the Jesuit Père du Lac at the house of a *salonnière*, Mme Dreyfus-Gonzales, he felt that some deal between the clericalists and the Dreyfusards had been done behind his back.

Mathieu Dreyfus, the co-ordinator of his brother's defence, regret-ted that the man who had so ably and eloquently defended Zola should now be sidelined, but Labori's policy of confrontation with the army was proving counter-productive. Mathieu understood how the judges, middle-ranking officers in the army, 'must find it difficult to believe in so much villainy, in so many perjuries on the part of people they esteem',[30] and agreed with Demange that the defence had to be conducted with this in mind.

It was clearly the most propitious line to take. Two weeks into the trial, three of the judges told Paléologue of 'their inability to see any light about the crime of 1894' and asked him if there was not some way in which conclusive evidence could not be obtained from the Germans. The same possibility had been mooted by the Prime Minister, Waldeck-Rousseau, in Paris; and it had been suggested to Schwartzkoppen by his former chief, Graf Münster von Derneburg, back in December 1898 that perhaps he, Schwartzkoppen, should intervene – to help not Dreyfus but Picquart when he faced a court martial and five years in prison: 'for you must not forget that what is at issue is the liberty and future of an officer whom you, be he French or German, must always regard as a brother officer'.[31] Schwartzkoppen had replied that he had been 'forbidden to make any admission' by his superiors, and added: 'For that matter, the unfortunate Captain Dreyfus should be as close a concern of mine as officer and comrade as Colonel Picquart, and nothing was ever done for the former on our part to free him from his tragic situation.'[32]

Six months later, the situation remained the same. The German government felt that the formal statements already made by its Ambassador and the Chancellor himself that it had had no dealings with Dreyfus sufficed, and that if these were doubted then why would the same protestations by lesser officers be believed? The only intervention from abroad came when Major Carrière, the prosecutor, produced as a witness an Austrian officer, like a white rabbit out of a hat. This was a Lieutenant Eugen Lazare von Czernuski who gave evidence through the clerk of the court (he could barely speak French) that a friend who served as a section head in the Ministry of Foreign Affairs in Vienna had told him that there were four persons spying for the 'Germanic powers' in France, and Alfred Dreyfus was top of the list. A high-ranking officer on the German General Staff had confirmed this information.

Even those predisposed to believe what he said found Czernuski an unconvincing witness. 'His appearance should have been enough to discredit him,' wrote Paléologue. 'His complexion was haggard, there was a shifty look in his rheumy, twitching eyes, his ears were asymmetrical and he was continually grimacing. His face was that of a rogue and vagabond; the man was obviously a social outcast.'[33] At a second session, held in camera, Czernuski broke down under cross-examination and subsequently said he was sick and left Rennes; but this introduction of a foreign witness provoked Labori, without consulting Demange, to demand that Schwartzkoppen and Panizzardi be summoned through diplomatic channels to give evidence. He sent telegrams to Kaiser Wilhelm II and the King of Italy to this effect.*

Labori's request was rejected by the judges of the court martial as being beyond their powers to enforce, and on 8 September an official communiqué of the German government confirmed the position already taken: that previous statements must suffice. 'Secretary of State von Bülow expressed himself in these terms on 24 January 1898 before the Reichstag Commission: "I declare as formally as possible that between the French ex-Captain Dreyfus, presently imprisoned on Devil's Island, and any German agency, there has never existed any relation or connection of any sort whatsoever."'[34]

———

The only other intervention from abroad came with the arrival in Rennes of Lord Russell of Killowen, the Lord Chief Justice of England, sent to report on the trial by Queen Victoria herself. He was received with the appropriate respect and seated on the platform behind the judges between Maurice Paléologue and General Chamoin. 'What an unattractive-looking man,' he whispered to Paléologue when he first saw Dreyfus. He later told Paléologue, who had been told to take care of him, that he was appalled by the patent bias of the judges against the accused and by the total confusion in the evidence between fact, hearsay and opinion; and he said he was amazed that the crucial role of prosecutor, in a trial that had the attention of the world, should have been given to 'such a grotesque figure' as Major Carrière. Stung by these criticisms of the French judicial system 'stated with an entirely British arrogance and abruptness', Paléologue assured his guest that if he knew the judges as well as he now did, he would accord them his respect and esteem.

However, later that evening, dining with Russell in a country inn, and finding him in a less xenophobic frame of mind, Paléologue came

———

* Dreyfus was later told that 25,000 francs had been withdrawn from the account of the Intelligence Department at the War Ministry at just the time Czernuski appeared at Rennes.

to appreciate 'the extent to which the French mind, which is so open to the sense of justice, is so closed to the notion of law'.[35] But was the French mind open to a sense of justice? On his way to the court martial Lord Russell had told his coachman that he thought Dreyfus innocent. 'And the generals?' the coachman had replied. 'Are they guilty?'[36]

'The choice is clear,' wrote Barrès. 'Dreyfus or our principal leaders. On the one hand there is Dreyfus's honour; on the other, there is the honour of all the ministers who have sworn to Dreyfus's guilt.' 'If the innocence of Dreyfus is established,' wrote Déroulède, 'there can be no punishments sufficiently terrible for the Ministers who either accused or allowed him to be accused. Every reprisal would be excusable . . . If Dreyfus is innocent, the generals are scoundrels.'[37]

'Between the Jew and the General, choose!' The General was Mercier, the alpha and omega of the Dreyfus Affair, the man who had brought the prosecution of Alfred Dreyfus in the autumn of 1894 to secure his position as Minister of War, and who was there in Rennes to stiffen the resolve of those like Boisdeffre and Gonse who had been broken by the Affair – 'all those', as Paléologue put it, 'whom the Dreyfus case has morally killed'. Mercier was not a cadaver in this 'necropolis'; he was not just alive but vigorous and commanding. He 'dominated the drama at Rennes and . . . outranked every one of the prisoner's seven judges'.[38] From the home in Rennes of his friend General de Saint-Germain, Mercier had co-ordinated the campaign of the anti-Dreyfusards, insisting upon 'rigorous discipline' throughout the camp. Even before the trial opened, he had thrown his own character on to the scales of justice. 'Dreyfus will certainly be condemned once again,' he had written in *L'Intransigeant* on 3 August 1899, 'because in this affair someone is guilty, and either it is him or it is me.'[39]

Unwavering in his insistence that Dreyfus was guilty, and as much in command in 1899 as he had been in 1894, Mercier's political affiliations had changed. As Jean Doise has pointed out, it was Mercier who started the Affair, a man who was said to be inspired by anti-Semitism, but in October 1894 he had been a staunch republican, a free-thinker, married to a Protestant Englishwoman, and 'had nothing about him of the *chouan*' (see p. 298).[40] Now he was the hero of the nationalist and royalist anti-Dreyfusards, although among these, as the trial had proceeded, there was a growing impatience at Mercier's delay in producing the document that would settle things once and for all – the photograph of the *bordereau* annotated in the hand of the Kaiser and mentioning Dreyfus by name. Was not the letter from Panizzardi, asked *La Libre Parole* and *La Croix*, forged by Henry to take its place at a time when revealing the real thing would have led to war? Now the time had come to end all procrastination. Mercier must play his trump card.

There was no trump card. Mercier's confidence that his view would prevail depended not on evidence but on authority. 'Nothing has been able to shake his faith in his own infallibility,' wrote Paléologue. 'The ruins that have accumulated round his handiwork, the most categorical denials, the most devastating disclosures, the troubled consciences of many of the most upright and able men, left him unmoved.'[41] On Saturday, 12 August, General Mercier took the stand. 'The hall was all agog', wrote Paléologue, 'for the dramatic and devastating disclosure that would end the case once and for all. But nothing came but a commonplace account of the case.' However, General Mercier concluded his four and a half hours of evidence with a personal statement.

> I shall now end my deposition, already very long, in thanking you for allowing me to speak for so long.
>
> I want to add only one word. I have not reached my age without learning from sad experience that all that is human is subject to error. In any case, if I am feeble-minded as Monsieur Zola has said, I am at least an honest man and the son of an honest man. Therefore, when I saw the start of the campaign for a retrial, I followed with acute anxiety all the polemics, all the debates which took place during the campaign. If the least doubt had entered my mind, gentlemen, I would be the first to declare and to say before you, Captain Dreyfus: 'I made an honest mistake.'

Hearing this, Dreyfus got to his feet. 'That is just what you must say.'

'I would say to Captain Dreyfus,' Mercier went on, '"I made an honest mistake, and with the same good faith I recognise that mistake, and I will do all that is humanly possible to make up for a terrible error.'"

'It is your duty,' shouted Dreyfus.

'But no. My conviction since 1894 has not changed one jot, and it has been strengthened by a deeper study of the dossier, and also by the futility of the efforts made to prove the innocence of the man convicted in 1894, despite the enormous effort and the many millions foolishly spent.'[42]

Mercier would make other interventions in the course of the trial, contradicting the evidence of the former President of the Republic, Jean Casimir-Perier 'with cold, poisonous – and cruel – impertinence' on the question of whether France and Germany were close to war on the night of 6 January 1895. But from Dreyfus himself there would be no further outbursts: he was beyond outrage. Paléologue found 'nothing sadder' than the spectacle of Dreyfus's 'old friends, or rather his old comrades, for even in the days of his prosperity he never had a friend', giving evidence against him, twisting what he had once said, or questions he had put to them, into evidence of treasonous intent. Dreyfus's passivity was baffling.

> If he were to leap from his chair and protest, the members of the court would be grateful to him. But no, he remains seated, phlegmatic or slightly contemptuous. He is the Jew, accustomed for so many centuries not to rise in protest against outrage. However, two or three times he raised his head, with a strange smile, as if he was saying to himself: 'Insult me! Humiliate me! What does it matter? Is not my cause that of justice and reason? Am I not at this moment the representative of the race which had the signal privilege of announcing the reign of justice in the world? What contempt all these *goyim* inspire me with.' Is not this the specific characteristic of Israel through the ages? An immense pride under the mask of humility?[43]

On Thursday, 7 September, General Mercier made a final 'moving' statement; he was the last witness to be heard. Colonel Jouaust then announced that the hearing of evidence was now concluded, at which point the hundred or so officers in the court rose as one man and marched out of the *salle des fêtes* in good order, 'with machine-like precision, with measured step and holding their heads erect, as if they were on manoeuvres'.[44] The prosecutor, Major Carrière, then made his closing speech. It was a fiasco – described by the correspondent for *Le Figaro*, Jules Cornély, as 'more or less incomprehensible drivel'[45] and by Paléologue as 'twaddle'. 'The twaddle that he inflicted on us for an hour and a half was so absurd, so flabby, so disjointed, so flat and incoherent, that at least twenty times the shorthand-writers, having hopelessly lost the thread, put down their pens in despair.' When the court rose, General Chamoin telephoned General Galliffet,* the Minister of War, to say that an acquittal was certain.

Then it was the turn of the defence. The differences between Labori and Demange remained, and each had his supporters in the Dreyfusard high command. Picquart and Georges Clemenceau wanted Labori to take the lead and denounce the conspiracy by Mercier and the General Staff. Joseph Reinach and Bernard Lazare wanted Labori to step back; so too did Victor Basch and Jean Jaurès. It was for Mathieu to decide, and he dithered, as conflicting advice came from all directions. Demange thought his colleague should take part in the final peroration, but in the end Labori himself decided that he would remain silent. 'If I speak,' he told Mathieu, 'and if, as I no longer doubt, your poor brother is convicted, they will say that it is my fault, that everything would have been saved without me. I shall remain silent.'[46]

Demange started to speak in defence of his client, Alfred Dreyfus, at 7.35 on the morning of Friday, 8 September. His peroration lasted for five hours. All agreed that he spoke well – 'a fine speech', judged Paléologue, 'with no gratuitous eloquence but solid, clear, prudent, moderate, imbued with common sense, and pity'. Lord Russell, too, thought the speech 'clear, sensible, well constructed'. However,

---

* 'The Butcher of the Communards' (see p. 20, above): appointed Minister of War by Pierre Waldeck-Rousseau to gain support on the right.

Demange's strategy remained that of showing great respect for the army and going no further than demonstrating that there was a reasonable doubt. 'I am sure that doubt will at least have entered your minds,' he said to the judges, 'and doubt is enough for you to acquit Dreyfus.'

Had doubt entered their minds? Paléologue, who in the course of the trial had got to know the seven judges, was pessimistic about an acquittal. The presiding judge, Colonel Jouaust, with his 'hard, martial and intelligent face', had shown a marked antagonism towards Dreyfus from the beginning. Brogniart, his deputy, and Bréon had confided in Paléologue at the start of the trial the unfavourable impression made on them by the accused. Paléologue had observed the difficulty faced by the judges in their effort 'to demilitarise their minds'. He was sure the effort would be too great for Commandant Merle who had taken part in the court's proceedings 'as he would a review, his head erect, his eyes looking straight to the front and empty. He is not a judge, but a sabre.' The devout Bréon looked to a higher authority: 'Every morning and every night the major spends a long time in prayer, praying to God to reveal to him whether Dreyfus is guilty or not.'[47] Profillet and Parfait were thought to favour a conviction, Beauvais to be undecided.

That afternoon, at three o'clock, Carrière, the prosecutor, responded to Demange in a short speech prepared by his assistant, Jules Auffray. 'The law does not ask jurors to account for the ways in which they have reached their beliefs,' he told the judges. 'It does not prescribe rules to which they are obliged to submit their sense of the sufficiency of evidence. It asks them only one question, which comprises the full measure of their duty: are you convinced?'

Demange begged Labori to have the final word, but Labori refused. An exhausted Demange therefore made a final plea in favour of Dreyfus: 'I know . . . that men of the loyalty and rectitude of these military judges will never raise to the level of proof mere possibilities and presumptions . . . Consequently, my last word is the one I have uttered before all of you. I have confidence in you because you are soldiers.' Dreyfus was asked by Jouaust if he had anything to add.

Pale, patently upset, Dreyfus managed only a few words in a hoarse voice. 'I am innocent . . . The honour of the name my children bear . . . Your loyalty . . .' He fell back on his chair, sweat pouring down his face.

'Is that all you have to say?' asked Jouaust.

'Yes, *mon colonel.*'

At 3.15 p.m., the judges withdrew to consider their verdict. While waiting, Maurice Paléologue and General Chamoin walked up and down in a small courtyard smoking cigarettes, as Commandant Carrière tried to keep them amused by telling 'inept jokes'. At 4.45 a bell rang to signal that the session was due to resume. Paléologue and Chamoin took their seats behind the judges. The auditorium quickly filled with silent spectators. A line of gendarmes had been stationed in front of the platform, and soldiers at the entrance to the hall. The chair in which Alfred Dreyfus had sat throughout the long court martial remained empty: the Military Code stipulated that the accused should not be present when the verdict was given. The judges filed in, 'all horribly pale'. Choking as he pronounced his first words, Colonel Jouaust declared, 'In the name of the French people! The court martial, by a majority of five votes to two, declares: Yes, the prisoner is guilty. By a majority, there are attenuating circumstances. As a result of this, the court sentences Alfred Dreyfus to ten years' detention.'

4: Pardon

Alfred Dreyfus, under guard in a small room, was told of his second conviction by Fernand Labori. 'You tell him,' Demange said to Labori. 'I can't bring myself to do it.' 'Two votes for you,' Labori told Dreyfus, 'plus attenuating circumstances. It is a conviction but you won't return to Devil's Island, I can promise you that.'

Dreyfus showed no emotion. 'Take care of my wife and my children,' he said to Labori.

The same impassive expression remained on his face when, in the corridor outside the room where he had been held, the clerk of the court, Coupois, formally read the sentence. Dreyfus stood, motionless, at attention, then he marched back to his cell in the military prison.

The two votes for an acquittal had been cast by the presiding judge, Colonel Jouaust, and the devout Catholic, Commandant de Bréon. It was no doubt they who had persuaded a majority to mention 'attenuating circumstances' which justified the sentence of ten years' imprisonment rather a return to Devil's Island. But, as was quickly realised, the concept of 'attenuating circumstances' was absurd: if Dreyfus was guilty, he was an out-and-out traitor and merited no mercy.

The tight control of his emotions that Alfred Dreyfus had shown upon hearing of his second conviction was not sustained. When Mathieu visited him the following day, he found him 'ravaged by suffering' – his mouth set in a grimace, his features convulsed. He shuddered at the mention of a second degradation: 'I will never tolerate a new condemnation. I will not put on my uniform again. They will have to drag me out. They will have to take me there by force.'[48] The brothers agreed that he should appeal. Henri Mornard drew up the papers which Alfred Dreyfus signed on 9 September 1899.

In Paris, the Prime Minister, Pierre Waldeck-Rousseau, also planned to appeal on behalf of the government on the grounds that the court martial had gone beyond its terms of reference in considering questions, such as Dreyfus's alleged confession, which had already been dealt with by the Combined Chambers of the Cour de Cassation. His Minister of War, General Galliffet, urged caution: the government should take care not to create a polarity – 'on one side the entire Army, a majority of the French, and all the agitators; on the other, the cabinet, the Dreyfusards, and the international community'.[49]

The international community mattered more than Galliffet supposed, and upon hearing the verdict Waldeck-Rousseau consulted not just his Minister of War and the President of the Republic, but also the Foreign Minister, Théophile Delcassé. The news of Dreyfus's second conviction had produced 'absolute amazement' abroad, followed by an outburst of extreme indignation.[50] There were demonstrations in Milan, Naples, Trieste, London and New York. The Germans were baffled: even the ultra-Catholic *Popular Gazette of Cologne* asked if the French had gone mad. The correspondent of *Le Figaro* in London wrote that the news of the verdict 'produced a profound stupefaction, followed at once by expressions of indignation from everyone that went beyond anything one could imagine. Never have I witnessed such an outburst of anger against our country. I do not approve of them, I merely report faithfully what I have seen and heard in journalistic circles as in the street.'[51]

The court martial had been followed closely, particularly in Britain and the United States, and there had been consternation at the way it had been conducted with witnesses not so much giving evidence as expressing their opinions and making emotive speeches. What a contrast to the strict rules of evidence found in the courts of the Anglo-Saxon nations.* This criticism of the French judicial system became criticism of French society and civilisation as such.[52] British public opinion blamed the whole French nation for the iniquities of the army's High Command, and bundled it with every other evil perpetrated throughout French history – the massacre of Protestants on St Bartholomew's Day and of aristocrats during the Terror, and the aggressive wars of Louis XIV and Napoleon. The heroes of the Dreyfus Affair – Picquart, Zola, Scheurer-Kestner, Demange – were perceived as exceptions that proved the rule. The fact that Dreyfus was a Jew was irrelevant: 'Dreyfus is, to the untainted conscience of humanity, no Semite,' editorialised *The Times*, 'but a human being.'[53] Queen Victoria referred to him as 'the poor martyr Dreyfus'.[54]

It was clear that the anti-Dreyfusards were also anti-British: Commandant de Bréon's anti-Dreyfusard cousin Colonel de Villebois-Mareuil would not be the only French volunteer to fight for the Boers. Should a coup of the kind planned by Déroulède succeed, France's policy towards Britain would change for the worse. 'I heard from a good source', the Dowager Empress of Germany wrote to her mother, Queen Victoria, on 22 August, in the middle of the Rennes court martial, 'that the French talk seriously of having a war with England in

* This complacency was premature. In Britain an Indian solicitor, George Edalji, was wrongfully convicted in 1903, as was a Silesian Jew, Oscar Slater, born Leschziner, in 1909. 'Racial prejudice, arbitrary judgement, and the corporate solidarity of corrupt and/or incompetent officialdom thus proved not to be exclusively cross-Channel phenomena' (Robert Tombs, '"Lesser Breeds without the Law": The British Establishment and the Dreyfus Affair, 1894–1899').

1900.'⁵⁵ Waldeck-Rousseau's government was deemed more pro-British than most, but the British Ambassador in Paris, Sir Edward Monson, had reported to the Foreign Office a few days before, on 14 August, that 'anything is possible' because a foreign quarrel would divert attention from France's 'internal discord and disgrace'.⁵⁶

Many in Britain blamed the Dreyfus Affair on the Catholic Church. In *The Times*, both editorial comment and readers' letters ascribed a moral responsibility to the Pope in Rome, the Roman *Curia* and the Catholic Archbishop of Westminster, Cardinal Vaughan. As in France, religious and tribal loyalties affected people's judgement. The Catholic periodical the *Tablet* condemned the hypocrisy of the British press 'in cases in which religious or national passions are involved' and ascribed the Affair not to 'religion or nationality' but to the mistakes made by amateur judges.

The report by Lord Russell of Killowen, the Lord Chief Justice, to Queen Victoria took a similar line. He told her that Dreyfus's second conviction was a result of mistakes made by inexperienced military judges under a system found 'in all countries of Europe in which the Roman Civil Law . . . prevails'. Passions had been inflamed by self-interested politicians such as Clemenceau and Jaurès, and the foreign, particularly the British, press. The French had rallied to defend the honour of their army and had been influenced by the views of its High Command. This was not a symptom, as had been suggested, of 'a general decadence of moral tone and sense'. Certainly, anti-Semitism had played a role, but Jews were unpopular in most countries where they resided, 'assuredly not on religious, but on racial and social grounds'.⁵⁷ The Dreyfus Affair was certainly not the fault of the Catholic Church, 'the religion of the mass of the people of France which is also the religion of a not unimportant section of her Majesty's subjects at home and in her empire abroad'. Lord Russell of Killowen was an Irish Catholic.

George Bernard Shaw was not a Catholic but he was Irish, and he concurred with his fellow countryman, the Lord Chief Justice; he thought the attacks on the Jesuits were no better than the anti-Semitism of 'Rochefort & Co.'. The failure of Catholics both in Britain and in the United States to go along with the British establishment's view of the Dreyfus Affair, wrote Robert Tombs, shows 'how clearly it was identified with Protestant and Anglo-Saxon ideology'.[58] To the French nationalists, it was a replay of the Damascus Affair: the Protestant British would always side with the Jews. Louis Martin's *L'Anglais, est-il un Juif?* (The Englishman, is he a Jew?) was published in France in 1895 and Martin Chagny's *La Sémitique Albion* (Semitic Albion) in 1898.[59]

The government of Pierre Waldeck-Rousseau might have felt able to shrug off foreign outrage at the verdict delivered at Rennes were it not for the Exposition Universelle due to be held in Paris in 1900. It was a re-run of the Exhibition held eleven years earlier which had seen the opening of the Eiffel Tower – but on a much grander scale. New public buildings to adorn Paris for the Exhibition were nearing completion – the Gare de Lyon and the Gare d'Orsay; the Pont Alexandre III; the Grand Palais, the Petit Palais; a wine rotunda designed by Gustave Eiffel, La Ruche; an indoor cycling circuit, the Vélodrome d'Hiver; and the first line of the new Paris Métro with a station at the Palais du Trocadéro.

What alarmed Waldeck-Rousseau were the increasing demands of liberal opinion abroad to boycott the Exposition Universelle. Images of the imprisoned Dreyfus appeared in newspapers under the title 'French Exhibit '99'. The French correspondent of *Le Figaro* was told, 'The Exhibition is finished. It won't take place.'[60] Waldeck-Rousseau was also dismayed by the thought that the divisions in French society caused by the Affair would continue. He looked for a way for the executive branch of government to cut through the Gordian knot which the judicial branch of government had failed to untie. On 11 September, in *Le Siècle*, Joseph Reinach proposed a solution. Alfred Dreyfus should be pardoned by presidential decree.

Later that day, Reinach held a meeting with Waldeck-Rousseau at the Élysée Palace. The two men were friends and political allies. The Prime Minister warmed to the idea of a pardon. But he foresaw difficulties. President Loubet might balk at doing something that could be seen as an insult to the army. General Galliffet might take the same line. When the idea was put to him, Galliffet did, indeed, point out the dangers inherent in pardoning Dreyfus – of alienating not just the army but many of the deputies and the French voters – but thought it would be more acceptable if it was combined with a general amnesty for anyone involved in the Affair.

The Socialist Minister Millerand, who was a Dreyfusard but also a lawyer, explained that Dreyfus could not be pardoned unless he withdrew his appeal. This could then be taken as an admission of guilt. That afternoon Millerand chaired a meeting of the Dreyfusard high command in his office on the rue de Lille – Mathieu Dreyfus, Georges Clemenceau, Jean Jaurès and Joseph Reinach. Mathieu at first thought it impossible to ask his brother, who valued honour more than life, to ask to be pardoned for a crime he did not commit. However, he was anxious about Alfred's state of health and doubted that he would survive further incarceration. 'Think,' said Reinach. 'In a couple of days, if you like, you and he can be far away in some peaceful place: he'll be with his wife, his children and a measure of happiness . . .' Clemenceau, on the other hand, argued against a pardon: 'you are humiliating the Republic before the sabre'. Jaurès, too, was reluctant, but was persuaded that a pardon need not mean an end to the campaign for full rehabilitation of an innocent man.[61]

The challenge now was to persuade Dreyfus himself to accept the idea of a pardon. Equipped with a promise from Millerand that he would resign from the cabinet if Dreyfus was not pardoned the next day, a statement drawn up by Jaurès stating that the struggle to establish his innocence would continue, and an order signed by General Galliffet that he should be allowed to see the prisoner alone, Mathieu took the night train to Rennes.

At six the following morning, 12 September, the meeting of the two brothers took place in Alfred's cell. Mathieu laid out the offer: Alfred would be pardoned if he withdrew his appeal. Alfred refused. Although he did not expect his appeal to be successful, he did not want to withdraw it because it would suggest that he accepted the verdict of the court martial. Mathieu persisted. Already in a poor state of health, Alfred might not survive if he returned to prison; free, he could continue to campaign for a review. He said that the idea of a pardon was supported by Reinach and Jaurès. Alfred demurred and finally he himself came up with the most persuasive argument of all for accepting a pardon: 'I thought of the sufferings of my wife and family, of the children I had not yet seen, and the thought of whom haunted me ever since my return to France.'[62] He agreed to withdraw his appeal.

Joseph Reinach, in his article in Le Siècle, had demanded an immediate pardon 'before the ink could dry' on the verdict delivered by the court martial in Rennes. Alexandre Millerand had said he would resign if Dreyfus was not pardoned the next day. President Loubet, however, procrastinated; he wanted, as a fig-leaf to cover the implicit repudiation of the authority of the army, a week's delay during which a doctor would report on Dreyfus's state of health. A thirty-eight-year-old physician at the Faculty of Medicine in Paris, Pierre Delbet, was sent to Rennes to examine Dreyfus – a man, Dreyfus judged, of high intelligence and goodwill.[63] Delbet's report was duly submitted to the Minister of War. 'It is clear from the information obtained that the health of the prisoner has been seriously affected and would not endure, without great danger, a prolonged period of detention.' This was enough for Loubet. At a meeting of the Council of Ministers, held on 19 September, the President of France acceded to the request made by the Minister of War and signed the decree pardoning Alfred Dreyfus for the crime of treason.

———

At two in the morning of 20 September 1899, Dreyfus left the military prison in Rennes wearing a navy-blue suit, a black overcoat and a black felt hat in the company of the Director of the Sûreté, Léopold Viguié, and four plain-clothes policemen. A car took Dreyfus and his escort to a small station at Vern, ten kilometres outside Rennes. Here they caught a train to Châteaubriant and then to Nantes, the first leg of a long journey to Carpentras in the south-east of France and the home of his much loved elder sister, Henriette, and her husband Joseph Valabrègue.

Mathieu Dreyfus and the Valabrègues' son Paul met Dreyfus at Nantes. The two brothers embraced and for a while held each other without saying a word.[64] Paul, too, embraced his uncle: it was Paul who had been subjected to du Paty de Clam's rant about adultery and treason back in 1894. With Mathieu and Paul was a reporter from *Le Figaro*, Jules Huret, who joined them for the rest of their journey.

'How beautiful the countryside is! Look at that little village, the cockerels, the chickens, the lovely trees in the mist! Can you believe that for a year all I saw was the sky and the sea, and then for four more years, the sky alone: a square of bright blue sky, hard, metallic and always the same, completely cloudless!'[65] If Dreyfus had had any doubts about accepting a pardon, they were now dispelled by the joy of freedom. He smoked one cigarette after another. 'You smoke too much,' Mathieu said to him.

'Let me smoke. Let me talk. Give me at least twenty-four hours of debauchery!'

Dreyfus talked while he smoked, and Huret, whom Dreyfus found 'a pleasant travelling companion', took notes for his exclusive story. How sad he was, said Dreyfus, to hear that Auguste Scheurer-Kestner, his great champion, had died on the very day of his pardon but without hearing the good news. How encouraged he had been by the 5,000 letters of support that he had received since returning to France – and this was not counting those sent to Lucie. 'Oh, that did me good. Even officers on active service sent me short notes: "Happy to see you back. Happy at the thought of your rehabilitation."'

When it came to his enemies, Dreyfus judged Mercier to be 'a bad and dishonest man', too 'lucid and perspicacious' not to be aware of what he had done. 'But if he is mentally aware, he is morally oblivious. He is amoral.' Dreyfus found excuses for his former comrades who had given evidence against him. 'I am sure it was not out of antagonism towards me. No, it was simply a low calculation of how to please their superiors. These are people who have a very strange idea of duty!'

When the travellers reached Bordeaux at half-past four, they ate a late lunch in the Hôtel Terminus, Dreyfus's first meal as a free man. The news of their arrival had leaked out and a crowd of journalists and the general public were held back by the men from the Sûreté. But unlike the throng that had bayed for blood when he had disembarked from the train at La Rochelle on his way to the Île de Ré five years before, the passions expressed were now mixed. As they went from the hotel to the platform to catch an overnight train to Narbonne and then Avignon, one man shouted 'Bravo!' and another 'Down with Dreyfus!' 'They cancel one another out,' said Dreyfus. '*Cela se balance.*'

When they finally arrived at Avignon, on the morning of 21 September, two landaus awaited Dreyfus and his companions. Here Jules Huret left them to return to Paris. Dreyfus, with his brother and nephew, got into the first landau; his escort from the Sûreté into the second. They then set out on the twenty-kilometre journey to Carpentras, the road passing through a landscape of olive trees and vines with Mont Ventoux in the distance, pink in the light of the morning sun.

The human landscape was equally benign: the mayor of Carpentras had been able to reassure the Prefect of the Vaucluse that there was no need to take special precautions to protect Dreyfus. The Valabrègue family were highly esteemed in a city that, governed by the popes until the French Revolution, had an ancient Jewish community and the oldest synagogue in France.

The Valabrègues' house, Villemarie, was outside the city, set in ten hectares of fields, orchards and vines, and surrounded by white walls. Dreyfus knew it well from his youth. Just as his sister Henriette had been a mother to him, so Villemarie had been a home. When he arrived at the end of the avenue leading to the house, he got down from the landau and was greeted by two of his sisters, Henriette and Louise. After them came their husbands.

Lucie was on her way from Paris, and reached Villemarie at midnight. 'This was the first real moment of reunion,' Dreyfus wrote later, 'because the situation in the prison at Rennes had been too agonizing, too sad, for us to be able to say what was in our hearts. Now, at last, after five years of the most cruel and unmerited martyrdom, we could speak freely.' The two children, Pierrot and Jeanne, arrived the next day with Lucie's parents, the Hadamards. It was the first time that Dreyfus had seen them since the day he had left his home on the avenue du Trocadéro in October 1894. He was apprehensive: 'My feelings were overwhelming in seeing once again these dear little creatures for whom I had kept myself alive, whose memory had enabled me to summon up such strength. I was afraid of that moment of astonishment, of their surprise, at finding themselves before a father whose face they no longer knew. But they immediately threw themselves into my arms and hugged and kissed me. Their mother had made sure they remembered their absent father. These few moments of joy helped me to forget so much sadness, so much grief.'[66]

The Last Act

1: Amnesty

On 17 November 1899, the French Prime Minister, Pierre Waldeck-Rousseau, introduced legislation into the Senate that would enact an amnesty for all crimes and misdemeanours connected with the Dreyfus Affair. This 'silent, stooping, myopic' man with 'the glazed look of a dead fish in his eyes'[1] had, the day before, been reconfirmed as Prime Minister in the Chamber of Deputies by a vote of 317 to 211. Given the narrow majority with which he had been first elected in 1899, this was a political triumph but one that had been achieved at a cost. The government now relied for its support on the Socialists: 'you have brought the enemy into the fort,' said the former Prime Minister Jules Méline, 'on the pretext of defending it'.[2]

The purpose of the amnesty was to remove the poison of the Dreyfus Affair from the body politic once and for all. It meant that the legal proceedings against Émile Zola and Georges Picquart would be dropped, as would the suit against Joseph Reinach by Berthe Henry. It would prevent any actions being taken against officers on the General Staff or Statistical Section for forging documents and telling lies. The legislation 'was not a matter of judging or absolving acts already accomplished', said Waldeck-Rousseau, 'but merely of making it impossible to revive a painful conflict'.

The amnesty outraged the Dreyfusards. Georges Picquart had demanded a judicial investigation into the conduct of General Gonse and Félix Gribelin, the archivist at the Statistical Section. Georges Clemenceau and Jean Jaurès thought it monstrous that General Mercier, 'the first of the criminals', should be exempt from prosecution. 'Waldeck-Rousseau's ministers', wrote Clemenceau in *L'Aurore*, 'are turning into the bandit's accomplices.'

'No one more ardently than myself wants an end to the tensions whose first victim was myself,' wrote Dreyfus in an address to the Senate sent from Villemarie. 'But only justice can allay tensions. Amnesty is a blow to my heart; the only person to profit from it would be General Mercier.'

There were also objections from the right. 'The amnesty is perfidious and shameful,' said *L'Écho de Paris*. 'It was prepared by Waldeck-Rousseau with the Dreyfusard confederates as traitors-in-chief and the apprentice traitors Picquart, Reinach, and Zola.' That the anti-Dreyfusards still held sway in some parts of the country was made clear when, on 28 January 1900, General Mercier himself was elected to the Senate for the Loire-Inférieure. He spoke in the debate on the amnesty, finally held on 1 June 1899, saying that it was of no interest to him but insisting yet again that what he had done in 1894 was for the sake of his country.

However, this 'cold crocodile who never smiled'[3] had met his match in Waldeck-Rousseau, a man with 'the frigid and distant impartiality of an English statesman'.[4] 'To those who think this law too indulgent and that we risk debilitating the Nation,' said Waldeck-Rousseau in his response to Mercier, 'I shall limit myself to observing that there are punishments more severe than those meted out by law, and that the justice of the court room is not the only justice. There is another, formed by public awareness, which traverses the ages, is the teaching of peoples, and is already entering into history.'[5] Mercier might have the support of the electors of the Loire-Inférieure but he would be condemned in due course by posterity.

The law was passed by a vote of 231 to 32 and the attention of the nation switched from the Dreyfus Affair to the pleasures of the Exposition Universelle. However, for Waldeck-Rousseau there remained unfinished business. Secure in office with the support of the left, he determined to 'bring the army to heel' – that army which had humiliated the nation with the verdict at Rennes. Immediately after Dreyfus's reconviction, on 29 September, General Galliffet had removed the power to appoint generals from the High Council of War and the High Commission of Promotion, and had reserved such appointments for the Minister of War. At the same time the government moved against the men who had attempted to suborn the army to overthrow the Republic: Paul Déroulède and Jules Guérin were once again charged with sedition. Though they had been triumphantly acquitted by a jury in May 1899, new warrants were issued for their arrest in September: Guérin and fifty of his supporters refused to give themselves up and were besieged by the police for five weeks in their headquarters on the rue de Chabrol. After the fall of this 'Fort Chabrol', Guérin and Déroulède were brought before the Senate, constituted as a High Court, on charges of sedition. The trial lasted for several months but, with a left majority in the upper chamber, the result was a foregone conclusion. The accused were found guilty: Guérin was sentenced to ten years' detention and Déroulède to ten years' exile. Deroulède left France for San Sebastián in Spain.

2: The Divided Dreyfusards

United in their condemnation of the amnesty, the Dreyfusards disagreed on the pardon – a difference of opinion that grew into an enmity that equalled and even exceeded that felt for the anti-Dreyfusards. Bernard Lazare, though he approved the pardon on humanitarian grounds, realised at once that accepting it meant the end of the 'heroic' phase of the Dreyfus Affair. In the previous two years, the campaign to free an innocent man, the victim of a miscarriage of justice, had grown into something far greater and grander: it had become a quest to append Justice to the Republic's three ideals of Liberty, Equality and Fraternity. The Dreyfusards had become an army fighting not so much for the rehabilitation of one man as for a supremely moral cause. 'If you recall the years 1897–1899 to a survivor of that period,' Dreyfus's son Pierre would write later in life, 'you will notice his face light up, his voice acquire a new harshness, his whole being tremble at the memory of that fierce struggle.'[6]

In the spring of 1900, Alfred and Lucie Dreyfus left Villemarie and moved to a villa at Coligny on the Lake of Geneva. Dreyfus had not abandoned his intention to seek full rehabilitation but, on the advice of his brother Mathieu, Joseph Reinach, Edgar Demange and Henri Mornard, he held back from taking any further action in the courts of law. The Criminal Chamber of the Cour de Cassation could review the verdict at Rennes only if there was new evidence that had not been made available to the judges. Even if such evidence was forthcoming, what could it lead to? A third court martial? What reason was there to think that it would return a different verdict from the first two?

Opposed to this view were Georges Picquart, Georges Clemenceau and Fernand Labori. They believed that Joseph Reinach, a political ally of Waldeck-Rousseau, and Edgar Demange, his old friend, had abandoned the struggle in order to calm the country and so keep him in power. Mathieu was accused of being interested only in 'saving his brother's skin', and that this egocentric attitude was typical of Jews.[7] They tried to persuade Dreyfus to send Mathieu back to Mulhouse and dismiss Edgar Demange – even though these were the two men who had come to his aid in his darkest hour. Dreyfus refused.

As the months passed, however, it began to look as if Alfred, by remaining in Switzerland, was somehow lying low; and his self-imposed exile was compared in the press to that of Esterhazy in England. As a result, in November 1900, Alfred and Lucie returned to Paris. With no apartment of their own, they stayed with Lucie's parents, the Hadamards, on the rue de Châteaudun. When Mathieu sent word to Fernand Labori that his brother was in Paris, Labori replied coldly: 'You have no doubt told M. Waldeck-Rousseau.' The amnesty law had not yet been passed and, as tabled, it exempted Alfred Dreyfus from its ban on any further legal action associated with the Affair; he would remain free to pursue his quest for a total rehabilitation. But Labori was convinced that by accepting the pardon Dreyfus had deserted his own cause. He had bartered his freedom for his 'legal honour' and in so doing was 'acting purely as an individual, not as a member of the human collective, in solidarity of his fellow men . . . However great the role he played may have been, he is no longer representative of anything.'[8]

Labori accused Mathieu, who had secured his brother's pardon, of being the government's tool in this ignominious compromise. At a meeting held on 14 December 1900, Mathieu was provoked by Labori's recriminations to break off relations. 'All is over between us,' he said. 'Au revoir, Monsieur.' Later, he later expressed regret for calling Labori 'Monsieur' when he still considered him a friend. A further meeting was arranged between Alfred, Mathieu and Labori in the presence of Georges Picquart. Nothing was resolved. Labori refused to be reconciled with the Dreyfus family; he would no longer act as their lawyer. Dreyfus pleaded with him to reconsider: 'Look, that's not your last word, is it? Look, stay, do it for me, do it for me.'[9] He got nowhere. Picquart suggested that they should simply agree to differ. When Dreyfus left, he was in tears. He would never see Labori again.

Losing the custom of the Dreyfus family had serious financial implications for Fernand Labori, whose legal practice had suffered as a result of the Affair – losing him clients and taking up all of his time. In January 1901, Labori received 40,000 francs in fees from Mathieu Dreyfus, half of which was paid through the Chief Rabbi, Zadoc Kahn. Zadoc Kahn asked for a receipt, which enraged Labori: 'never must an advocate give a receipt for his fee, and never would one think of asking him for one'. Beyond his fees, Labori had also received subsidies, from Émile Straus, Joseph Reinach and Mathieu Dreyfus in the form of a purchase of shares in Labori's journal *La Grande Revue*. In the wake of the breach, he sacked a protégé of Reinach's as political editor of the revue, which in turn led Reinach to dismiss Labori as *his* lawyer in the case for defamation that he had brought against Berthe Henry. Labori then submitted a bill to Reinach for 90,000 francs.

The squalid aftermath to the breach between Labori and the Dreyfus family was leaked to the press. An anonymous article in *L'Écho de Paris* attacked Labori for his ingratitude towards those who had paid his fees promptly and made up the losses he had incurred. The article also accused Georges Picquart of cold-shouldering Alfred Dreyfus, refusing a request that they should meet. It was implied that Picquart was now 'energetically anti-Semitic'. The anonymous author turned out to be Bernard Lazare. When Dreyfus learned this, he asked Lazare to publish a retraction and wrote to *L'Écho de Paris* to deny that he was behind what had been said.[10]

'I *knew* one day I would be attacked by the Jews and notably by the Dreyfuses,' Picquart now wrote to Louis Havet, a professor of Classics at the Collège de France who, with his wife Olympe, was a close friend of both Picquart and the Dreyfus family. At issue was not simply the choice between saving Dreyfus from a third court martial and fighting *à l'outrance* for justice, but also the extent to which Dreyfus's suffering had been because he was a Jew. Lazare's experience of the Dreyfus Affair had led him to abandon his belief in the progressive assimilation of Jews in European societies in favour of the idea, now espoused by his friend Theodor Herzl, of a separate state in Palestine for the Jews. The anarchist was now also a Zionist: his anarchism antagonised social conservatives such as Georges Picquart, and his Zionism provoked most French Jews who had no wish to move from *fin-de-siècle* France to an obscure and inhospitable province of the Turkish Empire. Both Alfred Dreyfus and Joseph Reinach considered Zionism 'an anachronism' in modern society, Reinach describing it as 'a trap set by anti-Semites for naive or unreflective minds'.[11]

Many Dreyfusards were antagonised by the way in which Bernard Lazare portrayed the Dreyfus Affair as the persecution of a Jew by gentiles rather than as a straightforward struggle for justice and legality. Labori insisted that 'the Jewish question is far from having played the principal role' in the Affair. Scheurer-Kestner, too, before his death, had been been keen to distance himself from the Jewish syndicate and considered it wrong to reduce the Affair to a case of ethnic hatred.[12] Now, the gentile Dreyfusards (Labori, Picquart, Clemenceau) saw what they perceived as the cowardice of the Dreyfus family – their decision to 'save their own skins' rather than pursue the common good – as a Jewish trait: 'here is where the pusillanimity of the Jews has brought us', wrote Picquart to Havet. 'We have done enough for Dreyfus.'[13]

Picquart, who had sacrificed his career, lost many of his friends and spent a year in prison, now felt let down. The reflex anti-Semitism evident in his remarks to Captain Tassin at Dreyfus's degradation (see p. 115 above), but which he had sought to suppress, now resurfaced. He alienated the Dreyfusard *salonnière*, the Marquise Arconati-Visconti, with his anti-Semitic remarks and took to reading *La Libre Parole*. 'If Drumont hadn't got in first,' said Clemenceau, 'what a splendid anti-Semitic newspaper Picquart and I could have run!'[14]

While in Paris, Dreyfus was lionised in the Dreyfusard salons. 'How do you do, Captain,' Geneviève Straus said upon receiving him in her house. 'I've been hearing such a lot about you.' Later she was heard to remark, 'What a pity we can't choose someone else for our innocent' – words which Marcel Proust put in the mouth of the Duchesse de Guermantes in *À la recherche du temps perdu*.[15] Dreyfus was no Kossuth or Garibaldi, and many were as disappointed by his dreary manner in the drawing rooms as they had been in court. 'They wanted him to show off, to indulge in theatrical poses and speeches, to beat the big drum,' wrote Arthur Ranc in the *Radical*, 'in a word, to behave like a second rate actor,' or, as 'a woman once replied, with a little acid on her tongue, "to be an Esterhazy"'.[16] He became a rich source of witticisms: Léon Daudet claimed that Dreyfus had complained, 'I've never had a moment's peace since I left Devil's Island,' and had stopped the arguments going on around him by saying, 'Shut up, all of you, or I'll confess.'[17]

Lucie Dreyfus took no pleasure in these social occasions and, when Dreyfus went to the soirées of the Marquise Arconati-Visconti on a Thursday, he went on his own.[18] Ruth Harris writes that Lucie, having been so strong while Alfred was on Devil's Island, was now 'broken' by the failure to secure a complete rehabilitation for her husband but considers that somehow this reflected well on him: 'it was the measure of the man that, when he returned, he created a space in which she could finally collapse'.[19] From the tenor of the letters she had written to Alfred while he was on Devil's Island, one gets the sense that Lucie, in her anxiety and distress, had somewhat idealised her marriage to him, forgetting his 'mercurial moods', closed nature and 'relentless perfectionism'.[20]

Upon his return, after what Alfred had been through, it was never going to be possible to go back to the *status quo ante*, particularly if that *status quo ante* had not been as Lucie remembered it. The confident, masterful man who had left his home in October 1894 was now physically enfeebled and psychologically scarred. Yet some traits in his character had not changed, one being his enjoyment of the company of other women. 'Lucie knew that side of her husband's character well,' wrote Michael Burns. She had 'been forced to deal with the lingering habits of his bachelorhood'.[21] His close friendship with the Marquise Arconati-Visconti, and the pleasure he took in escaping from the family circle to attend her Thursday-evening receptions, no doubt fulfilled the need met by the company of *femmes galantes* in the early years of his marriage.

Although Dreyfus remained preoccupied with his case, and was determined to pursue a final rehabilitation, he was remarkably detached and dispassionate in his analysis of what he had endured. He was uncomfortable in the role of martyr: 'I hate all this moaning about my suffering,' he told Julien Benda. 'I like to talk about my case *objectively*.' The interview with Jules Huret conducted while he travelled across France from Rennes to Carpentras, and subsequently published in *Le Figaro*, showed how objective he could be. When asked by Huret why he had aroused such antipathy in the General Staff, he did not ascribe it wholly to anti-Semitism. 'I believe the cause is fairly complex,' he told Huret.

First, and above all, they thought I was guilty. It is unimaginable that anyone would lightly make such a mistake. Then, there was a latent anti-Semitism; and my character may have played a role. Yes, I was a little brusque – with my superior officers, that is, because I always showed the greatest respect for my inferiors . . . I didn't lick any boots, and always retained in respect to my chiefs a frankness and independence. If a plan or a project seemed to me to be ill conceived, I did not stop myself from saying so rather than going along with things as others did when it was a superior officer who was speaking or in charge. I know that that was not popular with the General Staff.

It was not, then, because he was Jewish but because, like Picquart, he was an officer who thought for himself.

> Colonel Bertin-Mourot said something very true in relation to Colonel Picquart: 'One felt that this officer did not march behind his chiefs.' That is the whole of their psychology and their morality. Fall in behind the leaders. Ah! If it was during a war or during manoeuvres, so be it. But when it was a matter of honour and of duty, should one really march behind someone else? Doesn't a man have a conscience of his own?[22]

It was therefore not anti-Semitism as such that had made Dreyfus unpopular with the General Staff but the reactionary mind-set in the army, a mind-set no doubt formed by a 'clerical' formation – the dogmatic and hierarchical nature of the Catholic Church. Dreyfus was not such a reactionary – he was a progressive – but he remained, as he had always been, instinctively conservative. 'Had he not been Dreyfus,' asked Léon Blum, 'would he have been a Dreyfusard?'[23]

Dreyfus's unwillingness to be presented as a 'victim'[24] or a Jewish scapegoat led to him distancing himself from Bernard Lazare. Lazare's understanding of what was at the heart of the Dreyfus Affair differed from that of both sides in the acrimonious dispute among the other Dreyfusards. To Lazare, Dreyfus had suffered because he was a Jew, and the campaign for his rehabilitation was simply a part of a world-wide struggle for the emancipation of the Jews. Lazare had been welcomed at the first Zionist Congress held in Basel in 1897, and was both a friend and travelling companion of Theodor Herzl; but his anarchist ideals led him to denounce Herzl and the Zionist Action Committee as 'bourgeois in your thoughts, bourgeois in your feelings, bourgeois in your ideas, bourgeois in your conception of society'.

In 1900 and again in 1902 Lazare visited Jewish communities in Romania and upon his return described their pitiful condition in Clemenceau's *L'Aurore*. However, in 1903 he was diagnosed with colon cancer and, following an unsuccessful operation, died on 1 September in Nîmes, the town where he had been born thirty-eight years before.

Mathieu attended his funeral but not Alfred. Charles Péguy, who would claim that 'during the last years, during this past period of his life, I was his only friend', wrote bitterly in his memoir of the Dreyfus Affair, *Notre jeunesse*, of the way Lazare – 'a saint' – had been treated 'immediately after the resolution and apparent triumph, the false triumph of the Dreyfus Affair. The failure to appreciate, the ignorance, even, the solitude, the forgetting, the contempt in which one let him fall, or made him fall, or let him perish. In which one let him die.'

Péguy was particularly harsh in his judgement of Dreyfus himself. 'He did not die for himself, but a number died for him . . . He did not suffer ruin in his own cause . . . But many were ruined for him. Many sacrificed for him their career, their bread, even their life, the bread of their wives and children . . . The greatest of them all, Bernard Lazare who lived for him, died for him, died thinking of him.'[25] However, Péguy was writing some years after the event when subsequent political developments and a change of heart had perhaps coloured his judgement of the man who had inspired a whole generation to do great things. 'Our Dreyfusism was a religion,' wrote Péguy,[26] but in 1905 the Socialist poet had espoused an older faith with different martyrs. He had been received into the Catholic Church.

3: Retribution

'The physical conspiracy has vanished,' said the Prime Minister Pierre Waldeck-Rousseau after the conviction and sentencing of Jules Guérin and Paul Déroulède, 'but the moral conspiracy remains.'[27] The reactionary, anti-republican and therefore seditious influence of the Catholic Church should now be extirpated from the nation once and for all. French Catholics would now pay the price for backing the losing side in the Dreyfus Affair.

Waldeck-Rousseau's target was not the institutional Church – the bishops and curés who, under the Concordat, were salaried officials of the state – but the religious orders (*congrégations*) that were outside the control of the bishops and answered only to the Pope in Rome. These, he believed, endangered the Republic on two counts. The first was their political activism – surreptitious on the part of the Jesuits, but flagrant in the case of the Assumptionists during the election of 1898. The second was the more pervasive and therefore more insidious influence they exercised through their highly successful schools.

The government lost no time in mounting its attack. On 22 January 1900, less than two weeks after the conviction of Guérin and Déroulède, twelve members of the Assumptionist Order were arraigned before the Correctional Tribunal in Paris – priests in soutanes standing in the dock normally occupied by thieves and prostitutes. The charge was sedition or, more precisely, breaking a law passed under the First Empire prohibiting unauthorised associations of more than twenty people. But the substance of the indictment was that the order had used the vast funds collected for charitable purposes to interfere in elections and indoctrinate the young with reactionary, undemocratic and anti-republican opinions. 'The court case', wrote Ruth Harris, 'enabled the government to trot out the most elaborate fantasies of clerical subversion and financial corruption.'[28]

The trial ended in a conviction. The Assumptionist Order was judged to have broken the Law on Associations and was dissolved. Its newspaper, *La Croix*, was saved by transferring its ownership to a Catholic industrialist, Paul Féron-Vrau; but the Assumptionist priests were dispersed, many moving abroad, others remaining in France, permitted only to live in pairs and so without the support of a communal life. 'Lonely, sometimes ill and impoverished, they often died before their time or carried on in a state of disorientated discouragement.'[29] The Assumptionists had greatly underestimated the power of their enemies, and had counted too much on the power or just the willingness to protect them of the Pope, and perhaps also of God.

————

The Law on Associations, successfully used against the Assumptionist Order, was one which governments in the Third Republic had in the past applied selectively and at their discretion. Masonic Lodges were exempt: when Jules Guérin was prosecuted for failing to register his Anti-Semitic League he simply changed its name to Grand Occident of

France.[30] The rights of workers to form trades unions had been granted by Waldeck-Rousseau when he served in the cabinet of Jules Ferry back in 1884.[31] Now, in 1901, he proposed legislation that would specifically target the religious orders. As Dreyfus would later recognise, with a certain measure of satisfaction, his Affair had prepared public opinion for this move.[32] The perception now among republicans was that the Catholic religious orders had, by their support of criminals on the General Staff and their supposed sympathy with Guérin and Déroulède, forfeited their rights to freedom of action.

The dispute over religious education, however, long pre-dated the Affair and had little as such to do with recent political events. Jules Ferry had secularised primary schools twenty years before but had left French parents free to choose between the state lycées and Catholic colleges for their children's secondary education. The assumption by the republicans had been that free education in the secular lycées would cause the Catholic colleges to wither away. This had proved false: the number of pupils attending lycées had in fact declined from 56 per cent in 1887 to 51 per cent in 1899, whereas the number attending private schools, most of which were run by the religious orders, had risen from 44 per cent in 1887 to 49 per cent in 1899.[33]

To Waldeck-Rousseau it was this fissure in French education which was responsible for the political division in the country. The two systems were teaching different curricula and, above all, different values: they were creating, he said – using the phrase coined by the historian Ernest Lavisse in the 1880s – *deux jeunesses*, two childhoods, that grew into two hostile camps within one nation.[34] New laws prohibited all associations that were not specifically authorised by the state. Henceforward rights enjoyed by Socialists and Freemasons did not apply to monks and nuns. The new law, wrote Denis Brogan, 'created a new class of Frenchman with fewer rights than any other . . . Those French men or French women who wished to exercise this privilege to live in common for religious motives were only allowed to do so if a special law were passed.'[35]

These anti-clerical statutes, designed to silence 'propagandists for the Counter-Revolution', were 'the defining and only significant issue' during the general election of 1902.[36] Economic and fiscal questions such as tariffs and income tax roused no passions; the cement of the left-wing coalition, said the Comte de Mun, was 'religious war'.[37] If Waldeck-Rousseau, the bourgeois republican par excellence, had, as some suggested, promoted anti-clericalism to divert his Socialist allies in the Bloc des Gauches from their more revolutionary demands, he succeeded. Gambetta's cry, 'Le cléricalisme, voilà l'ennemi,' was as effective a rallying cry now as it had been twenty years before.

The French Catholics, chastened by the Affair, formed a new moderate party, Action Libérale, led by supporters of the *ralliement*, Jacques Piou and Albert de Mun; candidates were also put forward by the diehard anti-Dreyfusard Ligue de la Patrie Française. The popular vote was close; in the first round of the elections, the right trailed the left by only 200,000 votes, but the second round returned a majority of between eighty and ninety in the Chamber of Deputies for the Bloc des Gauches.[38]

If women had had the vote, the result might have been different. However, even without female suffrage, it is a paradox that a majority in a supposedly Catholic country should vote for the anti-clerical parties of the left. Roman Catholicism remained the faith of the majority of the French. There was a curé in every village, and most of the French still used Catholic ceremonies for the rites of passage through life – birth, marriage and death. The philosophical differences between Christianity and the Enlightenment that exercised the intellectuals were of little interest to the peasants in rural France. The explanation lies rather in the fact that, at a time of increasing social discontents, Catholicism was seen as the party of the established social order and therefore the enemy of both the urban and rural poor. 'The clergy of France has finally convinced everyone who believes in things popular and democratic', said the Abbé Frémont, 'that between the Church on the one hand and progress, the Republic and the future on the other, there is no possible relationship but the most deadly hatred.'[39]

This deadly hatred of French Catholicism is skilfully depicted in the novels of Octave Mirbeau. The anti-clerical Julien Sorel in Stendhal's *Le Rouge et le noir* was a Bonapartist; the same class antagonism in

Mirbeau's *Sébastien Roch*, *Abbé Jules* and *The Diary of a Chambermaid* leads to a darker, embittered anarchism. Mirbeau was among the Dreyfusards who met at the Trois Marches during Dreyfus's second court martial in Rennes. His depiction of Catholicism as the hypocritical ideology of a pretentious bourgeoisie, cold-hearted clergy and arrogant nobility is of more use in the understanding of the aftermath of the Dreyfus Affair than Marcel Proust's *À la recherche du temps perdu*.

The dichotomy between the Catholic Church's strict views on sexual morality and a growing eroticisation and permissiveness in French society was another cause of anti-clerical sentiment in the exclusively male electorate. Mirbeau's portrayal of priests as sex-obsessed hypocrites is almost certainly a distortion: 'the vast majority of the clergy in the nineteenth century', wrote Ralph Gibson, 'were pious and chaste and did their best to get on with their religious duties'.[40] However, among these duties was an attempt to enforce chastity through the confessional, and this undoubtedly contributed to the de-Christianisation of France.

First there were the clergy's strictures about dancing. In the course of the nineteenth century, traditional dances in which there was little physical contact between the sexes had been replaced by the waltz and the polka which placed a man and woman in one another's arms – effectively a lingering, perambulatory embrace. The moral dangers of such an 'occasion of sin' obsessed the nineteenth-century clergy. Girls were made to sign pledges not to dance, which alienated the young, 'particularly young men in the countryside who deeply resented the curé's role in cutting off the supply of girls for the village *bal*'.[41]

Secondly, among married Frenchmen, there was widespread resentment against the Church's teaching on birth control. The principal method employed by married couples to avoid conception was withdrawal prior to ejaculation – the sin of Onan[42] – a practice which was confessed by women but blamed on men.* Many French husbands

---

* Cf. Marcel Jouhandeau in *Marcel and Élise*: 'Thus Élise does not confess her sins but mine . . .'

deeply resented not just the Church's ruling but also the prying of the curé into the intimate details of their conjugal life. They themselves refused to submit to such an interrogation and abandoned the sacrament of confession; they were therefore barred from Easter communion and so effectively excluded from the Church. The Bishop of Le Mans, Jean-Baptiste Bouvier, in a letter to Pope Pius IX, asserted 'without hesitation that the prying by confessors into sexual habits and their prohibition of birth control was producing protests and driving people away from the Church'.[43]

It was, then, not so much the indifference to justice shown by so many French Catholics during the Dreyfus Affair that had made the Church unpopular as the widespread perception that it was the ally of the rich, the enemy of progress and a prurient killjoy when it came to sex. A majority of Frenchmen voted for the anti-clerical agenda of the Bloc des Gauches in the general election of 1902; Pierre Waldeck-Rousseau's strategy was vindicated. But, in his moment of triumph, he resigned on grounds of ill-health, exhausted after running the government for three momentous years – a longer period than any other in the history of the Third Republic. He was replaced as Prime Minister by Émile Combes.

Combes, born in the Tarn, had studied in a Catholic seminary for the priesthood but had been rejected because he was judged 'too proud'.[44] Spurned by the Church, Combes lost his faith, joined the Freemasons, studied medicine and practised as a doctor in the country town of Pons in the Charente-Inférieure. Here he espoused 'all the ideas, prejudices, hates, and principles of the small town anticlerical'.[45] He was typical of those in the French provinces who worked to ensure that the village priest was 'banished from the school, excluded from the committee directing official charities, regarded with malicious distrust or jealous hatred by the mayor and the school-master, kept at arm's length as a compromising neighbour by all the minor officials employed by the commune or the state, spied on by the innkeeper, exposed to the anonymous denunciations of the local newspaper' and left to spending 'his mornings reciting prayers to empty pews and his afternoons plant-ing cabbages and pruning roses'.[46]

What had been done on a small scale in a provincial town, Combes now enacted for the whole nation. He formed a cabinet which included ten fellow Freemasons, and in his first days in office signed decrees clos-ing down more than a hundred Catholic schools.[47] His provincial roots, and his disdain for the moderating blandishments of the metropolis such as a seat in the Académie Française, endeared this 'obstinate and self-satisfied little man'[48] to his admiring disciples, who called him the 'little father'. One of his few excursions into society was to attend the soirées of the Marquise Arconati-Visconti, where other regulars were Joseph Reinach and Alfred Dreyfus.[49]

On 1 July 1901, a new Law on Associations was passed which obliged every religious order to obtain 'a legislative authorising' act which would determine its function. All but five of the religious orders that applied for authorisation were refused.* The unauthorised orders were either dissolved or forced to move abroad. There were in France at that time 159,628 members of religious orders living in 19,424 establish-ments of one kind or another. Of these 3,126 were run by men, 16,298 by women. There were 30,136 members of male religious orders, of whom 23,327 taught in schools and colleges.[50]

However, it was women who were particularly affected by the new laws. As Katrin Schultheiss observed, 'membership in an active reli-gious congregation afforded single women of all classes the opportunity to perform a vast array of social services, including nursing and teach-ing'.[51] As many as 100,000 girls and single women were employed in enterprises in the silk and clothing industries run by religious orders; these were now closed down. In Catholic Brittany, there was popular resistance to the closures: 1,500 colonial troops were sent to deal with three convents in the province, and 3,000 laid siege to a monastery near Tarascon.[52] Expelling the nursing orders from French hospitals was particularly unpopular. The extraordinary expansion of active rather

---

* Those exempt were mostly missionary orders considered useful for the *mission civilisatrice* in the French Empire.

than contemplative religious orders in France in the nineteenth century
– the *congrégations* – had met a growing demand for social services
that the penny-pinching republican politicians had been unwilling to
satisfy.

> The *congrégations hospitalières* . . . rapidly developed their own paramed-
> ical establishments (pharmacies, sanatoria, home nursing, etc.) and then
> moved into a bewildering variety of social services: old people's homes,
> orphanages, homes for the blind and deaf-mutes, lunatic asylums,
> homes for ex-prostitutes, prison services, soup kitchens, job placements
> for domestic servants and so on, almost *ad infinitum* . . . They were
> prepared to take on the repulsive, the incurable, and the financially
> unrewarding in a way that doctors were often not.[53]

Now anti-clerical zeal overrode republican parsimony. 'It is the
strict duty of every republican', said the Parisian doctor and politician
Désiré Bourneville, 'to remove from the priests and nuns every means
of action accorded them in civil society of which they are the implacable adversaries.' Bourneville led a protracted campaign to replace nuns
with lay nurses in French hospitals and succeeded thanks to the anti-
clerical majority on Paris's Municipal Council. Katrin Schultheiss esti-
mates that there were, at the turn of the century, approximately 20,000
Catholic nuns providing nursing care in French hospitals. Sacking
them was not popular. In both Paris and Lyon, 'anti-clerical doctors,
hospital administrators and politicians – many of whom unequivocally
supported the laicization of the nation's schools – rallied in the defence
of the congregational nurses'.[54] On 15 January 1908, several thousand
Parisians, among them doctors, councillors and politicians, assembled
outside the historic Hôtel-Dieu hospital to take leave of the Augustine
Sisters who had served there as nurses for more than a hundred years.[55]
However, the prime target of the anti-clerical legislation was the
Catholic schools. By a law of 7 July 1904, members of religious orders
were prohibited from the 'teaching of every grade and every kind in
France'. The members of the few authorised congregations came under
this ban. Every religious, man or woman, who wanted to continue to

teach children had to renounce their religious calling, and it was left to the courts to decide whether such a renunciation was sincere. Henri de Gaulle, the father of Charles de Gaulle, lost his job as the lay headmaster of the Jesuit school in Paris and sent his son Charles to be educated by the Jesuits in Belgium.[56]

Here, for French Catholics, was the persecution which they had feared: it might not be as cruel and sanguinary as that of the Jacobins, but it was, all the same, a determined effort by a government of atheists and Freemasons to prevent the education of French children in a faith that had flourished in France since the baptism of Clovis 1,400 years before, and to root out significant aspects of Catholic practice from the life of the French nation. Many devout customs were now criminalised. Monastic life was unlawful and religious processions, dating from the Middle Ages, were banned by anti-clerical local authorities.[57]

What could the Catholic Church do in the face of this persecution? In 1901, Pope Leo XIII was ninety-one years old. With a government in Paris led by a Freemason and dominated by Freemasons, all that he had foreseen in his encyclical *Humanus Genus* had come to pass. He had held out an olive branch to the French republicans but they had rejected it: his policy of *ralliement* had failed. Leo died in 1903. His successor, Giuseppe Melchiore Sarto, the son of a village postman and a seamstress, took the name Pius in honour of the two popes, Pius VI and VII, who had been bullied and mistreated by Napoleon. If they had stood up to the military genius and Emperor of the French, Pius X was unlikely to retreat before the little doctor from the Tarn.

Disputes between the French government and the Vatican on a number of matters led to a diplomatic rupture and to the disestablishment of the Catholic Church in France. There was no formal denunciation of the Concordat, but a motion was passed in the Chamber of Deputies on 10 February 1905 declaring that 'the attitude of the Vatican' had rendered the separation of Church and state inevitable; and on 11 December 1905 the Separation Law was passed and published in the *Journal Officiel*.

For Charles Péguy, the fact that the struggle of the Dreyfusards should lead to this 'Combes demagogy' was a catastrophic perversion of the movement's ideals. 'The Dreyfusards who became Combists were already inflated with pride, and did evil.'[58] Certainly, the Church itself was partly to blame for its defeat by the French secularists. 'It was not the arguments that it lacks but charity. All the reasons, all the systems, all the pseudoscientific arguments weigh for nothing in the scales against an ounce of charity.'[59]

However, the Catholic Church had survived worse bouts of persecution before, and in some ways the persecution by the Combes government had a salutary outcome. Denis Brogan describes the effect as 'bracing'.[60] The disciples of Compte and Michelet, who had assumed that the Catholic faith itself would wither and die, were to be disappointed. In the world of letters there was a Catholic renaissance with authors such as Charles Péguy, Ferdinand Brunetière, Joris-Karl Huysmans, Paul Bourget, Paul Claudel, Georges Bernanos and François Mauriac, and philosophers and theologians such as Lucien Laberthonnière, Maurice Blondel, Louis Duchesne, Henri Brémond, Jacques Maritain and Ernest Psichari.

Some, certainly, remained anti-Semitic. 'I am an anti-Semite,' wrote Huysmans, 'because I am convinced that it is the Jews who have turned France into a sad country, agitated by the lowest passions, the sad country without God that we now see.'[61] But others, such as Péguy, Claudel, Bernanos or Mauriac, abhorred anti-Semitism; and the anti-Semitism of the Assumptionists that had contaminated, by association, the shrine at Lourdes and the message of Bernadette Soubirous was wholly absent in the cult of another Catholic girl, Thérèse Martin, a Carmelite nun, who died of consumption at Lisieux at the age of twenty-four in 1897. Her *Story of a Soul*, published posthumously, revealed a spirituality far removed from the polemics of Action Française or diplomatic disputes over the disestablishment of the Church. She was, as Ruth Harris writes, 'no anti-Semite, despite having grown up in an ultra-Catholic and right-wing family'.[62] Canonised by Pope Pius XI in 1925, Thérèse became 'the most widely loved Catholic intercessor of modern times'.

4: The Case Reopened

In a debate in the Chamber of Deputies on 6 April 1903, almost four years after Alfred Dreyfus had been pardoned by President Loubet, the Socialist leader Jean Jaurès ascended the podium to reintroduce the question of his unjust conviction. Taking up the whole session of 6 April, and speaking for two hours on the following day, he yet again presented the overwhelming proof of Dreyfus's innocence and the guilt of those who had conspired to thwart his rehabilitation. Throughout his address he was heckled by nationalist deputies, but he rose above the insults and interruptions, demonstrating once again his oratorical powers and his ability to rouse the passions of his followers with lofty appeals to justice and truth and 'accusations against the Church'.[63]

Jaurès demanded that the case be reopened; his motion was opposed by that most zealous of anti-Dreyfusards, the former Minister of War Godefroy Cavaignac. Dying of liver cancer, and taking his certainty of Dreyfus's guilt to the grave, Cavaignac's eloquence might not equal that of Jaurès but his assurance gave a morbid force to what he said. 'Our conscience is worth every bit as much as yours . . . You are not judges. You are not here as servants of the truth but as the slaves of your passions . . . Your project is to cause chaos and repudiation of the nation.' Insults were traded between the two sides. Cavaignac called Jaurès a coward; Jaurès said that Cavaignac filled him with contempt.

Cavaignac's objections were ignored. The Combes government, acting in concert with its staunch Socialist supporter Jaurès, had already decided to accede to his request. 'The government is eager to facilitate the search for the truth in this matter,' the Minister of War, General Louis André, announced to the Chamber, 'and agrees to proceed with an administrative investigation.' Quite what was meant by this was unclear, but Dreyfus did not wait for the politicians to decide. He immediately applied for a review based on the emergence of new evidence in his case. Combes then charged General André with making a 'personal investigation' into the case: the Dreyfus file was taken out and dusted down, and an examination of the evidence started all over again.

General André's investigation was conducted by a Captain Targe, who claimed an open mind. To find his way through the voluminous and often obscure documentation, Targe enlisted the help of its original author, the archivist from the Statistical Section, Félix Gribelin. Gribelin had been as complicit as any in the conspiracy against Dreyfus, had venerated Henry and had not changed his mind about Dreyfus's guilt; but he was astute enough to see that the wind was now blowing in a new direction. He co-operated with Targe. 'He had become truthful with age,' Joseph Reinach would write, 'as one becomes obese or bald.'[64]

With Gribelin's help, Targe quickly uncovered the numerous forgeries undertaken by Henry to incriminate both Dreyfus and Picquart. Here was the new evidence required to reopen the case. On 19 October 1903, General André presented his report based on the findings of Captain Targe to the Prime Minister, Émile Combes. On 27 November, the cabinet referred the request to the Review Commission, and on 24 December the Commission accepted the grounds for a review with no dissenting vote. The next day, while the clericalists celebrated the birth of Christ, the Minister of Justice referred the judgment made at Rennes to the Cour de Cassation.

———

Nine years had passed since Dreyfus's first conviction, and a number of the legal officers involved in the Affair had either died or retired. The presiding judge of the Criminal Chamber was now Jean-Antoine Chambareaud and the public prosecutor Manuel Baudouin – a man with a distinguished legal pedigree and one of the few Frenchmen who had not yet decided whether he thought Dreyfus innocent or guilty.

Examination of the evidence convinced Baudouin that Dreyfus had been convicted by the judges at the Rennes court martial on charges 'not one of which appears to resist scrutiny' and on the basis of documents 'which, after the conviction, were acknowledged to be forged'. His report was presented to the Criminal Chamber of the Cour de Cassation in January 1904; public hearings of the request opened on 3 March. The Criminal Chamber accepted the petition and its

re-examination of the evidence began on 7 March, continuing until
19 November.

All the protagonists were summoned once again to give evidence
and all the old files were reopened; even Mme Bastian made an appearance, and the love letters between Maximilian von Schwarzkoppen and
Hermance de Weede were brought back into court. Like a play in reper-
tory at the end of a long run, the same players recited the same lines but
many lacked conviction. General Mercier, now that his bluff had been
called on the annotated *bordereau*, fell back on the preposterous 'proof'
of the expert witness Bertillon that the *bordereau* had been written by
Dreyfus in a forged hand. General Billot was now forgetful; General
Roget trimmed his views; Captain Lauth distanced himself from his
deceased friend, Colonel Henry; while General Gonse struck Dreyfus
as 'pitiful, a luckless wretch crushed beneath the weight of all the infa-
mies he had committed'.[65] Only Captain Cuignet, a recent convert to
anti-Dreyfusism, and Commandant du Paty de Clam, who had been
one from the start, expressed their views with any conviction – though
the former, Cuignet, could not conceal his rancour and the latter,
du Paty, appeared mentally unstable. Even Maurice Weil was called
before the court and harshly questioned by Baudouin, but he bridled
at being treated as a suspect and gave nothing away.

When Dreyfus gave evidence on 22 June 1904, he made as poor
an impression as he had done at every court appearance since his first
court martial in 1894. Maître Mornard had prepared the court for his
client's inability to meet the expectations of others when playing his
role. 'His spirit, described as haughty and imperious . . . is in fact that
of a shy man fighting his own timidity; I know what lies behind this
allegedly unfeeling heart that has suffered so cruelly in obeying a self-
imposed rule not to show its suffering.' Dreyfus himself complained
of how unjust it was to judge by appearances: 'I believe in reason, I
believed that reason in such matters, in which the heart's emotions can
never contribute any explanation, any attenuation, was supposed to be
the judges' sole guide.'[66]

As in the judiciary, there had been a change of personnel in the
General Staff. A report it now submitted at the request of the judges

of the Criminal Chamber, drawn up by a number of senior officers including the commandant of the École de Guerre, demonstrated that the *bordereau* exonerated rather than incriminated Dreyfus. The phrase 'the way in which it performs' relating to the hydraulic brake on the 120mm cannon would have been 'utterly abnormal' coming from a trained artillery officer; and *Proposal for a Firing Manual* was not a confidential document: the claim that it was 'extremely difficult to get hold of' must have been inserted by Esterhazy to enhance his value in the eyes of Schwartzkoppen.

The conclusion of a second report requested by the court from three leading academics on Bertillon's expertise was that 'the absurdity of his system is self-evident'. The *bordereau* was not a careful forgery; it had been written spontaneously by a 'fluent hand'. On 19 November, 1904, the Criminal Chamber of the Cour de Cassation forwarded the case to the Combined Chambers in accordance with the law of dispossession that had been passed five years before. The presiding judge of the Combined Chambers, Alexis Ballot-Beaupré, appointed as *rapporteur* Judge Clément Moras. The full rehabilitation of Alfred Dreyfus seemed imminent. But then the political situation changed and a final judgment was delayed.

5: L'Affaire des Fiches

On 17 January 1905, Émile Combes resigned as Prime Minister, compromised by another scandal, *L'Affaire des Fiches* – the card-index affair. This was a covert system that had been set up by the Minister of War, General André, to purge the army officer corps of its 'Jesuits' – those officers who, republicans believed, owed their positions to the old-boy network established in the Jesuit school on the rue des Postes and later at Saint-Cyr. Despite the fact that General Mercier had been a staunch republican, and that there was a larger proportion of Jewish officers in the officer corps than in the population at large, it remained a republican *idée fixe* that the influence of these aristocratic Catholic officers meant that 'a good Republican, above all a good Republican who was also a Jew or a Protestant, had little chance of rising in the army'.[67]

How was General André to change this state of affairs? High-ranking promotions were now in the hands of the Minister, but lower down the scale they remained the prerogative of the promotion boards which were themselves composed of just the kind of clericalist officers that André abhorred. Of course, the boards, too, could be abolished and all promotions reserved for the Minister, but how could he hope to know the political and religious sympathies of so many men?

The solution was to seek information from outside the army – from civilian officials such as the departmental prefects or republican activists on the ground. General André delegated this task to his personal adjutant, Captain Mollin, who was the son-in-law of the great Dreyfusard author Anatole France. Mollin, like André, was a Freemason, a member of a notably political and anti-Catholic Lodge, the Grand Orient, with its headquarters on the rue Cadet in Paris. Here was a ready-made network of informers and a building where the information could be assembled and, in the person of the secretary of the Grand Orient, Narcisse-Amédée Vadecard and his assistant, Jean Bidegain, a staff to co-ordinate and collate the research.

The information, as it came in, was entered on cards or *fiches*. These would be marked either 'Corinth' or 'Carthage' – the Corinthians being the sheep who should be promoted and the Carthaginians the goats who should be held back. An officer reported to be 'perfect in all respects; excellent opinions' would be marked as a Corinthian; another who, 'though a good officer, well reported on, takes no part in politics' would nonetheless be designated a Carthaginian because he went 'to Mass with his family' and sent his six children to Catholic schools. A bachelor officer who went to Mass was by definition of a reactionary disposition. Officers loyal to the republican ideals were encouraged to report on the opinions voiced by their colleagues in the mess.

Despite the clandestine methods of the Grand Orient, such an extensive network of internal espionage could not be kept wholly secret, if only because it quickly became clear that atheist officers were being promoted while Catholic officers were not. Mollin was delighted to see 'an officer who in 1901 had his sons at a Jesuit school and openly displayed sentiments hostile to the Government, in 1902 sending his

sons to the lycée, and in 1903 displaying his respect for our institutions'. However, a system that led to military matters being affected
by civilian informers disturbed some of those who became aware of
what was going on. General Alexandre Percin alerted the former Prime
Minister, Pierre Waldeck-Rousseau, who then raised the matter with
his successor as Prime Minister, Émile Combes, saying that the practice
was both politically hazardous and morally wrong.

Combes did nothing: he felt confident that the practice, should it
be exposed, would meet with the approval of his Radical supporters.
It was a miscalculation. It turned out that Jean Bidegain, the assistant to Vadecard, the secretary of the Grand Orient, was not as loyal a
Mason as Vadecard and Mollin had supposed. In 1904 he made contact
with Gabriel Syveton, the secretary of the still active Ligue de la Patrie
Française, and sold him a selection of the *fiches* for 40,000 francs. The
most damning were read out in the Chamber of Deputies by Count
Jean Guyot de Villeneuve, a former protégé of General de Boisdeffre,
driven out of the army for his nationalist affiliations. In two dramatic
interventions, on 28 October and 4 November 1904, he exposed a
Masonic influence over the army – as real as that of the Jesuits had been
fictitious. In the Chamber Combes was evasive, while General André
lied about what he had known. In a vote of confidence on 17 January
1905, Combes's majority was reduced to six. Technically it was a victory
but morally a defeat. The 'little father' resigned.

6: Vindication

Émile Combes was replaced as Prime Minister by Pierre Maurice
Rouvier, a politician who had been out of office for the previous ten
years because of his links with Baron Reinach and Cornelius Herz
during the Panama scandal. His cabinet was unstable. With the
Catholic religious orders now dissolved and the Church disestablished,
anti-clericalism was no longer proving sufficient to hold the left-wing
coalition together. Increasing industrial unrest set the Socialists against
the bourgeois Radicals, and a visit to Tangiers by the German Kaiser,
hoping to frustrate France's plans to incorporate Morocco into its

North African empire, meant a renewed threat of war. It was not a time to alienate the army or its natural constituency on the right by pursuing the rehabilitation of Alfred Dreyfus.

Moreover, skirmishes continued between the Catholics and the anti-clericals. It was now that the government started its inventory of Church assets, including the sacred vessels reserved in tabernacles. There were riots; a Catholic was killed in northern France; support for Rouvier ebbed away and his government fell on 7 March 1906. Ferdinand Sarrien, the former Minister of Justice, took his place and appointed Georges Clemenceau as his Minister of the Interior.

Now sixty-five years old, it was the first time that this arch-Dreyfusard had held office. In contrast to his indecisive Prime Minister, Clemenceau took to power with an exceptional zest. He used the gendarmerie to subdue striking coal miners in the Pas de Calais; and when the postal workers went on strike in Paris, Clemenceau sacked them and made clear that he would not allow organised labour to challenge the state. To shore up support on the right, he instructed the departmental prefects to suspend the inventories of Church property: 'Knowing how many chandeliers there are in a church is not worth a human life.'

With Clemenceau moving to the right and Jaurès still of the left, the Dreyfusard alliance was falling apart. The general election of May 1906 confirmed the realignment. The Socialists did well, but the Radicals did better and could now form a majority without Socialist support. All the Dreyfusard candidates were returned thanks to the surge of support for the left.

The Affair itself was hardly mentioned in the course of the campaign; but if it was absent from the minds of the voters, it remained the pre-eminent cause of those now in power. The political climate was finally favourable for justice to be done. On 15 and 16 June 1906, the Combined Chambers of the Cour de Cassation met in camera to consider their verdict. On 18–22 June, in open session, it heard the report of Judge Clément Moras. The atmosphere was calm, almost boring. There were no angry crowds surrounding the Palais de Justice, no need for troops or gendarmes to keep order. Once again, but now for the last time, the case against Dreyfus was laid out, analysed and shown to be without substance.

Moras was followed by the public prosecutor, Baudouin, who addressed the court for eight consecutive sessions. It was he who tackled the difficult question of whether Dreyfus should be retried by a third court martial or be declared innocent by the court. Baudouin argued forcefully against a retrial. So too did Henri Mornard, who spoke on behalf of Dreyfus. He argued that with Henry dead and Esterhazy beyond the reach of French justice, crucial evidence would be unavailable; and, more importantly, that the court's reasons for annulling the verdict meant not just that Captain Alfred Dreyfus might be the victim of a miscarriage of justice, but that he had no case to answer.

The judges of the Combined Chambers withdrew to consider their judgment. On 12 July 1906, the presiding judge Ballot-Beaupré – surrounded by the other judges, all dressed in black and gold robes with ermine capes – delivered their ruling. The verdict of the court martial held at Rennes was annulled and 'given that, in the final analysis, nothing remains of the charges made against Dreyfus', he was declared innocent. An announcement of their judgment was to be posted in Paris and in Rennes and was to be inserted in the *Journal Officiel* as well as in fifty Parisian and provincial newspapers chosen by Dreyfus. Finally, after five years of incarceration, and a further seven years in a legal limbo, any taint of treason had been removed from his record, and the honour that had meant more to Alfred Dreyfus than life itself had been restored to him.

Dreyfus, his family and his supporters were exultant. 'I had never doubted that justice and truth would eventually triumph against error, deception and crime,' wrote Dreyfus. 'What sustained me . . . was the unshakable faith that France would one day proclaim my innocence to the world.' A celebratory dinner was held at the Hadamards' apartment: there were tears and embraces; flowers and telegrams were delivered to the door. Journalists were turned away. 'Excuse my brother,' Mathieu said to them. 'Today he wants to keep for his friends.'

Yet the triumph was not total. 'I can imagine your joy, and that of those close to you,' wrote Georges Picquart in a curt response to a note sent to him by Dreyfus giving him the good news. 'I would have preferred, as you know, a court martial, but I won't be stubborn. Perhaps it is better like this.'[68] Dreyfus, too, had always hoped to be declared innocent by his fellow officers – his peers. The rump of the anti-Dreyfusards were not slow to point out that the decision, strictly speaking, was illegal: the Cour de Cassation only had the power to 'break' or quash a verdict of a lower court, not to usurp the powers of the Attorney General in deciding whether or not there was a case to answer. General Mercier, in the Senate, accused the Cour de Cassation of resorting to an 'irregular' procedure. To the die-hards the verdict only confirmed what they had always known – that the Jewish syndicate which controlled both the executive and judicial branches of government had ignored legal niceties to save the skin of one of their own.

Dreyfus had renounced the right to claim monetary compensation for wrongful imprisonment, but he expected and was granted by an overwhelming vote in the Senate reinstatement in the officer corps of the French Army with the rank of major – a position he could reasonably have expected to have reached at that stage in his career. He was also awarded the Knight's Cross of the Légion d'Honneur. However, his promotion was gazetted from the date of the passing of the resolution in the National Assembly, 13 July 1906, whereas Georges Picquart was reinstated in the army as a brigadier-general, his promotion to be backdated to 10 July 1903. 'I was surprised', wrote Dreyfus, 'and so were many of my friends that my promotion to the rank of major was to date only from the day the resolution was passed. In all fairness, they should have applied the same principle to me as they did to Picquart who was given promotion over all those who had been junior to him as Lieutenant-Colonels at the time when he left the army.'[69]

The fissure among the Dreyfusards had not healed. Émile Zola had died from asphyxiation as a result of a blocked chimney in September 1902, but his widow, attending the hearings at the Cour de Cassation, was appalled to see Georges Picquart ostentatiously turn his back when Mathieu Dreyfus approached him to shake his hand.[70] However, Picquart was present when, on 21 July 1906, Alfred Dreyfus was made a member of the Légion d'Honneur. Dreyfus had turned down the idea of holding the ceremony in the main courtyard of the École Militaire, the scene of his degradation eleven years before, unsure of how he would bear up to such painful memories; he chose instead a smaller courtyard in the presence of a select group of invited guests. Besides Picquart, watching from an open window, were Mathieu, Lucie, Pierre and Jeanne Dreyfus; the public prosecutor, Manuel Baudouin, and the great Dreyfusard author Anatole France; but not the lawyers, Demange and Mornard, nor the politicians, Reinach, Jaurès and General André.

At 1.30 in the afternoon Dreyfus entered the courtyard in full military dress – 'the four-braided black hussar's dolman and grenade-adorned cap of unassigned officers' – before two squadrons of cavalry and two mounted batteries of artillery. To a fanfare of trumpets, he marched forward with the same stilted step as at his degradation, his stooped body straining to stand straight. With Dreyfus was Commandant Targe, who had assisted General André in laying the ground for the final rehabilitation; he was also to be honoured. Targe stepped forward first to receive an officer's rosette. Then it was the turn of Dreyfus. General Gillain, Commander of the 1st Cavalry Division, in full ceremonial dress, with an unsheathed sword, dubbed Dreyfus three times on the shoulders. 'In the name of the President of the Republic, I hereby name you Knight of the Légion d'Honneur.' Gillain then pinned the cross on Dreyfus's breast and embraced him. 'Commandant Dreyfus, I am honoured to have performed this task.' The contingents assembled in the courtyard now marched past the podium on which stood General Gillain and Major Dreyfus, the soldiers raising their hands and the cuirassiers their sabres to salute the once despised traitor who had now had his innocence re-established and his honour restored.

Epilogue

After his reinstatement, Major Alfred Dreyfus was put in command of the artillery depot at Vincennes. However, he had neither the strength nor the will to resume a military career and the following year he applied to take early retirement. He renounced his pension and, since he had not served as a major for two years, reverted in retirement to the rank of captain in the army reserve.

Dreyfus retreated, in so far as his celebrity permitted, into the family life that he had come to value above all else during his years of suffering on Devil's Island. His hope was 'to forget in calm all the sadness of the past and be born again to life',[1] but his health remained frail – he suffered from recurrent tropical fevers and long periods of chronic fatigue. Nor was he able to recover the zest for life that he had enjoyed before his arrest. His son Pierre would recall that during the seven-year wait for his final rehabilitation, 'the constant tension in the mind of my father . . . weighed upon us all, and lent a certain heaviness to the general atmosphere of family life'.[2]

My father was not, by nature, very demonstrative. Five years of torture and solitude had made him even more introspective. He lived an intense inner life, but was no longer capable of externalising his emotions. He had lost the habit of self-expression and since, moreover, he loathed self-pity and the display of his sufferings, he seemed very cold and distant to those who did not know him well.[3]

While at home, Dreyfus would work on a dossier of his Affair, collecting, classifying, annotating and arranging the large number of documents and cuttings. Receiving many letters from outside France, he started to collect stamps, and would help Lucie with her sewing – simple, methodical pastimes that kept his hands busy while his mind churned. He received visits from his family and close friends, and every Thursday would attend, without Lucie, the salon of the Marquise Arconati-Visconti – 'a change of scenery for a man who had always been restless', and one tolerated by Lucie who 'understood his impatience with family gatherings'.[4]

The passions aroused by the Affair had diminished but were not dead. Politically, the further polarisation resulting from the anti-clerical laws meant that the right would be excluded from government until 1919. The opposition from the right became extra-parliamentary: the Ligue de la Patrie Française was supplanted by the more combative Action Française – a movement which attracted the eloquent monarchist and anti-Semite Charles Maurras, and also his friend Léon Daudet, the son of the novelist Alphonse Daudet, who was married to the granddaughter of Victor Hugo and enjoyed a reputation as a great wit and gossip, 'a more coherent Rochefort, a less solemn Drumont'. Radicalism went out of fashion: it became smart to be right-wing.

In the spring of 1908, the government of Georges Clemenceau announced that the ashes of Émile Zola would be transferred to the Panthéon with all the solemnity of a republican ritual. The ceremony, which took place on 4 June that year, was attended by the Prime Minister, Clemenceau, Georges Picquart and Alfred Dreyfus. Among the spectators was a young journalist, Louis-Anthelme Grégori. He had a revolver which he fired at Dreyfus, the bullet hitting his arm. Dreyfus was taken to a police station. His wound was treated and found to be superficial.

The unsuccessful assassin, Grégori, apprehended and placed under arrest, turned out to be a member of Maurras's Action Française. He was charged with attempted murder and went on trial in September. Commandant du Paty de Clam and Captain Lebrun-Renault testified in his defence. When, in the course of the proceedings, the judge stated that the proclamation of Dreyfus's innocence by the Cour de Cassation was 'formal, definitive, irrefutable', the editor of the newspaper *Action*

Française shouted that it had been illegal and a fraud. Louis-Anthelme Grégori was acquitted, and left the court shouting triumphantly: 'it's a review of the review'.[5] Shortly afterwards the die-hard anti-Dreyfusards demonstrated against another Dreyfusard, the deceased Bernard Lazare, at the inauguration of a monument erected in his memory in Nîmes.

––––––

Georges Picquart, having been restored to the army with the rank of brigadier-general, was made Minister of War by Georges Clemenceau in October 1906. The bitterness both had felt at Dreyfus's acceptance of a pardon had forged a personal bond between Clemenceau and Picquart that led to this political alliance. No doubt had Picquart never become involved with Dreyfus he might have risen on his own merits to become Chief of the General Staff; but it was the politicisation of the Affair that had brought him this position of Minister of War. The anti-Dreyfusard elements in the army had fought a rearguard action against him: General de Pellieux put about rumours picked up from his contacts on *La Libre Parole* that Picquart went in for spiritualism and hypnotism and that his morals were 'bad, very bad'. The charges were taken sufficiently seriously for Picquart to be placed under surveillance by the police. Clemenceau, as Minister of the Interior, had read their reports; Waldeck-Rousseau, then Prime Minister, had thrown them into the waste-paper basket.[6]

Insinuations that Picquart was homosexual were disproved by Picquart's increasingly open liaison with Pauline Romazzotti, who had finally divorced her husband, Monnier, and was now Picquart's regular companion. She and Picquart would stay with Eugène and Hélène Naville at their villa at Coligny on Lake Léman where they would be seen walking hand in hand. 'He preferred not to define more formally the more intimate nature of their relationship,' wrote Christian Vigouroux, but Pauline accompanied him on his travels and acted as hostess at the receptions he gave as Minister of War.

––––––

Charles Esterhazy remained in England. It was said that he received secret subventions from sympathisers in France, but ostensibly he earned his living as a journalist – the profession for which he was best suited and which he had, in a sense, practised while pretending to be a spy. He had made some money selling his story to English newspapers, and wrote for them under the name Fitzgerald. He set up house in the small town of Harpenden in Hertfordshire, forty-eight kilometres north of London, as Count Jean-Marie de Voilemont and, when he died in 1923, was buried in the graveyard of the parish church. Édouard Drumont was put up for a place in the French Academy in 1909 but lost to Marcel Prévost, author of the mildly porno-graphic *The Demi-Vierges*. Drumont died in 1917. Père Stanislas du Lac spent his last years organising the Syndicat de l'Aiguille, a self-help associa-tion for poor seamstresses and dressmakers, the *midinettes*. He died in 1909.

The divisions and enmities in French society that had been exposed by the Dreyfus Affair were laid aside during the First World War. The religious orders were permitted to return to France and a *union sacrée* – sacred union – was formed to fight the war against Germany for which the French Army had been bracing itself for so many years. Its cause was absurd – a dispute between the Austro-Hungarian Empire and Slav nationalists. However, the interlocking alliances, in particular that between France and Russia so carefully negotiated in its military permutations by General de Boisdeffre, pitched the armies of France and Germany against one another in a line of blood and mud stretching from the plains of Picardy to the Vosges.

Under pressure of war, political prejudices had to be abandoned. Many of the officers promoted for their political correctness during the *Affaire des Fiches* were sacked and more competent Catholics put in their place. Fourteen of the nineteen senior officers whose courage and competence in the field won them promotion in late 1914 had previously been victims of Masonic detraction.[7] The *union sacrée* brought about a spirit of ecumeni-cal reconciliation. A painting by a Jewish artist showed a rabbi, Abraham Bloch, wearing a Red Cross armband and holding up a crucifix for a dying Catholic soldier shortly before he expired in the arms of a Jesuit.[8]

Death made no distinction between Dreyfusards and anti-Drey-fusards. Mathieu Dreyfus, Joseph Reinach and Berthe Henry all lost sons in the first days of the war. Charles Péguy was killed on

4 September 1914 at the start of the Battle of the Marne. Colonel du Paty de Clam, readmitted to the army, was wounded twice, was cited for giving 'the most beautiful examples of courage and authority'[9] and was awarded the Légion d'Honneur. Deemed unfit for further active service, he enlisted as a private in a unit commanded by his son. He was again wounded, this time fatally, and died in Versailles on 3 September 1916; on his death certificate it stated that he had 'died for France'.

Maximilian von Schwartzkoppen had married Luise Gräfin von Wedel in 1902, who subsequently gave birth to two daughters. He retired from the army with the rank of general in the autumn of 1908 and went to live on an estate he had bought at Polkwitz in the Altmark. At the outbreak of war he returned to the colours and was given command of the 233rd Infantry Brigade, which saw heavy action on the heights of Loretto. In October 1916, he took command of the 202nd Infantry Division on the eastern front. He contracted pneumonia and was taken to the Elisabeth Hospital in Berlin. His condition deteriorated. In a delirium, with his wife sitting at his bedside, Schwartzkoppen suddenly sat up and said, as if giving evidence in court: 'Frenchmen, listen to me! Dreyfus is innocent! There is no evidence whatsoever against him!' His wife took down what he had said. On 8 January 1917, Schwartzkoppen died from acute inflammation of the kidneys and heart failure.[10]

Georges Picquart died six months before the outbreak of the First World War on 19 January 1914, as the result of a riding accident. A proposal by the Minister of War in the Chamber of Deputies that funds should be voted for a state funeral met with angry opposition on the nationalist benches.[11] Picquart had not seen Alfred Dreyfus since the ceremony at the École Militaire eight years before. Jean Jaurès, the Socialist champion of Dreyfus, was assassinated on 31 July 1914 in a Parisian café by a twenty-nine-year-old nationalist, Raoul, enraged by Jaurès's attempts to persuade both French and Germans to come out on strike to prevent a war. Georges Clemenceau, by contrast, built on his reputation as 'the tiger' gained in smashing the trades unions to become a vigorous supporter of the war, serving as Prime Minister from November 1917, leading France to victory and imposing crushing terms on the Germans at the Treaty of Versailles, among them the return to French sovereignty of Alsace and Lorraine.

During the last months of the war, to demonstrate his ruthlessness, Clemenceau prosecuted the former Prime Minister, Joseph Caillaux, for treason. Caillaux was defended by the now bent and aged Maître Edgar Demange, who died at his desk, 'very old and very poor', on 10 February 1925. Fernand Labori had pleaded for Caillaux's wife, who had shot the editor of *Le Figaro*, and secured her acquittal; he himself died of natural causes on 14 March 1917.

Mathieu Dreyfus, after devoting six years of his life to his brother's rehabilitation, returned to manage the family's factories in Mulhouse. No definitive calculation was ever made of what it had cost to save Dreyfus, but the disbursements by Mathieu and Joseph Reinach on legal fees, sweeteners for journalists, travel expenses, fees for experts and private detectives 'far exceeded one million francs'.[12] Émile, the son of Mathieu and Suzanne, died from wounds received in the trenches in October 1915. Their daugher Marguerite married Adolphe Reinach, the son of Joseph Reinach, who was killed on the front in 1917. After the war, Mathieu and Suzanne moved to Paris to help care for their grandchildren. Mathieu died in October 1930, Suzanne in 1964.

Alfred outlived his elder brother by five years. As a reservist, he was mobilised in 1914, stationed first as an artillery officer in Paris, then attached to the 168th Division which took part in the battles of the Chemin des Dames and Verdun. In September 1918, he was promoted to the rank of lieutenant-colonel in the reserve and in July 1919 raised to the rank of an officer in the Légion d'Honneur.

In the years following the war, he continued assembling and annotating the dossier on his Affair. Now living with Lucie in a flat on the rue des Renaudes, he spent his days at his desk, going through his papers, sticking stamps into albums and smoking a pipe. He still suffered from nightmares, hearing in his dreams the cries of loathing at his degradation and feeling the torments on Devil's Island – the heat, the fever, the double shackles, the spider-crabs. He took long walks for the sake of his health – his grandson remembered him 'fragile, stooped, nervous, walking rapidly, his large pocketwatch always within reach'.[13]

Alfred and Lucie's son Pierre married Marie Baur and they had four children, a son and three daughters. Their daughter Jeanne married Pierre Paul Lévy and had two sons and two daughters. The grandchildren were brought to visit their grandparents. Alfred was impatient if they were unpunctual but was affectionate and never burdened them with painful reminiscences. 'I have a quite precise memory of my grandfather,' wrote Jean-Louis Lévy, 'but I must say first of all that Alfred Dreyfus never said a word about the Affair to his grandchildren, and not a word about his suffering.'[14] Dreyfus died peacefully, surrounded by his family, at five in the afternoon on 11 July 1935.

The *union sacrée* – the truce between left and right – did not survive the end of the First World War. The polarities became more extreme with further scandals such as the Stavisky Affair leading to riots, and militants on both wings growing impatient with parliamentary democracy and testing their strength in the streets. When, in June 1940, German armies once again attacked France through Belgium, the French Army could not hold them. It was a replay of 1870 with Hitler playing the role of Bismarck. To save the nation in its hour of need, the politicians turned to a marshal of France, Henri Pétain, the former classmate of the Marquis de Morès at Saint-Cyr. Only eighty deputies, Léon Blum among them, voted against giving Pétain full powers to negotiate an armistice and govern France.

France was saved from *polonisation* – the fate of Poland, placed under a gauleiter by Hitler and its population enslaved: half the country remained unoccupied until 1942, ruled by Pétain and his appointed Prime Ministers from the spa town of Vichy in the Auvergne. The right was now in power. The slogan of 'Liberty, Equality and Fraternity' was replaced by 'Work, Family, Nation'. The government quickly passed laws that discriminated against Jews: a statute of 3 October 1940 excluded Jews, defined on religious and racial grounds, from all political positions, from posts in the governmental and judicial administration, the armed services and the media and from French schools and universities.[15] The exclusion was later extended to banking, finance, advertising and real-estate; the law passed by Adolphe Crémieux giving French citizenship to Algerian Jews was repealed.

Hannah Arendt, in *The Origins of Totalitarianism*, judged that French anti-Semitism was not 'an active historical factor in the final catastrophe' that overwhelmed European Jews during the Second World War; however, the Vichy government was undoubtedly complicit in the implementation of Hitler's 'Final Solution'. The legal definition of who was a Jew applied by the Vichy government cast a wider net than that of the Nazis, and the administrative structures of the French state were used to round up Jews living in France and intern them in Drancy prior to their deportation. Vichy may have successfully opposed the German demand that Jews wear a yellow star, but its opposition to the deportation of French Jews to the extermination camps was ineffective: '6,000 of the 65,000 deported from France to the death camps were French citizens.'[16]

Alfred and Lucie's son, Pierre Dreyfus, spent the first two years following the defeat of France hiding in Marseille and the villages behind the city. His wife Marie had relatives in the United States, and it was decided that because of his status as the son of Alfred Dreyfus, and the work he had done for Jewish groups, Pierre and his family should be granted visas.[17] He left France for America in 1943. His sister Jeanne and her husband Pierre Lévy remained in Toulouse. Their daughter Madeleine, aged twenty-two, joined the Resistance, was arrested in Toulouse by French police and deported via Drancy to Auschwitz where she was killed.

In March 1941, the Vichy government set up a Commissariat Général to administer Jewish affairs in France. Its first director was Xavier Vallat; the second Louis Darquier; the third Charles du Paty de Clam, the son of Commandant Ferdinand du Paty de Clam. Among the tasks of the Commissariat was the sequestration of funds and property belonging to Jews. Twenty thousand francs was taken from a bank account held by Lucie Dreyfus.[18] Lucie lived with her daughter Jeanne in Toulouse until the Germans moved into the unoccupied zone in November 1942. She then went to her younger sister Alice in Valence, adopted Alice's married name, Duteil, and was hidden for the rest of the war by a community of retired nuns in a convent in Valence;[19] only the Mother Superior knew who she was.[20] At the Liberation, Lucie left the convent and returned to her flat in Paris where she died on 14 December 1945.

Principal Characters

Aboville, Commandant Albert d'
Second-in-command of the Fourth Bureau of the General Staff. Suggested that the author of the incriminating *bordereau* may have been one of the interns (*stagiaires*).

André, General Louis
Minister of War, 1900–November 1904.

Arconati-Visconti, Marquise Marie (née Peyrat)
Dreyfusard *salonnière* who befriended Dreyfus after his pardon. Both Joseph Reinach and Émile Combes belonged to her circle.

Barrès, Maurice
Anti-Dreyfusard journalist and intellectual. Covered the Rennes court martial for *Le Journal*. One of the founders in 1899 of the Ligue de la Patrie Française to oppose the Ligue des Droits de l'Homme.

Bastian, Mme Marie-Caudron
Cleaning lady at the German Embassy on the rue de Lille. Recruited by Martin-Joseph Brücker as an agent for the French secret service. Delivered the contents of the Embassy's waste-paper baskets to Commandant Joseph Henry.

Beauvais, Captain Charles
Judge at the Rennes court martial.

Bertillon, Alphonse
Chief of the Judicial Identification Department at the Paris Prefecture of Police. Judged the *bordereau* to have been written by Alfred Dreyfus.

Bertulus, Judge Paul
A civilian examining magistrate. Consulted by General de Pellieux on the legality of seizing Esterhazy's letters to Mme de Boulancy, and the first civilian legal officer to be drawn into the Affair.

Billot, General Jean-Baptiste
Minister of War, April 1896–June 1898. Friend of Auguste Scheurer-Kestner. Anti-Dreyfusard.

Biot, Commandant Octave
Former officer in the territorial army who wrote for *La Libre Parole* on military matters under the pseudonym Commandant Z, often in collaboration with Esterhazy.

Boisdeffre, General Raoul François Charles le Mouton de
Chief of the Army General Staff, September 1893–September 1898. Architect of the Franco-Russian alliance.

Boulancy, Mme de
One-time mistress of Charles Esterhazy.

Bréon, Major Lancrau de
A judge at the Rennes court martial. Devout Catholic.

Brogniart, Lieutenant-Colonel François
A judge at the Rennes court martial.

Brücker, Martin-Joseph
Low-life agent working for Commandant Henry. He recruited Mme Bastian.

Casimir-Perier, Jean
Prime Minister, April–December 1893. Chosen as President in June 1894 after assassination of Sadi Carnot. Resigned in January 1895, disillusioned by his inability to control or influence government.

Cassagnac, Paul de
Editor of *L'Autorité*. Member of anti-Semitic faction in the Chamber of Deputies.

Castro, Jacques de
Parisian stockbroker of South American origin.

Cavaignac, Godefroy
Minister of War, November 1895–April 1896. Anti-Dreyfusard.

Chamoin, General Eugène
Representative of the Ministry of War at Dreyfus's second court martial in Rennes.

Chanoine, General Charles
Minister of War, September–October 1898.

Clemenceau, Georges
Radical politician. Compromised by the Panama Canal scandal. Founder of *L'Aurore*. Prominent Dreyfusard.

Cochefert, Commissaire Armand
Head of CID at the Sûreté Générale seconded to the Statistical Section.

Combes, Émile
Prime Minister, June 1902–January 1905. Militant anti-clerical.

Cordier, Commandant Albert
Deputy Commander of the Statistical Section at the time of Dreyfus's arrest.

Cuers, Richard
French spy working for German military intelligence, the Nachrichtenbureau.

Cuignet, Captain Louis
Officer who collated the secret dossier for the Ministers of War Billot and Cavaignac. Anti-Dreyfusard.

Demange, Edgar
Dreyfus's first lawyer.

Déroulède, Paul
Poet and politician. Founded the Ligue des Patriotes. Anti-Dreyfusard but not anti-Semitic.

Dreyfus, Alfred
Captain in the artillery. Candidate for the General Staff.

Dreyfus, Camille
Radical Deputy. Fought a duel with Marquis de Morès. Founded *Le Matin*.

Dreyfus, Jacques
Eldest brother of Albert Dreyfus.

Dreyfus, Jeanne
Daughter of Alfred Dreyfus, born 1893.

Dreyfus, Lucie
Née Hadamard. Wife of Alfred Dreyfus.

Dreyfus, Mathieu
Elder brother of Alfred Dreyfus.

Dreyfus, Pierre
Son of Alfred Dreyfus, born 1891.

Dreyfus, Raphaël
Father of Alfred Dreyfus.

Drumont, Édouard
Author of *La France juive*. Founder of anti-Semitic newspaper *La Libre Parole*.

Dupuy, Charles
Prime Minister, May 1894–January 1895.

Esterhazy, Commandant Marie-Charles-Ferdinand Walsin
Infantry officer, son of a French general of remote Hungarian descent. Acted as second to André Crémieu-Foa in his duel with Édouard Drumont.

Faure, Félix
President of France, January 1895–February 1899.

Forzinetti, Commandant Ferdinand
Governor of the Cherche-Midi military prison.

Freycinet, Charles de
Reforming Minister of War, April 1888–January 1893 and November 1898–May 1899.

Freystaetter, Captain Martin
Judge at the first court martial.

Galliffet, General le Marquis de
Minister of War, June 1899–May 1900. Succeeded by General André.

Gambetta, Léon
Radical politician. Proclaimed a republic after the defeat of Napoleon III at Sedan. Escaped from Paris besieged by the Prussians in 1869 in a hot-air balloon. Anti-clerical.

Gobert, Alfred
Handwriting expert from the Banque de France. Judged that the handwriting of the *bordereau* was not that of Alfred Dreyfus.

Gonse, General Charles-Arthur
Deputy Chief of the General Staff, 1893–1899.

Gribelin, Félix
Archivist at the Statistical Section. Served as clerk to Commandant du Paty de Clam during his investigations.

Guénée, François
Former undercover police officer working for the Statistical Section. Controller of the French agent in the Spanish Embassy, the Marquis de Val Carlos.

Guérin, Jules
Active anti-Semite. Supported by the royalist pretender, the Duc d'Orléans; founded the Ligue Antisémitique in 1897 and the newspaper, *L'Antijuif.*

Hanotaux, Gabriel
Minister of Foreign Affairs in 1894. Retired from politics after Fashoda crisis in 1898. Friend of Dr Adrien Proust, father of Marcel.

Henry, Commandant Hubert Joseph
Third-in-command at the Statistical Section, the only officer who had risen from the ranks.

Jaurès, Jean
Leader of the Socialist Party.

Jouaust, Colonel Albert
Presiding judge at the second court martial.

Lac de Fugères, Père Stanislas du
French Jesuit, Rector of the École Sainte-Geneviève on the rue des Postes between 1872 and 1881.

Lauth, Captain Jules
Officer serving in the Statistical Section. Protestant from Alsace.

Lazare, Bernard
Jewish journalist recruited by Mathieu Dreyfus to promote the case of his brother Alfred. Author of *L'Antisémitisme, son histoire et ses causes* (*Anti-Semitism: Its History and Causes*).

Leblois, Louis
Lawyer. Friend of Georges Picquart from their schooldays in Alsace.

Lebrun-Renault, Captain Charles-Gustave
Officer in charge of Alfred Dreyfus prior to his degradation who later claimed that he had confessed.

Lépine, Commissaire Louis
Prefect of the Paris Police.

Loubet, Émile
President of France, February 1899–February 1906.

Matton, Captain Pierre
Italian specialist in the Statistical Section. Played a minor role in the Panizzardi telegram.

Maurel, Colonel E.
Presiding judge at the first court martial.

Maurras, Charles
Nationalist writer and journalist.

Mayer, Captain Armand
Jewish officer killed by the Marquis de Morès in a duel.

Mercier, General Auguste
Minister of War, December 1893–January 1895.

Merle, Commandant Émile
Judge at second court martial.

Meyer, Arthur
Jewish convert to Catholicism; editor of *Le Gaulois*.

Monnier, Pauline
Née Romazzotti. Wife of a civil servant in the Ministry of Foreign Affairs, mistress of Colonel Georges Picquart.

Morès, Marquis Antoine de
Co-founder with Jules Guérin of the Ligue Antisémitique. Killed the Jewish Captain Armand Mayer in a duel in 1894.

Müller, Major
Chief of German military intelligence, the Nachrichtenbureau.

Mun, Comte Albert de
Right-wing deputy and monarchist who supported Pope Leo XIII's *ralliement* – the acceptance of a republican form of government.

Münster von Derneburg, Graf Georges-Herbert
German Ambassador to France.

Nisard, Armand
Director of Political Affairs at the French Foreign Office, the Quai d'Orsay.

Ormescheville, Major Besson d'
Judge advocate (investigating magistrate) at the first court martial held in Paris. Cross-examined Alfred Dreyfus on 14 November 1894.

Paléologue, Maurice
Assistant to Armand Nisard at the French Foreign Office with responsibility for liaison with military intelligence (the Statistical Section). Witnessed Dreyfus's degradation in 1895 and was both witness and observer at his second court martial in Rennes.

Panizzardi, Major Alessandro
Military attaché at the Italian Embassy in Paris. Friend and lover of Maximilian von Schwartzkoppen.

Parfait, Captain
Judge at the Rennes court martial.

Paty de Clam, Commandant Ferdinand du
Officer of the General Staff. Ordered by his cousin, General de Boisdeffre, to investigate the *bordereau* and subsequently to build up a case against Alfred Dreyfus.

Pays, Marguerite
Esterhazy's mistress; previously the mistress of the journalist Ponchon de Saint-André, alias Boisandré of *La Libre Parole*.

Péguy, Charles
Socialist poet and essayist. Ardent Dreyfusard. Later converted to Catholicism. Close friend of Bernard Lazare.

Pelletier, Eugène
Handwriting expert. Judged that the handwriting of the *bordereau* was not that of Alfred Dreyfus.

Pellieux, General Georges de
Commander of the army in the department of the Seine. Ordered by General Saussier to conduct the investigation into Esterhazy after he was accused by Mathieu Dreyfus of being the traitor. Became a convinced anti-Dreyfusard.

Picard, Captain Ernest
Jewish officer marked down at the École de Guerre at the same time as Dreyfus.

Picquart, Colonel Georges
Succeeded Colonel Sandherr as head of the Statistical Section in July 1895. Attended the first court martial as representative of the Ministry of War.

Poincaré, Raymond
Minister of Finance at the time of Dreyfus's arrest. Belated Dreyfusard. President of France during the First World War.

Profillet, Major
Judge at the second court martial at Rennes.

Reinach, Joseph
Radical politician and early Dreyfusard. Nephew of Baron Jacques de Reinach, compromised by the Panama Canal scandal. Wrote *Histoire de l'Affaire Dreyfus*.

Roche, Jules
Nationalist Deputy. Patron of Esterhazy. Possible Minister of War.

Rochefort, Henri Marquis de
Former Communard who escaped from the penal colony in New Caledonia. Nationalist and anti-Semite. Founded *L'Intransigeant*.

Roget, General Gaudérique
Assessor of Dreyfus at the École Militaire; chief of the Fourth Bureau of the General Staff; Adjutant to Cavaignac at the Ministry of War. Anti-Dreyfusard.

Rothschild, Baron Edmond de
Fellow pupil of Charles Walsin-Esterhazy at the Lycée Condorcet. Sent him 2,000 francs.

Sandherr, Colonel Jean
Chief of French military intelligence, the Statistical Section. Replaced by Picquart on 1 July 1895. Died in 1897.

Saussier, General Félix
Military Governor of Paris from 1884 and later Vice-President of Army Council, i.e. commander-in-chief designate in the event of war. Friend and patron of Commandant Maurice Weil.

Scheurer-Kestner, Auguste
Deputy for Haut-Rhin (Alsace) in National Assembly in 1871, last representative from Alsace before its annexation by Germany. Vice-President of the Senate and Senator for Life. Early Dreyfusard. Died in 1899.

Schwartzkoppen, Lieutenant-Colonel Maximilian von
Military attaché at the German Embassy in Paris, 1891–7.

Schwob, Suzanne
Wife of Mathieu Dreyfus.

Straus, Geneviève (née Halévy)
Dreyfusard *salonnière*. Widow of the composer Georges Bizet; wife of the Rothschilds' lawyer Émile Straus.

Targe, Captain Antoine
Officer charged with the final analysis of the Dreyfus file.

Teysonnières, Pierre
Handwriting expert. Judged that the handwriting of the *bordereau* was that of Dreyfus.

Trarieux, Ludovic
Minister of Justice in 1894. Founder and first President of the League of the Rights of Man.

Val Carlos, Raimundo Marquis de
Second military attaché in the Spanish Embassy in Paris. Supplied information to the Statistical Section.

Waldeck-Rousseau, Pierre
Lawyer and politician. Prime Minister, June 1899–June 1902.

Walsin-Esterhazy, Commandant Marie-Charles-Ferdinand
See Esterhazy, Commandant Marie-Charles-Ferdinand Walsin.

Weil, Major Maurice
A Jewish officer serving on the staff of General Saussier. His wife was Saussier's mistress.

Zola, Émile
Novelist and journalist who took up the cause of Dreyfus.

Zurlinden, General Émile
Minister of War, 5–17 September 1898. Later Military Governor of Paris.

Notes

Preface

1 Michael Burns, *Rural Society and French Politics*, p. 7
2 Marcel Thomas, *L'Affaire sans Dreyfus*, p. 524
3 See Jacqueline Rose, 'J'accuse: Dreyfus in our Times', *London Review of Books*, vol. 32, no. 11, June 2010
4 Charles Péguy, *Notre jeunesse*, p. 14
5 Hannah Arendt, *The Origins of Totalitarianism*, p. 10
6 Ruth Harris, *The Man on Devil's Island*, p. 376
7 Stephen Wilson, *Ideology and Experience*, p. xiii
8 Vincent Duclert, *Alfred Dreyfus: l'honneur d'un patriote*, p. 102
9 Alain Pagès, *Emile Zola: un intellectuel dans l'Affaire Dreyfus*, p. 282, quoted in Marie-Christine Leps, 'Normal Deviance: The Dreyfus Affair', Actes de Colloque
10 See David Seznec in David Canard, ed., *Partir au bagne*, p. 2
11 Pierre Dreyfus, *Dreyfus: His Life and Letters*, p. 13
12 Duclert, op. cit., p. 111
13 Leps, op. cit.
14 Jean-Louis Lévy internet interview
15 Quoted in Wilson, op. cit., p. xiii
16 Albert S. Lindemann, *The Jew Accused*, p. 94
17 Ruth Harris, op. cit., p. xvii
18 Michael R. Marrus, *Times Literary Supplement*, 20 and 27 August 2010, p. 29
19 Lindemann, op. cit., pp. 7–8

Chapter 1: The French Revolution

1 Christopher Hibbert, *The French Revolution*, p. 45
2 Michael Burleigh, *Earthly Powers*, p. 39
3 Linda Colley, *Britons*, p. 369
4 Max Dimont, *Jews, God and History*, p. 210
5 Quoted in Michael Burns, *Dreyfus: A Family Affair*, p. 11
6 Duclert, op. cit., p. 33
7 Yakov M. Rabkin, *A Threat from Within*, p. 23
8 Abram Sacher, quoted in Edward H. Flannery, *The Anguish of the Jews*, p. 167
9 Flannery, op. cit., p. 167
10 *Encyclopaedia Britannica*, vol. 7, p. 666
11 Adam Zamoyski, *Rites of Peace*, p. 379
12 Count Ratti-Menton to Marshal Soult, quoted in Jonathan Frankel, *The Damascus Affair*, p. 24
13 Frankel, op. cit., p. 273
14 Ibid., p. 207
15 Lindemann, op. cit., p. 38
16 Frankel, op. cit., p. 390
17 Zamoyski, op. cit., p. 436
18 Burleigh, op. cit., p. 25
19 Ralph Gibson, *A Social History of French Catholicism, 1789–1914*, p. 16
20 Burleigh, op. cit., p. 64
21 Hibbert, op. cit., p. 170
22 Burleigh, op. cit., p. 107
23 Ibid., p. 101
24 Ibid., p. 97
25 Ibid., p. 47
26 Gibson, op. cit., p. 44
27 Ibid., p. 60
28 Ibid., p. 52
29 Ibid., p. 121
30 François-René de Chateaubriand, *The Beauties of Christianity*, p. 277
31 Geoffrey Wawro, *The Franco-Prussian War*, p. 2
32 Edmond and Jules de Goncourt, *Pages from the Goncourt Journals*, p. 179
33 Wawro, op. cit., p. 66
34 Ibid., p. 309
35 Ibid., p. 279
36 D. W. Brogan, *The Development of Modern France*, p. 56
37 Ibid., p. 67
38 Wawro, op. cit., p. 310
39 Ibid., p. 311

Chapter 2: The Third Republic

1 Robert Anderson, 'The Conflict in Education', p. 51
2 Decree 52 of 5th General Congregation, 1592, confirmed by Decree 28 of 6th General Congregation, 1608, and Decree 27 of 27th General Congregation, 1927, which referred only to 'all who are descended from the Jewish race'
3 *Catholic Encyclopaedia*
4 Ruth Harris, *Lourdes*, p. 213
5 Katrin Schultheiss, *Bodies and Souls*, p. 3
6 Quoted in Brogan, op. cit., p.175
7 John McManners, *Church and State in France, 1870–1914*, p. 16
8 Brogan, op. cit., p. 141
9 Anderson, op. cit., p. 71
10 Evelyn M. Acomb, *The French Laic Laws (1879–1889)*, p. 56
11 Brogan, op. cit., p. 150
12 Acomb, op. cit., p. 255
13 Brogan, op. cit., p. 155
14 Lindemann, op. cit., pp. 67–8, 276
15 Gibson, op. cit., p. 230
16 Robert Tombs, *France, 1814–1914*, p. 89
17 Wilson, op. cit., p. 419
18 Ibid., p. 546
19 Wawro, op. cit., p. 310
20 Jean-Louis Bredin, *The Affair*, p. 16
21 Brogan, op. cit., p. 380
22 Quoted in Wilson, op. cit., p. 402
23 Lindemann, op. cit., p. 64
24 McManners, op. cit., p. 126
25 Pierre Miquel, *L'Affaire Dreyfus*, p. 18
26 Quoted in Duclert, op. cit., p. 85
27 Ibid., p. 84

Chapter 3: Édouard Drumont

1 Édouard Drumont, *La France juive*, vol. I, p. 8
2 Jean-Paul Sartre, *Anti-Semite and Jew*, p. 45
3 Drumont, op. cit., p. 451
4 Ibid., p. 123
5 Brogan, op. cit., p. 367
6 Drumont, op. cit., p. 309
7 McManners, op. cit., p. 122
8 Quoted in Wilson, op. cit., p. 537

9 See McManners, op. cit., p. 122
10 Brogan, op. cit., p. 277
11 Quoted in Wilson, op. cit., p. 174
12 Brogan, op. cit., p. 271
13 Ibid., p. 272
14 Ibid., p. 274
15 Ibid., p. 284
16 See Anthony Levi, *Cardinal Richelieu and the Making of France*, pp. 104 et seq.
17 Burns, *Dreyfus: A Family Affair*, p. 188
18 Lindemann, op. cit., p. 91
19 Goncourt, op. cit., p. 319
20 Ibid., p. 332
21 Drumont, op. cit., p. 18
22 Quoted in Miquel, op. cit., p. 18
23 Maurice Paléologue, *My Secret Diary of the Dreyfus Case, 1894–1899*, p. 64
24 Ibid.
25 Quoted in Wilson, op. cit., p. 319
26 Donald Dresden, *The Marquis de Morès*, p. 226
27 Wilson, op. cit., p. 619
28 Quoted in Duclert, op. cit., p. 66
29 Dresden, op. cit., p. 249
30 Quoted in Thomas, op. cit., p. 43
31 Ibid., p. 152

Chapter 4: Evidence of Treason

1 Allan Mitchell, 'The Xenophobic Style: French Counterespionage and the Emergence of the Dreyfus Affair', p. 416
2 Ibid., p. 417
3 Ibid., p. 18
4 Thomas, op. cit., p. 71
5 Douglas Porch, *French Secret Service*, p. 30
6 Mitchell, op. cit., p. 424
7 Miquel, op. cit., p. 18
8 Quoted in Porch, op. cit., p. 30
9 Thomas, op. cit., p. 61
10 Ibid., p. 61
11 Paléologue, op. cit., p. 162
12 Quoted in Bredin, op. cit., p. 49
13 Thomas, op. cit., p. 73
14 Ibid.
15 Paléologue, op. cit., p. 101
16 Thomas, op. cit., p. 74

17 Paléologue, op. cit., p. 101
18 Thomas, op. cit., p. 119
19 Ibid., p. 76
20 Ibid., p. 110
21 Jean Doise, *Un Secret bien gardé: histoire militaire de l'affaire Dreyfus*, p. 26
22 Thomas, op. cit., p. 124
23 Bredin, op. cit., p. 64
24 Duclert, op. cit., p. 113
25 Jacqueline Rose, 'J'accuse: Dreyfus in our Times'
26 Lindemann, op. cit., p. 102
27 Robert Louis Hoffman, *More than a Trial*, p. 4
28 Thomas, op. cit., p. 130
29 Ibid., p. 128
30 Bredin, op. cit., p. 65
31 Burns, *Dreyfus: A Family Affair*, p. 123
32 Pierre Dreyfus, op. cit., p. 84
33 Thomas, op. cit., p. 132
34 Bernhard Schwertfeger, ed., *The Truth about Dreyfus from the Schwartzkoppen Papers*, p. 33
35 Ibid., p. 34
36 Thomas, op. cit., p. 137
37 Ibid., p. 134
38 Ibid.
39 Quoted in Bredin, op. cit., p. 68
40 Leps, op. cit.
41 Bredin, op. cit., p. 69

Chapter 5: Dreyfus Accused

1 Alfred Dreyfus, *Five Years of my Life*, p. 3
2 Duclert, op. cit., p. 63
3 Thomas, op. cit., p. 148
4 Pierre Dreyfus, op. cit., p. 37
5 Burns, *Dreyfus: A Family Affair*, p. 41
6 Ibid., p. 37
7 Ruth Harris, *The Man on Devil's Island*, p. 62
8 Burns, *Dreyfus: A Family Affair*, p. 36
9 Duclert, op. cit., p. 37
10 Burns, *Dreyfus: A Family Affair*, p. 131
11 Quoted in Pierre Dreyfus, op. cit., p. 40
12 Ibid., p. 38
13 Burns, *Dreyfus: A Family Affair*, p. 98
14 Duclert, op. cit., p. 44
15 Ibid., p. 45

16 Burns, *Dreyfus: A Family Affair*, p. 76
17 Ibid., p. 79
18 Ibid., p. 103
19 Ibid., p. 75
20 Quoted in Ruth Harris, *The Man on Devil's Island*, p. 68
21 Burns, *Dreyfus: A Family Affair*, p. 79
22 Duclert, op. cit., p. 64
23 Burns, *Dreyfus: A Family Affair*, p. 79
24 Ruth Harris, *The Man on Devil's Island*, p. 67
25 Duclert, op. cit., p. 55
26 Joseph Reinach, quoted in *ibid.*, p. 264
27 Burns, *Dreyfus: A Family Affair*, p. 88
28 Ibid., p. 80
29 Duclert, op. cit., p. 59
30 Burns, *Dreyfus: A Family Affair*, p. 97
31 Duclert, op. cit., p. 38
32 Burns, *Dreyfus: A Family Affair*, p. 83
33 Duclert, op. cit., p. 45
34 Ibid., p. 99
35 Burns, *Dreyfus: A Family Affair*, p. 89
36 Ruth Harris, *The Man on Devil's Island*, p. 67
37 Duclert, op. cit., p. 80
38 Douglas Johnson, *France and the Dreyfus Affair*, p. 214
39 Lindemann, op. cit., p. 60
40 Quoted in George D. Painter, *Marcel Proust: A Biography*, vol. I, p. 74
41 Duclert, op. cit., p. 107
42 Ibid., p. 108
43 Ibid., p. 97
44 Ibid., pp. 94–5
45 Ibid., p. 110
46 Ibid., p. 105

Chapter 6: Dreyfus Condemned

1 Commissaire Cochefert's evidence at Rennes, quoted in Duclert, op. cit., p. 16
2 Quoted in ibid., p. 18
3 Quoted in Bredin, op. cit., p. 57
4 Quoted in Duclert, op. cit., p. 23
5 Pierre Dreyfus, op. cit., p. 25
6 Duclert, op. cit., p. 139
7 Ibid., p. 320
8 Quoted in ibid., p. 277
9 Thomas, op. cit., p. 148

10 Quoted in Duclert, op. cit., p. 133
11 Ibid., p. 320
12 Pierre Dreyfus, op. cit., p. 27
13 Quoted in ibid., p. 28
14 Duclert, op. cit., p. 317
15 Burns, *Dreyfus: A Family Affair*, p. 117
16 Quoted in Miquel, op. cit., p. 31
17 Bredin, op. cit., p. 84
18 Ibid.
19 Ibid., p. 76
20 Quoted in Burns, *Dreyfus: A Family Affair*, p. 117
21 Duclert, op. cit., p. 197
22 Thomas, op. cit., p. 171
23 Ibid., p. 174; Duclert, op. cit., p. 325
24 Duclert, op. cit., p. 324
25 Paléologue, op. cit., p. 158
26 Porch, op. cit., pp. 36–7
27 Quoted in Bredin, op. cit., p. 89
28 Ibid., p. 125
29 Quoted in Duclert, op. cit., p. 278
30 Burns, *Dreyfus: A Family Affair*, p. 99
31 Ibid., p. 76
32 Ibid., p. 81
33 Ibid., p. 115
34 Bredin, op. cit., p. 77
35 Duclert, op. cit., p. 279
36 See Norman Stone, *Europe Transformed, 1878–1919*, p. 218
37 Bredin, op. cit., p. 77
38 Burns, *Dreyfus: A Family Affair*, p. 120
39 Quoted in Duclert, op. cit., p. 155
40 Bredin, op. cit., p. 95
41 Lindemann, op. cit., p. 104
42 Quoted in Duclert, op. cit., p. 151
43 Ibid., p. 153
44 Ibid., p. 355
45 Burns, *Dreyfus: A Family Affair*, p. 133
46 Alfred Dreyfus, *Memoirs of Captain Dreyfus*, p. 357
47 Duclert, op. cit., p. 165
48 Bredin, op. cit., p. 95
49 Paléologue, op. cit., p. 33
50 Duclert, op. cit., p. 250
51 Ibid., p. 253
52 Bredin, op. cit., p. 97

53 Ibid., p. 4
54 Duclert, op. cit., p. 212
55 Quoted in Bredin, op. cit., p. 7
56 Alfred Dreyfus, *Five Years of my Life*, p. 46
57 Ibid., p. 43
58 Ibid., p. 57
59 Duclert, op. cit., p. 203
60 Ruth Harris, *The Man on Devil's Island*, p. 35
61 Burns, *Dreyfus: A Family Affair*, p. 152
62 Christian Vigouroux, *Georges Picquart*, p. 356
63 See Aaron Manson in a letter to the *New Yorker*, 26 October 2009
64 See Shlomo Avinerei, *Herzl*, Zalman Shazar Center, 2008
65 Burns, *Dreyfus: A Family Affair*, p. 153
66 Goncourt, op. cit., p. 398
67 Bredin, op. cit., p. 107
68 Burns, *Dreyfus: A Family Affair*, p. 153
69 Duclert, op. cit., p. 390
70 Ibid., p. 125

Chapter 7: The Isles of Salvation

1   Alfred Dreyfus, *Five Years of my Life*, p. 67
2   Quoted in Burns, *Dreyfus: A Family Affair*, p. 143
3   Duclert, op. cit., p. 269
4   Ruth Harris, *The Man on Devil's Island*, p. 269
5   Quoted in Pierre Dreyfus, op. cit., p. 44
6   Quoted in ibid.
7   Quoted in ibid., p. 51
8   Alfred Dreyfus, *Five Years of my Life*, p. 26
9   Duclert, op. cit., p. 272
10 Alfred Dreyfus, *Five Years of my Life*, p. 163
11 Duclert, op. cit., p. 396
12 Bredin, op. cit., p. 100
13 Quoted in ibid.
14 Brogan, op. cit., p. 303
15 Alfred Dreyfus, *Five Years of my Life*, p. 63
16 Canard, *Partir au bagne*, p. 75
17 Ibid., p. 72
18 Ibid., p. 93
19 Alfred Dreyfus, *Five Years of my Life*, p. 110
20 Ibid., p. 136
21 Burns, *Dreyfus: A Family Affair*, p. 198
22 Alfred Dreyfus, *Five Years of my Life*, p. 158

23 Ibid., pp. 246–7
24 Pierre Dreyfus, op. cit., p. 93
25 Alfred Dreyfus, *Five Years of my Life*, p. 169
26 Ibid., p. 283
27 Ibid., p. 162
28 Ibid., p. 208
29 Ibid., p. 163
30 Ibid., p. 189
31 Ibid., p. 224
32 Ibid., p. 114
33 *Othello*, Act III, scene iii
34 Burns, *Dreyfus: A Family Affair*, p. 217
35 Duclert, op. cit., p. 459
36 Alfred Dreyfus, *Five Years of my Life*, p. 246
37 Ibid., p. 163
38 Ibid., p. 172
39 Quoted in Pierre Dreyfus, op. cit., p. 148
40 Ibid., p. 144
41 Quoted in Duclert, op. cit., p. 471
42 Alfred Dreyfus, *Five Years of my Life*, p. 107
43 Ibid.
44 Quoted in Duclert, op. cit., p. 527
45 Alfred Dreyfus, *Five Years of my Life*, p. 111
46 Ibid., p. 187
47 Bredin, op. cit., p. 130
48 Quoted in Duclert, op. cit., p. 522
49 Drumont, op. cit., p. 222
50 Alfred Dreyfus, *Five Years of my Life*, p. 274
51 Ibid., p. 274
52 Ibid., p. 310
53 Ibid., p. 275
54 Pierre Dreyfus, op. cit., p. 95
55 Alfred Dreyfus, *Five Years of my Life*, p. 231
56 Ibid., p. 232
57 See Clément Duval, *Moi, Clément Duval, bagnard et Anarchiste*, Éditions Ouvriers, 1991; also *Black Flag Quarterly*, vol. 7, no. 5 (Winter 1984)
58 Alfred Dreyfus, *Five Years of my Life*, p. 117
59 Ibid., p. 186
60 Quoted in Duclert, op. cit., p. 475
61 Alfred Dreyfus, *Five Years of my Life*, p. 234
62 Duclert, op. cit., p. 476
63 Alfred Dreyfus, *Five Years of my Life*, p. 277
64 Pierre Dreyfus, op. cit., p. 144

65 Alfred Dreyfus, *Five Years of my Life*, p. 304
66 Ibid., p. 288
67 Ibid., p. 293
68 Quoted in Duclert, op. cit., p. 478
69 Alfred Dreyfus, *Five Years of my Life*, p. 310
70 Ibid., p. 321

Chapter 8: The First Dreyfusards

1 Burns, *Dreyfus: A Family Affair*, p. 132
2 Lindemann, op. cit., p. 109
3 Burns, *Dreyfus: A Family Affair*, p. 176
4 Ibid.
5 Wilson, op. cit., p. 699
6 Lindemann, op. cit., p. 109
7 Burns, *Dreyfus: A Family Affair*, p. 174
8 Quoted in Bredin, op. cit., p. 115
9 Duclert, op. cit., p. 258
10 Bredin, op. cit., p. 115
11 Quoted in ibid., p. 117
12 Quoted in Alfred Dreyfus, *Memoirs of Captain Dreyfus*, p. 291
13 Bredin, op. cit., p. 119
14 Ibid., p. 134
15 Bernard Lazare, *Anti-Semitism: Its History and Causes*, p. 92 (www.indiana.edu)
16 *La Libre Parole*, 10 January 1895, quoted in Bredin, op. cit., p. 134
17 Lazare, op. cit., p. 4
18 Ibid., p. 22
19 Ibid., p. 45
20 Ibid., p. 117
21 Ibid., p. 83
22 Ibid., p. 132
23 Ibid., p. 108
24 Ibid., p. 118
25 Ibid., p. 124
26 Ibid., p. 136
27 See Bredin, op. cit., p. 139
28 Ibid., p. 138
29 Quoted in Rose, op. cit.
30 Ruth Harris, *The Man on Devil's Island*, p. 95
31 Quoted in Corinne Casset, *Joseph Reinach avant l'Affaire Dreyfus*, p. 172: see Ruth Harris, *The Man on Devil's Island*, p. 94
32 Quoted in Bredin, op. cit., p. 136
33 Ibid., p. 137

34 Ruth Harris, *The Man on Devil's Island*, p. 304
35 Goncourt, op. cit., p. 211
36 Burns, *Dreyfus: A Family Affair*, p. 179
37 Thomas, op. cit., p. 286
38 Duclert, op. cit., p. 589

Chapter 9: Colonel Picquart

1   Louis Begley, *Why the Dreyfus Affair Matters*, p. 92
2   Paléologue, op. cit., p. 101
3   Thomas, op. cit., p. 235
4   Vigouroux, op. cit., p. 352
5   Thomas, op. cit., p. 203
6   See Vigouroux, op. cit., p. 346
7   Bredin, op. cit., p. 141n.
8   Ibid., p. 141
9   Ibid., p. 151
10 Ibid., p. 162
11 Miquel, op. cit., p. 18
12 Thomas, op. cit., p. 252
13 Begley, op. cit., p. 97
14 Thomas, op. cit., p. 280
15 See Bredin, op. cit., p. 165
16 John, 11: 49
17 Thomas, op. cit., p. 274
18 Ibid., p. 278
19 Ibid., p. 274
20 Ibid., p. 321
21 Bredin, op. cit., p. 177
22 Ibid., p. 142
23 Ibid., p. 183
24 Thomas, op. cit., p. 392
25 Ruth Harris, *The Man on Devil's Island*, p. 196
26 Quoted in Bredin, op. cit., p. 185
27 Ibid., p. 180
28 Ruth Harris, *The Man on Devil's Island*, p. 90
29 Burns, *Dreyfus: A Family Affair*, p. 192

Chapter 10: Commandant Esterhazy

1   Zamoyski, op. cit., p. 276
2   Quoted in Bredin, op. cit., p. 222

3 Thomas, op. cit., p. 34
4 Ibid., p. 35
5 Quoted in Bredin, op. cit., p. 155
6 Quoted in Arendt, op. cit., p. 104
7 Quoted in Thomas, op. cit., p. 24
8 Duclert, op. cit., p. 345
9 Quoted in Thomas, op. cit., p. 41
10 Ibid., p. 52
11 Schwertfeger, op. cit., p. 5
12 Ibid., p. 15
13 Ibid., p. 16
14 Thomas, op. cit., p. 100
15 Ibid., p. 96
16 Ibid., p. 95
17 Ibid., p. 196
18 Ibid., p. 204
19 Bredin, op. cit., p. 187
20 Thomas, op. cit., p. 196
21 Bredin, op. cit., p. 188
22 Ibid., p. 187; also Thomas, *op. cit.*, p. 415
23 Arendt, op. cit., p. 101
24 Duclert, op. cit., p. 412
25 Thomas, op. cit., p. 465
26 Quoted in Bredin, op. cit., p. 190
27 Ibid., p. 191
28 Schwertfeger, op. cit., p. 109
29 Bredin, op. cit., p. 218
30 Wilson, op. cit., p. 360
31 Ibid., p. 520
32 McManners, op. cit., p. 91
33 Quoted in Ruth Harris, *The Man on Devil's Island*, p. 181
34 Ibid., p. 183
35 Quoted in Bredin, op. cit., p. 229
36 Ibid., p. 230
37 Ibid., p. 241

Chapter 11: Émile Zola

1 Miquel, op. cit., p. 7
2 Goncourt, op. cit., p. 320
3 Quoted in Wilson, op. cit., p. 204
4 Quoted in Rose, op. cit.
5 Quoted in Bredin, op. cit., p. 246

6 Émile Zola, *L'Affaire Dreyfus: la vérité en marche*, p. 103

7 Ibid., p. 105

8 See Duclert, op. cit., p. 596

9 Zola, op. cit., p. 115

10 Miquel, op. cit., p. 43

11 Quoted in Bredin, op. cit., p. 250

12 Quoted in Thomas, op. cit., p. 502

13 Lindemann, op. cit., p. 116

14 Thomas, op. cit., p. 501

15 Ruth Harris, *Lourdes*, p. 247

16 Ibid., p. 361

17 Ibid., p. 304

18 Ibid., p. 277

19 Goncourt, op. cit., p. 369

20 Ibid., p. 317

21 Burns, *Dreyfus: A Family Affair*, p. 144

22 Wilson, op. cit., p. 474

23 Bredin, op. cit., p. 286

24 Quoted in Bredin, op. cit., p. 255

25 Ibid., p. 259

26 Marcel Proust, *Jean Santeuil*, p. 350

27 Quoted in Bredin, op. cit., p. 261

28 Proust, op. cit., p. 359

29 Quoted in Bredin, op. cit., p. 266

30 Thomas, op. cit., p. 504

31 Pierre Dreyfus, op. cit., p. 179

Chapter 12: The Pen versus the Sword

1 Painter, op. cit., vol. I, p. 233

2 Quoted in Bredin, op. cit., p. 277

3 Ruth Harris, *The Man on Devil's Island*, p. 149

4 Quoted in ibid., p. 148

5 Bredin, op. cit., p. 281

6 See Ruth Harris, *The Man on Devil's Island*, p. 142

7 See Charles Péguy, op. cit., p. 54

8 Painter, op. cit., p. 108

9 Ibid., p. 142

10 Quoted in Wilson, op. cit., p. 309n.

11 Ibid., p. 278

12 Painter, op. cit., p. 161

13 Ibid., p. 243

14 Ibid., p. 118

15 Ruth Harris, *The Man on Devil's Island*, p. 273; Painter, op. cit., p. 223

16 Painter, op. cit., p. 223

17 Ruth Harris, *The Man on Devil's Island*, p. 251

18 Robert Tombs, '"Lesser Breeds without the Law": The British Establishment and the Dreyfus Affair, 1894–1899', p. 498

19 Quoted in Bredin, op. cit., p. 272

20 Tombs, '"Lesser Breeds without the Law"', p. 497

21 Frederick C. Conybeare, *The Dreyfus Case*, p. 154

22 Paléologue, op. cit., p. 95

23 Schwertfeger, op. cit., p. 104

24 Ibid., p. 94

25 Ibid., p. 108

26 Ibid., p. 110

27 Quoted in Bredin, op. cit., p. 300

28 See Ruth Harris, 'The Assumptionists and the Dreyfus Affair', p. 177

29 Bredin, op. cit., p. 306

30 Ibid., p. 309

31 Ibid., p. 312

32 Quoted in ibid., p. 316

33 Ibid., p. 320

Chapter 13: The Road to Rennes

1 Bredin, op. cit., p. 325

2 Thomas, op. cit., p. 518

3 Quoted in Bredin, op. cit., p. 329

4 Burns, *Rural Society and French Politics*, p. 45

5 Thomas, op. cit., p.108

6 Quoted in Bredin, op. cit., p. 330

7 Ruth Harris, *The Man on Devil's Island*, p. 236

8 Quoted in Bredin, op. cit., p. 345

9 *L'Intransigeant*, 18 October 1898, quoted in ibid., p. 361

10 Brogan, op. cit., p. 342

11 Burleigh, op. cit., p. 314

12 Ruth Harris, *The Man on Devil's Island*, p. 191

13 Bredin, op. cit., p. 304n.

14 Arendt, op. cit., p. 102

15 Ibid., p. 115

16 Tombs, *France, 1814–1914*, p. 93

17 Gibson, op. cit., p. 110

18 Ruth Harris, *The Man on Devil's Island*, p. 171

19 Vigouroux, op. cit., p. 346

20 Ruth Harris, *The Man on Devil's Island*, p. 171

21 Wilson, op. cit., p. 524.

22 Ruth Harris, *The Man on Devil's Island*, p. 185

23 Quoted in Burleigh, op. cit., p. 354

24 McManners, op. cit., p. 126

25 *The Times*, 17 January 1899

26 Paléologue, op. cit., p. 135

27 'The Jesuits and the Dreyfus Case', *The Month*, February 1899, p. 124

28 Flannery, op. cit., pp. 188–9

29 Quoted in Burleigh, op. cit., p. 430

30 Quoted in Wilson, op. cit., p. 418

31 Brogan, op. cit., p. 367

32 Tombs, *France, 1814–1914*, p. 63

33 Quoted in Bredin, op. cit., p. 338

34 Wilson, op. cit., p. 137

35 Burleigh, op. cit., p. 427

36 Quoted in Wilson, op. cit., p. 148

37 Ibid., p. 150

38 Ibid., p. 156

39 Ruth Harris, *The Man on Devil's Island*, p. 242

40 Brogan, op. cit., p. 334

41 Quoted in Bredin, op. cit., p. 351

42 Ruth Harris, *The Man on Devil's Island*, p. 243

43 Duclert, op. cit., p. 573

44 Painter, op. cit., vol. II, p. 30

45 Schwertfeger, op. cit., p. 109

46 Alfred Dreyfus, *Memoirs of Captain Dreyfus*, p. 227

47 Miquel, op. cit., p. 83

48 Vigouroux, op. cit., p. 357

49 Quoted in Bredin, op. cit., p. 363

50 Paléologue, op. cit., p. 189

51 Vigouroux, op. cit., p. 347

52 Bredin, op. cit., p. 366

53 Ibid., p. 371

54 Paléologue, op. cit., p. 150

55 Ibid., p. 152

56 Quoted in Bredin, op. cit., p. 373

57 Ibid., p. 376

58 Paléologue, op. cit., p. 156

59 Ibid., p. 158

60 Ibid., p. 161

61 Bredin, op. cit., p. 385

62 Ibid., p. 387

Chapter 14: Rennes

1 Alfred Dreyfus, *Five Years of my Life*, p. 326
2 Burns, *Dreyfus: A Family Affair*, p. 219
3 Alfred Dreyfus, *Five Years of my Life*, p. 337
4 Thomas, op. cit., p. 507
5 Alfred Dreyfus, *Five Years of my Life*, p. 341
6 Duclert, op. cit., p. 556
7 Paléologue, op. cit., p. 167
8 Ibid., p. 192
9 Brogan, op. cit., p. 355
10 Paléologue, op. cit., p. 171
11 Ruth Harris, *The Man on Devil's Island*, p. 326. Bredin says seventy
12 Quoted in Bredin, op. cit., p. 403
13 Ibid., p. 402
14 Paléologue, op. cit., p. 195
15 Ibid., p. 169
16 Maurice Barrès, *Scènes et doctrines du nationalisme*, p. 138, quoted in Bredin, op. cit., p. 405
17 Paléologue, op. cit., p. 169
18 Ibid., p. 170
19 Ibid., p. 173
20 Ibid., p. 175
21 Duclert, op. cit., p. 707
22 Paléologue, op. cit., p. 185
23 Ibid., p. 186
24 Ibid., p. 196
25 Duclert, op. cit., p. 708
26 Ibid., p. 705
27 Paléologue, op. cit., p. 198
28 Ibid., p. 177
29 Maurice Barrès, quoted in Bredin, op. cit., p. 413
30 Quoted in Ruth Harris, *The Man on Devil's Island*, p. 327
31 Schwertfeger, op. cit., p. 143
32 Ibid., p. 147
33 Paléologue, op. cit., p. 209
34 Quoted in Bredin, op. cit., p. 420
35 Paléologue, op. cit., p. 221
36 Burns, *Dreyfus: A Family Affair*, p. 256
37 Quoted in Miquel, op. cit., p. 110
38 Burns, op. cit., p. 248
39 Miguel, op. cit., p. 107
40 Doise, op. cit., p. 61

41 Paléologue, op. cit., p. 148
42 Duclert, op. cit., p. 661
43 Paléologue, op. cit., p. 205
44 Ibid., p. 218
45 Duclert, op. cit., p. 422
46 Bredin, op. cit., p. 425
47 Paléologue, op. cit., p. 189
48 Quoted in Bredin, op. cit., p. 429
49 Ibid., p. 430
50 Duclert, op. cit., p. 756
51 Ibid.
52 Tombs, "'Lesser Breeds without the Law'", p. 495
53 Ibid., p. 505
54 Ibid., p. 502
55 Ibid., p. 506
56 Ibid.
57 Ibid., p. 508
58 Ibid.
59 Wilson, op. cit., p. 423
60 Duclert, op. cit., p. 756
61 Bredin, op. cit., p. 433
62 Alfred Dreyfus, *Five Years of my Life*, p. 344
63 Duclert, op. cit., p. 772
64 Ibid., p. 793
65 Ibid., p. 795
66 Alfred Dreyfus, *Carnets*, p. 30, quoted in ibid., p. 802

Chapter 15: The Last Act

 1 McManners, op. cit., p. 127
 2 Quoted in Bredin, op. cit., p. 439
 3 Doise, op. cit., p. 61
 4 McManners, op. cit., p. 127
 5 Quoted in Bredin, op. cit., p. 443
 6 Pierre Dreyfus, op. cit., dedication
 7 Ruth Harris, *The Man on Devil's Island*, p. 350
 8 *Le Journal*, 4 December 1901, quoted in Bredin, op. cit., p. 449
 9 Ibid., p. 448
10 Ruth Harris, *The Man on Devil's Island*, p. 356
11 Ibid., p. 193
12 Ibid., p. 352
13 Burns, *Dreyfus: A Family Affair*, p. 325
14 Painter, op. cit., vol. I, p. 248

15 Ibid.
16 Alfred Dreyfus, *Memoirs of Captain Dreyfus*, p. 322
17 Painter, op. cit., p. 248
18 Burns, *Dreyfus: A Family Affair*, p. 319
19 Ruth Harris, *The Man on Devil's Island*, p. 359
20 Burns, *Dreyfus: A Family Affair*, p. 83
21 *Ibid.*, p. 319
22 Quoted in Duclert, op. cit., p. 797
23 Burns, *Dreyfus: A Family Affair*, p. 445
24 Ruth Harris, *The Man on Devil's Island*, p. 359
25 Péguy, op. cit., pp. 65–6
26 Ibid., p. 113
27 Quoted in McManners, op. cit., p. 127
28 Ruth Harris, 'The Assumptionists and the Dreyfus Affair', *Past and Present*, p. 208
29 Ibid.
30 Wilson, op. cit., p. 187
31 Miquel, op. cit., p. 104
32 Ruth Harris, *The Man on Devil's Island*, p. 369
33 Anderson, op. cit., p. 59
34 Ibid., p. 51
35 Brogan, op. cit., p. 361
36 Tombs, *France, 1814–1914*, p. 465
37 McManners, op. cit., p. 125
38 Tombs, op. cit., p. 465
39 Quoted in McManners, op. cit., p. 44
40 Gibson, op. cit., p. 103
41 Ibid., p. 93
42 Genesis, 38: 8–10
43 Theodore Zeldin, *Conflicts in French Society*, p. 49
44 McManners, op. cit., p. 133
45 Brogan, op. cit., p. 362
46 *Revue des Deux Mondes*, quoted in McManners, op. cit., p. 133
47 Burns, *Dreyfus: A Family Affair*, p. 296
48 Brogan, op. cit., p. 362
49 Ruth Harris, *The Man on Devil's Island*, p. 359
50 *The Catholic Encylopaedia* (1913)
51 Schultheiss, op. cit., p. 10. See also the scathing satire of such an institution in Octave Mirbeau's *Diary of a Chambermaid*
52 Tombs, op. cit., p. 469
53 Gibson, op. cit., p. 126
54 Schultheiss, op. cit., p. 11
55 Ibid., p. 20
56 See Don Cook, *Charles de Gaulle*, p. 27

57 Brogan, op. cit., p. 378

58 Péguy, op. cit., p. 96

59 Ibid., p. 134

60 Brogan, op. cit., p. 378

61 Quoted in Wilson, op. cit., p. 555

62 Ruth Harris, *The Man on Devil's Island*, p. 229

63 Bredin, op. cit., p. 459

64 Joseph Reinach, *Histoire de l'Affaire Dreyfus*, vol. VI, p. 200, quoted in ibid., p. 461

65 Quoted in ibid., p. 467

66 Ibid., p. 468

67 Brogan, op. cit., p. 380

68 Bredin, op. cit., p. 481

69 Alfred Dreyfus, *Memoirs of Captain Dreyfus*, p. 359

70 Burns, *Dreyfus: A Family Affair*, p. 309

Epilogue

1   Alfred Dreyfus, *Cinq années de ma vie*, p. 228, quoted in Bredin, op. cit., p. 486

2   Pierre Dreyfus, op. cit., p. 8

3   Ibid., p. 9

4   Burns, *Dreyfus: A Family Affair*, p. 319

5   Duclert, op. cit., p. 1011

6   Vigouroux, op. cit., p. 347

7   Burleigh, op. cit., p. 454

8   Ibid., p. 455

9   Bredin, op. cit., p. 501

10 Schwertfeger, op. cit., pp. viii, 243

11 Vigouroux, op. cit., p. 4

12 Burns, *Dreyfus: A Family Affair*, p. 401

13 Bredin, op. cit., p. 488

14 Jean-Louis Lévy, internet interview

15 Wilson, op. cit., p. 740

16 Ibid., p. 741

17 Burns, *Dreyfus: A Family Affair*, p. 466

18 Leps, op. cit.

19 Burns, *Dreyfus: A Family Affair*, p. 466

20 Jean-Louis Lévy, internet interview

Bibliography

Acomb, Evelyn M., *The French Laic Laws (1879–1889): The First Anti-Clerical Campaign of the Third French Republic*, New York, Columbia University Press, 1941

Anderson, Robert, 'The Conflict in Education: Catholic Secondary Schools (1850–1870): A Reappraisal', in Theodore Zeldin, ed., *Conflicts in French Society: Anticlericalism, Education and Morals in the Nineteenth Century*, London, George Allen & Unwin, 1970

Arendt, Hannah, *The Origins of Totalitarianism*, London, George Allen & Unwin, 1958

Begley, Louis, *Why the Dreyfus Affair Matters*, New Haven and London, Yale University Press, 2009

Bredin, Jean-Louis, *The Affair: The Case of Alfred Dreyfus*, trans. Jeffrey Mehlman, London, Sidgwick & Jackson, 1987

Brogan, D. W., *The Development of Modern France, 1870–1939*, London, Hamish Hamilton, 1940

Brown, Frederick, *For the Soul of France: Culture Wars in the Age of Dreyfus*, New York, Alfred A. Knopf, 2010

Burleigh, Michael, *Earthly Powers: The Clash of Religion and Politics in Europe, from the French Revolution to the Great War*, London, HarperCollins, 2005

Burns, Michael, *Dreyfus: A Family Affair, 1789–1945*, London, HarperCollins, 1991

—, *Rural Society and French Politics: Boulangism and the Dreyfus Affair, 1886–1900*, Princeton, Princeton University Press, 1984

Canard, David, ed., *Partir au bagne*, La Crèche, Geste Éditions, 2005

Chateaubriand, François-René de, *The Beauties of Christianity*, trans. Frederic Shoberl, London, Henry Colburn, 1813

—, *The Memoirs of Chateaubriand*, trans. Robert Baldick, London, Hamish Hamilton, 1961

Colley, Linda, *Britons: Forging the Nations, 1707–1837*, London, Yale University Press, 1992

Conybeare, Frederick C., *The Dreyfus Case*, London, George Allen, 1898

Cook, Don, *Charles de Gaulle: A Biography*, London, Secker & Warburg, 1984

Dimont, Max I., *Jews, God and History*, New York, New American Library, 1962

Doise, Jean, *Un Secret bien gardé: histoire militaire de l'affaire Dreyfus*, Paris, Éditions du Seuil, 1994

Dresden, Donald, *The Marquis de Morès: Emperor of the Bad Lands*, Norman, University of Oklahoma Press, 1970

Dreyfus, Alfred, *Five Years of my Life*, trans. James Mortimer, London, George Newnes, 1901

—, *Memoirs of Captain Dreyfus, 1899–1906*, trans. Dr Betty Morgan, London, Hutchinson, 1937

Dreyfus, Pierre, *Dreyfus: His Life and Letters*, trans. Dr Betty Morgan, London, Hutchinson, 1937

Drumont, Édouard, *La France juive: essai d'histoire contemporaine*, vols I and II, Paris, C. Marpon & E. Flammarion, 1886

Duclert, Vincent, *Alfred Dreyfus: l'honneur d'un patriote*, Paris, Fayard, 2006.

Flannery, Edward H., *The Anguish of the Jews: Twenty-three Centuries of Anti-Semitism*, New York, Paulist Press, 1985

Frankel, Jonathan, *The Damascus Affair: 'Ritual Murder', Politics and the Jews in 1840*, Cambridge, Cambridge University Press, 1997

Gibson, Ralph, *A Social History of French Catholicism, 1789–1914*, London, Routledge, 1989

Goncourt, Edmond and Jules de, *Pages from the Goncourt Journals*, ed. and trans. Robert Baldick, New York, New York Review Books, 1962

Guillemin, Henri, *L'Énigme Esterhazy*, Paris, Gallimard, 1962

Halfond, Irwin, *Maurice Paléologue: The Diplomat, the Writer, the Man, and the Third French Republic*, Lanham, University Press of America, 2007

Harris, Robin, *Talleyrand: Betrayer and Saviour of France*, London, John Murray, 2007

Harris, Ruth, 'The Assumptionists and the Dreyfus Affair', *Past and Present*, vol. 194, issue 1, 2007, pp. 175–211

—, *Lourdes: Body and Spirit in the Secular Age*, London, Allen Lane, 1989

—, *The Man on Devil's Island: Alfred Dreyfus and the Affair that Divided France*, London, Allen Lane, 2010

Hibbert, Christopher, *The French Revolution*, London, Allen Lane, 1980

Hoffman, Robert Louis, *More than a Trial: The Struggle over Captain Dreyfus*, New York, Free Press, 1980

Jennings, Jeremy, *Revolution and the Republic: A History of Political Thought in France since the Eighteenth Century*, Cambridge, Cambridge University Press, 2011

Johnson, Douglas, *France and the Dreyfus Affair*, London, Blandford Press, 1966

Lazare, Bernard, *Anti-Semitism: Its History and Causes*, Jewish History Sourcebooks, Halsall History Websites

Leps, Marie-Christine, 'Normal Deviance: The Dreyfus Affair', Actes de Colloque, Maison Française d'Oxford, Social Deviance in England and in France (c. 1830–1900), 2003, www.mfo.ac.uk

Levi, Anthony, *Cardinal Richelieu and the Making of France*, London, Constable, 2000

Lévy, Jean-Louis, interview with Marc Knobel posted on website of Conseil Répresentatif des Institutions Juives de France, www.crif.org

Lindemann, Albert S., *The Jew Accused: Three Anti-Semitic Affairs (Dreyfus, Beilis, Frank), 1894–1915*, Cambridge, Cambridge University Press, 1991

McManners, John, *Church and State in France, 1870–1914*, London, SPCK, 1972

Miquel, Pierre, *L'Affair Dreyfus*, Paris, Presses Universitaires de France, 1961

Mitchell, Alan, 'The Xenophobic Style: French Counterespionage and the Emergence of the Dreyfus Affair', *Journal of Modern History*, vol. 52, no. 3, 1980

Painter, George D., *Marcel Proust: A Biography*, London, Chatto & Windus, 1959 (vol. I), 1965 (vol. II)

Paléologue, Maurice, *My Secret Diary of the Dreyfus Case, 1894–1899*, trans. Eric Mosbacher, London, Secker & Warburg, 1957

Péguy, Charles, *Notre jeunesse*, Paris, Gallimard, 1942

Porch, Douglas, *French Secret Service: From the Dreyfus Affair to the Gulf War*, London, Macmillan, 1996

Proust, Marcel, *Jean Santeuil*, trans. Gerard Hopkins, London, Weidenfeld & Nicolson, 1955

Rabkin, Yakov M., *A Threat from Within: A Century of Jewish Opposition to Zionism*, trans. Fred. A. Reed, London, Zed Books, 2006

Reinach, Joseph, *Histoire de l'affaire Dreyfus*, 7 vols, Paris, Éditions de la Revue Blanche, 1901–11

Rose, Jacqueline, 'J'accuse: Dreyfus in our Times', *London Review of Books*, vol. 32, no. 11, June 2010

Sartre, Jean-Paul, *Anti-Semite and Jew*, trans. George J. Becker, New York, Schocken Books, 1976

Schultheiss, Katrin, *Bodies and Souls: Politics and Professionalization of Nursing in France, 1880–1922*, Cambridge, Mass., Harvard University Press, 2001

Schwertfeger, Bernhard, ed., *The Truth about Dreyfus from the Schwartzkoppen Papers*, London, Putnam, 1931

Sharif, Regina S., *Non-Jewish Zionism: Its Roots in Western History*, London, Zed Press, 1983

Stone, Norman, *Europe Transformed, 1878–1919*, Oxford, Blackwell, 1999

Thomas, Marcel, *L'Affaire sans Dreyfus*, Paris, Fayard, 1961

Tombs, Robert, *France, 1814–1914*, London, Longman, 1996

—, '"Lesser Breeds without the Law": The British Establishment and the Dreyfus Affair, 1894–1899', *Historical Journal*, vol. 41, no. 2, 1998

Vigouroux, Christian, *Georges Picquart, Dreyfusard, proscrit, ministre: la justice par l'exactitude*, Paris, Dalloz, 2009

Wawro, Geoffrey, *The Franco-Prussian War: The German Conquest of France in 1870–1871*, Cambridge, Cambridge University Press, 2003

Wilson, Stephen, *Ideology and Experience: Antisemitism in France at the Time of the Dreyfus Affair*, London and Toronto, Associated University Presses, 1982

Zamoyski, Adam, *Rites of Peace: The Fall of Napoleon and the Congress of Vienna*, London, HarperPress, 2007

Zeldin, Theodore, ed., *Conflicts in French Society: Anticlericalism, Education and Morals in the Nineteenth Century*, London, George Allen & Unwin, 1970

Zola, Émile, *L'Affaire Dreyfus: la vérité en marche*, Paris, Garnier Flammarion, 1969

Acknowledgements

My thanks are due to the many historians of nineteenth-century France and the Dreyfus Affair whose works have furnished material for this book. I am particularly grateful to Dr Ruth Harris, who generously answered my queries over lunch at New College, Oxford; and to Professor Jeremy Jennings, who kindly gave me a preview of a chapter of his *Revolution and the Republic: A History of Political Thought in France since the Eighteenth Century*. I should like to acknowledge the help of the staff at the London Library whose comprehensive collection of books on the Dreyfus Affair proved invaluable.

I should also like to thank my wife Emily for her help in translating difficult passages from French sources; my agent, Gillon Aitken, who encouraged me to write about the Dreyfus Affair; and Michael Fishwick, my editor at Bloomsbury, who commissioned this book and gave sound advice on the revision of my first draft. I am grateful to Anna Simpson for shepherding my manuscript through its different stages; to Peter James for his superb copy-editing, Catherine Best for reading the proofs and Alan Rutter for the index. I should like to thank Henry Jeffreys, Alexa von Hirschberg, Tess Viljoen, Paul Nash, Polly Napper and all at Bloomsbury who helped in the publication of this book. My thanks also go to Peter Ginna and Pete Beatty of Bloomsbury Press in New York.

I am grateful for permission to quote from the following works by other authors: Ralph Gibson, *A Social History of French Catholicism*,

1789–1914 (Routledge, 1989); Edmond and Jules de Goncourt, *Pages from the Goncourt Journal*, ed. and trans. Robert Baldick (New York Review Books, 1962); Albert S. Lindemann, *The Jew Accused: Three Anti-Semitic Affairs (Dreyfus, Beilis, Frank), 1894–1915* (Cambridge University Press, 1991); Maurice Paléologue, *My Secret Diary of the Dreyfus Case, 1894–1899*, trans. Eric Mosbacher (Secker & Warburg, 1957), reprinted by permission of The Random House Group; Ruth Harris, *The Man on Devil's Island: Alfred Dreyfus and the Affair that Divided France* (Allen Lane), by permission of the Penguin Group; and Vincent Duclert, *Alfred Dreyfus: L'honneur d'un patriote*, reprinted by permission of Libraire Arthème Fayard.

Index